Test Item

to Accompany

PSYCHOLOGY

Seventh Edition

John W. Santrock

University of Texas at Dallas

Ron Mulson

Hudson Valley Community College

Boston   Burr Ridge, IL   Dubuque, IA   Madison, WI   New York   San Francisco   St. Louis
Bangkok   Bogotá   Caracas   Lisbon   London   Madrid
Mexico City   Milan   New Delhi   Seoul   Singapore   Sydney   Taipei   Toronto

McGraw-Hill Higher Education

*A Division of The **McGraw-Hill** Companies*

Test Item File I to Accompany
PSYCHOLOGY

Published by McGraw-Hill, an imprint of The McGraw-Hill Companies, Inc., 1221
Avenue of the Americas, New York, NY 10020. Copyright 2003, 2000, 1997 by
The McGraw-Hill Companies, Inc. All rights reserved.

2 3 4 5 6 7 8 9 0 BKM/BKM   0 9 8 7 6 5 4 3

ISBN 0-07-249420-4

www.mhhe.com

Contents

Preface

About This Test Item File

At McGraw-Hill, we try to publish high-quality test items that fairly and accurately measure your students' achievement. We ask our authors to adhere to the following principles:

- Test the important instructional objectives from each chapter of the text.
- Make sure the number of items written for each objective is in proportion to its importance.
- Write items that are grammatically correct, free of mechanical impediments, and appropriate for the students being tested.

Each item in this test item file is keyed to a learning goal. The content, or learning goals, for this text open each chapter in this test item file. These learning goals outline the important topics covered in each chapter.

Behavioral objectives help to identify the student's level of achievement, ranging from recognition to generalization and application of course material. There are many ways to classify behavioral objectives. The system most commonly used, and the one used with this test item file, is the *Taxonomy of Educational Objectives, Cognitive Domain*, developed by Benjamin Bloom and his colleagues. We ask our authors to write items that test at Bloom's first three cognitive levels. *Factual* or *knowledge* questions (F) require students to recognize or recall certain facts, terms, rules, classifications, principles, and methods. *Conceptual* or *comprehension* questions (C) require students to consider more than one fact to arrive at the correct answer. Specifically, these items may involve the identification of examples of psychological concepts or the translation, interpretation, prediction, generalization, and explanation of the material that has been studied. *Applied* questions (A) require students to employ psychological concepts, methods, and principles in unique problem-solving situations. This system has been utilized to categorize the learning goals of this test bank.

Key to Item Information

Each test item is accompanied by the following information:

> *Ans.:*   Correct answer to the question.
> *LG:*   The chapter learning goal addressed by this question.
> *Page:*   The page in the textbook where the correct answer may be found.
> *QT:*   The question type identifying the level of this question according to Bloom et al.'s *Taxonomy of Educational Objectives, Cognitive Domain*

Connections

Encourage your students to test their knowledge of this chapter's material by taking the different practice quizzes found in the *Student Study Guide*, on the text's *website* (www.mhhe.com/Santrockp7), or on the *Student CD-ROM* packaged with their text. To reinforce students' use of these valuable study tools, try selecting a few questions from these sources and including them on your in-class tests.

A Note from the Author

Introductory psychology is as important as any class that we may ever have the opportunity to teach. If one of the aims of education is to improve the quality of the lives of students, than one would be hard pressed to find a more suitable blueprint from which to work. As John Santrock says in his preface, this course and this textbook will help students understand themselves and others better. Students will be given the opportunity to not only learn about human thought and behavior but will be provided with critical thinking guidelines that will allow them to see the difference between science and speculation. This information and approach to thinking can transcend the limits of the classroom to put them in a better position to succeed in life.

We, as teachers, choose what we feel are the most important points from any textbook to emphasize in our classes. Both this text, and hopefully this test bank will provide enough of a diverse coverage of topics to meet your teaching needs. The questions in the test bank have been written to match the text, and to assess knowledge at different levels of understanding. For each chapter, there are multiple-choice, true-false, fill-in-the-blank, matching, and essay questions. Keep in mind that the students in your class may not only have different learning styles, but also different test taking styles. The test bank should provide enough different types of questions that you can create a well-balanced test for your students. I am confident that it will provide you with questions that will provide support for the high quality of both your tests and your class.

Your approach to testing should be consistent with the scientific approach to psychology that you have emphasized during the semester. And you should be as sensitive to the effectiveness of your tests as you are to teaching your subject. Item analysis of questions should take place every time you give an objective test. I have always felt that it is easier to find money on the street than it is to find a good test question. Often the questions that make perfect sense to us will fail miserably when put to use with students. When I give a test to students, I am just as interested in how well the test worked as I am in how the individual students performed on it. If by some chance you construct the perfect test, please let me know because I am still searching for it.

Acknowledgments

I have to thank a number of others who contributed to this project including Cheri Dellelo, the Developmental Editor who managed to pull this all together, and Malvine Litten and her staff for their patience and hard work in editing my one or two errors. Special thanks to Jutta M. Street, the author of the previous edition. Her work provided an excellent foundation to extend upon. And to Susan Swithers, at Purdue University, who stepped in and offered her expert assistance to help complete four of the chapters. I especially have to mention my wife Linda, and our children Jessica and Derek, who patiently waited for me to come out of the office this spring.

Ron Mulson
Hudson Valley Community College

The McGraw-Hill Companies
DIPLOMA$^©$ Testing Software
from the Brownstone Research Group

Diploma's testing capability is consistently ranked number one in evaluations over other products. With its Test Generator, On-Line Testing Program, Internet Testing, and Grade Management Systems, Diploma is very instructor-friendly software. Below are just some of the features offered by the Diploma software:

Exam Generator Features:
- Individual questions can be added to tests simply by double clicking them or you may randomly select your test questions.
- Instructors may edit current questions or enter new questions into the test bank with the use of the question editor.
- Instructors may filter questions by any available field (such as Topic, Difficulty, Objective, Page, etc.) to quickly find exactly the questions they want to incorporate into the test.
- Instructions to students can be added to any location within a test.
- Answer Keys can be printed independently.
- Questions in the printed test can be scrambled to create many different versions and printed with the version number on each test page.
- Users can preview tests before printing them.

On-Line Testing Program Features:
- Supports multiple choice, true/false, short answer, and fill-in-the-blank question types.
- Results are displayed with graphs at the test's completion.
- Student logins can be required by instructors.
- Time limits, start times, and completion times can be set.
- Results can be saved for importing into a gradebook.

Internet Testing Program Features:
- Exam's Internet tests include a Grade button that allows students to grade their tests and review their results immediately.
- Internet tests are created in one simple step from with the Exam program. The test is published in HTML format.
- Internet tests can be posted on any Web site.
- The self-grading feature is automatically incorporated into Internet tests.

Gradebook Features:
- Thousands of students and hundreds of assignments can be stored within one file.
- Grades can be organized into related groups such as tests, papers, homework, etc.
- Assignments can be independently weighted.
- Grades can be entered as points, percentages, letters or custom grades.
- Scores and averages can be curved.
- Results from intranet-, internet- or network-based tests can be merged.
- Student rosters can be imported and exported.

This computerized testing software is currently available for use with this test bank. For more information on how to obtain your copy of this instructor-friendly software, contact your local sales representative.

Chapter 1: What Is Psychology?

Learning Goals

1. Explain what psychology is and how it developed.
2. Describe six contemporary approaches to psychology.
3. Describe two movements that reflect a positive approach to psychology.
4. Evaluate careers and areas of specialization in psychology.
5. Apply some strategies that will help you succeed in psychology.

Multiple-Choice Items

Learning Goal 1: Explain what psychology is and how it developed.

1. Psychology is considered a(n)
   a. behavioral science.
   b. natural science.
   c. physical science.
   d. philosophy.
   Ans.: a   LG: 1   Page: 6   QT: F

2. Psychology is the study of
   a. behavior.
   b. mental processes.
   c. the mind.
   d. behavior and mental processes.
   Ans.: d   LG: 1   Page: 5   QT: F

3. Which of the following would be the best example of a behavior?
   a. thinking of the words in this question
   b. thinking of the answer to this question
   c. critical thinking about this question
   d. writing the answer to this question
   Ans.: d   LG: 1   Page: 6   QT: A

4. Which of the following would be the best example of a mental process?
   a. asking your professor for clarification of a concept
   b. telling your professor potential solutions to a problem
   c. considering potential solutions to a problem
   d. putting your thoughts on paper
   Ans.: c   LG: 1   Page: 6   QT: A

5. Which of the following is true of psychology?
   a. It uses the scientific method.
   b. It describes behavior from the same perspective as did the philosophers.
   c. All psychology is developed from myth.
   d. It is based upon common sense.
   Ans.: a   LG: 1   Page: 6   QT: C

6. Which of the following is *not* an important part of a behavioral science?
    a. observation
    b. prediction
    c. controversy
    d. certainty
    Ans.: d   LG: 1   Page: 6   QT: C

7. When we are observing others, we are paying attention to their
    a. thoughts.
    b. motivations.
    c. behaviors.
    d. mental processes.
    Ans.: c   LG: 1   Page: 6   QT: C

8. Damon is trying to predict the behavior of television talk show hosts. What must he keep in mind during his observations?
    a. He must use objective data collection.
    b. He should only look for behaviors that support his initial assumptions.
    c. He should focus on the talk show hosts that he does not like.
    d. He should focus on what the hosts are thinking during the show.
    Ans.: a   LG: 1   Page: 6   QT: C

9. Which of the following is not an important component of the field of psychology?
    a. science
    b. behavior
    c. mental processes
    d. common sense
    Ans.: d   LG: 1   Page: 6   QT: F

10. Which of the following would be the easiest to study scientifically?
    a. thoughts
    b. behaviors
    c. motives
    d. feelings
    Ans.: b   LG: 1   Page: 6   QT: F

11. Which of the following would not be considered a mental process?
    a. thoughts
    b. feelings
    c. motives
    d. behavior
    Ans.: d   LG: 1   Page: 6   QT: F

12. Which of the following would be easiest to study scientifically?
    a. a person trying to remember a name
    b. a person feeling sad
    c. a person saying "thank you" after receiving a gift
    d. a person who is going to give a gift
    Ans.: c   LG: 1   Page: 6   QT: C

13. A number of areas of study have played important parts in the development of psychology as a field. Which of the following played the least important part?
   a. physics
   b. philosophy
   c. biology
   d. physiology
   Ans.: a   LG: 1   Page: 7   QT: F

14. The psychological concept of the mind as something other than a physical entity came from
   a. philosophy.
   b. evolution.
   c. natural science.
   d. biology.
   Ans.: a   LG: 1   Page: 7   QT: F

15. What is the difference between how a psychologist would approach an issue and how a philosopher would address the same issue?
   a. A philosopher would discuss an issue and a psychologist would not.
   b. A psychologist would use the scientific method and a philosopher would not.
   c. A psychologist would look for causes of human behavior and a philosopher would not.
   d. A philosopher would consider more potential explanations for human behavior than a psychologist.
   Ans.: b   LG: 1   Page: 7   QT: C

16. The official birth of psychology as a science is attributed to
   a. Freud's book "The Interpretation of Dreams."
   b. William James' "Principles of Psychology."
   c. John Watson's "Psychology as a Behaviorist Views It."
   d. Wilhelm Wundt's lab in Leipzig, Germany.
   Ans.: d   LG: 1   Page: 8   QT: F

17. In 1879, in Leipzig, Germany, Wilhelm Wundt established the first psychological laboratory. The theory that resulted from his work was called
   a. functionalism.
   b. structuralism.
   c. natural selection.
   d. behaviorism.
   Ans.: b   LG: 1   Page: 8   QT: F

18. The psychologist who named the study of the conscious mind and its structures *structuralism* was
   a. Sigmund Freud.
   b. Edward Titchener.
   c. Wolfgang Kohler.
   d. Albert Bandura.
   Ans.: b   LG: 1   Page: 8   QT: F

19. Structuralism utilized a technique in which subjects were placed in a laboratory setting and asked to think about what was going on mentally while different events were taking place. This technique was known as
   a. inner analysis.
   b. introspection.
   c. self analysis.
   d. inside/outside therapy.
   Ans.: b   LG: 1   Page: 8   QT: F

20. When someone asks you how you are feeling, they are asking for a(n)
   a. introspection.
   b. conditioned response.
   c. scientific response.
   d. cognitive assessment.
   Ans.: a   LG: 1   Page: 8   QT: C

21. Contrary to the structuralists, who described the components of the mind, functionalism emphasized the
   a. functions of the mind and behavior in adapting to the environment.
   b. neurological functions of the brain.
   c. function of the environment in dictating human behavior.
   d. function of the unconscious in determining human personality.
   Ans.: a   LG: 1   Page: 8   QT: C

22. William James was known for which of the following
   a. behaviorist
   b. developer of the stream of consciousness.
   c. structuralist
   d. someone who was interested in the rigid structures of the mind.
   Ans.: b   LG: 1   Page: 8   QT: F

23. When studying the development of the field of psychology, which of the following is *not* true?
   a. Psychology was heavily influenced by historical events.
   b. Psychological theories were often developed in opposition to another.
   c. No one theory explains all human thought and behavior.
   d. After more than a century of research, there are no other theories to discover.
   Ans.: d   LG: 1   Page: 7   QT: C

24. The process by which organisms that are best adapted to their world are most likely to survive is known as
   a. natural selection.
   b. survival of the fittest.
   c. evolutionary theory.
   d. all of the above
   Ans.: d   LG: 1   Page: 7   QT: F

4

25. Which of the following best describes the theory of natural selection?
    a. survival of the fittest
    b. Organisms that are best adapted to their world are most likely to survive.
    c. Adaptation to the environment follows a species specific plan of changes.
    d. Organisms that are best adapted to their environments are most likely to survive, reproduce, and pass on their characteristics to their offspring.
    Ans.: d   LG: 1   Page: 7   QT: C

26. The early theory of psychology developed by Wundt and Titchener was known as *structuralism.* Which of the following best describes structuralism?
    a. the classification of the components of the mind and the importance of conscious thought
    b. the emphasis on man's adaptations to a changing environment
    c. the study of the unconscious mind
    d. the classification of the components of the unconscious mind
    Ans.: a   LG: 1   Page: 8   QT: C

27. William James' functionalism was most interested in which of the following?
    a. The adaptation of the mind to the environment.
    b. The unconscious.
    c. The structure of the mind.
    d. The internal workings of the mind.
    Ans.: a   LG: 1   Page: 8   QT: F

28. It is the late 1800's. John has been performing scientific research from the structural perspective. Which of the following would best describe his work?
    a. John has been investigating subconscious motives that have influenced a subject's behavior.
    b. John has been investigating to find how his subject's mind and behavior have adapted to the environment.
    c. John has been looking for the origin of the mind.
    d. John has been using introspection to investigate sensation and perception.
    Ans.: d   LG: 1   Page: 8   QT: C

29. It is the late 1800's. William has been performing scientific research from the functionalist perspective. Which of the following would best describe his work?
    a. William has been investigating subconscious motives that have influenced a subject's behavior.
    b. William has been investigating to find how his subject's mind and behavior have adapted to the environment.
    c. William has been looking for the origin of the mind.
    d. William has been using introspection to investigate sensation and perception.
    Ans.: b   LG: 1   Page: 8   QT: C

30. When comparing the structuralists and functionalists, one could say that
    a. the structuralists were interested in what went on inside the mind, and the functionalists were more concerned with a person's interactions with the outside world.
    b. the functionalists were concerned with what went on inside the mind, and the structuralists were more concerned with a person's interactions with the outside world.
    c. both the structuralists and functionalists were interested in the components of the mind.
    d. only the functionalists were interested with the components of the mind.
    Ans.: a   LG: 1   Page: 8   QT: C

31. Which of the following individuals gave an American perspective to the field of psychology?
    a. Wundt
    b. James
    c. Titchener
    d. Freud
    Ans.: b   LG: 1   Page: 8   QT: F

Learning Goal 2: Describe six contemporary approaches to psychology.

32. An interest in measurable responses led to the _____ perspective of John Watson.
    a. psychodynamic
    b. cognitive
    c. functionalist
    d. behavioral
    Ans.: b   LG: 2   Page: 10   QT: F

33. Which of the following theorists is associated with the start of behaviorism?
    a. Albert Bandura
    b. William James
    c. John Watson
    d. Sigmund Freud
    Ans.: c   LG: 2   Page: 10   QT: F

34. What did Skinner say was most important in the study of human psychology?
    a. What we think about.
    b. What is in our unconscious.
    c. What we do.
    d. All of the above
    Ans.: c   LG: 2   Page: 11   QT: F

35. Which of the following theorists was actively working with behaviorism for much of the twentieth century?
    a. Albert Bandura
    b. Ivan Pavlov
    c. Sigmund Freud
    d. B. F. Skinner
    Ans.: d   LG: 2   Page: 11   QT: F

36. Missouri is known as the "Show Me State" because the residents are proud of being skeptical of believing anything unless they actually see it. Which of the following psychological theories would share this sentiment?
    a. psychodynamic
    b. gestalt
    c. behaviorism
    d. structuralism
    Ans.: c   LG: 2   Page: 10   QT: C

37. George says that the thought process is insignificant and our actions are dictated by our desire to obtain rewards and avoid punishment. If you were to name which psychological approach would best match George's perspective, it would be
    a. humanistic.
    b. cognitive.
    c. behavioral.
    d. psychodynamic.
    Ans.: c   LG: 2   Page: 11   QT: A

38. Maryanne has always been a very good employee at her company. She is always on time and is the first to volunteer for any overtime. How would a behaviorist explain her actions?
    a. She is driven to succeed because of her internal motivation.
    b. As a small child, she was often told how she was incapable of doing things well. She has spent the rest of her life trying to prove that she can succeed.
    c. Her behavior is a result of an inborn aggressive tendency, which would have provided an advantage for our ancestors' chances for survival.
    d. She is being rewarded with money for her efforts.
    Ans.: d   LG: 2   Page: 11   QT: A

39. The social cognitive theory is an outgrowth of
    a. behaviorism.
    b. functionalism.
    c. structuralism.
    d. evolutionary theory.
    Ans.: a   LG: 2   Page: 11   QT: F

40. A key component of the social cognitive theory is
    a. direct reinforcement.
    b. introspection.
    c. observational learning.
    d. delayed reinforcement.
    Ans.: c   LG: 2   Page: 11   QT: F

41. The social cognitive theory, as proposed by Albert Bandura, would provide an explanation for which of the following?
    a. Sharon is given a time-out for taking candy, so does not do it again.
    b. Giles is not allowed to watch television because he took a cookie.
    c. Alyssa sees Sharon get in trouble for taking candy and makes up her mind not to repeat Sharon's behavior.
    d. Giles and Sharon make a decision to both take candy together. They believe that because of their social cooperation in the task, they will not get in trouble.
    Ans.: c   LG: 2   Page: 11   QT: A

42. Which of the following theorists is associated with psychodynamic theory?
    a. John Watson
    b. Edward Titchener
    c. B.F. Skinner
    d. Sigmund Freud
    Ans.: d   LG: 2   Page: 11   QT: F

43. Lindsey believes that her personality is influenced by hidden feelings deep inside her that she has no control over. She feels that her mother's early interactions with her have somehow made her the way she is. Which theorist would be most interested in meeting with Lindsey to discuss her problems?
    a. B. F. Skinner
    b. John Watson
    c. Albert Bandura
    d. Sigmund Freud
    Ans.: d   LG: 2   Page: 11   QT: C

44. Which of the following would not be emphasized in psychodynamic theory?
    a. unconscious thought
    b. reinforcement
    c. biological instincts and society's demands
    d. family experiences
    Ans.: b   LG: 2   Page: 11   QT: F

45. Whereas _____ focused on experimental research, _____ focused on clinical applications.
    a. Watson, Freud
    b. Freud, Bandura
    c. Watson, Wundt
    d. Freud, Watson
    Ans.: a   LG: 2   Page: 11   QT: F

46. George is a very unfocused and disorganized individual. He has a great deal of ability, but never seems to be able to apply himself to any one task long enough to succeed. How would Sigmund Freud explain his behavior?
    a. A poor relationship with his parents when he was a child has had an effect on his personality.
    b. He has never been rewarded for applying himself.
    c. He has observed others not applying themselves and has seen that they have not suffered as a result.
    d. Humans are disorganized and unfocused by nature. It may be an important ability that leads to our survival, because if we focused too closely on any one thing, we would not be aware of other potential dangers.
    Ans.: a   LG: 2   Page: 11   QT: A

47. Shamika is a very unfocused and disorganized individual. She has a great deal of ability, but never seems to be able to apply herself to any one task long enough to succeed.   How would John Watson explain her behavior?
    a. A poor relationship with her parents when she was a child has had an effect on her personality.
    b. She has never been rewarded for applying herself.
    c. She has observed others not applying themselves and has seen that they have not suffered as a result.
    d. Humans are disorganized and unfocused by nature. It may be an important ability that leads to our survival, because if we focused too closely on any one thing, we would not be aware of other potential dangers
    Ans.: b   LG: 2   Page: 11   QT: A

48. Rosemary has found that her son gets better grades when she promises him a reward for high test scores. Though Rosemary is not a psychologist, her approach is consistent with the _____ approach.
    a. behavioral
    b. humanist
    c. cognitive
    d. psychodynamic
    Ans.: a   LG: 2   Page: 11   QT: A

49. Which of the following perspectives would be most difficult to validate scientifically?
    a. behaviorism
    b. evolutionary
    c. psychodynamic
    d. social cognitive
    Ans.: c   LG: 2   Page: 11   QT: C

50. The psychological approach that emphasizes the mental processes of the mind is the
    a. humanistic approach.
    b. cognitive approach.
    c. functional approach.
    d. behavioral approach.
    Ans.: b   LG: 2   Page: 12   QT: F

51. Which of the following psychological approaches would be most interested in mental imagery?
    a. cognitive
    b. evolutionary
    c. sociocultural
    d. behavioral
    Ans.: a   LG: 2   Page: 12   QT: C

52. Which of the following psychological approaches would be *least* interested in mental imagery?
    a. cognitive
    b. evolutionary
    c. sociocultural
    d. behavioral
    Ans.: d   LG: 2   Page: 11   QT: C

53. Cognitive theorists are interested in the concept of
    a. the unconscious.
    b. instincts.
    c. the mind.
    d. rewards.
    Ans.: c   LG: 2   Page: 12   QT: F

54. _____ theorists see human behavior as being controlled by unconscious forces, whereas _____ theorists believe that mental processes are in control of behavior.
    a. Psychodynamic, behavioral
    b. Cognitive, psychodynamic
    c. Psychodynamic, cognitive
    d. Behavioral, cognitive
    Ans.: c   LG: 2   Page: 12   QT: F

55. _____ theorists see human behavior as being controlled by external environmental forces, whereas _____ theorists believe that mental processes are in control of behavior.
    a. Psychodynamic, behavioral
    b. Cognitive, psychodynamic
    c. Psychodynamic, cognitive
    d. Behavioral, cognitive
    Ans.: d   LG: 2   Page: 12   QT: F

56. Juan is interested in how the mind functions. If you were to name the psychological perspective that best describes Juan's area of study, it would be
    a. functionalist.
    b. cognitive.
    c. psychodynamic.
    b. behaviorist.
    Ans.: b   LG: 2   Page: 12   QT: C

57. Damien is interested in improving his memory. He has begun to consider how we process information in order to put it to long term memory. Damien's interest is very consistent with which of the following psychological approaches?
    a. cognitive
    b. psychodynamic
    c. behavioral
    d. structuralism
    Ans.: a   LG: 2   Page: 12   QT: C

58. Maria is interested in studying human cognition. Which of the following subjects would she find most interesting?
    a. the development of attentional skills
    b. how unconscious forces effect our behavior
    c. how external forces influence our physical skills
    d. the role of instincts in our behavior
    Ans.: a   LG: 2   Page: 12   QT: C

59. Phillip takes a behavioral neuroscience approach to psychology. Which of the following would best describe his perspective?
    a. Thoughts and emotions are the result of conditioning.
    b. Thoughts and emotions have a physical origin in the brain.
    c. Thoughts and emotions are the result of unconscious motives.
    d. Thoughts and emotions are influenced by the culture in which we live.
    Ans.: b   LG: 2   Page: 12   QT: C

60. One of the factors that has played a large role in the development of the field of behavioral neuroscience is
    a. the progression of research in behaviorism.
    b. the cognitive revolution.
    c. the humanist perspective as the third force in psychology.
    d. the development of technology.
    Ans.: d   LG: 2   Page: 12   QT: C

61. Willie is interested in the technical aspects of how the brain functions. He has always had a strong ability in biology and is also interested in psychology. Which of the following areas of psychology would you recommend that he look into?
    a. cognitive
    b. behaviorism
    c. humanism
    d. behavioral neuroscience
    Ans.: d   LG: 2   Page: 12   QT: C

62. The evolutionary psychology approach would obviously be influenced by the work of Charles Darwin. What other early psychological perspective would also be of influence?
    a. structuralism
    b. functionalism
    c. behaviorism
    d. psychodynamic
    Ans.: b   LG: 2   Page: 13   QT: C

63. The evolutionary approach emphasizes all of the following *except*
    a. adaptation.
    b. reproduction.
    c. unconscious.
    d. survival of the fittest.
    Ans.: c   LG: 2   Page: 13   QT: F

64. From an evolutionary perspective, which of the following human characteristics would be most important?
    a. hair length
    b. color vision
    c. attractiveness to the opposite sex
    d. height
    Ans.: c   LG: 2   Page: 14   QT: C

65. From an evolutionary perspective, which of the following human characteristics would be least important?
    a. physical attractiveness to the opposite sex
    b. ability to defend oneself
    c. good sensory perception
    d. hair color
    Ans.: d   LG: 2   Page: 14   QT: C

66. All but which of the following human actions may be explained by the evolutionary perspective?
    a. the attraction between members of the opposite sex
    b. cultural diversity
    c. the presence of emotions such as fear
    d. the computing capability of the mind
    Ans.: b   LG: 2   Page: 14   QT: C

67. Joe has recently moved from the city, where things are fast paced, to a small town, where things progress at a slower rate. He is having difficulty adjusting because classmates find him too pushy and hurried. Which of the following perspectives would best explain these differences?
   a. cognitive
   b. behavioral
   c. evolutionary
   d. sociocultural
   Ans.: d   LG: 2   Page: 15   QT: A

68. The psychological approach which examines how the behavior patterns, beliefs, and other products of a particular group of people influence human thought and behavior is the
   a. sociocultural.
   b. cognitive.
   c. behavioral.
   d. psychodynamic.
   Ans.: a   LG: 2   Page: 15   QT: C

69. Judy is investigating the mathematics achievement of children from countries such as the U.S., Germany, Taiwan, and South Africa. What type of psychological approach is Judy utilizing?
   a. cognitive
   b. information processing
   c. psychodynamic
   d. sociocultural
   Ans.: d   LG: 2   Page: 15   QT: A

70. Ramon has been interested in how different ethnic groups in America have coped and adapted to living in a predominately white society. What area of psychology should Ramon study?
   a. psychodynamic
   b. behavioral
   c. sociocultural
   d. cognitive
   Ans.: c   LG: 2   Page: 15   QT: C

71. When different theories consider the influence of internal versus external forces on psychological development, which of the following would be a correct grouping?
   a. Cognitive and behavioral emphasize outside influence.
   b. Behavioral and sociocultural emphasize outside influence.
   c. Cognitive and sociocultural emphasize inside influence.
   d. Cognitive and behavioral emphasize inside influence.
   Ans.: b   LG: 2   Page: 15   QT: C

Learning Goal 3: Describe two movements that reflect a positive approach to psychology.

72. The humanistic perspective became the third force in psychology in response to the influence of
   a. the structural and behavioral movements.
   b. the functional and behavioral movements.
   c. the psychodynamic and behavioral movements.
   d. the cognitive and behavioral movements.
   Ans.: c   LG: 3   Page: 16   QT: F

73. During the Second World War, humans suffered horribly when placed in concentration camps. In spite of this terrible environmental influence, many left with both a sense of humor and their sense of dignity intact. Which of the following perspectives would best explain this?
   a. behaviorism
   b. cognitive
   c. humanist
   d. psychodynamic
   Ans.: c   LG: 3   Page: 16   QT: C

74. An important part of the humanist perspective is
   a. conditioning.
   b. the unconscious.
   c. survival of the fittest.
   d. free will.
   Ans.: d   LG: 3   Page: 16   QT: F

75. Which of the following events had a direct influence on the development of the humanistic perspective of psychology?
   a. behaviorism's emphasis on external rewards.
   b. the focus on the unconscious of the psychodynamic perspective
   c. a need for a more positive perspective.
   d. all of the above
   Ans.: d   LG: 3   Page: 16   QT: C

76. Three psychologists are in a discussion. One is a humanist, one a behaviorist, and one takes the psychodynamic perspective. They are discussing why a particular subject would act a certain way. Which of the following would summarize their perspectives?
   a. The psychodynamic and humanist would argue that the subject had free will and the behaviorist would disagree.
   b. The humanist would argue that the subject had free will; the behaviorist and psychodynamic would disagree.
   c. The humanist and the behaviorist would argue that the subject had free will and the psychodynamic theorist would disagree.
   d. The psychodynamic and the behaviorist would argue that the subjects had free will and the humanist would disagree.
   Ans.: b   LG: 3   Page: 16   QT: A

77. What initiated the positive psychology movement that is currently receiving a great deal of attention?
   a. Sloppy research methods left researchers far from positive (certain) about their results.
   b. There was an inability to positively identify the one theory that explained all human behavior.
   c. With the advancements of technology, researchers can now positively identify neurological activity that was speculative in the past.
   d. Psychology in the 20th century had become too negative, not focusing enough on positive human behaviors.
   Ans.: d   LG: 3   Page: 17   QT: C

78. The positive psychology movement developed as a result of the more negative emphasis on people's lives that psychological research seemed to focus on during the 20th century. Which of the following perspectives placed the least emphasis on negative human behavior?
    a. psychodynamic
    b. evolutionary
    c. behaviorist
    d. humanist
    Ans.: d   LG: 3   Page: 16   QT: C

79. Researchers interested in investigating the aspects of positive psychology would be least interested in which of the following?
    a. hope
    b. love
    c. responsibility
    d. aggression
    Ans.: d   LG: 3   Page: 17   QT: F

80. A researcher who is interested in learning more about subjective human experience would be most interested in which of the following perspectives?
    a. functionalism
    b. evolutionary
    c. positive psychology movement
    d. behaviorism
    Ans.: c   LG: 3   Page: 17   QT: C

Learning Goal 4: Evaluate careers and areas of specialization in psychology.

81. William is considering studying psychology as a major, but is concerned that he does not want to spend his life working with the mentally ill in a clinical setting. What advise could you offer him?
    a. Do not study psychology because it primarily involves just such work.
    b. Study psychology because you can use the understanding of human thought and behavior in many other occupational fields.
    c. Study psychology because there are many other areas of psychology that do not involve such work.
    d. both b and c
    Ans.: d   LG: 4   Page: 19   QT: A

82. Which of the following fields of study would involve acquiring an M.D.?
    a. clinical psychology
    b. counseling psychology
    c. behavioral neuroscience
    d. psychiatry
    Ans.: d   LG: 4   Page: 20   QT: F

83. A patient has been diagnosed as suffering from a psychological disorder and her therapist prescribes a drug that will block reuptake of neurotransmitters. The therapist is most likely a
    a. counseling psychologist.
    b. clinical psychologist.
    c. psychiatrist.
    d. behavioral neuroscientist.
    Ans.: c   LG: 4   Page: 20   QT: A

84. Some psychologists diagnose and treat people with psychological problems. Which of these would assist people with more serious problems?
   a. clinical psychologists
   b. counseling psychologists
   c. developmental psychologists
   d. personality psychologists
   Ans.: a   LG: 4   Page: 20   QT: C

85. Devon would like to work in an institutional setting with the mentally ill. Devon would be most interested in
   a. clinical psychology.
   b. developmental psychology.
   c. personality psychology.
   d. institutional psychology.
   Ans.: a   LG: 4   Page: 20   QT: A

86. While the field of psychology interests Chris a great deal, he would like to focus on research, rather than therapy. Which of the following fields would appeal to Chris?
   a. clinical psychology
   b. experimental psychology
   c. developmental psychology
   d. industrial and organizational psychology
   Ans.: b   LG: 4   Page: 21   QT: A

87. Raphael has talent in both biology and psychology. He cannot decide on a major but knows that he is interested in research. Which of the following fields of psychology would you urge him to learn more about?
   a. clinical psychology
   b. behavioral neuroscience
   c. developmental psychology
   d. industrial organizational psychology
   Ans.: b   LG: 4   Page: 21   QT: A

88. Cherie has developed an interest in how the brain functions. She wants to study the structures of the brain and try to determine how each works at the neurological level. Cherie would be most interested in which of the following areas of study?
   a. behavioral neuroscience
   b. cognitive psychology
   c. behavioral psychology
   d. all of the above
   Ans.: a   LG: 4   Page: 21   QT: A

89. William is the president of a company with over fifty employees. He is concerned that their productivity is not all it could be and wonders if motivation could be a problem. Which of the following types of psychologists should William consult?
   a. experimental psychologist
   b. social psychologist
   c. industrial organizational psychologist
   d. counseling psychologist
   Ans.: c   LG: 4   Page: 23   QT: A

90. Theresa is working as a consultant to provide information on what an employer should look for in a potential employee. It has been found through research that certain types of individuals tend to become better long-term employees than others. What type of psychologist is Theresa?
   a. cognitive psychologist
   b. social psychologist
   c. behavioral psychologist
   d. industrial organizational psychologist
   Ans.: d   LG: 4   Page: 23   QT: A

91. The field of psychology that would be interested in the biological, cognitive, and social domains of aging would be
   a. developmental psychology.
   b. experimental psychology.
   c. behavioral neuroscience.
   d. counseling psychology.
   Ans.: a   LG: 4   Page: 21   QT: F

92. The field of psychology that has been most greatly influenced by longer human life expectancy is
   a. humanistic psychology.
   b. developmental psychology.
   c. cognitive psychology.
   d. social psychology.
   Ans.: b   LG: 4   Page: 21   QT: F

93. Which of the following would be most interested in the enduring traits and characteristics of individuals?
   a. developmental psychologists
   b. personality psychologists
   c. humanistic psychologists
   d. experimental psychologists
   Ans.: b   LG: 4   Page: 21   QT: F

94. Luanda would like to study what it is that makes each of us uniquely different from each other. She knows of your extensive background in psychology and asks you which part of the field would be of most interest to her. Which of the following would you recommend?
   a. humanistic psychology
   b. cognitive psychology
   c. developmental psychology
   d. personality psychology
   Ans.: d   LG: 4   Page: 21   QT: A

95. Dr. Farison has performed extensive research on how to motivate sexually active teens to utilize condoms in order to avoid sexually transmitted diseases. Dr Farison is most likely a
   a. clinical psychologist.
   b. counseling psychologist.
   c. health psychologist.
   d. personality psychologist.
   Ans.: c   LG: 4   Page: 22   QT: A

96. Which of the following specialists would be most interested in how subjects cope with stress?
    a. health psychologists
    b. personality psychologists
    c. humanistic psychologists
    d. none of the above
    Ans.: a   LG: 4   Page: 22   QT: F

97. Fred and Wilma would like to find ways to improve their marriage. Each realizes that they may not be interacting as well as they could and would like some insight into potential solutions. They should consult with a
    a. clinical psychologist.
    b. counseling psychologist.
    c. health psychologist.
    d. personality psychologist.
    Ans.: b   LG: 4   Page: 20   QT: A

98. Tom is getting help with his ability to deal with his anger. A psychologist is teaching him skills to utilize when he feels himself losing control. The type of psychologist that Tom is seeing is most likely a
    a. counseling psychologist.
    b. behavioral neuroscientist.
    c. developmental psychologist.
    d. humanistic psychologist.
    Ans.: a   LG: 4   Page: 20   QT: A

99. Which of the following psychologists would be most interested in how students learn in the classroom?
    a. educational psychologist
    b. school psychologist
    c. counseling psychologist
    d. humanistic psychologist
    Ans.: a   LG: 4   Page: 22   QT: F

100. Sally is a teacher who is having a great deal of trouble controlling the students in her class. She took over the class midway through the semester from another teacher who resigned and left. Which of the following areas of psychological study would provide information that would be most helpful to her?
    a. school psychology
    b. counseling psychology
    c. humanistic psychology
    d. educational psychology
    Ans.: d   LG: 4   Page: 22   QT: A

101. Which of the following areas of psychology would be most involved in testing children and placing them in appropriate educational settings?
    a. educational psychology
    b. school psychology
    c. forensic psychology
    d. developmental psychology
    Ans.: b   LG: 4   Page: 22   QT: F

102. A field of psychology that is linked with human sensitivity to destruction of natural resources is
    a. educational psychology
    b. forensic psychology
    c. environmental psychology
    d. humanistic psychology
    Ans.: c   LG: 4   Page: 23   QT: F

103. Psychologists who are most interested in studying whether human psychological phenomena are universal or specific to one group would be
    a. humanistic psychologists
    b. environmental psychologists
    c. forensic psychologists
    d. cross-cultural psychologists
    Ans.: d   LG: 4   Page: 24   QT: F

104. Diane is investigating to find if there is a relationship between national origin and dissatisfaction in life among teens. Which of the following areas of psychology do you think Diane is trained in?
    a. humanistic psychology
    b. the positive psychology movement
    c. behaviorism
    d. cross-cultural psychology
    Ans.: d   LG: 4   Page: 24   QT: A

105. Researchers investigating the psychology of women would be most interested in
    a. promoting research on the study of women.
    b. integrating information about women with current psychological beliefs.
    c. applying information about the psychology of women to society and its institutions.
    d. all of the above
    Ans.: d   LG: 4   Page: 24   QT: C

106. The formal study of the psychology of women is a relatively new area. Which of the following would help to explain this?
    a. The field of psychology was dominated by men for many years.
    b. It was assumed that women think the same way that men do.
    c. Social and cultural expectations changed over the years, allowing women to become more involved in both education and careers.
    d. all of the above
    Ans.: d   LG: 4   Page: 24   QT: C

107. The field of psychology that applies psychological concepts to the legal system is
    a. humanistic psychology.
    b. forensic psychology.
    c. the positive psychology movement.
    d. environmental psychology.
    Ans.: b   LG: 4   Page: 24   QT: F

108. A law firm has retained Dr. Smith to consult on what type of jurist would be most sympathetic to their defendant's plight. Dr Smith would be a
    a. humanistic psychologist.
    b. cognitive psychologist.
    c. personality psychologist.
    d. forensic psychologist.
    Ans.: d   LG: 4   Page: 24   QT: A

109. The field of psychology which would be most interested in spectator response at an athletic event would be
    a. forensic psychology.
    b. sport psychology.
    c. industrial/organizational psychology.
    d. humanistic psychology.
    Ans.: b   LG: 4   Page: 24   QT: F

110. Jermaine is interested in the effects of visualization techniques on athletic performance. Jermaine is most likely a
    a. forensic psychologist.
    b. industrial/organizational psychologist.
    c. sport psychologist.
    d. humanistic psychologist.
    Ans.: c   LG: 4   Page: 24   QT: A

Learning Goal 5: Apply some strategies that will help you succeed in psychology.

111. The process of thinking reflectively, productively, and examining evidence is called
    a. common sense.
    b. culture bias.
    c. introspection.
    d. critical thinking.
    Ans.: d   LG: 5   Page: 29   QT: F

112. Which of the following is not a guideline for critical thinkers to follow?
    a. Be open minded.
    b. Use common sense.
    c. Be intellectually curious and careful.
    d. All of the above are guidelines for critical thinkers.
    Ans.: b   LG: 5   Page: 29   QT: F

113. Which of the following is a component of critical thinking?
    a. skepticism
    b. curiosity
    c. open mindedness
    d. All of the above are components of critical thinking.
    Ans.: d   LG: 5   Page: 29   QT: F

114. Which of the following would be the best example of the use of critical thinking?
    a. Rather than just rely on a horoscope, get a second opinion from a telephone psychic.
    b. Watch an individual who communicates with the dead on television more than once to ensure that their accuracy rate is high.
    c. Consult published research on a topic that you initially became interested in while watching a television show.
    d. Rather than study for the next test, rely on a friend who did study to communicate telepathically with you to give you the correct answers.
    Ans.: c   LG: 5   Page: 30   QT: A

115. Which of the following is true regarding channeling, horoscopes, and clairvoyance?
    a. They are money-making enterprises.
    b. They are meaningful to critical thinkers.
    c. They do not take advantage of people looking for answers.
    d. They are usually accurate.
    Ans.: a   LG: 5   Page: 31   QT: F

116. What would be the best strategy to use when trying to convince friends that horoscopes have no scientific basis for validity?
    a. Explain to them that many people believe in horoscopes but horoscopes have no scientific evidence to support their validity.
    b. Show them how each of the predictions for the day are very vague and could apply to anyone.
    c. Access a peer-reviewed psychological journal that contains a scientific study on the topic.
    d. all of the above
    Ans.: d   LG: 5   Page: 31   QT: C

117. Many ideas regarding the content of dreams have lasted for generations. One involves the idea that if are falling in your dream and hit the ground, you will really die that evening. Which of the following would be the perspective of a critical thinker regarding this?
    a. If someone really did die as a result of this dream, how could they have told anyone what they had dreamed?
    b. This is probably true, because you have heard it in the past.
    c. This is probably true, because you had heard it before and read it in a book on dream interpretation.
    d. This is probably true, because you had heard it before, read it in a book on dream interpretation, and saw it on a television show with a channeling expert communicating with the dead.
    Ans.: a   LG: 5   Page: 30   QT: C

118. Which of the following would provide the least amount of useful information for someone using critical thinking skills?
    a. professional journal
    b. psychological dictionary
    c. a television news report
    d. a psychological encyclopedia
    Ans.: c   LG: 5   Page: 30   QT: C

119. Which of the following verbs are associated with the use of critical thinking?
    a. analyze
    b. recite
    c. state
    d. list
    Ans.: a   LG: 5   Page: 29   QT: C

120. Which of the following verbs would be *least* associated with the use of critical thinking?
    a. rethink
    b. evaluate
    c. describe
    d. synthesize
    Ans.: c   LG: 5   Page: 29   QT: C

121. A news report relates that a child in a school setting has been arrested for bringing a weapon to school. A critical thinker would most likely approach this problem in which of the following ways?
    a. Point to the availability of weapons as the cause.
    b. Blame television violence.
    c. Point a finger at poor parenting.
    d. Look for multiple determinants of behavior.
    Ans.: d   LG: 5   Page: 29   QT: A

122. The use of critical thinking skills
    a. can be learned.
    b. makes decision making more difficult.
    c. often may not lead to concrete solutions.
    d. all of the above
    Ans.: d   LG: 5   Page: 29   QT: C

123. Which of the following would a critical thinker be least skeptical of?
    a. evolution
    b. astrology
    c. plant consciousness
    d. pre-cognition
    Ans.: a   LG: 5   Page: 31   QT: A

124. Which of the following would give a student the most balanced perspective on the topic of foreign policy?
    a. listening to a political leader regarding foreign policy
    b. listening to a professor about foreign policy
    c. applying critical thinking to foreign policy
    d. using common sense about foreign policy
    Ans.: c   LG: 5   Page: 30   QT: C

125. Which of the following study habits would be important to academic success?
    a. time management skills
    b. maximizing reading effectiveness
    c. classroom participation and interaction
    d. all of the above
    Ans.: d   LG: 5   Page: 26   QT: C

True/False Items

___ 126. The field of philosophy provides the origins for many psychological theories.
___ 127. Psychology is considered a natural science.
___ 128. Structuralism was based upon Darwin's theory of natural selection.
___ 129. Structuralism used introspection as a primary source of data.
___ 130. Wilhelm Wundt is credited with establishing the first psychological laboratory in 1879.
___ 131. Titchener is considered to be the founder of behaviorism.
___ 132. Social cognitive theory is based upon behaviorism.
___ 133. The unconscious plays an important role in psychodynamic theories.
___ 134. Cognitive theorists are interested in how the mind processes information.
___ 135. Most contemporary psychologists prefer the behavioral neuroscience approach.
___ 136. Evolutionary psychology theory has been influenced by the work of Darwin.
___ 137. The humanistic perspective is known as the "third force" in response to behaviorism and functionalism.
___ 138. One major difference between clinical and counseling psychologists is the severity of the problems that their clients have experienced
___ 139. Critical thinking involves thinking reflectively, productively, and examining evidence.
___ 140. Following critical thinking guidelines will always lead to a correct answer for a problem.

Answer Key for True/False Items

126.	Ans.: T	LG: 1	Page: 7	134.	Ans.: T	LG: 2	Page: 12
127.	Ans.: F	LG: 1	Page: 7	135.	Ans.: F	LG: 2	Page: 12
128.	Ans.: F	LG: 1	Page: 8	136.	Ans.: T	LG: 2	Page: 13
129.	Ans.: T	LG: 1	Page: 8	137.	Ans.: F	LG: 3	Page: 16
130.	Ans.: T	LG: 1	Page: 8	138.	Ans.: T	LG: 4	Page: 20
131.	Ans.: F	LG: 2	Page: 10	139.	Ans.: T	LG: 5	Page: 29
132.	Ans.: T	LG: 2	Page: 11	140.	Ans.: F	LG: 5	Page: 31
133.	Ans.: T	LG: 2	Page: 11				

Fill-in-the-Blank Items

141. Psychology is known as a _____ science.
142. The official beginning of the study of psychology in a laboratory is attributed to Wilhelm Wundt's work on perception. Wundt's work would lead to what became known as the _____ approach.
143. Thinking of the answer to this question would be called a _____ .
144. Writing the answer to this question would be a _____.
145. William James was a pragmatist who was most interested in useful knowledge. Rather than focus on components of the mind, he was more interested in how man adapts to and interacts with the environment. James was a _____.
146. John Watson proposed that the mental processes could not be studied scientifically. Instead he suggested that what should be monitored is _____.
147. _____ theory suggested that thoughts have an influence on how the environment influences behavior.
148. Dr. Stutz believes that our personalities are largely affected by unconscious forces. Dr. Stutz takes a _____ approach to human psychology.

149. If one were to take an interest in the process and sequence of events that contribute to information being stored in memory, _____ psychology would be their field of choice.
150. Professor Smith's area of research involves how neurotransmitters and neurological activity are linked to emotion. Professor Smith is researching from the_____ approach.
151. _____ psychology investigates the functional purpose and the role of adaptation to a changing environment in explaining human behavior.
152. Dr. Smith would like to know if there is a difference in the occurrence of depressive symptoms between different socioeconomic classes. Dr. Smith takes a _____ approach to the study of psychology.
153. Abraham argues with his friend Burhus that what is learned in conditioning rats and pigeons cannot be generalized to people because people think at a higher level. Abraham is most likely takes a _____ psychological perspective.
154. A relatively newer perspective that does not place an emphasis on the negatives of human thought and behavior is the _____.
155. Fred claims that he does not want to hear anyone criticize psychics because they have been consistently accurate for world events. It would appear that Fred is not utilizing the skill of _____.

Answer Key for Fill-in-the-Blank Items

141.	Ans.: behavioral	LG: 1	Page: 6
142.	Ans.: structural	LG: 1	Page: 8
143.	Ans.: mental process	LG: 1	Page: 6
144.	Ans.: behavior	LG: 1	Page: 6
145.	Ans.: functionalist	LG: 1	Page: 8
146.	Ans.: behavior	LG: 2	Page: 10
147.	Ans.: Social cognitive	LG: 2	Page: 11
148.	Ans.: psychodynamic	LG: 2	Page: 11
149.	Ans.: cognitive	LG: 2	Page: 12
150.	Ans.: behavioral neuroscience	LG: 2	Page: 13
151.	Ans.: Evolutionary	LG: 2	Page: 13
152.	Ans.: sociocultural	LG: 2	Page: 15
153.	Ans.: humanist	LG: 3	Page: 16
154.	Ans.: positive psychology movement	LG: 3	Page: 17
155.	Ans.: critical thinking	LG: 5	Page: 31

Matching Items

___	156. Adaptation	a. humanistic psychology
___	157. Stress and coping	b. health psychology
___	158. Underlying issues	c. forensic psychology
___	159. Effective teaching	d. industrial/organizational psychology
___	160. What we do	e. behaviorism
___	161. Athletic issues	f. cognitive psychology
___	162. Legal issues	g. psychodynamic approach
___	163. What we think	h. evolutionary psychology
___	164. Free will	i. educational psychology
___	165. Business success	j. sport psychology

Answer Key for Matching Items

156.	Ans.: h	LG: 2	Page: 13		161.	Ans.: j	LG: 4	Page: 24
157.	Ans.: b	LG: 4	Page: 22		162.	Ans.: c	LG: 4	Page: 24
158.	Ans.: g	LG: 2	Page: 11		163.	Ans.: f	LG: 2	Page: 12
159.	Ans.: i	LG: 4	Page: 22		164.	Ans.: a	LG: 3	Page: 16
160.	Ans.: e	LG: 2	Page: 11		165.	Ans.: d	LG: 4	Page: 23

Essay Questions

166. Explain how myth, philosophy, and science have all contributed to the development of the field of psychology. (LG: 1)

Answer Guidelines: Ancient myths gave way to philosophy. People attempted to explain phenomena in natural rather than supernatural causes. Eventually, use of the scientific method was incorporated to tests these causes.

167. Explain the difference between mental processes and behavior and give an example of each. In your answer, include the study of each and use of the scientific method. (LG: 1)

Answer Guidelines: Answers should reflect an understanding of the difference between mental processes (thoughts, feelings, motives) and behavior (what we actually do). Study of behavior is relatively straightforward, whereas for many years the study of mental processes was often speculative. Technology may be closing the gap between the two and someday may allow us to scientifically trace mental activity.

168. The functionalist perspective was one of the earliest schools of psychology. What was the primary emphasis of the functionalist perspective and what theory provided the foundation for this? Include the name of at least one prominent functionalist in your answer. (LG: 1)

Answer Guidelines: The functionalists emphasized the interactions between the mind and the outside environment. This was in opposition to the structuralists who were most interested in the components of the mind. Charles Darwin had a very large influence on the functionalists. . William James is the most prominent of the functionalists.

169. Compare the behavioral approach with the psychodynamic approach. In your answer, please include the names of at least one major proponent or each. (LG: 2)

Answer Guidelines: While the psychodynamic approach focuses on unconscious motives, the behavioral perspective stressed a more scientific approach to the study of psychology. The behaviorists stressed that the unconscious could not be studied scientifically, whereas behavior could be observed and quantified. Sigmund Freud was the father of the psychodynamic approach, and John Watson was the major proponent of behaviorism.

170. Compare the cognitive approach with the behavioral approach. How would each differ in their perspective on the human mind and thought process? (LG: 2)

Answer Guidelines: The behaviorists stressed the study of observable, quantifiable behaviors to the point where radical behaviorists believed that the thought process was not significant. In the middle part of the 20th century, researchers began to notice that not all learning was demonstrated and resurgence in interest in the thought process grew. The behaviorists would say that the thoughts behind behavior are insignificant. The cognitive theorists would argue that the study of the mind and thought process are the key to our understanding human psychology.

171. What is the evolutionary psychology approach and how does it attempt to explain human thought and behavior? (LG: 2)

Answer Guidelines: Evolutionary psychology is a relatively new resurgence in interest in Darwin's framework applied to humans. Evolutionary psychology emphasizes the importance of the adaptation, reproduction, and "survival of the fittest" in explaining behavior. This would include our appearance, our decisions, aggression, our fears, and our mating patterns.

172. Explain the sociocultural approach to psychology and describe its relevance to the field today. Why would this approach be receiving so much attention at the present time? (LG: 2)

Answer Guidelines: The sociocultural approach examines the ways in which the social and cultural environments influence behavior. If we are to fully understand a person's behavior, we must have knowledge of the cultural context in which that behavior occurs. In our own multicultural society and in the contrasts in different approaches to culture that are apparent worldwide, this is an extremely relevant and timely approach to the study of human psychology.

173. Explain the origins of the positive approach to psychology. Include the development of the humanistic perspective in your answer. (LG: 3)

Answer Guidelines: Recently, some psychologists have proposed that the study of human thought and behavior has become too negative. They believe that too often we place an emphasis on what people do wrong, rather than what they do right. The humanistic perspective of psychology was considered to be the "third force" in psychology, in response to the psychodynamic and behavioral theories. The humanists stressed positive qualities, the capacity for positive growth, and the freedom to choose a destiny.

174. List five different areas of specialization in psychology and briefly describe the function of each. (LG: 4)

Answer Guidelines: The answers to this could mention any of the different areas of psychology that are mentioned in the text and a brief description of what people in these fields really do.

175. Why is critical thinking important to the behavioral sciences? In your answer, please include four guidelines for critical thinking and give examples of how each could apply to the field of psychology. (LG: 5)

Answer Guidelines: Understanding the complex nature of the mind and behavior requires thinking reflectively and productively, and evaluating evidence to keep the field from sliding back to the use of myth. Guidelines for critical thinking include being open minded, being intellectually curious, being intellectually careful, looking for multiple determinants of behavior, and thinking like a scientist.

Chapter 2: Psychology's Scientific Methods

Learning Goals

1. Explain what makes psychology a science.
2. Discuss the three types of research that are used in psychology.
3. Distinguish between descriptive statistics and inferential statistics.
4. Discuss some research challenges that involve ethics, bias, and information.

Multiple-Choice Items

Learning Goal 1: Explain what makes psychology a science.

1. Which of the following is not central to the scientific approach?
   a. curiosity
   b. understanding
   c. skepticism
   d. objectivity
   Ans.: b   LG: 1   Page: 40   QT: F

2. The public dissemination of psychological findings in journals is an important component of which of the following aspects of science?
   a. collaboration
   b. professional requirements
   c. publishing sales
   d. none of the above
   Ans.: a   LG: 1   Page: 42   QT: F

3. Scientific journals are
   a. highly selective about what they publish.
   b. often peer reviewed.
   c. an important part of collaboration.
   d. all of the above
   Ans.: d   LG: 1   Page: 42   QT: F

4. Which of the following best describes the scientific method?
   a. conceptualizing a problem, collecting data, analyzing data, and drawing conclusions
   b. conceptualizing a problem, drawing conclusions, and then finding data to prove your conclusions
   c. conceptualizing a problem and drawing conclusions
   d. all of the above
   Ans.: a   LG: 1   Page: 42   QT: C

5. If one were to conceptualize a problem, which of the following would be most important?
   a. investigating relevant theories
   b. creating a hypothesis
   c. operationally defining terms
   d. all of the above
   Ans.: d   LG: 1   Page: 44   QT: C

6. Which of the following is the best example of a theory?
   a. Humans learn by observing others who are reinforced for their behaviors.
   b. Television is bad for children.
   c. Television is good for children.
   d. Children who watch television do not do well in school.
   Ans.: a   LG: 1   Page: 42   QT: A

7. A hypothesis in the behavioral sciences would also be referred to as
   a. an educated guess.
   b. a testable guess.
   c. a theory.
   d. both a and b
   Ans.: d   LG: 1   Page: 43   QT: C

8. Which of the following is the best example of a good hypothesis?
   a. Students who take classes early in the day will not learn as much.
   b. Students who stay up late at night will not pay as much attention the next day.
   c. Students who take classes early in the day and stay up late at night will not pay attention so they will not learn as much.
   d. Students who average less than six hours of sleep the nights before classes will not score as high on classroom tests as those students who average eight hours of sleep or more.
   Ans.: d   LG: 1   Page: 43   QT: A

9. Geraldine believes that if she has a cup of coffee in the morning, she may be able to pay more attention in her eight o'clock class. She plans to have a cup of coffee each day for a week before class and rate her level of alertness with a letter grade at the end of class. The best explanation for what Geraldine is utilizing is
   a. common sense.
   b. a theory.
   c. an informal use of the scientific method to test a hypothesis.
   d. the scientific method.
   Ans.: c   LG: 1   Page: 43   QT: A

10. What is the relationship between a theory and a hypothesis?
    a. Theories generate hypotheses.
    b. Hypotheses lead to theories.
    c. Theories are permanently correct.
    d. both a and b
    Ans.: d   LG: 1   Page: 43   QT: F

11. Which of the following is not true regarding theories and hypotheses?
    a. By the time a hypothesis gets to be a theory, it is known as a fact.
    b. Hypotheses may become theories if they are supported by research.
    c. A theory may lead to other hypotheses.
    d. A theory is only as good as the current research that supports it.
    Ans.: a   LG: 1   Page: 43   QT: C

12. Leslie believes that she may start feeling poorly as a result of eating certain foods. Recently she has noticed a slight rash that appears after she ingests some types of salads. She predicts that she will feel poorly the next time that she eats uncooked vegetables with preservatives. She has developed a(n) _____ about the origins of her rash. Her prediction that when she eats another salad with preservatives she will get another rash is a(n) _____.
    a. theory, hypothesis
    b. data, operational definition
    c. hypothesis, theory
    d. operational definition, theory
    Ans.: a   LG: 1   Page: 43   QT: A

13. Randy notices that the women's soccer team at his school tends to play the game at a better technical level than the boy's team. Though they are not as athletic, they move the ball better and work to be in position to make the correct play. Randy has a _____ about how women play soccer.
    a. hypothesis
    b. data
    c. theory
    d. operational definition
    Ans.: c   LG: 1   Page: 42   QT: A

14. When a research hypothesis is created, the terms must be
    a. correlated.
    b. defined by the dictionary.
    c. operationally defined in the context of the research.
    d. new terms.
    Ans.: c   LG: 1   Page: 44   QT: F

15. What does the term *operational definition* mean?
    a. an objective description of how a variable will be measured
    b. the rules of the scientific method
    c. the definition of the terms in each chapter
    d. how reliable the study will be
    Ans.: a   LG: 1   Page: 44   QT: F

16. Which of the following could be a good operational definition for *fast runner*?
    a. Olympic gold medallist
    b. one who breaks a world record
    c. school record holder
    d. all of the above
    Ans.: d   LG: 1   Page: 44   QT: A

17. Which of the following is the worst example of an operational definition?
    a. Intelligent—over the 98th percentile on a standardized test of intelligence
    b. Intelligent—over a 130 on a standardized test of intelligence
    c. Intelligent—class valedictorian
    d. Intelligent—very, very, smart
    Ans.: d   LG: 1   Page: 44   QT: A

18. Which of the following is the best operational definition for *bright*?
    a. extremely quick witted
    b. scoring two standard deviations above the average on a standardized test of intelligence
    c. class valedictorian
    d. extensive vocabulary
    Ans.: b   LG: 1   Page: 44   QT: A

19. Professor Thomas is researching marital disharmony. Which of the following would be the best operational definition of marital disharmony for his research study?
    a. lack of communication
    b. extramarital affairs
    c. scoring low on a psychological measure of marital harmony
    d. loss of the feeling of being in love
    Ans.: c   LG: 1   Page: 44   QT: A

20. Research information is known as
    a. facts.
    b. details.
    c. empirical facts.
    d. data.
    Ans.: d   LG: 1   Page: 45   QT: F

21. Which of the following is an example of data?
    a. scores on an IQ test
    b. number of times an infant smiles in a one-hour period
    c. how often a subject will put money in a slot machine
    d. all of the above
    Ans.: d   LG: 1   Page: 45   QT: F

22. When researchers collect data, they must consider
    a. who the subjects are.
    b. what research methods will be used.
    c. both a and b
    d. none of the above
    Ans.: c   LG: 1   Page: 45   QT: F

23. Which of the following is the best source of data?
    a. the thought process involved in decision making
    b. the conflicts of the unconscious
    c. introspective reflections
    d. the number of students that get this question correct on this test
    Ans.: d   LG: 1   Page: 45   QT: F

24. Professor Harper is speaking to his college class about his interest in learning strategies for elementary school students. The students in the elementary schools would be called a
    a. population.
    b. sample.
    c. random sample.
    d. stratified sample.
    Ans.: a   LG: 1   Page: 45   QT: A

25. Professor Harper decides to perform some research on the use of learning strategies for elementary school students. He chooses a school district in Vermont to see if teaching the students learning strategies will make a significant difference in their learning. These students would be called a
    a. random sample.
    b. sample.
    c. population.
    d. stratified sample.
    Ans.: b   LG: 1   Page: 45   QT: A

26. What is the relationship of a population and a sample?
    a. Populations are the same as samples.
    b. Samples are a subgroup of populations.
    c. Populations are subgroups of populations.
    d. What is learned from a population can be inferred to a sample.
    Ans.: b   LG: 1   Page: 45   QT: C

27. The entire group that a researcher would like to learn about is called a
    a. sample.
    b. random sample.
    c. population.
    d. population sample.
    Ans.: c   LG: 1   Page: 45   QT: F

28. A subset of the population that a researcher has chosen to study would be called a
    a. group.
    b. grouping variable.
    c. segmented population.
    d. sample.
    Ans.: d   LG: 1   Page: 45   QT: F

29. What is the best definition for a random sample?
    a. a sample of a population
    b. a sample of a population in which every subject has an equal chance of getting selected
    c. a sample of the population in which subjects are divided into one of two treatment conditions so that both groups are equal in ability
    d. a sample which ensures that the research hypothesis will be supported.
    Ans.: b   LG: 1   Page: 45   QT: F

30. Why is a random sample important to psychological research?
    a. It ensures that researcher bias did not play a part in the selection of the subjects.
    b. It provides better grounds for generalizing findings to the overall population.
    c. It provides a representative sample of the population of interest.
    d. all of the above
    Ans.: d   LG: 1   Page: 45   QT: C

31. A researcher wants to study motivation in the general high school population. Assuming she has equal access to all of them, which of the following groups of students would be a good representative sample?
    a. students in a remedial reading class
    b. members of the school debate team
    c. students in a required Library Sciences class
    d. students in after-school detention
    Ans.: c   LG: 1   Page: 46   QT: A

Learning Goal 2: Discuss the three types of research that are used in psychology.

32. What is the fundamental means of testing a hypothesis?
    a. observation
    b. description
    c. operationally defining
    d. collecting data
    Ans.: d   LG: 2   Page: 47   QT: F

33. Research that has the purpose of observing and recording behavior, but not proving any inferences is called
    a. descriptive research.
    b. correlational research.
    c. experimental research.
    d. quasi-experimental research.
    Ans.: a   LG: 2   Page: 47   QT: F

34. Observations and case studies would be considered which of the following types of research?
    a. experimental
    b. descriptive
    c. correlational
    d. none of the above
    Ans.: b   LG: 2   Page: 47   QT: F

35. Jillian has a pet rat that is extremely bright. She finds that the rat tends to follow the same routines as her pet dog. When the refrigerator is opened, both the dog and rat come to see if they will get rewarded with food. Jillian is using the _____ method of research.
    a. descriptive
    b. laboratory observation
    c. case study
    d. both a and c
    Ans.: d   LG: 2   Page: 47   QT: A

36. For observations to be effective in gathering data, they must be
    a. systematic.
    b. performed by someone who knows what they are looking for.
    c. precisely recorded.
    d. all of the above
    Ans.: d   LG: 2   Page: 48   QT: F

37. Which of the following would be considered an observational study?
    a. Dr. Lang gives two groups different amounts of caffeine to see if there are significant differences in the ability to recall words from a list.
    b. Dr. Howard analyzes test scores to see if there is a relationship between socioeconomic status and academic achievement.
    c. Dr. Fine looks at test scores from two different classes to see if there is a significant difference as a result of classes meeting at 8:00 A.M. or 11:00 A.M.
    d. Dr. Fine watches preschoolers interact to see if there are differences in socialization patterns between boys and girls.
    Ans.: d   LG: 2   Page: 48   QT: A

38. Which of the following is a drawback of laboratory observation?
    a. The researcher has a lack of control.
    b. The subjects are aware that they are being studied.
    c. Outside influences may be minimized.
    d. The laboratory is a controlled setting.
    Ans.: b   LG: 2   Page: 49   QT: C

39. Which of the following is an advantage of a laboratory observation?
    a. The subjects will act as they do in real life.
    b. Subjects are generally from a diverse background.
    c. The "mind" is very well matched to laboratory observation.
    d. The researcher has more control over outside distractions.
    Ans.: d   LG: 2   Page: 49   QT: C

40. Albert Bandura's famous study of observational learning was a
    a. naturalistic observation.
    b. laboratory observation.
    c. correlational study.
    d. quasi-experiment.
    Ans.: b   LG: 2   Page: 49   QT: A

41. Which of the following would be the best example of a laboratory observation?
    a. In a room in the college psychology department, children of the faculty were observed to see if the type of toy they played with had an effect on their social interactions.
    b. Graduate students went to a local mall to monitor how children from three to five years old interacted with their parents in the toy store.
    c. Graduate students monitored their own interactions with their professors both while working together in the college psychology laboratory and later at the school cafeteria to see if there was a difference in the demeanor of the professor during the interactions.
    d. Students monitor the entrance to the psychology building to see how often a person who has had the door held open for them holds the door for the next person.
    Ans.: a   LG: 2   Page: 49   QT: A

42. When researchers observe behavior in a real world setting, making no effort to control the situation, it is called a
    a. naturalistic observation.
    b. laboratory observation.
    c. correlational study.
    d. quasi-experiment.
    Ans.: a   LG: 2   Page: 50   QT: F

43. Which of the following would be not be an advantage of a naturalistic observation?
    a. Researchers would get a variety of subjects to observe.
    b. Subjects would act as they normally do.
    c. Researchers would give up some control over variables.
    d. Subjects would behave differently than in the laboratory.
    Ans.: c   LG: 2   Page: 50   QT: C

44. Which of the following would be an example of a naturalistic observation?
    a. Researchers watch parents react at a youth soccer game in a study of spectator behavior in sports.
    b. Students observe the race car section of a toy store to see if there is a difference in the number of boys and girls that spend time there.
    c. Dr. Fine observes a classroom to determine if students who sit in the front of the class interact with the teacher more frequently.
    d. all of the above
    Ans.: d   LG: 2   Page: 50   QT: C

45. When comparing naturalistic observations with laboratory observations, it can be said that with laboratory observations, researchers _____ and with naturalistic observations, researchers _____.
    a. give up control of variables, gain control of variables
    b. can generalize what they find to the overall population, are limited in their ability to generalize
    c. gain control of variables, give up control of variables
    d. both a and b
    Ans.: c   LG: 2   Page: 50   QT: C

46. When attempting to obtain a large sample for gathering data, a good source of information involves the use of
    a. naturalistic observations.
    b. laboratory observations.
    c. case studies.
    d. surveys and interviews.
    Ans.: d   LG: 2   Page: 51   QT: F

47. Which of the following would support use of a survey to gather data?
    a. mail
    b. telephone
    c. internet
    d. all of the above
    Ans.: d   LG: 2   Page: 51   QT: F

48. Which of the following is a disadvantage of using the survey method?
    a. Subjects are anonymous.
    b. Results can easily be quantified.
    c. It is possible to obtain large numbers of responses.
    d. Subjects may give socially desirable answers.
    Ans.: d   LG: 2   Page: 51   QT: C

49. Which of the following is true when comparing the interview and survey methods of data acquisition?
    a. Surveys can be done over the internet.
    b. Interviews can use open-ended questions and surveys can not.
    c. Surveys cannot be conducted over the telephone.
    d. All of the above are true.
    Ans.: d   LG: 2   Page: 51   QT: C

50. If one were concerned that the survey they were using was not written well enough to test subjects in a particular area, one approach to gathering data would be to use a(n)
    a. interview.
    b. standardized test.
    c. telephone survey.
    d. case study.
    Ans.: b   LG: 2   Page: 51   QT: C

51. Which of the following is not a property of a standardized test?
    a. Subjects are required to answer a series of written or oral questions.
    b. An individual's answers are tallied to yield a single score.
    c. The individual's score is compared with a large group of similar people.
    d. All standardized tests are based upon intelligence.
    Ans.: d   LG: 2   Page: 51   QT: F

52. Which of the following is false regarding standardized tests?
    a. They provide information about individual differences among people.
    b. They provide information about the person in non-test situations.
    c. They assume that behavior is consistent and stable.
    d. There have been criticisms of bias toward different cultural groups.
    Ans.: b   LG: 2   Page: 52   QT: C

53. A case study is most often
    a. an in-depth look at a single individual, used when the aspects of a person's life experiences cannot be duplicated.
    b. an experimental study.
    c. used to infer causation.
    d. an in-depth look at a single individual in the laboratory setting.
    Ans.: a   LG: 2   Page: 52   QT: F

54. Dr. Momambo has been studying the social development of a subject who has suffered through a horrific childhood. She is trying to learn as much as possible to help others who may have comparable experiences. Dr. Momambo is working on a
    a. naturalistic observation.
    b. correlational study.
    c. laboratory observation.
    d. case study.
    Ans.: d   LG: 2   Page: 52   QT: A

55. Which of the following statements is false regarding case studies?
    a. Researchers may learn a great deal about the individual they are studying.
    b. Often case studies look at situations which could not be ethically duplicated.
    c. What is learned in case studies is usually generalizable to the overall population.
    d. Subjects in case studies are often unique.
    Ans.: c   LG: 2   Page: 52   QT: C

56. If one were to investigate the strength of the relationship between two variables, they would be doing _____ research.
    a. descriptive
    b. experimental
    c. correlational
    d. case study
    Ans.: c   LG: 2   Page: 53   QT: F

57. If a correlation is positive, what does it mean?
    a. As one variable increased, the other variable increased.
    b. As one variable decreased, the other variable decreased.
    c. As one variable increased, the other variable decreased.
    d. both a and b
    Ans.: d   LG: 2   Page: 54   QT: C

58. Which of the following is true in determining the strength of a correlation?
    a. The closer the correlation is to 0.00, the weaker the correlation.
    b. Positive correlations are stronger than negative correlations.
    c. Negative correlations are stronger than positive correlations.
    d. The closer the correlation is to 1.00, the weaker the correlation.
    Ans.: a   LG: 2   Page: 54   QT: C

59. A student in statistics class was looking at the data that linked hours studied for a test and test score. They calculated a correlation coefficient of a positive 4.7. What does this mean?
    a. The student made an error in calculation
    b. There is an extremely strong relationship between hours studied and test scores.
    c. The number of hours studied causes test scores to be higher.
    d. both b and c
    Ans.: a   LG: 2   Page: 53   QT: C

60. Which of the following is not true regarding correlational studies?
    a. A positive correlation means that both factors vary in the same direction.
    b. A negative correlation means that both factors vary in different directions.
    c. The closer to 0.00 the correlation is, the weaker the strength of relationship.
    d. If the correlation is close to 1.00, causation can be inferred.
    Ans.: d   LG: 2   Page: 55   QT: C

61. Which is the strongest of the following correlations?
    a. + .1
    b. + .01
    c. − .4
    d. + 2.5
    Ans.: c   LG: 2   Page: 53   QT: F

62. In a two-day adult business training course, a number of students were sent by companies to sharpen their business skills. On the second day of the course, at 8:00 in the morning, they were given a pop quiz. Many of the students had attended a company social the previous night and researchers decided to try to determine if test scores were related to the number of drinks consumed the evening before. The correlation that resulted was a − .73. What does this infer?
    a. As the number of drinks consumed the evening before increased, so did the test scores.
    b. As the number of drinks consumed the evening before increased, test scores decreased.
    c. There is a very weak relationship between test scores and drinks consumed.
    d. Drinking the night before the test caused the test scores to decrease.
    Ans.: b   LG: 2   Page: 54   QT: A

63. John finds a study that has investigated the relationship between classroom seating position and academic achievement. The study finds a strong positive relationship between how close you sit to the front and center of the room and your class average. John, who sits in the back, is not the most motivated or successful student, but he decides to try this for himself. Without changing anything else in his approach to the class, he grabs a front seat the next time the class meets. When John takes his next test, as usual he had not studied, but he is shocked to find that his grade is no better than before. What could you tell John?
    a. Correlation does not infer causation.
    b. There were other variables at work besides seating position.
    c. both a and b
    d. His outcome is a statistical outlier, and his next test will be higher.
    Ans.: c   LG: 2   Page: 55   QT: A

64. When one variable has a direct effect on another, it is referred to as
    a. a strong positive correlation.
    b. a strong negative correlation.
    c. either a strong positive or a strong negative correlation.
    d. causation.
    Ans.: d   LG: 2   Page: 55   QT: F

65. Naturalistic observation may allow psychologists to _____ behavior whereas experiments may allow psychologists to _____ behavior.
    a. describe, explain
    b. explain, describe
    c. explain, control
    d. explain, explain
    Ans.: a   LG: 2   Page: 56   QT: C

66. What type of research must be utilized to infer causation?
    a. case study
    b. laboratory observation
    c. correlational
    d. experimental
    Ans.: d   LG: 2   Page: 56   QT: F

67. _____ research is a carefully regulated procedure in which one or more factors believed to influence the behavior being studied are manipulated while all other factors are held constant.
    a. Descriptive
    b. Correlational
    c. Experimental
    d. Standardized
    Ans.: c   LG: 2   Page: 56   QT: F

68. In experimental research, the _____ is manipulated by the researcher to be an influential factor.
    a. dependent variable
    b. independent variable
    c. correlational variable
    d. extraneous variable
    Ans.: b   LG: 2   Page: 56   QT: F

69. In experimental research, the _____ can change in an experiment as a result of the treatment.
    a. dependent variable
    b. independent variable
    c. correlational variable
    d. extraneous variable
    Ans.: a   LG: 2   Page: 56   QT: F

70. The change of the _____ is subject to the influence of the
    _____.
    a. extraneous variable, dependent variable
    b. dependent variable, independent variable
    c. independent variable, dependent variable
    d. independent variable, extraneous variable
    Ans.: b   LG: 2   Page: 56   QT: F

71. Jana is investigating the effects of expectation of task difficulty on task performance. She has randomly assigned her subjects to one of two groups. In group one, the subjects are told that the puzzle that they are going to solve is very difficult. In group two, the subjects are told that the puzzle is only of moderate difficulty. Jana has decided to time the subjects to find if there is a significant difference in the time that it takes the members of each group to solve the puzzle. Jana is using which kind of research method?
    a. an experiment
    b. a case study
    c. naturalistic observation
    d. a case study
    Ans.: a   LG: 2   Page: 56   QT: A

72. Jana is investigating the effects of expectation of task difficulty on task performance. She has randomly assigned her subjects to one of two groups. In group one, the subjects are told that the puzzle that they are going to solve is very difficult. In group two, the subjects are told that the puzzle is only of moderate difficulty. Jana has decided to time the subjects to find if there is a significant difference in the time that it takes the members of each group to solve the puzzle. In this study, what is the independent variable?
    a. the puzzle that each subject tries to solve
    b. the time that it takes to solve the puzzle
    c. the number of mistakes the subjects make solving the puzzle
    d. what each group is told about the difficulty of the puzzle prior to solving it
    Ans.: d   LG: 2   Page: 56   QT: A

73. A researcher is interested in determining if alcohol will have a negative effect on rats' ability to complete a maze. One group of rats is fed a measured amount of alcohol and a second group is not. Both groups are observed in the maze to see how many mistakes (wrong turns) that they make before they complete the task. The researcher hypothesizes that the rats that have ingested the alcohol will have a more difficult time getting through the maze. What is the dependent variable in this experiment?
    a. the maze
    b. the amount of alcohol ingested
    c. the group that the rat is in
    d. the number of errors made in the maze
    Ans.: d   LG: 2   Page: 56   QT: A

74. In an experiment, the group that receives a manipulation of the independent variable is known as the
    a. experimental group.
    b. treatment group.
    c. control group.
    d. random group.
    Ans.: a   LG: 2   Page: 56   QT: F

75. In an experiment, the group that does not receive manipulation of the independent variable, but establishes a baseline for comparison is known as the
    a. non-treatment group.
    b. experimental group.
    c. random group.
    d. control group.
    Ans.: d   LG: 2   Page: 56   QT: F

76. A researcher is interested in determining if alcohol will have a negative effect on rats' ability to complete a maze. One group of rats is fed a measured amount of alcohol and a second group is not. Both groups are observed in the maze to see how many mistakes (wrong turns) that they make before they complete the task. The researcher hypothesizes that the rats that have ingested the alcohol will have a more difficult time getting through the maze. Which is the control group in this study?
   a. the rats who have ingested the alcohol
   b. the rats who have not ingested alcohol
   c. the researchers who are monitoring the experiment
   d. This experiment does not have a control group.
   Ans.: b   LG: 2   Page: 56   QT: A

77. A researcher is interested in determining if alcohol will have a negative effect on rats' ability to complete a maze. One group of rats is fed a measured amount of alcohol and a second group is not. Both groups are observed in the maze to see how many mistakes (wrong turns) that they make before they complete the task. The researcher hypothesizes that the rats that have ingested the alcohol will have a more difficult time getting through the maze. Which is the experimental group in this study?
   a. the rats who have ingested the alcohol
   b. the rats who have not ingested alcohol
   c. the researchers who are monitoring the experiment
   d. This experiment does not have a control group.
   Ans.: a   LG: 2   Page: 56   QT: A

78. A diabolical psychology professor decides to perform an experiment with two of his classes. He believes that students who are in a classroom that is too hot will not learn well. In one class, he leaves the temperature of the room at 70 degrees, which is normal room temperature. In another class, each day before they enter, he turns the thermostat up to 85 degrees. At the end of that particular semester, he tests them both with the same exam to see if one group has learned significantly more than the other. In this highly unethical study, what class would be the experimental group?
   a. the 70-degree class
   b. the 85-degree class
   c. Both groups are in the experiment.
   d. Because of ethics, there was no experimental group.
   Ans.: b   LG: 2   Page: 56   QT: A

79. A diabolical psychology professor decides to perform an experiment with two of his classes. He believes that students who are in a classroom that is too hot will not learn well. In one class, he leaves the temperature of the room at 70 degrees, which is normal room temperature. In another class, each day before they enter, he turns the thermostat up to 85 degrees. At the end of that particular semester, he tests them both with the same exam to see if one group has learned significantly more than the other. In this highly unethical study, the students in the 70-degree classroom would be the _____ and the students in the 85-degree classroom would be the _____.
   a. experimental group, control group
   b. independent variable, dependent variable
   c. dependent variable, independent variable
   d. control group, experimental group
   Ans.: d   LG: 2   Page: 56   QT: A

80. Which of the following is not true of random assignment?
   a. It reduces the likelihood that the experiment's results will be due to any preexisting differences between groups.
   b. It is an important consideration when performing experimental research.
   c. It prevents the researcher from intentionally making the groups different before the treatment.
   d. It guarantees that both groups will be equal at the start of the experiment.
   Ans.: d   LG: 2   Page: 56   QT: C

81. Experimenter bias is demonstrated in the text by the classic Rosenthal study with the "maze-bright" and "maze-dull rats". In this study,
   a. experimenter expectations influenced the performance of the rats.
   b. students were compelled to help the "maze-dull" rats because of their lack of ability.
   c. "maze-dull" rats actually outperformed the "maze-bright" rats.
   d. one group of students started with rats that really were brighter than others but the students were told that the abilities were equal.
   Ans.: a   LG: 2   Page: 57   QT: F

82. Which of the following would help reduce the effects of experimenter bias or research participant bias?
   a. random sampling
   b. double blind experiments
   c. use of a placebo
   d. all of the above
   Ans.: d   LG: 2   Page: 57   QT: F

83. What is the difference between experimenter bias and research participant bias?
   a. Experimenter bias is based upon researcher expectations; participant bias is a result of poor selection of subjects.
   b. Participant bias is when subjects act upon a preconceived expectation; experimenter bias is based upon researcher expectations.
   c. Experimenter bias is when the subjects do not like the experimenter; participant bias is a result of a poor selection of subjects.
   d. There is no difference between experimenter bias and participant bias.
   Ans.: b   LG: 2   Page: 57   QT: C

84. Which of the following does not apply to a placebo?
   a. innocuous
   b. inert
   c. physiological effect
   d. no physiological effect
   Ans.: c   LG: 2   Page: 58   QT: F

85. When research participant expectations, rather than the treatment, produce an experimental outcome, it is called a(n)
   a. blind effect.
   b. double blind effect.
   c. experimenter bias.
   d. placebo effect.
   Ans.: d   LG: 2   Page: 58   QT: F

86. Sam needs a cup of coffee to get himself going in the morning. His wife does not think that the ingestion of caffeine is good for him, so she gradually switches his coffee from caffeinated to decaffeinated without telling him. Sam never notices the difference and, in fact, remarks that his coffee really gives him a boost for his day. What might best explain this?
    a. placebo effect
    b. double blind effect
    c. experimenter bias
    d. all of the above
    Ans.: a   LG: 2   Page: 58   QT: A

87. Which of the following procedures would be the best example of a double blind experiment? Dr. Jones randomly chooses two groups of subjects for a study on the effects of ginseng on memory. He would like to test the idea that ginseng may improve memory.
    a. He gives one group ginseng and gives the other nothing. He then gives each group the same memory test.
    b. He gives one group ginseng and the other group a placebo. The subjects do not know which one they have received. He then gives each group the same memory test.
    c. He has an associate give one group ginseng and the other group a placebo. He therefore never knows which group got the ginseng and neither do the subjects. He then gives each group the same memory test.
    d. He gives one group ginseng and the other group a placebo. The subjects do not know which they have received. He then gives each group a different memory test.
    Ans.: c   LG: 2   Page: 58   QT: A

88. Dr. Ramirez has developed a new drug that will make subjects feel more alert and better about themselves. She randomly selects two groups of participants and gives one group a capsule that contains the compound every day for one month. The other group does not take any medication. After one month, the experimental group reports feeling more healthy than normal. The control group does not report any difference. As a critical thinker, who is familiar with research fundamentals, what might you consider in analyzing Dr. Ramirez's study?
    a. The experimental group could be experiencing a placebo effect.
    b. The doctor's drug worked.
    c. The sampling of groups was biased.
    d. The drug must have some sort of stimulant in it.
    Ans.: a   LG: 2   Page: 58   QT: A

Learning Goal 3: Distinguish between descriptive statistics and inferential statistics.

89. How would one describe statistics in behavioral sciences?
    a. mathematical methods used to report data
    b. descriptive
    c. inferential
    d. all of the above
    Ans.: d   LG: 3   Page: 59   QT: F

90. The mathematical procedures used to summarize and describe data are called
    a. inferential statistics.
    b. descriptive statistics.
    c. probabilities.
    d. regression.
    Ans.: b   LG: 3   Page: 59   QT: F

91. Which of the following would not be a good example of descriptive statistics?
    a. the mean of a set of personality scores
    b. the median of intelligence test scores
    c. a predicted intelligence test score
    d. the standard deviation of a set of intelligence test scores
    Ans.: c   LG: 3   Page: 59   QT: F

92. Which of the following types of studies would best utilize descriptive statistics?
    a. a report of the class average and standard deviation of this test
    b. a predictive study using the regression formula that forecasts the scores on this test
    c. experiment testing a hypothesis regarding rat behavior under the influence of alcohol
    d. all of the above
    Ans.: a   LG: 3   Page: 59   QT: A

93. A single number that tells you the overall characteristics for a set of data would be called
    a. an inferential statistic.
    b. a measure of central tendency.
    c. a correlation coefficient.
    d. all of the above.
    Ans.: b   LG: 3   Page: 59   QT: F

94. The measure of central tendency that is used most often is the
    a. standard deviation.
    b. variance.
    c. mean.
    d. median.
    Ans.: c   LG: 3   Page: 59   QT: F

95. The measure of central tendency that is the average of all of the scores is the
    a. mean.
    b. median.
    c. mode.
    d. standard deviation.
    Ans.: a   LG: 3   Page: 59   QT: F

96. The _____ is the measure of central tendency that falls exactly in the middle of the distribution of scores.
    a. mean
    b. median
    c. mode
    d. standard deviation
    Ans.: b   LG: 3   Page: 60   QT: F

97. Considering a distribution of the following scores (8, 9, 11, 48, 73), which measure of central tendency does the number 11 represent?
   a. mean
   b. median
   c. mode
   d. standard deviation
   Ans.: b   LG: 3   Page: 60   QT: F

98. Considering the distribution of the following scores (8, 9, 10, 11, 73), which measure of central tendency would you choose to represent the distribution?
   a. mean
   b. median
   c. mode
   d. none of the above
   Ans.: b   LG: 3   Page: 60   QT: C

99. The most frequently occurring score in a distribution is called the
   a. mean.
   b. median.
   c. mode.
   d. standard deviation.
   Ans.: c   LG: 3   Page: 60   QT: F

100. Considering a distribution of the following scores (8, 8, 11, 48, 73), which measure of central tendency does the number 8 represent?
   a. mean
   b. median
   c. mode
   d. standard deviation
   Ans.: c   LG: 3   Page: 60   QT: A

101. A friend approaches you and asks you to donate to a particular cause. You ask the friend how much everyone else has been giving. You are asking for which measure of central tendency?
   a. mean
   b. median
   c. mode
   d. standard deviation
   Ans.: c   LG: 3   Page: 60   QT: A

102. Which of the following would not be considered a measure of variability?
   a. range
   b. standard deviation
   c. variance
   d. mean
   Ans.: d   LG: 3   Page: 60   QT: C

103. The descriptive statistic that will give an indication of how much the scores are spread out is the
    a. mean.
    b. median.
    c. range.
    d. standard deviation.
    Ans.: c   LG: 3   Page: 61   QT: C

104. The _____ gives an idea of how far the scores vary on average from the mean of the sample.
    a. mean
    b. median
    c. range
    d. standard deviation
    Ans.: d   LG: 3   Page: 61   QT: C

105. Group A has taken a memory test and the resultant scores have a mean of 78 and a standard deviation of 12. Group B has taken the same test and has a mean of 72 and a standard deviation of 20. Based upon this information, which of the following is true?
    a. Group A scored higher on average and the scores were more spread out from the average than Group B.
    b. Group B scored higher on average and the scores were more spread out from the average than Group A.
    c. Group A scored higher on average and the scores were less spread out from the average than Group B.
    d. Group B scored higher on average and the scores were less spread out from the average than Group B.
    Ans.: c   LG: 3   Page: 61   QT: A

106. The mathematical method that is used to draw conclusions about data and to test a hypothesis is called
    a. central tendency.
    b. descriptive statistics.
    c. range.
    d. inferential statistics.
    Ans.: d   LG: 3   Page: 62   QT: F

107. Which of the following would not utilize inferential statistics methods?
    a. Jana is testing a hypothesis on expectations and problem solving.
    b. Mark would like to see if there is a significant difference in male and female scores on this test.
    c. Duval would like to know if the 11:00 class did better on this test than the 8:00 class.
    d. Marvin wants to know the overall class average.
    Ans.: d   LG: 3   Page: 62   QT: A

108. When research findings are found to be statistically significant, we can say that our hypothesis has a high level of _____ of being correct.
    a. probability
    b. certainty
    c. proof
    d. doubt
    Ans.: a   LG: 3   Page: 62   QT: C

109. Researchers have decided to investigate the hypothesis that token economies can be used to improve classroom behavior in elementary school. One class of students will get a star each time they behave well each morning or afternoon. At the end of the week, if they have accumulated 8 stars, they will get an extended play period on Friday afternoon. Another class will not be offered the stars or the extended play period. Classroom observers will monitor behavior to see if there is a difference in disruptive acts at the end of the week. They found that there is indeed a large statistical difference between groups as a result of the treatment, with the class who was rewarded having significantly fewer disruptive behaviors. Which of the following can be said about our results?
    a. This proves that token economies improve behavior.
    b. This proves that students do not behave as well when they are not rewarded.
    c. Our findings are statistically significant and support our hypothesis.
    d. both a and b
    Ans.: c   LG: 3   Page: 62   QT: A

Learning Goal 4: Discuss some research challenges that involve ethics, bias, and information.

110. Which of the following is not true about ethics in psychological research?
    a. The participant's best interests must be kept foremost in the researcher's mind.
    b. Technology has been linked to new questions in ethics.
    c. There are no famous studies that would be considered unethical today.
    d. Research must often be altered to meet ethical standards.
    Ans.: c   LG: 4   Page: 63   QT: C

111. Which of the following is not an ethical issue addressed by American Psychological Association guidelines?
    a. informed consent
    b. subjects being paid for participation
    c. debriefing
    d. deception
    Ans.: b   LG: 4   Page: 64   QT: F

112. Which of the following is true regarding ethical research with animals?
    a. Animal research has led to some very beneficial outcomes for human application.
    b. Rats and mice account for the vast majority of animals in psychological research.
    c. Animal research is guided by a set of ethical standards.
    d. all of the above
    Ans.: d   LG: 4   Page: 66   QT: F

113. Fred has decided to do research on the effects of ingestion of caffeine on the ability to run quickly. He has decided to trap neighbors' cats and feed half of them milk with caffeine added to it. The other half will drink milk without caffeine. After exactly 30 minutes, he plans to open the cage door and frighten them. He will then time them with a stopwatch to see how quickly they cross his yard to the exit point. What is the major problem with Fred's plan?
    a. He does not plan to randomly choose the subjects.
    b. There is no guarantee the cats will run directly to the exit.
    c. He may not be able to generalize what he has learned about cats to humans.
    d. There are some ethical problems with this study.
    Ans.: d   LG: 4   Page: 66   QT: A

114. Prior to being involved in a study, all research participants must know what their participation will involve and what risks might develop. This is called
    a. debriefing.
    b. confidentiality.
    c. informed consent.
    d. deception.
    Ans.: c   LG: 4   Page: 64   QT: F

115. Following the conclusion of research, all participants must be informed of its purpose and the methods that were used. This is referred to as
    a. debriefing.
    b. confidentiality.
    c. informed consent.
    d. deception.
    Ans.: a   LG: 4   Page: 64   QT: F

116. Which of the following was prevalent in society and in psychology for a long time?
    a. gender bias
    b. cultural bias
    c. ethnic bias
    d. all of the above
    Ans.: d   LG: 4   Page: 67   QT: F

117. The term "ethnic gloss" refers to which of the following?
    a. making a particular ethnic group look better than they really are
    b. portraying an ethnic group as less diverse than they really are
    c. covering up imperfections in an ethnic group
    d. portraying an ethnic group as more diverse than they really are
    Ans.: b   LG: 4   Page: 67   QT: F

118. John decided to compare test scores of a particular cultural group with the scores of his own group. He knew that many students of the other group could be found in one of the poorer schools in the district, so he went there to get the data. He also knew of students from his own group who were enrolled in one of the better districts in his area, so he gathered data from them. His comparisons did support his hypothesis that his group did much better in that standardized test. Which of the following problem with John's research could be associated with ethnic gloss?
    a. He assumed that all members of his culture were similar to those he tested in ability.
    b. He assumed that all members of the other culture were similar in ability to those that he tested.
    c. both a and b
    d. none of the above
    Ans.: c   LG: 4   Page: 68   QT: A

119. If a researcher is investigating differences in children's behavior based on cultural background and is aware of ethnic gloss, she would
    a. realize that members of each group are very similar to each other because of genetics.
    b. understand that within each group there will be individual differences.
    c. realize that there really are no differences between the groups.
    d. understand that ethnic groups are very homogeneous.
    Ans.: b   LG: 4   Page: 67   QT: C

120. When we read research studies, we may have a tendency to overgeneralize. This means
    a. we assume that the results of this study are correct.
    b. we assume that there is a causation factor when there is not.
    c. we assume that what we learned from a small sample would apply to the population.
    d. we use critical thinking too much.
    Ans.: c   LG: 4   Page: 70   QT: C

121. Imagine that a woman named Jane Doe is the foremost proponent of one psychological perspective on human motivation. As we read the writings of Jane Doe on the topic, what must we keep in mind as critical thinkers?
    a. Jane Doe has certainly considered other perspectives that disagree with what she is writing and they must be incorrect.
    b. Jane Doe would not be published if her writings addressed only one perspective.
    c. Jane Doe is an expert in the field and what she writes must be true.
    d. Jane Doe may be correct, but we must also consider potential bias as we read the article.
    Ans.: d   LG: 4   Page: 71   QT: C

122. Which of the following would be the best source of a scientific study in psychology?
    a. tabloid
    b. magazine
    c. television
    d. professional journal
    Ans.: d   LG: 4   Page: 71   QT: F

123. If we were to rank sources of information from low to high in level of credibility, which of the following would be correct?
    a. magazine, tabloid, television, professional journal
    b. tabloid, magazine, professional journal, television
    c. television, magazine, tabloid, professional journal
    d. tabloid, television, magazine, professional journal
    Ans.: d   LG: 4   Page: 71   QT: C

124. Which of the following is the best statement regarding values in the field of psychology?
    a. Psychology is a science and values do not exist in science.
    b. Psychologists are able to separate their own views and values from their research.
    c. Psychology professors intentionally keep their values out of their lectures.
    d. Because psychologists are humans, their values are often reflected in their work. It is therefore important to utilize critical thinking in being a wise consumer of information about psychology.
    Ans.: d   LG: 4   Page: 66   QT: C

125. Which of the following statements is important to being a wise consumer of information about psychology?
    a. Do not overgeneralize from a small sample.
    b. Do not attribute causation where it has not been found.
    c. Always consider the source of psychological information.
    d. all of the above
    Ans.: d   LG: 4   Page: 70   QT: C

True/False Items

_____ 126. Science is a collaborative effort in which colleagues share their research in academic journals.
_____ 127. A hypothesis is a testable assumption.
_____ 128. Hypotheses lead to theories, which can then lead to other hypotheses.
_____ 129. Descriptive studies are used primarily in hypothesis testing.
_____ 130. Causation may be inferred from correlational research if the correlation is positive enough.
_____ 131. A correlation coefficient operationally defines strength of relationship.
_____ 132. An experimental study can be used to prove a hypothesis.
_____ 133. In an experimental study, the dependent variable is manipulated by the researcher.
_____ 134. In experimental research, the control group is used as a comparison group to determine if the treatment has had a significant effect on the experimental group.
_____ 135. If we were to give a group a treatment that changes their outcomes so much that our treatment is recognized as effective by the rules of science, it has created results that would be called statistically significant.
_____ 136. The standard deviation is a descriptive statistic that gives us the range of our scores.
_____ 137. Inferential statistics are used to describe what has occurred in a study.
_____ 138. The most common measure of central tendency is the median.
_____ 139. In all psychological research, the highest priority is always placed upon making certain that our treatment has an no adverse effects on subjects.
_____ 140. We are more aware of gender, ethnic, and cultural bias today than we have been in the past.

Answer Key for True/False Items

126.	Ans.: T	LG: 1	Page: 42		134.	Ans.: T	LG: 2	Page: 56
127.	Ans.: T	LG: 1	Page: 43		135.	Ans.: T	LG: 3	Page: 62
128.	Ans.: T	LG: 1	Page: 43		136.	Ans.: F	LG: 3	Page: 61
129.	Ans.: F	LG: 2	Page: 47		137.	Ans.: F	LG: 3	Page: 62
130.	Ans.: F	LG: 2	Page: 55		138.	Ans.: F	LG: 3	Page: 60
131.	Ans.: T	LG: 2	Page: 53		139.	Ans.: F	LG: 4	Page: 63
132.	Ans.: F	LG: 2	Page: 56		140.	Ans.: T	LG: 4	Page: 67
133.	Ans.: F	LG: 2	Page: 56					

Fill-in-the-Blank Items

141. The _____ is essentially a four-step process involving conceptualizing a problem, collecting data, analyzing data, and drawing conclusions.

142. A _____ is a possible explanation for past observations that can also be used to predict future observations.

143. _____ research involves systematically observing and recording behavior.

144. One of the disadvantages of a _____ observation is that the researcher gives up control over variables.

145. One of the disadvantages of a _____ observation is that subjects may not respond as they normally would.

146. Using a _____ is a way to gather large responses, but is susceptible to social desirability effects in subjects' responses.

147. _____ research quantifies the strength of relationship between two variables.

148. Only with the experimental method can researchers infer _____.
149. In an experiment, the variable that is measured to determine if the treatment had an effect is called the _____ variable.
150. When all subjects have an equal probability of being selected for a study, it is called _____ assignment.
151. _____ is what takes place when subjects' expectations, rather than the actual treatment, influence research outcomes.
152. _____ statistics are mathematical procedures that are used to summarize data.
153. _____ is the statistical measure that is the distance between the highest and lowest scores in the distribution.
154. _____ statistics are mathematical methods that are commonly used in hypothesis testing.
155. _____ _____ involves assuming that there are less individual differences within ethnic groups than there really are.

Answer Key for Fill-in-the-Blank Items

141.	Ans.: scientific method	LG: 1	Page: 42
142.	Ans.: theory	LG: 1	Page: 42
143.	Ans.: Descriptive	LG: 2	Page: 47
144.	Ans.: naturalistic	LG: 2	Page: 50
145.	Ans.: laboratory	LG: 2	Page: 49
146.	Ans.: survey	LG: 2	Page: 51
147.	Ans.: Correlational	LG: 2	Page: 53
148.	Ans.: causation	LG: 2	Page: 56
149.	Ans.: dependent	LG: 2	Page: 56
150.	Ans.: random	LG: 2	Page: 56
151.	Ans.: Placebo effect	LG: 2	Page: 58
152.	Ans.: Descriptive	LG: 3	Page: 59
153.	Ans.: Range	LG: 3	Page: 60
154.	Ans.: Inferential	LG: 3	Page: 62
155.	Ans.: Ethnic gloss	LG: 4	Page: 67

Matching Items

___	156. Hypothesis	A.	most frequent score
___	157. Operational definition	B.	specifies variables
___	158. Population	C.	all those of interest
___	159. Case study	D.	average of distances from the mean
___	160. Mean	E.	subjects aware
___	161. Median	F.	middle score
___	162. Standard deviation	G.	average
___	163. Double blind experiment	H.	subjects, researcher unaware
___	164. Research participant bias	I.	testable guess
___	165. Mode	J.	population of one

Answer Key for Matching Items

156.	Ans.: I	LG: 1	Page: 43	161.	Ans.: F	LG: 3	Page: 60
157.	Ans.: B	LG: 1	Page: 44	162.	Ans.: D	LG: 4	Page: 61
158.	Ans.: C	LG: 1	Page: 45	163.	Ans.: H	LG: 2	Page: 58
159.	Ans.: J	LG: 2	Page: 52	164.	Ans.: E	LG: 2	Page: 57
160.	Ans.: G	LG: 3	Page: 59	165.	Ans.: A	LG: 3	Page: 60

Essay Questions

166. What are the four steps of the scientific method as applied to psychological research? Create a hypothetical research situation and describe how each of the steps would be applied to developing your study. (LG: 1)

> Answer Guidelines: The four steps of the scientific method, as listed in the text, are:
> 1. conceptualize a problem.
> 2. collect research information (data),
> 3. analyze data, and
> 4. draw conclusions.
> The students should be able to construct their own hypothetical study, using application of the aforementioned terms to the study to show understanding of both.

167. Explain the relationship between hypotheses and theories in the constant development of psychological research. Explain the importance of operationally defining terms in your answer. (LG: 1)

> Answer Guidelines: Answers should reflect an understanding of how theory and hypothesis development constantly interact to advance the field of psychology. A theory is a set of ideas that attempt to explain certain observations and a hypothesis is a testable guess. A large part of what makes a hypothesis testable is operationally defining the terms of the study. Theories lead to hypotheses, which lead to more theories, which lead to more hypotheses and so on.

168. What is descriptive research? List three types of descriptive studies and create a research scenario for each of them. (LG: 2)

> Answer Guidelines: Descriptive research has the purpose of systematically observing and recording behavior. Four types of descriptive research are observations, surveys or interviews, standardized tests, and case studies. Students should show their understanding of each by generating their own example of each.

169. Explain correlational research. In your answer, address each of the following:
    a. Strengths and limitations of correlational studies.
    b. An example of a correlational study, including a hypothetical correlation coefficient, and an explanation of what this number means. (LG: 2)

    Answer Guidelines: Correlational research investigates the relationship between two variables. One of the strengths of a correlational study is that it quantifies this relationship as positive or negative and by how closely the two variables follow trends in relationship to each other. A disadvantage is that often correlational studies are inferred to be causational, which they are not. Students should demonstrate their understanding by creating a hypothetical study and explaining how their correlation coefficient reflects what has taken place in the study.

170. Explain the concept of experimental research in psychology, including causation. As a part of your answer, create a hypothetical experiment and include an independent variable, dependent variable, experimental group, control group, and random sampling. Be certain to utilize some controls for outside influences in your study. (LG: 2)

    Answer Guidelines: In order to infer causation from this study, students should mention some control of other variables that could have an influence on the dependent variable in addition to the effects of the independent variable. Again, by applying these terms to a research scenario, students are demonstrating their understanding of the language of research.

171. What are descriptive statistics? In your answer include an explanation of central tendency and variability, listing and describing three of the measures of central tendency and two measures of variability. (LG: 3)

    Answer Guidelines: Descriptive statistics describe and summarize data. A measure of central tendency is a single number that represents the overall characteristics of a set of data. Three measures of central tendency would be the mean, median, and mode. Variability describes how each set of data varies in its scores and how they are distributed. The range and standard deviation would be measures of variability.

172. Explain the use of inferential statistics in psychological research. Include the concept of statistical significance and give an example of a research situation when the use of inferential statistics would be appropriate. (LG: 3)

    Answer Guidelines: Inferential statistics are used to draw conclusions about data that has been collected. Inferential statistics would be used in hypothesis testing. When we speak of statistical significance, it infers that the differences between the two groups are so large that there is a very small statistical probability the outcomes are the result of chance. The key to the student example would be that it reflects hypothesis testing.

173. What are ethics and why are they important to psychological research? Include four of the APA ethical guidelines in your answer. (LG: 4)

Answer Guidelines: Ethics requirements are constantly evolving along with the science of psychology. Ethical guidelines keep psychological research within the standards of what is acceptable and what is not by the current culture. Ethical issues covered in the book include informed consent, confidentiality, debriefing, and deception.

174. Why are potential gender, cultural, and ethnic biases important to consider in the field of psychology? In your answer describe the role of overgeneralization and ethnic gloss in bias. (LG: 4)

Answer Guidelines: For decades, psychology demonstrated both a gender bias and a lack of inclusion of more people from diverse ethnic groups. Today, there is more awareness of this, and researchers are more conscious of such concepts as overgeneralization and assuming that every one from a particular ethnic background is more similar than they really are.

175. Why is critical thinking in reading research important to being a wise consumer of psychological information? List three considerations that should be kept in mind when considering psychological findings. (LG: 4)

Answer Guidelines: Critical thinking in reading research will keep the reader aware of potential bias or values of the researcher, which could limit the use of their findings. Considerations to keep in mind would be distinguishing between group results and individual needs, not overgeneralizing based upon a small sample, understanding that a single study is rarely the defining word about a problem, not inferring causation from correlation, and evaluating the source of the information for values, bias, or credibility.

Chapter 3: Biological Foundations of Behavior

Learning Goals

1. Discuss the nature and basic functions of the nervous system.
2. Explain what neurons are and how they process information.
3. Identify the brain's levels and structures, and summarize the functions of its structures.
4. State what the endocrine system is and how it affects behavior.
5. Describe the brain's capacity for recovery and repair.
6. Explain how genetics and evolutionary psychology increase our understanding of behavior.

Multiple-Choice Questions

Learning Goal 1: Discuss the nature and basic functions of the nervous system.

1. The body's electrochemical communication circuitry that is made up of billions of neurons is called
    a. the brain.
    b. the spinal cord.
    c. the peripheral system.
    d. the nervous system.
    Ans.: d   LG: 1   Page: 78   QT: F

2. From an evolutionary perspective, the human brain evolved because _____ gave some humans an advantage in survival.
    a. being able to anticipate adversity
    b. planning for ways to avoid adversity
    c. finding ways to cope with adversity
    d. all of the above
    Ans.: d   LG: 1   Page: 78   QT: F

3. The brain and the spinal cord comprise the
    a. central nervous system (CNS).
    b. peripheral nervous system (PNS).
    c. autonomic nervous system.
    d. sympathetic nervous system.
    Ans.: a   LG: 1   Page: 81   QT: F

4. Robin is interested specifically in the nervous system and wishes to study further on the topic. Her field of interest is called
    a. physiology.
    b. neuroscience.
    c. behavioral science.
    d. biology.
    Ans.: b   LG: 1   Page: 78   QT: F

5. The term _____ denotes the brain's capacity for modification and change.
   a. malleability
   b. plasticity
   c. flexibility
   d. non-rigidity
   Ans.: b   LG: 1   Page: 79   QT: F

6. Which of the following would *not* be an example of cognitive plasticity?
   a. A baby learns to reach for objects.
   b. A school child pronounces a complex word for the first time.
   c. A student cannot remember the name of a term for a test.
   d. A child rides a bicycle without training wheels for the first time.
   Ans.: c   LG: 1   Page: 79   QT: A

7. Afferent nerves
   a. carry information to the brain.
   b. are sensory nerves.
   c. carry information away from the brain to affect movement.
   d. both a and b
   Ans.: d   LG: 1   Page: 80   QT: F

8. Efferent nerves
   a. are motor nerves.
   b. carry information to the brain.
   c. are sensory nerves.
   d. both b and c
   Ans.: a   LG: 1   Page: 80   QT: F

9. Afferent nerves are _____ and efferent nerves are _____.
   a. motor nerves, sensory nerves
   b. sensory nerves, motor nerves
   c. motor nerves, internerves
   d. sensory nerves, internerves
   Ans.: b   LG: 1   Page: 80   QT: F

10. The sensory neurons and motor neurons are parts of the
    a. afferent neuron.
    b. neural network
    c. efferent neuron.
    d. transmitter neuron.
    Ans.: b   LG: 1   Page: 80   QT: F

11. Sean stepped on a tack. The sensation of the pain is carried to his central nervous system by
    a. efferent neurons.
    b. association neurons.
    c. glial neurons.
    d. afferent neurons.
    Ans.: d   LG: 1   Page: 80   QT: C

12. While driving, you see a light flashing red and step on the brakes. The instructions to press on the brakes were conveyed to the muscles by
    a. afferent neurons.
    b. sympathetic neurons.
    c. efferent neurons.
    d. parasympathetic neurons.
    Ans.: c   LG: 1   Page: 80   QT: C

13. Afferent is to efferent as _____ is to _____.
    a. peripheral, central
    b. central, peripheral
    c. motor, sensory
    d. sensory, motor
    Ans.: d   LG: 1   Page: 80   QT: C

14. Most information processing occurs when information moves through _____ in the central nervous system.
    a. neural networks
    b. pathways
    c. interneurons
    d. associations
    Ans.: a   LG: 1   Page: 80   QT: F

15. The brain and spinal cord make up the
    a. central nervous system.
    b. peripheral nervous system.
    c. nervous system.
    d. somatic nervous system.
    Ans.: a   LG: 1   Page: 81   QT: C

16. All nerve fibers outside of the central nervous system are part of the
    a. autonomic nervous system.
    b. voluntary nervous system.
    c. peripheral nervous system.
    d. spinal nervous system.
    Ans.: c   LG: 1   Page: 81   QT: F

17. What is the main function of the peripheral nervous system?
    a. to direct communication between the brain and the spinal cord
    b. to connect the central nervous system to the rest of the body
    c. to balance the activities of the central nervous system
    d. to send information from the skin and muscles to the CNS
    Ans.: b   LG: 1   Page: 81   QT: C

18. On the news you hear of an individual who was injured in a diving accident and lost the use of their body from the neck down. From what you know about the human nervous system, where would you hypothesize that the damage was done?
    a. central nervous system
    b. peripheral nervous system
    c. synaptic cleft
    d. myelin sheath
    Ans.: a   LG: 1   Page: 81   QT: A

19. Fred was using a power tool and mangled the end of one of his fingers. Even though doctors were able to reconstruct the finger for use, he has no feeling in the finger. Which part of the human nervous system would you say was most affected?
    a. central nervous system
    b. peripheral nervous system
    c. synaptic cleft
    d. myelin sheath
    Ans.: b   LG: 1   Page: 81   QT: A

20. The majority of nerve cells in the human body are located in the
    a. sympathetic nervous system.
    b. autonomic nervous system.
    c. peripheral nervous system (PNS).
    d. central nervous system (CNS).
    Ans.: d   LG: 1   Page: 81   QT: F

21. Which of the following is not a part of the peripheral nervous system?
    a. somatic nervous system
    b. sympathetic nervous system
    c. spinal cord
    d. autonomic nervous system
    Ans.: c   LG: 1   Page: 81   QT: F

22. As you drive down the interstate, a car approaches you traveling the wrong way in your lane. Which part of your nervous system goes into action?
    a. the parasympathetic division of the central nervous system
    b. the sympathetic division of the autonomic nervous system
    c. the sympathetic division of the somatic nervous system
    d. the somatic division of the central nervous system
    Ans.: b   LG: 1   Page: 81   QT: C

23. The division of the nervous system that helps conserve energy by calming the body is the
    a. central nervous system.
    b. sensory nervous system.
    c. parasympathetic nervous system.
    d. sympathetic nervous system.
    Ans.: c   LG: 1   Page: 81   QT: F

24. The sympathetic and parasympathetic nervous system comprise the
    a. autonomic nervous system.
    b. somatic nervous system.
    c. peripheral nervous system.
    d. voluntary nervous system.
    Ans.: a   LG: 1   Page: 81   QT: F

25. When you accidentally touch a hot burner on a stove, which part of your nervous system carries the pain message from your skin to your brain?
    a. the autonomic nervous system
    b. the sympathetic nervous system
    c. the parasympathetic nervous system
    d. the somatic nervous system
    Ans.: d   LG: 1   Page: 81   QT: F

26. Breathing, heart rate, and digestion are monitored by the
    a. central nervous system.
    b. autonomic nervous system.
    c. somatic nervous system.
    d. brain.
    Ans.: b   LG: 1   Page: 81   QT: F

Learning Goal 2: Explain what neurons are and how they process information.

27. Approximately how many neurons are in the human brain?
    a. 100 million
    b. 5 billion
    c. 10 billion
    d. 100 billion
    Ans.: d   LG: 2   Page: 82   QT: F

28. Information is transmitted in the nervous system at speeds as fast as
    a. 760 miles per hour (speed of sound).
    b. 186,000 miles per second (speed of light).
    c. a few hundred miles per hour.
    d. a few thousand miles per hour.
    Ans.: c   LG: 2   Page: 82   QT: F

29. The _____ provide support and nutritional benefits in the nervous system.
    a. worker neurons
    b. glial cells
    c. interneurons
    d. dendrites
    Ans.: b   LG: 2   Page: 82   QT: F

30. What is the relationship between neurons and glial cells?
    a. Glial cells cannot develop without neurons.
    b. Neurons need the support of glial cells.
    c. Glial cells destroy neurons.
    d. Neurons make glial cells stronger.
    Ans.: b   LG: 2   Page: 82   QT: C

31. Which of the following statements is not true regarding glial cells?
    a. Glial cells are specialized to process information.
    b. There are more glial cells in the nervous system than neurons.
    c. Glial cells function in a supportive role for neurons.
    d. Glial cells function in a nutritive role for neurons.
    Ans.: a   LG: 2   Page: 82   QT: C

32. What are the three basic parts of the neuron?
    a. cell body, axon, myelin sheath
    b. dendrites, cell body, axon
    c. nucleus, cell body, synapse
    d. cell body, myelin sheath, terminal button
    Ans.: b   LG: 2   Page: 82   QT: F

33. The part of the neuron that receives messages is the
    a. dendrite.
    b. synapse.
    c. axon.
    d. myelin sheath.
    Ans.: a   LG: 2   Page: 82   QT: F

34. The part of the neuron that carries messages away from the cell bodysoma and toward the terminal buttons is called the
    a. nucleus.
    b. axon.
    c. dendrite.
    d. cell body.
    Ans.: b   LG: 2   Page: 82   QT: F

35. A message travels from one neuron to the next in which sequence?
    a. dendrite, axon, cell body
    b. axon, dendrite, synapse
    c. synapse, axon, dendrite
    d. cell body, axon, dendrite
    Ans.: d   LG: 2   Page: 82   QT: C

36. Dendrites contribute to neurological networks by
    a. providing more surface area for other axons to link to.
    b. sending information to more axons.
    c. interpreting transferred information in complex combinations.
    d. firing signals.
    Ans.: a   LG: 2   Page: 82   QT: F

37. A layer of fat cells that encases and insulates most axons is called
    a. a myelin sheath.
    b. insulation.
    c. axon plasticity.
    d. neuron sheathing.
    Ans.: a   LG: 2   Page: 82   QT: F

38. The speed at which a neuron sends its message along the axon is faster if the
    a. neuron is unmyelinated.
    b. nodes of Ranvier are missing.
    c. neuron is myelinated.
    d. axon has dendrites.
    Ans.: c   LG: 2   Page: 83   QT: C

39. Damaged or insufficient myelin sheath would cause which of the following?
    a. slowed nerve impulses
    b. rapid nerve impulses
    c. accelerated nerve impulses
    d. exaggerated nerve impulses
    Ans.: a   LG: 2   Page: 83   QT: C

40. Neuron number one is unmyelinated. Neuron number two is myelinated. Which neuron will conduct signals faster?
    a. neuron one
    b. neuron two
    c. Neurons do not conduct at different speeds.
    d. All neurons conduct at the same speed.
    Ans.: b   LG: 2   Page: 83   QT: C

41. William has Multiple Sclerosis (MS). MS is associated with damage or deterioration to the myelin sheath. What effect will this destruction have on William's neurological functioning?
    a. William will suffer from seizures.
    b. William will not experience many neurological deficits from his multiple sclerosis.
    c. William's neural impulses will be more efficient due to the lack of myelin.
    d. William's neural impulses will be slowed down due to the damaging of the myelin tissue.
    Ans.: d   LG: 2   Page: 83   QT: A

42. The conduction of nerve impulses abides by which principle?
    a. some-or-all principle
    b. negative-positive principle
    c. all-or-none principle
    d. relativity principle
    Ans.: c   LG: 2   Page: 84   QT: F

43. The all-or-none principle describes which of the following events?
    a. All of the chemicals must be in place for a neuron to fire.
    b. Neurons either fire or not; there is no partial firing.
    c. When you cannot remember something, it is because some neurons are firing at less than half capacity.
    d. All neurons must fire at once, or none of them will fire.
    Ans.: b   LG: 2   Page: 84   QT: C

44. While a neuron is actively sending a message, its electrical charge is
    a. negative.
    b. indeterminate.
    c. positive.
    d. neutral.
    Ans.: c   LG: 2   Page: 84   QT: C

45. The term given to the stable, negative charge of an inactive neuron is
    a. dormant.
    b. afferent.
    c. somatic.
    d. resting potential.
    Ans.: d   LG: 2   Page: 84   QT: F

46. Which of the following conditions is present when a neuron is at rest?
    a. There are more positive ions within the neuron.
    b. The neuron is regenerating neurotransmitters.
    c. The neuron lacks an electrical charge.
    d. There are negative ions within the neuron.
    Ans.: d   LG: 2   Page: 84   QT: F

47. Action potential is the term that refers to a neuron
    a. that is prepared to send an electrochemical signal.
    b. that has just "fired."
    c. that is "firing."
    d. that is about to "fire."
    Ans.: c   LG: 2   Page: 84   QT: F

48. The term used to describe the brief wave of electrical charge that sweeps down the axon is
    a. firing.
    b. action potential.
    c. resting potential.
    d. both a and b
    Ans.: b   LG: 2   Page: 84   QT: F

49. In the neuron's resting state, some ions can pass through the cell membrane and some cannot; this is possible because the membrane is
    a. fatty.
    b. permeable.
    c. semipermeable.
    d. depolarized.
    Ans.: c   LG: 2   Page: 84   QT: F

50. Which of the following types of ion are most significant to the neural impulse?
    a. sodium and potassium
    b. calcium and sodium
    c. potassium and ginseng
    d. ginseng and magnesium
    Ans.: a   LG: 2   Page: 83   QT: F

51. The tiny junctions between neurons are called
    a. receptor gaps.
    b. dendrite gaps.
    c. synapses.
    d. interneurons.
    Ans.: c   LG: 2   Page: 85   QT: F

52. Before the _____ neural impulse can cross the _____, it must be converted
    to a(n) _____ impulse.
    a. electrical, synaptic gap, chemical
    b. chemical, interneuron, electrical
    c. electrical, interneuron, chemical
    d. chemical, synaptic gap, electrical
    Ans.: a   LG: 2   Page: 85   QT: C

53. Neurotransmitters are stored
    a. inside the myelin sheath.
    b. in the vesicles of terminal buttons.
    c. in the cell body.
    d. at the end of the dendrites.
    Ans.: b   LG: 2   Page: 86   QT: F

54. The function of synaptic vesicles is to
    a. break down neurotransmitters.
    b. restore the electrical balance of the cell after an action potential has occurred.
    c. receive information from other cells and store it for later use.
    d. store neurotransmitter molecules.
    Ans.: d   LG: 2   Page: 86   QT: F

55. Substances that make possible the transmission of a nerve impulse from one neuron to another are
    called
    a. depolarization substances.
    b. synaptic transmitters.
    c. neurotransmitters.
    d. electrical transmitters.
    Ans.: c   LG: 2   Page: 86   QT: F

56. A neural impulse continues to travel through the receiving neuron only after
    a. neurotransmitter molecules have been locked into the receptor sites of the receiving neuron.
    b. neurotransmitter molecules have been released into the synapse between the two neurons.
    c. neurotransmitter molecules have been released by the synaptic vesicles of the first neuron.
    d. neurotransmitter molecules have been stored in the terminal buttons of the receiving neuron.
    Ans.: a   LG: 2   Page: 86   QT: C

57. Neurotransmitters _____ neurons to fire.
    a. excite or inhibit
    b. inhibit
    c. always cause
    d. excite
    Ans.: a   LG: 2   Page: 86   QT: F

58. What is the relationship between inhibitory neurotransmitters and excitatory neurotransmitters?
    a. Inhibitory neurotransmitters inhibit the nervous system to calm the individual.
    b. Excitatory neurotransmitters excite the nervous system to make the subject more alert.
    c. Excitatory neurotransmitters make the receiving cell more likely to fire a signal and inhibitory neurotransmitters make the receiving cell less likely to fire a signal.
    d. both a and b
    Ans.: c   LG: 2   Page: 86   QT: C

59. According to your text, how many neurotransmitters have been identified?
    a. about 5
    b. about 10
    c. more than 50
    d. more than 1,000
    Ans.: c   LG: 2   Page: 86   QT: F

60. Sarah has recently started taking an antianxiety drug prescribed by her doctor. She was most likely suffering from which of the following?
    a. a dopamine deficiency
    b. a GABA deficiency
    c. an excess of serotonin
    d. an excess of endorphins
    Ans.: b   LG: 2   Page: 87   QT: C

61. Which of the following neurotransmitters is *not* inhibitory?
    a. norepinephrine
    b. serotonin
    c. dopamine
    d. acetylcholine
    Ans.: d   LG: 2   Page: 86   QT: F

62. Research has found that low levels of GABA are linked with
    a. anxiety.
    b. depression.
    c. decreased pain sensations.
    d. Down's syndrome.
    Ans.: a   LG: 2   Page: 87   QT: F

63. If a poison causes severe, uncontrollable muscle spasms, that poison probably _____ activity in the neurotransmitter _____.
   a. increases; dopamine
   b. decreases; serotonin
   c. increases; acetylcholine (ACh)
   d. decreases; GABA
   Ans.: c   LG: 2   Page: 86   QT: C

64. Too little of this neurotransmitter is associated with depression and too much of it is associated with manic states. The neurotransmitter in question is
   a. norepinephrine.
   b. acetylcholine (ACh).
   c. GABA.
   d. dopamine.
   Ans.: a   LG: 2   Page: 87   QT: F

65. If a person has a low level of dopamine, this would most likely cause which problem?
   a. The person would have difficulty walking.
   b. The person would suffer from anxiety.
   c. The person would suffer from depression.
   d. The person would have sleep problems.
   Ans.: a   LG: 2   Page: 87   QT: C

66. Cross-country runners often experience a great deal of pain in the middle of a run. Coaches advise that if a runner can make it through this "wall of pain," some relief will occur naturally. This relief, sometimes called "runner's high," occurs due to neurotransmitters called
   a. serotonins.
   b. GABA inhibitors.
   c. epinephrines.
   d. endorphins.
   Ans.: d   LG: 2   Page: 87   QT: C

67. Endorphins can be described as all of the following *except*
   a. pain killers.
   b. natural opiates.
   c. pain inhibitors.
   d. GABA inhibitors.
   Ans.: d   LG: 2   Page: 87   QT: C

68. You may twist your foot and not feel any pain until some time after the injury occurred. This initial lack of pain is due to which of the following?
   a. the release of dopamine
   b. the release of serotonin
   c. the release of endorphins
   d. the inhibition of GABA
   Ans.: c   LG: 2   Page: 87   QT: C

69. People with an unusually high pain threshold most likely have high levels of which neurotransmitter?
    a. endorphins
    b. serotonins
    c. dopamines
    d. epinephrines
    Ans.: a   LG: 2   Page: 87   QT: C

70. Charles has been given Prozac to help with his depression. In this kind of situation, it is hoped that Prozac will do which of the following?
    a. increase the inhibitory effect of GABA
    b. increase levels of serotonin
    c. decrease the norepinephrine level
    d. reduce the activity of endorphins
    Ans.: b   LG: 2   Page: 87   QT: C

71. What do serotonin, dopamine, and norepinephrine have in common?
    a. All regulate the sleep/wake cycle.
    b. All stimulate the firing of neurons in the central nervous system.
    c. All affect mental health.
    d. All are involved in muscular control.
    Ans.: c   LG: 2   Page: 87   QT: C

72. Your friend, who has been feeling pretty low lately, has been diagnosed with a neurotransmitter imbalance. What can you tell your friend to alleviate her worries about this diagnosis?
    a. Neurotransmitter imbalances are no cause for worry.
    b. Neurotransmitter imbalances only affect behavior in elderly people.
    c. Most neurotransmitter imbalances will correct themselves.
    d. Many neurotransmitter imbalances can be effectively treated with medication.
    Ans.: d   LG: 2   Page:87-88   QT: A

73. Some neurotransmitters are excitatory whereas others are
    a. inhibitory.
    b. resting.
    c. charged.
    d. agitory.
    Ans.: a   LG: 2   Page: 86   QT: F

74. A drug that mimics or increases a neurotransmitter's effects is known as a(n)
    a. antagonist.
    b. protagonist.
    c. agonist.
    d. agitator.
    Ans.: c   LG: 2   Page: 88   QT: F

Learning Goal 3. Identify the brain's levels and structures, and summarize the functions of its structures.

75. An abnormal disruption in the brain caused by injury or disease is called a
    a. lesion.
    b. brain stain.
    c. peroxidase.
    d. neuro stain.
    Ans.: a   LG: 3   Page: 89   QT: F

76. Howard Gardner studied subjects who had received trauma to areas of their brain tissue to determine its effects on their function. This would be called a _____ study.
    a. biological
    b. lesion
    c. neuro stain
    d. physiological
    Ans.: b   LG: 3   Page: 89   QT: A

77. Identifying pathways of connectivity in the brain and nervous system is enabled by using
    a. electroencephalographs.
    b. stains.
    c. lesion studies.
    d. X-rays.
    Ans.: b   LG: 3   Page: 90   QT: F

78. Dr. Fine would like to monitor brain activity during the sleep cycle in an attempt to determine if brain waves change significantly during dreams. Dr. Fine would be most interested in using a(n) _____ to monitor this activity.
    a. lesion study
    b. MRI
    c. EEG
    d. peroxidase
    Ans.: c   LG: 3   Page: 90   QT: A

79. A three-dimensional image obtained from a computer to assemble X-rays of the head is called a(n)
    a. electroencephalograph (EEG).
    b. magnetic resonance imaging (MRI).
    c. positron-emission tomography (PET).
    d. computerized tomography (CT scan).
    Ans.: d   LG: 3   Page: 91   QT: F

80. Dr. Howard would like to observe the parts of the brain that are active when a subject is engaged in problem solving. She uses a tracer that is responsive to glucose levels in order to monitor the brain's activity. Which of the following tests would she be using?
    a. electroencephalograph (EEG)
    b. magnetic resonance imaging (MRI)
    c. positron-emission tomography (PET)
    d. computerized tomography (CT scan)
    Ans.: c   LG: 3   Page: 91   QT: A

81. Dr. Smith needs to obtain a detailed view of internal brain tissue in a subject. He believes that there may be a tumor, and would like for medical technology to assist him in pinpointing it. Which of the following tests would he want to use?
    a. electroencephalograph (EEG)
    b. magnetic resonance imaging (MRI)
    c. positron-emission tomography (PET)
    d. lesion study
    Ans.: b   LG: 3   Page: 91   QT: A

82. Electrical activity of the brain is commonly recorded by a(n)
    a. PET scan.
    b. action potential.
    c. electroencephalograph.
    d. quantum interference device.
    Ans.: c   LG: 3   Page: 90   QT: F

83. Why is a CT scan superior to a regular X ray of the brain?
    a. It measures the glucose levels in the brain.
    b. It does not pose a problem of radiation overexposure.
    c. It results in a chart of brain-wave activity.
    d. It provides a three-dimensional image.
    Ans.: d   LG: 3   Page: 91   QT: C

84. What do an EEG, a CT scan, a PET scan, and a MRI have in common?
    a. They have to be performed when the subject is asleep.
    b. They provide a visual representation of activity throughout the brain.
    c. They produce specific information about neurotransmitters.
    d. They are dangerous and used only in extreme cases.
    Ans.: b   LG: 3   Page: 91   QT: C

85. What are the three main parts of the hindbrain?
    a. medulla, reticular formation, and thalamus
    b. medulla, pons, and cerebellum
    c. pons, cerebellum, and hippocampus
    d. hippocampus, thalamus, and amygdala
    Ans.: b   LG: 3   Page: 91   QT: F

86. Which part of the hindbrain is involved in sleep and arousal?
    a. pons
    b. cerebellum
    c. hippocampus
    d. amygdala
    Ans.: a   LG: 3   Page: 92   QT: F

87. If a person's cerebellum were damaged in an accident, you would expect that person to have problems with
    a. breathing.
    b. seeing and hearing.
    c. speaking.
    d. muscle coordination.
    Ans.: d   LG: 3   Page: 92   QT: C

88. A blow to the back of the head can be dangerous because the
    a. thalamus is there.
    b. medulla, which regulates breathing, is there.
    c. substantia nigra, which regulates movement, is there.
    d. memories are stored there.
    Ans.: b   LG: 3   Page: 92   QT: C

89. The medulla, the cerebellum, and the pons are found in the
    a. hindbrain.
    b. midbrain.
    c. forebrain.
    d. antebrain.
    Ans.: a   LG: 3   Page: 91   QT: F

90. An area of the brain that regulates basic survival functions and is often referred to as the "reptilian brain" is called the
    a. thalamus.
    b. brain stem.
    c. medulla.
    d. cerebral cortex.
    Ans.: b   LG: 3   Page: 93   QT: F

91. The reticular formation is primarily involved in
    a. breathing and reflexes.
    b. arousal and attention.
    c. eating and drinking.
    d. thinking and learning.
    Ans.: b   LG: 3   Page: 92   QT: F

92. When someone calls your name, you turn to see who called you because of the activation of which brain structure?
    a. hypothalamus
    b. reticular formation
    c. medulla
    d. spinal cord
    Ans.: b   LG: 3   Page: 92   QT: C

93. The midbrain relays information between the
    a. brain and the eyes and ears.
    b. cerebellum and the pons.
    c. brain and the spinal cord.
    d. spinal cord and the thalamus.
    Ans.: a   LG: 3   Page: 92   QT: F

94. The amygdala and the hippocampus comprise which of the following?
    a. thalamus
    b. midbrain
    c. basal ganglia
    d. limbic system
    Ans.: d   LG: 3   Page: 93   QT: F

95. Andrea suffered a brain injury that damaged her hippocampus. Andrea will most likely have difficulties with which of the following?
    a. walking
    b. sleeping
    c. retention of new memories
    d. control of emotions
    Ans.: c   LG: 3   Page: 93   QT: C

96. Which part of the brain serves as the switching station for the brain's incoming and outgoing messages?
    a. hypothalamus
    b. thalamus
    c. hippocampus
    d. amygdala
    Ans.: b   LG: 3   Page: 94   QT: C

97. The part of the brain that mainly differentiates the human brain from the brains of animals like rats is the
    a. brain stem.
    b. hindbrain.
    c. midbrain.
    d. forebrain.
    Ans.: d   LG: 3   Page: 93   QT: F

98. The limbic system includes the
    a. cerebral cortex.
    b. amygdala.
    c. hippocampus.
    d. both b and c
    Ans.: d   LG: 3   Page: 93   QT: F

99. The part of the brain that is the shape of an almond and is involved with emotional awareness is the
   a. hippocampus.
   b. amygdala.
   c. thalamus.
   d. hypothalamus.
   Ans.: b   LG: 3   Page: 93   QT: F

100. The component of the limbic system that is involved with the processing of memories is the
   a. amygdala.
   b. hippocampus.
   c. brain stem.
   d. thalamus.
   Ans.: b   LG: 3   Page: 93   QT: F

101. The part of the forebrain that sits on top of the brain stem and functions as a relay station for information is the
   a. hypothalamus.
   b. thalamus.
   c. cerebral cortex.
   d. cerebrum.
   Ans.: b   LG: 3   Page: 94   QT: F

102. The small forebrain structure that monitors such pleasurable activities as eating, drinking and sex is called the
   a. thalamus.
   b. hippocampus.
   c. hypothalamus.
   d. cerebrum.
   Ans.: c   LG: 3   Page: 94   QT: F

103. The _____ is involved in the regulation of variables such as body temperature.
   a. hypothalamus
   b. thalamus
   c. cerebral cortex
   d. cerebrum
   Ans.: a   LG: 3   Page: 94   QT: F

104. The hypothalamus can be described best as a(n)
   a. screen.
   b. subordinate.
   c. regulator.
   d. advisor.
   Ans.: c   LG: 3   Page: 94   QT: C

105. The cerebral cortex is the _____ region of the forebrain and the _____ developed part of the brain in the evolution scheme.
    a. highest, most recently
    b. highest, least recently
    c. lowest, most recently
    d. lowest, least recently
    Ans.: a   LG: 3   Page: 95   QT: C

106. The cerebral cortex is made up of two nearly separate halves called
    a. cerebral lobes.
    b. hemispheres.
    c. the hypothalamus and the thalamus.
    d. reticular formations.
    Ans.: b   LG: 3   Page: 95   QT: F

107. Which of the following is *not* one of the lobes of the cerebral cortex?
    a. occipital
    b. frontal
    c. temporal
    d. posterior
    Ans.: d   LG: 3   Page: 95   QT: F

108. A person with damage to the occipital lobe would most likely experience problems with
    a. visual functioning.
    b. auditory functioning.
    c. bodily sensations.
    d. voluntary muscle movement.
    Ans.: a   LG: 3   Page: 95   QT: C

109. Which of the following lobes of the cerebral cortex would be involved in registering spatial location, attention, and motor control?
    a. frontal lobe
    b. parietal lobe
    c. temporal lobe
    d. occipital lobe
    Ans.: b   LG: 3   Page: 96   QT: F

110. Phineas Gage was once an easygoing person. However, after he sustained a severe brain injury, he became an obstinate, moody, irresponsible, often selfish individual. From this information, we can suspect that Phineas most likely suffered damage to which lobe of his cerebral cortex?
    a. parietal lobe
    b. frontal lobe
    c. temporal lobe
    d. occipital lobe
    Ans.: b   LG: 3   Page: 96   QT: C

111. The _____, which is just above the ears, is involved with hearing, language processing, and memory.
    a. parietal lobe
    b. frontal lobe
    c. temporal lobe
    d. occipital lobe
    Ans.: c   LG: 3   Page: 95   QT: C

112. The process of stimulating different areas of the brain and recording the resulting behavior is used to make a(n)
    a. mapping.
    b. EEG.
    c. MRI scan.
    d. CAT scan.
    Ans.: a   LG: 3   Page: 97   QT: F

113. Research about various brain areas indicates that higher mental processes like thinking and problem solving are located within the
    a. association areas.
    b. parietal sulcus.
    c. limbic system.
    d. thalamic nuclei.
    Ans.: a   LG: 3   Page: 98   QT: C

114. The image of a glass of iced tea is projected onto the left visual field of a split-brain patient. When asked what she saw, the patient cannot name the object. Which of the following is *not* a reason for this patient's inability to produce the correct response?
    a. The left hemisphere did not see the object.
    b. Only the left hemisphere can produce the language necessary for the correct response.
    c. The right hemisphere cannot communicate with the left hemisphere.
    d. The right hemisphere does not know what the object is called.
    Ans.: d   LG: 3   Page: 99   QT: C

115. The two hemispheres are connected by which structure?
    a. corpus callosum
    b. thalamus
    c. hypothalamus
    d. reticular formation
    Ans.: a   LG: 3   Page: 98   QT: F

116. Since she has sustained a brain injury, Cara has been having problems with comprehending language. Most likely, Cara suffered damage to which area of the brain?
    a. left hemisphere
    b. occipital lobe
    c. right hemisphere
    d. frontal lobe
    Ans.: a   LG: 3   Page: 98   QT: C

117. Broca's area is primarily responsible for which function?
    a. speech comprehension
    b. emotions
    c. memory
    d. speech production
    Ans.: d   LG: 3   Page: 98   QT: F

Learning Goal 4: State what the endocrine system is and how it affects behavior.

118. The _____ is a set of glands that regulate the activities of certain organs by releasing their chemical products into the bloodstream.
    a. reticular system
    b. endocrine system
    c. hydrosis system
    d. association system
    Ans.: b   LG: 4   Page: 102   QT: F

119. Chemical messengers manufactured by the endocrine glands are called
    a. neurotransmitters.
    b. endocrine fluids.
    c. hormones.
    d. hydroelectric fluids.
    Ans.: c   LG: 4   Page: 102   QT: F

120. Which endocrine gland regulates other glands?
    a. adrenal gland
    b. pituitary
    c. basal ganglia
    d. reticular formation
    Ans.: b   LG: 4   Page: 102   QT: F

121. Tyrone is a healthy, active six-year-old who happens to be significantly shorter than the average kid of his age. His parents, both of whom have normal height, consult a physician to find out what is wrong with their son. What might the physician most likely suggest?
    a. Tyrone may have a hormonal deficiency.
    b. Tyrone's neurons lack myelin sheath.
    c. Tyrone's adrenal glands are overactive.
    d. Tyrone may have a neurotransmitter imbalance.
    Ans.: a   LG: 4   Page: 102   QT: C

122. In a fit of road rage, which of an individual's endocrine glands would be *most* active?
    a. thyroid
    b. parathyroid
    c. pancreas
    d. adrenal
    Ans.: d   LG: 4   Page: 103   QT: C

123. Which division of the nervous system primarily acts on the endocrine system?
    a. somatic
    b. autonomic
    c. spinal cord
    d. forebrain
    Ans.: b   LG: 4   Page: 102   QT: F

Learning Goal 5. Describe the brain's capacity for recovery and repair.

124. A damaged brain can sometimes repair itself thorough _____, in which the axons of some healthy neurons adjacent to damaged cells grow new branches.
    a. collateral sprouting
    b. substitution of function
    c. neurogenesis
    d. lesions
    Ans.: a   LG: 5   Page: 104   QT: F

125. At times a function of a damaged region of the brain is taken over by another area or areas of the brain. This is called
    a. collateral sprouting.
    b. substitution of function.
    c. neurogenesis.
    d. lesions.
    Ans.: b   LG: 5   Page: 104   QT: F

126. For many years it was believed that humans had all of the brain cells that they were ever going to have at birth. Neuroscientists have recently found that human adults can create new neurons. This process is called
    a. collateral sprouting.
    b. substitution of function.
    c. neurogenesis.
    d. lesions.
    Ans.: c   LG: 5   Page: 104   QT: F

127. Which is the *best* synonym for *brain graft*?
    a. collateralization
    b. brain tissue implant
    c. substitution
    d. plasticity
    Ans.: b   LG: 5   Page: 104   QT: C

128. The research on the use of brain grafts to repair brain damage suggests all of the following *except* which one?
    a. Research results from animal studies may not apply to humans.
    b. There appear to be no substitutes for brain tissue.
    c. The best graft material would be brain tissue from fetuses.
    d. Even if this technique worked well, the problem would be getting donors.
    Ans.: b   LG: 5   Page: 105   QT: C

129. At its current status, research on brain grafts promises the *greatest* potential for individuals who suffer from
    a. Huntington's Chorea.
    b. Parkinson's disease or Alzheimer's disease.
    c. dopamine deficiencies.
    d. less severe forms of schizophrenia.
    Ans.: b   LG: 5   Page: 105   QT: F

Learning Goal 6: Explain how genetics and evolutionary psychology increase our understanding of behavior.

130. How many chromosomes does each human cell contain?
    a. 23
    b. 46
    c. 46 pairs
    d. trillions
    Ans.: b   LG: 6   Page: 106   QT: F

131. Which are the actual units of heredity?
    a. DNA
    b. chromosomes
    c. cells
    d. genes
    Ans.: d   LG: 6   Page: 106   QT: F

132. What has to happen in order for an individual to show a recessive trait?
    a. The individual must inherit two recessive genes for that trait.
    b. The individual must inherit at least one dominant gene for that trait.
    c. The individual must inherit two dominant genes for that trait.
    d. The individual must inherit at least one recessive gene for that trait.
    Ans.: a   LG: 6   Page: 106   QT: F

133. What is the relationship among genes, chromosomes, and DNA?
    a. DNA is composed of genes, which are also known as chromosomes.
    b. Chromosomes and genes are composed of DNA.
    c. DNA carries chromosomes and genes to each cell nucleus.
    d. Genes are segments of chromosomes composed of DNA.
    Ans.: d   LG: 6   Page: 106   QT: C

134. The dominant-recessive genes principle states all of the following except which one?
    a. A recessive gene exerts its influence only if both genes of a pair are recessive.
    b. Dominant genes override the effect of a recessive gene.
    c. If one gene of a pair is dominant and one is recessive, the dominant gene exerts its effect.
    d. If both genes of a pair are dominant, the effect converts into a recessive trait.
    Ans.: d   LG: 6   Page: 106   QT: F

135. Jacqueline and Matt both have brown eyes. They have a blue-eyed baby. If brown is dominant and blue is recessive, this means that
   a. Matt is not the baby's father.
   b. blue eyes are dominant.
   c. both parents are carriers of the recessive blue gene.
   d. both parents are carriers of the recessive brown gene.
   Ans.: c   LG: 6   Page: 106   QT: C

136. _____ involves actual manipulation of genes using technology to determine their effect on behavior.
   a. Molecular genetics
   b. Polygenetics
   c. Genotypes
   d. Technical genetics
   Ans.: a   LG: 6   Page: 107   QT: F

137. The term _____ is used to describe the complete set of instructions for making an organism.
   a. phenotype
   b. genome
   c. inheritance
   d. all of the above
   Ans.: b   LG: 6   Page: 107   QT: F

138. Robert Tryon mated rats who were maze bright and maze dull to find if their offspring would show similar abilities. This type of research is called
   a. molecular genetics.
   b. selective breeding.
   c. behavioral genetics.
   d. polygenetics.
   Ans.: b   LG: 6   Page: 108   QT: C

139. _____ use(s) methods such as twin studies to investigate the degree and nature of heredity's influence on behavior.
   a. Molecular genetics
   b. Selective breeding
   c. Behavioral genetics
   d. Polygenetics
   Ans.: c   LG: 6   Page: 108   QT: F

140. Evolutionary psychology is concerned with all of the following *except*
   a. importance of adaptation.
   b. survival of the fittest.
   c. reproduction.
   d. cultural diversity.
   Ans.: d   LG: 6   Page: 110   QT: F

141. According to evolutionary psychology, fears and phobias are related to
    a. the inheritance of recessive genes.
    b. the inheritance of dominant genes.
    c. successful survival and reproduction.
    d. low rate of survival and reproduction.
    Ans.: c   LG: 6   Page: 110   QT: C

142. An evolutionary psychologist would focus primarily on which aspect of the genetics versus environment question?
    a. the impact of genetics on human behavior
    b. the influence of the environment on human behavior
    c. the impact of both genetics and the environment on human behavior
    d. the impact of the environment on human behavior
    Ans.: c   LG: 6   Page: 105   QT: C

143. Which of the following is true regarding the evolutionary perspective?
    a. The evolutionary approach does not explain differences in human behavior due to cultural diversity.
    b. The evolutionary approach focuses exclusively on the impact of the environment.
    c. Evolutionary advances dictate human environments.
    d. The evolutionary approach provides the solution to all of the questions regarding human thought and behavior.
    Ans.: a   LG: 6   Page: 111   QT: C

144. Which of the following is the best set of synonyms for the terms *genetics* and *contexts* ?
    a. biology and psychology
    b. instincts and innate characteristics
    c. learning and instinct
    d. heredity and environment
    Ans.: d   LG: 6   Page: 111   QT: C

145. You and a few friends are discussing juvenile delinquency and what can be done to reduce this problem in our society. If you took the stand that the environment makes a big difference in people's behavior, which argument would you present in this discussion?
    a. Society can't do much to change the biological predispositions of juvenile delinquents.
    b. We need more youth programs that give kids a sense of belonging and accomplishment.
    c. Due to its genetic nature, delinquency runs in families.
    d. Youth programs are a waste of money because these kids are headed for delinquency no matter what we try to do with them or for them.
    Ans.: b   LG: 6   Page: 111   QT: A

146. Most psychologists agree that human behavior and mental processes are influenced
    a. mostly by evolution.
    b. predominantly by parents and society.
    c. by the interaction of genetics and the environment.
    d. predominantly by genetics.
    Ans.: c   LG: 6   Page: 111   QT: C

147. Methods for studying heredity include all of the following *except*
    a. molecular genetics.
    b. selective breeding of humans.
    c. behavioral genetics.
    d. twin studies.
    Ans.: b   LG: 6   Page: 108   QT: F

148. Researchers are investigating the similarities of and differences between identical twins and fraternal twins. They find that the in some traits, identical twins who were separated at birth are no more similar than fraternal twins who were reared apart. This would suggest that _____ plays a significant role in this characteristic.
    a. biological parents
    b. genetics
    c. environment
    d. genotype
    Ans.: c   LG: 6   Page: 109   QT: F

149. Identical twins who are reunited after separations lasting as long as thirty years often find that their lives are very similar. This is evidence that
    a. heredity has some effect on behavior.
    b. identical twins have telepathic capabilities.
    c. most of our interests are inherited.
    d. genetics are more important than the environment.
    Ans.: a   LG: 6   Page: 109   QT: C

150. A researcher measures shyness in identical and fraternal twins. She finds that both types of twins are equally shy. This implies that shyness
    a. has a strong genetic component.
    b. has a strong environmental component.
    c. is determined by both genetic and environmental influences.
    d. is determined by neither genetics nor environment.
    Ans.: c   LG: 6   Page: 109   QT: C

True/False Items

___ 151. Afferent nerves are sensory nerves.
___ 152. The central nervous system consists of the spinal cord and brain.
___ 153. The autonomic nervous system involves voluntary behaviors.
___ 154. Messages about temperature and pain are related to the CNS by the somatic nervous system.
___ 155. Glial cells are responsible for the perception of mood.
___ 156. Mylinated neurons require less time to fire than non-mylinated neurons.
___ 157. Axons are the receiving parts of the neuron.
___ 158. When neurons are at rest, they carry a positive charge.
___ 159. Neurons fire according to the all-or-none principle which means that all of the neurons must fire, or none do.
___ 160. The medulla, the cerebellum, and the pons are the main structures of the forebrain.
___ 161. The two hemispheres are separated by the corpus callosum.
___ 162. Endocrine glands release chemicals directly into the bloodstream.

_____ 163. Although neurons cannot be regenerated, the human brain appears to have mechanisms to repair itself after brain damage.
_____ 164. Twin studies allow us to study behavioral genetics.
_____ 165. Evolutionary psychology is concerned strictly with genetics.

Answer Key for True/False Items

151.	Ans.: T	LG: 1	Page: 80	159.	Ans.: F	LG: 2	Page: 84
152.	Ans.: T	LG: 1	Page: 81	160.	Ans.: F	LG: 3	Page: 91
153.	Ans.: F	LG: 1	Page: 81	161.	Ans.: T	LG: 3	Page: 98
154.	Ans.: T	LG: 1	Page: 81	162.	Ans.: T	LG: 4	Page: 102
155.	Ans.: F	LG: 2	Page: 82	163.	Ans.: T	LG: 5	Page: 104
156.	Ans.: T	LG: 2	Page: 82	164.	Ans.: T	LG: 6	Page: 108
157.	Ans.: F	LG: 2	Page: 82	165.	Ans.: F	LG: 6	Page: 110
158.	Ans.: F	LG: 2	Page: 84				

Fill-in-the-Blank Items

166. The brain's special capacity for modification and change is called _____.
167. The nervous system that is primarily responsible for communication between the brain and the spinal cord and the rest of the body is known as the _____ nervous system.
168. The system that functions to take messages to and from the body's internal organs is the _____ nervous system.
169. Each neuron has an axon, a dendrite, and a _____.
170. The _____ is covered by the myelin sheath.
171. The tiny junctions between neurons are called_____.
172. Chemicals that carry information across the gaps between neurons are called_____.
173. The _____ is the highest level in the forebrain where thinking and planning take place.
174. Damage to the _____ lobe could cause problems with motor movement.
175. The _____ is an important relay station.
176. A patient with severe _____ might improve with a split-brain operation.
177. _____ are chemical messengers manufactured by the endocrine glands.
178. The _____ gland controls growth and regulates other glands.
179. _____ psychology emphasizes the connection between behavior and adaptive problems.
180. A psychologist who studies identical twins is probably interested in the role of _____ in human behavior.

Answer Key for Fill-in-the-Blank Items

166.	Ans.: plasticity	LG: 1	Page: 79
167.	Ans.: peripheral	LG: 1	Page: 81
168.	Ans.: autonomic	LG: 1	Page: 81
169.	Ans.: cell body	LG: 2	Page: 82
170.	Ans.: axon	LG: 2	Page: 82
171.	Ans.: synapses	LG: 2	Page: 85
172.	Ans.: neurotransmitters	LG: 2	Page: 86
173.	Ans.: cerebral cortex	LG: 3	Page: 95

174.	Ans.: frontal	LG: 3	Page: 95
175.	Ans.: thalamus	LG: 3	Page: 94
176.	Ans.: epilepsy	LG: 3	Page: 99
177.	Ans.: Hormones	LG: 4	Page: 102
178.	Ans.: pituitary	LG: 4	Page: 102
179.	Ans.: Evolutionary	LG: 5	Page: 110
180.	Ans.: genetics	LG: 6	Page: 109

Matching Items

___ 181.	sympathetic nervous system	A. glands that release hormones
___ 182.	parasympathetic nervous system	B. action potential
___ 183.	part of the limbic system	C. afferent neurons (nerves)
___ 184.	cerebellum	D. glial cells
___ 185.	epinephrine	E. hippocampus
___ 186.	endocrine system	F. arouses the body
___ 187.	carry information to the brain	G. produced by the adrenal glands
___ 188.	electrical charge within a neuron	H. inhibitory neurotransmitter
___ 189.	supportive non-neuron cells of the brain	I. involved in motor behavior
___ 190.	serotonin	J. calms the body

Answer Key for Matching Items

181.	Ans.: F	LG: 1	Page: 81	186.	Ans.: A	LG: 4	Page: 102
182.	Ans.: J	LG: 1	Page: 81	187.	Ans.: C	LG: 1	Page: 80
183.	Ans.: E	LG: 3	Page: 93	188.	Ans.: B	LG: 2	Page: 84
184.	Ans.: I	LG: 3	Page: 92	189.	Ans.: D	LG: 2	Page: 82
185.	Ans.: G	LG: 4	Page: 103	190.	Ans.: H	LG: 2	Page: 87

Essay Questions

191. Explain the human nervous system and how it functions as a neural network. In your answer, include the terms *central nervous system, peripheral nervous system, afferent nerves,* and *efferent nerves.* (LG: 1)

Answer Guidelines: The answer should include an overview of the system and should explain how the central nervous system includes the brain and spinal cord and the peripheral nervous system connects the central nervous system to the rest of the body. In addition, afferent (sensory) nerves carry information to the brain and efferent (motor) nerves carry information away from the brain.

192. Explain the roles of the somatic nervous system, the autonomic nervous system, the sympathetic nervous system, and the parasympathetic nervous system in the daily functioning of our bodies. (LG: 1)

Answer Guidelines: The somatic nervous system consists of both sensory and motor nerves. The autonomic nervous system functions to take messages to and from the body's internal organs. The sympathetic nervous system arouses the body and the parasympathetic system calms the body.

193. List and describe the main structures of a neuron. You may want to add a sketch of a neuron to illustrate your discussion. (LG: 2)

Answer Guidelines: Possible options include mentioning the cell body, nucleus, dendrites, axon, myelin sheath, terminal buttons, and synapse.

194. Describe the process by which information is sent from one neuron to the next. Include in your answer the specific neuronal structures involved in this process. (LG: 2)

Answer Guidelines: Possible options include mentioning that neurons fire when they get activated by an electrical charge called the action potential. Once the neuron is activated, the electrical activity, or message, travels from the cell body down the axon (information travels faster in well-myelinated axons). When the message reaches the end of the axon, or terminal buttons, neurotransmitters are released from the synaptic vesicles into the synapse, a minute gap between the end of one neuron's axon and the next neuron's dendrites. While in the synapse, some neurotransmitter molecules lock onto the dendrites of the next neuron. The dendrites then orient the message toward the cell body of the second neuron, and the process of transmission starts over.

195. List three neurotransmitters and discuss their functions. (LG: 2)

Answer Guidelines: Possible options include mentioning GABA (inhibitory; low levels associated with anxiety), acetylcholine (excitatory; involved in muscle action, learning, and memory), norepinephrine (inhibitory; involved in control of alertness and wakefulness; low levels associated with depression; high levels associated with manic states), dopamine (inhibitory; involved in control of voluntary movement), serotonin (inhibitory; involved in the regulation of sleep and depression), or endorphins (excitatory; increase pleasure and decrease pain).

196. The brain is divided into four lobes. List these lobes and describe the location of each lobe. Finally, identify the brain functions that are associated with each lobe. (You may wish to construct a 3-column chart for your answer.) (LG: 3)

Answer Guidelines: Possible options include mentioning (a) occipital lobe, located at the back of the head, and associated with visual functioning; (b) temporal lobe, located at the side of the head just above the ear, and associated with hearing; (c) parietal lobe, located at the top of the head toward the rear, and associated with bodily sensation; and (d) frontal lobe, located behind the forehead, and associated with voluntary muscles, intelligence, and personality.

197. Discuss the similarities and differences of the two hemispheres of the brain. What happens when the corpus callosum is severed? Why would this procedure be performed? (LG: 3)

Answer Guidelines: Possible options include mentioning that the two hemispheres of the brain are asymmetrical, each controlling the opposite side of the body. Each hemisphere has primary areas of function, with the left hemisphere primarily responsible for verbal functioning and the right hemisphere primarily responsible for visual-spatial functioning and logical reasoning. For most complex human behaviors, however, the two hemispheres work together by communicating by way of the corpus callosum. The procedure of severing the corpus callosum, known as the split-brain operation, is performed only on patients who have severe epilepsy. The procedure reduces epileptic seizures, but it also disrupts the direct communication between the two hemispheres. Despite the severity of this procedure, split-brain patients generally function quite well after this surgery because the two hemispheres of the brain learn to operate independently.

198. Explain the endocrine system and how it affects behavior. In your answer include hormones, the pituitary gland, and the adrenal glands. (LG: 4)

Answer Guidelines: The endocrine glands release chemical products into the blood stream. Hormones are chemical messengers produced by the endocrine glands that travel throughout the body through the bloodstream. The pituitary gland is the master endocrine gland, controlling growth and regulating other glands. The adrenal glands regulate mood, energy level, and the ability to cope with stress.

199. Discuss the brain's plasticity and describe techniques that are used to repair damaged brains. (LG: 5)

Answer Guidelines: Possible options include mentioning that plasticity refers to the brain's ability to modify and reorganize itself after damage. Factors related to plasticity include the age of the person at time of the damage and the extent of the damage. The two mechanisms that affect plasticity are collateral sprouting and substitution of function. An experimental method for repairing severe damage involves brain grafts. This promising technique has thus far only been used in animals. One major ethical problem with this technique is finding donors for the required fetal tissue.

200. Compare and contrast the contributions of genetics and the environment to human behavior. Cite a specific example of how both interact in determining human behavior. (LG: 6)

Answer Guidelines: Possible options include mentioning that nature refers to the biological, inherited, genetic component that describes our behavior whereas nurture refers to the environmental, experiential component that describes our behavior. The example could consist of one individual whose behavior contradicts genetic predispositions due to an adverse or enhanced environment. The example could also consist of two individuals who experienced very similar environmental influences, but whose behaviors are very different due to possible genetic predisposition.

Chapter 4: Human Development

Learning Goals

1. Explain how psychologists think about development.
2. Describe children's development from conception to adolescence.
3. Identify the most important changes that occur in adolescence.
4. Discuss adult development and the positive dimensions of aging.

Multiple-Choice Items

Learning Goal 1: Explain how psychologists think about development.

1. Which of the following is *not* a primary process involved in development?
    a. physical processes
    b. cognitive processes
    c. socioemotional processes
    d. signal processes
    Ans.: d   LG: 1   Page: 119   QT: C

2. The hormonal changes at puberty and menopause are examples of which type of developmental processes?
    a. physical processes
    b. cognitive processes
    c. socioemotional processes
    d. signal processes
    Ans.: a   LG: 1   Page: 119   QT: C

3. Imagining yourself growing up to be a firefighter is an example of which type of developmental process?
    a. physical process
    b. cognitive process
    c. socioemotional process
    d. signal process
    Ans.: b   LG: 1   Page: 119   QT: C

4. A toddler's jealousy at the birth of a new sibling is an example of which type of developmental process?
    a. physical process
    b. cognitive process
    c. socioemotional process
    d. signal process
    Ans.: c   LG: 1   Page: 119   QT: C

5. The pattern of change in human capabilities that begins at conception and continues throughout the lifespan is known as
   a. maturation.
   b. development.
   c. phenotype.
   d. assimilation.
   Ans.: b   LG: 1   Page: 119   QT: F

6. Psychologists define development as
   a. the pattern of change in human capabilities that begins at conception and continues throughout the lifespan.
   b. the expression of an individual's genotype in observable, measurable characteristics.
   c. an individual's genetic heritage.
   d. an individual's behavioral style and characteristic way of responding.
   Ans.: a   LG: 1   Page: 119   QT: F

7. According to the early-experience doctrine,
   a. children are malleable, and later experiences are more important than earlier experiences.
   b. infants who are rocked frequently become better athletes.
   c. after a period of early development, we become fixed and permanent in our makeup.
   d. infants who do not experience warm, nurturing caregiving in the first year or so have no disadvantages compared to those infants that do.
   Ans.: c   LG: 1   Page: 120   QT: F

8. Which of the following ideas is most consistent with the later-experience perspective on development?
   a. Infants who are rocked frequently become better athletes.
   b. The way that infants are handled determines their future character.
   c. Infants who do not experience nurturing during the first year of life will not develop to their full potential.
   d. Early experiences are not more important than later experiences in shaping development.
   Ans.: d   LG: 1   Page: 120   QT: C

9. Which of the following has *not* been linked with depression in girls during adolescence?
   a. parents who were overly nurturing when the girls were 3 to 5 years old
   b. stressful experiences in adolescence
   c. parents who demanded high achievement when the girls were 3 to 5 years old
   d. parents who were overly controlling when the girls were 3 to 5 years old
   Ans.: a   LG: 1   Page: 121   QT: C

10. Genotype refers to
    a. the pattern of change in human capabilities that begins at conception and continues throughout the lifespan.
    b. the expression of an individual's genotype in observable, measurable characteristics.
    c. an individual's genetic heritage.
    d. an individual's behavioral style and characteristic way of responding.
    Ans.: c   LG: 1   Page: 121   QT: F

11. An individual's genetic heritage is known as
   a. development.
   b. schema.
   c. phenotype.
   d. genotype.
   Ans.: d   LG: 1   Page: 121   QT: F

12. The expression of an individual's genes in observable, measurable characteristics is known as
   a. development.
   b. schema.
   c. phenotype.
   d. genotype.
   Ans.: c   LG: 1   Page: 121   QT: F

13. Phenotype refers to
   a. the pattern of change in human capabilities that begins at conception and continues throughout the lifespan.
   b. the expression of an individual's genotype in observable, measurable characteristics.
   c. an individual's genetic heritage.
   d. an individual's behavioral style and characteristic way of responding.
   Ans.: b   LG: 1   Page: 121   QT: F

14. Which of the following is *not* an example of a phenotype?
   a. personality
   b. weight
   c. eye color
   d. having one X chromosome and one Y chromosome
   Ans.: d   LG: 1   Page: 121   QT: A

15. Which of the following terms is used to refer to an individual's biological inheritance?
   a. assimilation
   b. interaction
   c. nature
   d. nurture
   Ans.: c   LG: 1   Page: 122   QT: F

16. When considering processes of development, nature refers to
   a. an organism's environmental experiences.
   b. the pattern of change in human capabilities that begins at conception.
   c. the stage when individuals adjust their schemas to new information.
   d. an organism's biological inheritance.
   Ans.: d   LG: 1   Page: 122   QT: F

17. Which of the following would *not* be considered an environmental influence on development?
   a. your DNA
   b. family dynamics
   c. viruses
   d. both a and c
   Ans.: a   LG: 1   Page: 122   QT: C

18. Which of the following is *not* an example of a life theme?
    a. our activities
    b. our exposure to chicken pox
    c. our social relationships
    d. our life goals
    Ans.: b   LG: 1   Page: 122   QT: C

19. Life themes refer to
    a. the way individuals incorporate new information into existing knowledge.
    b. the way individuals adjust their schemas to new information.
    c. efforts to experience our lives in optimal ways.
    d. expressions of an individuals genotype in observable, measurable characteristics.
    Ans.: c   LG: 1   Page: 122   QT: F

20. Our efforts to experience our lives in optimal ways are known as
    a. life themes.
    b. schemas.
    c. phenotypes.
    d. accommodations.
    Ans.: a   LG: 1   Page: 122   QT: F

21. Which of the following is *not* an example of an optimal life theme?
    a. increasing tolerance
    b. selfish reproduction
    c. fostering understanding
    d. promoting cooperation
    Ans.: b   LG: 1   Page: 122   QT: C

Learning Goal 2: Describe children's development from conception to adolescence.

22. The germinal period of human development refers to
    a. weeks 3 through 8 following conception.
    b. weeks 1 and 2 following conception.
    c. months 3 through 9 following conception.
    d. the last year prior to death.
    Ans.: b   LG: 2   Page: 123   QT: F

23. The embryonic period refers to
    a. weeks 3 through 8 following conception.
    b. weeks 1 and 2 following conception.
    c. months 3 through 9 following conception.
    d. the last year prior to death.
    Ans.: a   LG: 2   Page: 123   QT: F

24. Which of the following occurs during the embryonic period of human development?
    a. conception
    b. formation of the neural tube
    c. irregular breathing
    d. appearance of the grasping reflex
    Ans.: b   LG: 2   Page: 123   QT: F

25. Which of the following occurs during the fetal period of human development?
    a. conception
    b. formation of the neural tube
    c. appearance of a heart beat
    d. appearance of the grasping reflex
    Ans.: d   LG: 2   Page: 124   QT: F

26. Teratogen refers to
    a. any agent that causes a birth defect.
    b. a concept or framework that organizes and interprets information.
    c. the expression of an individual's genotype in measurable characteristics.
    d. the tendency of an infant to form an attachment to the first moving object it encounters.
    Ans.: a   LG: 2   Page: 124   QT: C

27. Children who are born to mothers who are heavy drinkers are likely to show all of the following
    except
    a. a small head.
    b. increased intelligence.
    c. defective limbs.
    d. heart defects.
    Ans.: b   LG: 2   Page: 124   QT: C

28. Exposure to heroin during pregnancy has been linked to all of the following *except*
    a. premature birth.
    b. breathing problems.
    c. obesity at birth.
    d. death.
    Ans.: c   LG: 2   Page: 124   QT: C

29. Pre-term infants are those infants who
    a. were exposed to heroin before birth.
    b. were exposed to alcohol before birth.
    c. were born after 42 weeks of pregnancy.
    d. were born before 38 weeks of pregnancy.
    Ans.: d   LG: 2   Page: 124   QT: F

30. Which of the following pre-term infants is most likely to have developmental problems?
    a. an infant from a high-income family
    b. a large infant
    c. an infant who is massaged
    d. an infant born in poverty
    Ans.: d   LG: 2   Page: 125   QT: C

31. Which of the following is *not* an effect of infant massage that has been demonstrated?
    a. increased weight gain
    b. increased activity
    c. decreased alertness
    d. increased performance on developmental tests
    Ans.: c   LG: 2   Page: 125   QT: C

32. An infant who displays the grasping reflex is most likely
    a. arching its back, flinging out its arms and legs, then rapidly closing them to the center of its body.
    b. moving its feet as if to walk when held above a surface.
    c. curling its fingers around an object that touches its palm.
    d. automatically sucking an object that touches its mouth.
    Ans.: c   LG: 2   Page: 125   QT: C

33. Which of the following is a reflex that disappears during infancy?
    a. gagging
    b. stepping
    c. yawning
    d. blinking
    Ans.: b   LG: 2   Page: 125   QT: C

34. Your baby is able to roll over and support some weight with its legs, but cannot stand alone easily. She is most likely
    a. 1 month old.
    b. 14 months old.
    c. 4 months old.
    d. 11 months old.
    Ans.: c   LG: 2   Page: 126   QT: C

35. Your baby can pull herself to stand, walk using furniture for support, but cannot stand alone easily or walk alone. She is most likely
    a. 1 month old.
    b. 4 months old.
    c. 14 months old.
    d. 9 months old.
    Ans.: d   LG: 2   Page: 126   QT: C

36. Which of the following is the best description of the infant's brain at birth?
    a. It is fully connected.
    b. It has all of the dendrites it needs.
    c. It already contains 100 billion neurons.
    d. It has approximately half of the neurons it will need.
    Ans.: c   LG: 2   Page: 126   QT: C

37. Which of the following is *not* true of myelination in the human brain?
    a. Visual pathways are myelinated during the first 6 months.
    b. Myelination is completed by age 5.
    c. Myelination begins prenatally.
    d. Auditory myelination is not completed until at least 4 years of age.
    Ans.: b   LG: 2   Page: 127   QT: C

38. Which of the following is the *least* accurate statement?
    a. Babies have only half of the synaptic connections they will ever use.
    b. Myelination is not completed until adolescence.
    c. Children's brains undergo dramatic anatomical changes between 3 and 15 years of age.
    d. The most rapid growth in the brain between 3 and 6 years of age is in the frontal lobe.
    Ans.: a   LG: 2   Page: 127   QT: C

39. The process of the elimination of unused neural connections is known as
    a. imprinting.
    b. myelination.
    c. accommodation.
    d. pruning.
    Ans.: d   LG: 2   Page: 127   QT: F

40. A concept or framework that organizes information and provides a structure for interpreting it is known as a(n)
    a. schema.
    b. attachment.
    c. accommodation.
    d. assimilation.
    Ans.: a   LG: 2   Page: 128   QT: F

41. The process of incorporating new information into existing knowledge is known as
    a. schema.
    b. attachment.
    c. accommodation.
    d. assimilation.
    Ans.: d   LG: 2   Page: 128   QT: F

42. The process of adjusting existing schemas to new information is known as
    a. imprinting.
    b. attachment.
    c. accommodation.
    d. assimilation.
    Ans.: c   LG: 2   Page: 129   QT: F

43. An infant has just discovered that sucking on the cat's tail is not such a good idea, and has adjusted her schema of sucking accordingly. This infant is demonstrating Piaget's concept of
    a. imprinting.
    b. attachment.
    c. accommodation.
    d. assimilation.
    Ans.: c   LG: 2   Page: 129   QT: A

44. An infant has just sucked on a lollipop, discovered its pleasant taste, and incorporated sucking lollipops into his taste schema. This infant is demonstrating Piaget's concept of
   a. imprinting.
   b. attachment.
   c. accommodation.
   d. assimilation.
   Ans.: d   LG: 2   Page: 129   QT: A

45. During Piaget's sensorimotor stage,
   a. individuals coordinate experiences like seeing and hearing with physical actions.
   b. thought becomes more symbolic and egocentric.
   c. intuitive thought is replaced with logical reasoning in concrete situations.
   d. thinking becomes more abstract, logical, and idealistic.
   Ans.: a   LG: 2   Page: 129   QT: F

46. According to Piaget, the stage of cognitive development when individuals coordinate experiences like seeing and hearing with physical actions is known as the
   a. preoperational stage.
   b. concrete operational stage.
   c. sensorimotor stage.
   d. formal operational stage.
   Ans.: c   LG: 2   Page: 129   QT: F

47. The understanding that objects continue to exist even when they cannot be directly seen is known as
   a. conservation.
   b. imprinting.
   c. accommodation.
   d. object permanence.
   Ans.: d   LG: 2   Page: 130   QT: F

48. You show a ball to a small child, then hide it behind your back. The child shows no evidence of knowing that the ball still exists. The child is most likely in which of the following stages of Piaget's cognitive development?
   a. formal operational
   b. sensorimotor
   c. concrete operational
   d. preoperational
   Ans.: b   LG: 2   Page: 130   QT: A

49. During Piaget's preoperational stage,
   a. individuals coordinate experiences like seeing and hearing with physical actions.
   b. thought becomes more symbolic and egocentric.
   c. intuitive thought is replaced with logical reasoning in concrete situations.
   d. thinking becomes more abstract, logical, and idealistic.
   Ans.: b   LG: 2   Page: 130   QT: F

50. A child tells you that they always put their clothes on by themselves in the morning, but cannot take them off by themselves in the evening. The child is most likely in which of the following stages of Piaget's cognitive development?
   a. formal operational
   b. sensorimotor
   c. concrete operational
   d. preoperational
   Ans.: d   LG: 2   Page: 130   QT: A

51. Conservation refers to the concept that
   a. objects have permanent attributes that do not change in spite of superficial changes.
   b. an infant develops an attachment to the first moving object it sees.
   c. children are unable to distinguish between their' own perspective and someone else's perspective.
   d. objects and events continue to exist even when they cannot be directly seen.
   Ans.: a   LG: 2   Page: 130   QT: F

52. Egocentrism refers to the concept that
   a. objects have permanent attributes that do not change in spite of superficial changes.
   b. an infant develops an attachment to the first moving object it sees.
   c. children are unable to distinguish between their' own perspective and someone else's perspective.
   d. objects and events continue to exist even when they cannot be directly seen.
   Ans.: c   LG: 2   Page: 130   QT: F

53. A child tells you that the sky is green. You ask him how he knows that, and he says because that's what he thinks, and isn't bothered that his reasoning isn't logical. This child is most likely in which stage of cognitive development?
   a. formal operational
   b. sensorimotor
   c. concrete operational
   d. preoperational
   Ans.: d   LG: 2   Page: 131   QT: A

54. After learning about the structure of the United States government, a child is able to understand a chart of its organization, but can't yet apply the organizational principles to the government of a fictitious island. She is most likely in which stage of cognitive development?
   a. formal operational
   b. sensorimotor
   c. concrete operational
   d. preoperational
   Ans.: c   LG: 2   Page: 132   QT: A

55. According to Piaget, the stage of cognitive development when thought becomes operational and intuitive thought is replaced with logical reasoning in concrete situations is known as the
   a. preoperational stage.
   b. concrete operational stage.
   c. sensorimotor stage.
   d. formal operational stage.
   Ans.: b   LG: 2   Page: 132   QT: F

56. An individual is able to consider hypothetical possibilities and devises plans to solve problems. This individual is most likely in which stage of cognitive development?
    a. preoperational stage
    b. concrete operational stage
    c. sensorimotor stage
    d. formal operational stage
    Ans.: d   LG: 2   Page: 133   QT: A

57. According to Piaget, the stage of cognitive development when thinking becomes more abstract, idealistic, and logical is known as the
    a. preoperational stage.
    b. concrete operational stage.
    c. sensorimotor stage.
    d. formal operational stage.
    Ans.: d   LG: 2   Page: 133   QT: F

58. Which of the following is *not* a criticism of Piaget's theory of cognitive development?
    a. Cognitive abilities like object permanence emerge much later than Piaget thought.
    b. He emphasized grand stages too much.
    c. Some adults do not reason as logically as Piaget thought.
    d. He ignored individual differences.
    Ans.: a   LG: 2   Page: 133   QT: C

59. Compared to Piaget, information-processing psychologists are more likely to emphasize
    a. the role of culture in development.
    b. the importance of small steps in development.
    c. the earlier ages at which skills emerged.
    d. the failure of adults to reason logically.
    Ans.: b   LG: 2   Page: 133   QT: C

60. Compared to Piaget, Vygotsky placed more emphasis on
    a. the role of culture in development.
    b. the importance of small steps in development.
    c. the earlier ages at which skills emerged.
    d. the failure of adults to reason logically.
    Ans.: a   LG: 2   Page: 134   QT: C

61. According to Erik Erickson, which of the following stages of socioemotional development does *not* take place during childhood?
    a. trust versus mistrust
    b. autonomy versus shame and doubt
    c. intimacy versus isolation
    d. initiative versus guilt
    Ans.: c   LG: 2   Page: 134   QT: C

62. A baby who learns that needs like comfort, food, and warmth will be met by responsive caregivers has successfully resolved which of Erickson's developmental stages?
    a. trust versus mistrust
    b. intimacy versus isolation
    c. initiative versus guilt
    d. industry versus inferiority
    Ans.: a   LG: 2   Page: 134   QT: C

63. Children who master knowledge and intellectual skills have successfully resolved which of these socioemotional stages?
    a. trust versus mistrust
    b. intimacy versus isolation
    c. initiative versus guilt
    d. industry versus inferiority
    Ans.: d   LG: 2   Page: 136   QT: C

64. Which of the following is considered Erickson's main contribution to understanding development?
    a. demonstrating that children's minds change and develop in orderly sequential ways
    b. demonstrating the importance of psychosexual stages in development
    c. demonstrating that we must solve different socioemotional tasks at different ages
    d. demonstrating that children form close emotional bonds with caregivers
    Ans.: c   LG: 2   Page: 136   QT: C

65. According to development psychologists, attachment refers to
    a. the understanding that objects continue to exist even when they cannot be directly seen.
    b. the tendency of an infant to form an attachment to the first moving object it sees.
    c. the close emotional bond between an infant and caregiver.
    d. the formation of new synaptic connections in the frontal cortex.
    Ans.: c   LG: 2   Page: 136   QT: F

66. The close emotional bond between an infant and caregiver is known as
    a. attachment.
    b. imprinting.
    c. nurture.
    d. schema.
    Ans.: a   LG: 2   Page: 136   QT: F

67. Which of the following is the most critical element in the attachment process?
    a. food
    b. contact comfort
    c. movement
    d. indulgence
    Ans.: b   LG: 2   Page: 136   QT: C

68. Ethology refers to
    a. the study of the function and evolution of behavior.
    b. the close emotional bond between an infant and caregiver.
    c. any agent which causes birth defects.
    d. a period of rapid skeletal and sexual maturation.
    Ans.: a   LG: 2   Page: 136   QT: F

69. Imprinting refers to
    a. the understanding that objects continue to exist even when they cannot be directly seen.
    b. the tendency of an infant to form an attachment to the first moving object it sees.
    c. the close emotional bond between an infant and caregiver.
    d. the formation of new synaptic connections in the frontal cortex.
    Ans.: b   LG: 2   Page: 137   QT: F

70. Secure attachment refers to
    a. the tendency of infants to use a caregiver as a base from which to explore the environment.
    b. the understanding that objects continue to exist even when they cannot be directly seen.
    c. the tendency of an infant to form an attachment to the first moving object it sees.
    d. the formation of new synaptic connections in the frontal cortex.
    Ans.: a   LG: 2   Page: 138   QT: F

71. The tendency of infants to use a caregiver as a base from which to explore the environment is known as
    a. imprinting.
    b. accommodation.
    c. secure attachment.
    d. nurture.
    Ans.: c   LG: 2   Page: 138   QT: F

72. Temperament refers to
    a. an individual's tendency to use a caregiver as a base from which to explore the environment.
    b. the formation of new synaptic connections in the frontal cortex.
    c. the understanding that objects continue to exist even when they cannot be directly seen.
    d. an individual's behavioral style and characteristic way of responding.
    Ans.: d   LG: 2   Page: 138   QT: F

73. Which of the following is *not* a basic cluster of temperament in children?
    a. easy children
    b. slow-to-warm-up children
    c. quick-to-warm-up children
    d. difficult children
    Ans.: c   LG: 2   Page: 138   QT: C

74. A child who tends to react negatively, cry frequently, and is slow to accept new experiences has a temperament known as
    a. easy.
    b. slow-to-warm-up.
    c. quick-to-warm-up.
    d. difficult.
    Ans.: d   LG: 2   Page: 138   QT: C

75. Authoritative parenting refers to a style
    a. which is restrictive and punitive and limits and controls children.
    b. which encourages children to be independent but places limits and controls on their behavior.
    c. in which parents are uninvolved in their child's life.
    d. in which parents are involved but place few limits.
    Ans.: b   LG: 2   Page: 139   QT: F

76. Indulgent parenting refers to a style
    a. which is restrictive and punitive and limits and controls children.
    b. which encourages children to be independent but places limits and controls on their behavior.
    c. in which parents are uninvolved in their child's life.
    d. in which parents are involved but place few limits.
    Ans.: d   LG: 2   Page: 139   QT: F

77. Parents who are restrictive and punitive are displaying
    a. indulgent parenting.
    b. authoritative parenting.
    c. neglectful parenting.
    d. authoritarian parenting.
    Ans.: d   LG: 2   Page: 139   QT: F

78. Parents who are uninvolved in their child's life are displaying
    a. indulgent parenting.
    b. authoritative parenting.
    c. neglectful parenting.
    d. authoritarian parenting.
    Ans.: c   LG: 2   Page: 139   QT: F

79. A child with authoritarian parents is likely to display all of the following *except*
    a. failure to initiate activity.
    b. poor communication skills.
    c. self-reliance.
    d. social incompetence.
    Ans.: c   LG: 2   Page: 139   QT: F

80. Psychologists have found the highest social competence in children whose parents have which style?
    a. indulgent parenting
    b. authoritative parenting
    c. neglectful parenting
    d. authoritarian parenting
    Ans.: b   LG: 2   Page: 139   QT: C

81. Reciprocal socialization refers to the concept that
    a. children must be trained to fit into the social world.
    b. parenting style is a product of the parents alone.
    c. children socialize their parents and parents socialize their children.
    d. children are like blobs of clay from which a sculptor builds a statue.
    Ans.: c   LG: 2   Page: 140   QT: C

82. Psychologists studying the effects of divorce on children have found that
    a. 80% of children from divorced families have adjustment problems.
    b. these children are less likely to be aggressive.
    c. these children are more likely to be depressed.
    d. these children are less likely to have adjustment problems.
    Ans.: c   LG: 2   Page: 141   QT: C

83. Which of the following is *not* an aspect of positive parenting?
    a. utilizing quick and simple parenting tips like playing Mozart to infants
    b. coaching children to control their emotions
    c. using strategies to raise a moral child
    d. recognizing that parenting takes time and effort
    Ans.: a   LG: 2   Page: 142   QT: C

84. Emotion-coaching refers to parents who
    a. recognize that parenting takes time and effort.
    b. try to parent quickly with little inconvenience.
    c. raise a child who is considerate of others.
    d. provide guidance in effectively dealing with emotions.
    Ans.: d   LG: 2   Page: 142   QT: C

85. Which of the following strategies have *not* been found to be effective in raising a moral child?
    a. being punitive
    b. using reasoning a child can understand
    c. involving children in family decision making about moral decisions
    d. modeling moral behaviors
    Ans.: a   LG: 2   Page: 142   QT: C

86. In Kohlberg's preconventional level, moral judgments are made based on
    a. standards learned from parents.
    b. punishments.
    c. society's laws.
    d. personal moral codes.
    Ans.: b   LG: 2   Page: 144   QT: C

87. In Kohlberg's conventional level, moral judgments are made based on
    a. rewards.
    b. punishments.
    c. society's laws.
    d. personal moral codes.
    Ans.: c   LG: 2   Page: 144   QT: C

88. A person who makes moral judgments based on abstract principles for all of humanity is in Kohlberg's
    a. preoperational stage.
    b. postconventional stage.
    c. conventional stage.
    d. operational stage.
    Ans.: b   LG: 2   Page: 144   QT: C

89. Compared to Kohlberg's view, Gilligan's view of moral development emphasizes
    a. the rights of the individual.
    b. the justice perspective.
    c. the ability of people to independently make moral decisions.
    d. the care perspective.
    Ans.: d   LG: 2   Page: 145   QT: C

90. The care perspective of moral development emphasizes
    a. concern for others.
    b. moral behavior rather than moral judgments.
    c. the rights of the individual.
    d. the importance of justice.
    Ans.: a   LG: 2   Page: 145   QT: C

91. Estrogens refer to
    a. any agent that produces birth defects.
    b. the main class of male sex hormones.
    c. the main class of female sex hormones.
    d. an individual's genetic heritage.
    Ans.: c   LG: 2   Page: 146   QT: C

92. Which of the following has *not* been supported as having a role in affecting gender behavior?
    a. prenatal exposure of males to high levels of estrogens
    b. evolutionary pressures
    c. social experience
    d. prenatal exposure of females to an excess of androgens
    Ans.: a   LG: 2   Page: 146   QT: C

93. In the evolutionary view of gender development, men and women behave differently because of
    a. exposure to different levels of hormones prenatally.
    b. differences in successful reproductive strategies.
    c. society's expectations.
    d. interactions with peers.
    Ans.: b   LG: 2   Page: 146   QT: C

94. Biological views of gender development emphasize the role of which of these in gender development?
    a. exposure to different levels of hormones prenatally
    b. differences in successful reproductive strategies
    c. society's expectations
    d. interactions with peers
    Ans.: a   LG: 2   Page: 146   QT: C

95. Researchers have found that
    a. girls perform better on visuospatial skills than boys.
    b. boys and girls perform equally well on all cognitive tasks.
    c. boys perform better than girls on math skills at young ages, but these differences disappear as they age.
    d. girls perform better than boys on reading skills at young ages, but these differences disappear as they age.
    Ans.: c   LG: 2   Page: 148   QT: C

96. According to a recent theory on the role of gender schema in development,
    a. hormones determine gender roles.
    b. children develop cognitive frameworks based on what is considered appropriate behavior for males and females in their culture.
    c. parents are responsible for determining gender roles.
    d. males and females have different gender behaviors because of different evolutionary pressures.
    Ans.: b   LG: 2   Page: 148   QT: C

97. Which of the following factors contributes to resilient children?
    a. absence of parents
    b. low intellectual functioning
    c. low self-esteem
    d. bonds to supportive, competent adults
    Ans.: d   LG: 2   Page: 148   QT: C

98. Positive psychology has identified all of the following as contributors to optimal functioning in children *except*
    a. high intellectual functioning.
    b. presence of a supportive parent.
    c. bonds to competent adults outside the family.
    d. low self-esteem.
    Ans.: d   LG: 2   Page: 148   QT: C

99. Resilient children are most likely to have which of the following?
    a. supportive adults outside the family
    b. high intellectual functioning
    c. at least one supportive parent
    d. all of the above
    Ans.: d   LG: 2   Page: 148   QT: C

Learning Goal 3: Identify the most important changes that occur in adolescence.

100. The positive psychology perspective on adolescence emphasizes
    a. adolescents as sexually driven.
    b. the inherent conflicts of adolescence.
    c. adolescence as a time of evaluation and decision making.
    d. adolescents as radical, unnerving, and different.
    Ans.: c   LG: 3   Page: 150   QT: C

101. According to positive psychology, adolescence is characterized by all of the following *except*
    a. decision making.
    b. identity searching.
    c. evaluation.
    d. pathology and deviation.
    Ans.: d   LG: 3   Page: 150   QT: C

102. Puberty refers to
    a. any agent that causes birth defects.
    b. a period of rapid skeletal and sexual maturation.
    c. an individual's behavioral style.
    d. expectations for how males and females should think, act, and feel.
    Ans.: b   LG: 3   Page: 151   QT: C

103. The primary mechanism driving a decrease in the age of onset of puberty over the last century is
    a. increased hormones in the food supply.
    b. changes in the genetic makeup of the population.
    c. increased exposure to radiation.
    d. higher levels of nutrition and health.
    Ans.: d   LG: 3   Page: 151   QT: C

104. Testosterone is associated with all of the following *except*
    a. increases in height.
    b. changes in voice.
    c. breast development.
    d. changes in male genitals.
    Ans.: c   LG: 3   Page: 151   QT: C

105. Which of the following have been shown to have the highest relationship with depression and anger in adolescent girls?
    a. low levels of estrogens
    b. high levels of testosterone
    c. stress, bad grades, and relationship problems
    d. low levels of testosterone
    Ans.: c   LG: 3   Page: 152   QT: C

106. Individuals are most likely to enter which cognitive stage during adolescence?
    a. preoperational
    b. formal operational
    c. sensorimotor
    d. concrete operational
    Ans.: b   LG: 3   Page: 152   QT: C

107. Adolescent egocentrism is characterized by all of the following *except* the
    a. belief that others are as preoccupied with the individual as he or she is.
    b. belief that one is unique.
    c. belief that one is invincible.
    d. belief that one is superior to others.
    Ans.: d   LG: 3   Page: 152   QT: C

108. According to Erickson's theory of socioemotional development, adolescents struggle with which of the following crises?
    a. trust versus mistrust
    b. initative versus guilt
    c. identity versus identity confusion
    d. industry versus inferiority
    Ans.: c   LG: 3   Page: 153   QT: C

109. Identity status refers to
    a. a person's position in the development of an identity.
    b. the challenge adolescents face in finding out who they are.
    c. the bond between an adolescent and a caregiver.
    d. expectations about how adolescents should think, feel, and act.
    Ans.: a   LG: 3   Page: 154   QT: C

110. According to Marcia's ideas about identity status, a person who has not yet explored meaningful alternatives and has not made a commitment is in which stage?
    a. identity foreclosure
    b. identity moratorium
    c. identity achievement
    d. identity diffusion
    Ans.: d   LG: 3   Page: 154   QT: F

111. According to Marcia's ideas about identity status, a person who is exploring alternative paths but has not yet made a commitment is in which stage?
    a. identity foreclosure
    b. identity moratorium
    c. identity achievement
    d. identity diffusion
    Ans.: b   LG: 3   Page: 154   QT: F

112.. According to Marcia's ideas about identity status, a person who has explored alternative paths and made a commitment is in which stage?
    a. identity foreclosure
    b. identity moratorium
    c. identity achievement
    d. identity diffusion
    Ans.: c   LG: 3   Page: 154   QT: F

113. Which of the following does *not* contribute to the development of a positive identity?
    a. adopting your parent's identity
    b. recognizing that your identity is complex
    c. expecting your identity to change
    d. making the most of your college years
    Ans.: a   LG: 3   Page: 155   QT: C

114. Which of the following is *not* a key aspect of at-risk youths?
    a. delinquency
    b. self-identity
    c. substance abuse
    d. unprotected sex
    Ans.: b   LG: 3   Page: 155   QT: C

Learning Goal 4: Discuss adult development and the positive dimensions of aging.

115. Which of the following does *not* increase during early adulthood?
      a. use of cigarettes
      b. alcohol consumption
      c. marijuana use
      d. athletic ability
      Ans.: d   LG: 4   Page: 157   QT: C

116. Which of the following is the *least* likely consequence of binge drinking?
      a. unprotected sex
      b. higher grades
      c. physical injuries
      d. trouble with the police
      Ans.: b   LG: 4   Page: 157   QT: C

117. Which of the following physical changes is *not* associated with middle adulthood?
      a. skin wrinkles
      b. age spots
      c. thinning hair
      d. increased height
      Ans.: d   LG: 4   Page: 157   QT: C

118. Which of the following is *not* one of the three greatest health concerns of middle adulthood?
      a. cancer
      b. weight
      c. Alzheimer's disease
      d. heart disease
      Ans.: c   LG: 4   Page: 157   QT: C

119. Menopause results in
      a. dramatic increases in testosterone release.
      b. dramatic increases in estrogen release.
      c. dramatic decreases in testosterone release.
      d. dramatic decreases in estrogen release.
      Ans.: d   LG: 4   Page: 158   QT: C

120. Which of the following is *not* a benefit of estrogen replacement therapy?
      a. reduced risk of osteoporosis
      b. reduced risk of breast cancer
      c. reduced risk of coronary disease
      d. decrease in symptoms such as hot flashes and sweating
      Ans.: b   LG: 4   Page: 158   QT: C

121. Life span refers to
      a. the maximum number of years an individual can expect to live.
      b. the number of years that will probably be lived by the average person born in a given year.
      c. the average age at which an individual gives birth.
      d. the number of years between successive generations.
      Ans.: a   LG: 4   Page: 158   QT: C

122. The number of years that an average person born in a given year will probably live is known as
    a. life span.
    b. life expectancy.
    c. life term.
    d. life ideal.
    Ans.: b   LG: 4   Page: 158   QT: C

123. The average increase in life expectancy since 1900 is
    a. 10 years.
    b. 20 years.
    c. 30 years.
    d. 40 years.
    Ans.: c   LG: 4   Page: 158   QT: C

124. Which of the following is *not* an aspect of the cellular-clock theory of aging?
    a. Cells create unstable oxygen molecules that damage DNA.
    b. Cells can only divide about 100 times.
    c. As cells divide, telomeres become shorter.
    d. The upper limit of the human life span is about 120 years.
    Ans.: a   LG: 4   Page: 159   QT: C

125. Which of the following is *not* an aspect of the free-radical theory of aging?
    a. Unstable oxygen molecules are produced in cells.
    b. Molecules inside of cells damage DNA and other structures.
    c. Damage done by free radicals can lead to cancer and arthritis.
    d. Shortening of telomeres leads to the results of aging.
    Ans.: d   LG: 4   Page: 159   QT: C

126. Which of the following is *not* a physical change associated with late adulthood?
    a. weight gain
    b. increased blood pressure
    c. muscle loss
    d. bone loss
    Ans.: a   LG: 4   Page: 159   QT: C

127. Chronic diseases are most prevalent in
    a. adolescence.
    b. early adulthood.
    c. middle adulthood.
    d. late adulthood.
    Ans.: d   LG: 4   Page: 159   QT: C

128. The most common chronic disorder of late adulthood is
    a. Alzheimer's disease.
    b. diabetes.
    c. arthritis.
    d. depression.
    Ans.: c   LG: 4   Page: 160   QT: C

129. Studies of aging brains have shown all of the following *except* that
    a. older adult's brains rewire themselves to compensate for losses.
    b. all aging brains will eventually develop Alzheimer's disease.
    c. dendritic growth continues through the 70s.
    d. as brains age, they can shift function from one region to another.
    Ans.: b   LG: 4   Page: 160   QT: C

130. Alzheimer's disease is associated with all of these *except*
    a. deterioration in memory.
    b. decreased language ability.
    c. impaired reasoning.
    d. increased acetylcholine.
    Ans.: d   LG: 4   Page: 160   QT: C

131. Research on the brain and Alzheimer's disease has implicated all of the following *except*
    a. increased dendrites.
    b. increased plaques.
    c. decreased acetylcholine.
    d. increased tangles.
    Ans.: a   LG: 4   Page: 161   QT: C

132. Which is most true of the thinking of adolescents compared to adults?
    a. Adolescents have more knowledge in specific domains.
    b. Adolescents think more pragmatically than adults.
    c. Adults think more idealistically than adolescents.
    d. Adolescents think more in absolute terms.
    Ans.: d   LG: 4   Page: 162   QT: C

133. Crystallized intelligence refers to
    a. an individual's accumulated knowledge.
    b. one's ability to reason abstractly.
    c. expert knowledge about practical aspects of life.
    d. an individual's behavioral styles and ways of responding.
    Ans.: a   LG: 4   Page: 162   QT: C

134. Fluid intelligence refers to
    a. an individual's accumulated knowledge.
    b. one's ability to reason abstractly.
    c. expert knowledge about practical aspects of life.
    d. an individual's behavioral styles and ways of responding.
    Ans.: b   LG: 4   Page: 162   QT: C

135. In a longitudinal study,
    a. a number of different people are studied at the same time.
    b. the same people are studied over a lengthy period.
    c. cohort effects are very high.
    d. fluid intelligence is measured.
    Ans.: b   LG: 4   Page: 162   QT: C

136. In a cross-sectional study,
    a. a number of different people are studied at the same time.
    b. the same people are studied over a lengthy period.
    c. cohort effects are minimized.
    d. fluid intelligence is measured.
    Ans.: a   LG: 4   Page: 162   QT: C

137. When results of cross-sectional and longitudinal studies of cognitive function are compared,
    a. longitudinal studies show greater declines in middle adulthood.
    b. cross sectional studies show declines of inductive reasoning later than longitudinal studies.
    c. cross sectional studies show greater declines in early adulthood.
    d. longitudinal studies show lower declines in late adulthood.
    Ans.: d   LG: 4   Page: 163   QT: C

138. Wisdom refers to
    a. an individual's accumulated knowledge.
    b. one's ability to reason abstractly.
    c. expert knowledge about practical aspects of life.
    d. an individual's behavioral styles and ways of responding.
    Ans.: c   LG: 4   Page: 164   QT: C

139. Which of the following of Erickson's stages of life-span development does *not* occur during adulthood?
    a. integrity versus despair
    b. generativity versus stagnation
    c. autonomy versus shame and doubt
    d. intimacy versus isolation
    Ans.: c   LG: 4   Page: 164   QT: C

140. Which of the following of Erickson's stages of life-span development occurs during early adulthood?
    a. integrity versus despair
    b. generativity versus stagnation
    c. autonomy versus shame and doubt
    d. intimacy versus isolation
    Ans.: d   LG: 4   Page: 164   QT: C

141. Which of the following of Erickson's stages of life-span development occurs during late adulthood?
    a. integrity versus despair
    b. generativity versus stagnation
    c. autonomy versus shame and doubt
    d. intimacy versus isolation
    Ans.: a   LG: 4   Page: 164   QT: C

142. Research on careers and work has shown all of the following *except* that
    a. men are increasing the amount of housework they do.
    b. women are increasing the amount of money they earn.
    c. men are more interested in family and parenting.
    d. men bear most of the responsibilities for child care and home maintenance.
    Ans.: d   LG: 4   Page: 165   QT: C

143. Which of the following statements about marriage is most true?
    a. Men and women are from different planets.
    b. The average duration of a marriage in the United States is 25 years.
    c. The proportion of women who never married increased dramatically in the last 10 years.
    d. Overly idealistic expectations of marriage contribute to the high rate of divorce.
    Ans.: d   LG: 4   Page: 166   QT: C

144. Studies of successful marriages have demonstrated that all of the following are important to a successful marriage *except*
    a. nurturing fondness and admiration.
    b. relying on the spouse as a friend.
    c. concentrating power in one spouse.
    d. solving conflicts together.
    Ans.: c   LG: 4   Page: 167   QT: C

145. Which of the following is *not* a common benefit of being single?
    a. freedom to make one's own decisions
    b. involvement in intimate relationships
    c. opportunities to explore new places
    d. time to develop personal resources
    Ans.: b   LG: 4   Page: 167   QT: C

146. Which of the following is *not* one of the major conflicts that may contribute to mid-life crises?
    a. being destructive versus constructive
    b. being masculine versus being feminine
    c. being attached to others versus being separated from them
    d. being trusting versus mistrusting
    Ans.: d   LG: 4   Page: 168   QT: C

147. Recent studies of midlife in Americans have supported which of these?
    a. 90% experience a midlife crisis.
    b. Middle-aged individuals had lower anxiety levels than those under 40.
    c. Middle-aged adults report fewer negative life events than those under 40.
    d. Midlife individuals had many illnesses.
    Ans.: b   LG: 4   Page: 168   QT: C

148. When socioemotional aspects of aging are examined, researchers have found that
    a. older adults are more likely to report positive emotions.
    b. older adults are less likely to report positive emotions.
    c. older adults are less likely to report negative emotions.
    d. older adults are more likely to report negative emotions.
    Ans.: c   LG: 4   Page: 169   QT: C

149. Research on social relationships among older adults have supported which of the following?
    a. Older adults are more likely to widen their circle of acquaintances.
    b. Older adults are more likely to take emotional risks.
    c. Older adults spend more time with familiar individuals.
    d. Emotional lives of older adults are more bleak than previously thought.
    Ans.: c   LG: 4   Page: 169   QT: C

150. When researchers studied individuals at 50 years of age and again at 75–80 years of age, they found that which of the following contributed to health and happiness at age 75–80?
    a. heavy smoking
    b. alcohol abuse
    c. exercise
    d. unstable marriage
    Ans.: c   LG: 4   Page: 169   QT: C

True/False Items

____ 151. Socioemotional processes and cognitive processes interact during development, but physical processes are separate from them.
____ 152. Psychologists currently believe that genes are more important than environment in determining psychological development.
____ 153. Smaller pre-term infants are more likely to have developmental problems than larger pre-term infants.
____ 154. Piaget's theory of development argues that children merely receive information from the environment.
____ 155. Vygotsky emphasized the role of culture in development.
____ 156. According to Erickson's theory of development, children must master knowledge and intellectual skills to successfully resolve the initiative versus guilt stage.
____ 157. Harry Harlow found that contact comfort was more important than food for establishing infant attachment.
____ 158. Psychologists have found that children who are raised by authoritarian parents are the most socially competent.
____ 159. In Kohlberg's theory of moral development, moral decisions at the postconventional level are made based on rewards and punishments.
____ 160. Gender roles are quite similar across all cultures.
____ 161. In the absence of a nurturing parent, bonds to caring adults outside of the home can lead to the development of resilient children.
____ 162. Cross-cultural studies of adolescents have documented that 75% are unhappy and have poor self-images.
____ 163. Adolescent egocentrism refers to beliefs that one is unique, invincible, and superior to others.
____ 164. Men experience more radical changes in hormone levels in middle adulthood than women do.
____ 165. Cognitive skills of older adults benefit from engaging in challenging intellectual activities.

Answer Key for True/False Items

151.	Ans.: F	LG: 1	Page: 119	159.	Ans.: F	LG: 2	Page: 144
152.	Ans.: F	LG: 1	Page: 122	160.	Ans.: F	LG: 2	Page: 147
153.	Ans.: T	LG: 2	Page: 124	161.	Ans.: T	LG: 2	Page: 148
154.	Ans.: F	LG: 2	Page: 128	162.	Ans.: F	LG: 3	Page: 150
155.	Ans.: T	LG: 2	Page: 134	163.	Ans.: F	LG: 3	Page: 152
156.	Ans.: F	LG: 2	Page: 135	164.	Ans.: F	LG: 4	Page: 158
157.	Ans.: T	LG: 2	Page: 136	165.	Ans.: T	LG: 4	Page: 161
158.	Ans.: F	LG: 2	Page: 139				

Fill-in-the-Blank Items

166. The expression of a person's genes in measurable characteristics is known as _____.
167. An organism's environmental experiences are also known as _____.
168. Efforts to experience our lives in optimal ways may involve the development of _____ that involve our activities, social relationships and life goals.
169. During human development, the heart first begins to beat during the _____ period.
170. The process of elimination of unused neural connections is known as _____.
171. According to Piaget, the stage of cognitive development when thinking becomes abstract, idealistic, and logical is known as the _____.
172. Compared to Piaget, Vygotsky placed more emphasis on the role of _____ in development.
173. According to Erickson, children whose basic needs are not met by responsive sensitive caregivers will develop _____.
174. Infants who use the caregiver as a base from which to explore the environment are demonstrating _____.
175. Psychologists have found that children with _____ parents are most socially competent.
176. Expectations for how females and males should think, act, and feel are known as _____.
177. Adolescents with poor self-images can be helped by encouraging the capacity for _____.
178. The belief during adolescences that one is unique and invincible and that others are as preoccupied with you as you are yourself is known as _____.
179. The maximum number of years an individual can expect to live is known as _____.
180. Expert knowledge about the practical aspects of life is known as _____.

Answer Key for Fill-in-the-Blank Items

166.	Ans.: phenotype	LG: 1	Page: 121
167.	Ans.: nurture	LG: 1	Page: 122
168.	Ans.: life themes	LG: 1	Page: 122
169.	Ans.: embryonic	LG: 2	Page: 123
170.	Ans.: pruning	LG: 2	Page: 127
171.	Ans.: formal operational stage	LG: 2	Page: 133
172.	Ans.: culture	LG: 2	Page: 134
173.	Ans.: mistrust	LG: 2	Page: 134
174.	Ans.: secure attachment	LG: 2	Page: 138
175.	Ans.: authoritative	LG: 2	Page: 139
176.	Ans.: gender roles	LG: 2	Page: 147
177.	Ans.: initiative	LG: 3	Page: 151
178.	Ans.: adolescent egocentrism	LG: 3	Page: 152
179.	Ans.: life span	LG: 4	Page: 158
180.	Ans.: wisdom	LG: 4	Page: 164

Matching Items

___	181. physical	A.	heart beat
___	182. socioemotional	B.	doubt and shame
___	183. germinal period	C.	hormones
___	184. embryonic period	D.	stagnation
___	185. autonomy	E.	despair
___	186. initiative	F.	personality
___	187. adolescence	G.	identity confusion
___	188. identity status	H.	guilt
___	189. generativity	I.	conception
___	190. integrity	J.	identity diffusion

Answer Key for Matching Items

181.	Ans.: C	LG: 1	Page: 119		186.	Ans.: H	LG: 2	Page: 135
182.	Ans.: F	LG: 1	Page: 119		187.	Ans.: G	LG: 3	Page: 153
183.	Ans.: I	LG: 2	Page: 123		188.	Ans.: J	LG: 3	Page: 154
184.	Ans.: A	LG: 2	Page: 123		189.	Ans.: D	LG: 4	Page: 164
185.	Ans.: B	LG: 2	Page: 134		190.	Ans.: E	LG: 4	Page: 164

Essay Questions

191. Define genotype, phenotype, nature and nurture. Describe current psychological views on the role each plays in development. (LG: 1)

Answer Guidelines: Genotype: the individual's actual genetic makeup. Phenotype: observable or measurable characteristics that an individual has. Nature: biological inheritance. Nurture: environmental experiences.

Genotype may contribute to predispositions to behave in certain ways, or to have certain physical characteristics; genes don't turn on all at once, so the role of nature is not confined to a period around conception or birth, but instead genes produce proteins throughout life. Actual phenotypes depend on the interaction between the genotype (or nature) with the environmental experiences (or nurture). Psychologists' definitions of what constitutes an influence of environment are broader (parenting, family relationships, interactions with peers, education, but also exposure to viruses, birth complications, cellular activities). It no longer seems useful to try to determine whether nature or nurture contributes more than the other.

192. Describe the current perspective on how infant motor behavior develops. (LG: 2)

Answer Guidelines: Infants can create new motor behaviors if they are motivated to do something; the form of these behaviors will depend on the physical properties of the body, the goal that the infant is trying to achieve and the support available in the environment. Motor skills are also linked to perceptual skills; they use these links to learn how to maintain balance, reach for objects in space, and move across different terrains and surfaces. Motor skills also allow infants to learn about the texture, size, and hardness of objects, and provide different perceptual perspectives of objects.

193. Describe the conservation task and the three-mountains task, and discuss what results of the tests indicate about cognitive development. (LG: 2)

Answer Guidelines: Conservation task: Child is presented with two identical cups, each containing the same amount of liquid; the child watches the experimenter pour the contents of one of the cups into a third cup which is taller and thinner than the two identical cups. The experimenter asks the child whether the new cup has the same amount of liquid as the remaining identical cup. Children in the preoperational stage say no, and indicate that the taller cup has more liquid. They fail to understand that objects have properties (like volume) that are not altered by superficial changes.

Three-mountains task: Child is shown a 3-dimensional model of three mountains; the child walks around the model to see it from different perspectives. The child is then seated on one side of the model, and asked to identify photographs that would reflect the view from different perspectives. Preoperational children choose their own perspective regardless of which perspective they are asked to identify.

Both of these tasks demonstrate an inability to perform operations—to demonstrate the understanding that actions are reversible.

194. Describe four criticisms of Piaget's theory of cognitive development. (LG: 2)

Answer Guidelines: (1) Cognitive abilities in children emerge much earlier than Piaget thought (for example, object permanence, memory and other symbolic acitivity). (2) Formal operational thought does not emerge as consistently in early adolescence as Piaget thought; some adults don't reason as logically as Piaget thought. (3) He ignored individual differences. (4) He placed too much emphasis on big stages, and not enough on smaller steps in solving problems. (5) Piaget ignored the role of culture and education in children's development.

195. Describe 4 types of parenting styles, and discuss the effects of each style on children's social competence. (LG: 2)

Answer Guidelines:

(1) Authoritarian parenting—a restrictive, punitive style; parent expects the child to follow the parent's directions and to respect work and effort; parent firmly limits and controls the child with little verbal exchange; associated with children's social incompetence, including failure to initiate activity, poor communication skills, and comparison with others.

(2) Authoritative parenting—encourages children to be independent but still places limits and controls on their behavior; characterized by extensive verbal give-and-take; parents are warm and nurturing toward the child; children tend to be socially competent, self-reliant, and socially responsible.

(3) Neglectful parenting—a style in which parents are uninvolved in their child's life. Children whose parents are neglectful might develop a sense that other aspects of the parents' lives are more important than they are. Children whose parents are neglectful tend to be less competent socially, not handle independence well, and especially show poor self-control.

(4) Indulgent parenting—a style in which parents are involved with their children but place few limits on them; let their children do what they want; some parents deliberately rear their children in this way because they believe the combination of warm involvement with few restraints will produce a creative, confident child; in reality, children whose parents are indulgent often rate poorly in social competence. They fail to learn respect for others, expect to get their own way, and have difficulty controlling their behavior.

196. Describe two different perspectives on the development of gender in humans. (LG: 2)

Answer Guidelines:
Biological theories suggest that exposure to sex hormones can influence gender behavior; males who are exposed to insufficient levels of androgens or females who are exposed to high levels of androgens show atypical gender behavior; role of hormones is supported by animal experiments where prenatal exposure to hormones affects outcomes.

Evolutionary theories emphasize the different adaptive strategies for males versus females; as a result of these pressures, males are more likely to be aggressive, risk-taking and violent; females have evolved to be more nurturing and select mates who have characteristics that would contribute to long-term support for a family.

Social theories emphasize the role of culture, parents and peers in shaping gender behavior. Society produces gender roles which dictate how males and females should behave, and children learn the rules for each of these roles through interactions with parents, peers, and society as a whole.

197. Describe Erickson's identity versus identity confusion stage, and discuss how it applies to issues facing adolescents. (LG: 3)

Answer Guidelines: Adolescents face the challenges of finding out who they are, what they are all about, and where they are going in life; choosing among many new roles and adult statuses— from the vocational to the romantic. If they don't adequately explore their identity during this stage, they emerge with a sense of confusion about who they are; parents should allow adolescents to explore many different roles, not push an identity on them. Identity confusion is expressed in one of two ways: either individuals withdraw, isolating themselves from peers and family, or they lose themselves in the crowd.

In American culture, adolescents need to decide what careers they will pursue, whether they will go to college, and whether they will marry; they want to free themselves from the control of their parents and other adults and make their own choices, but may deeply fear making the wrong decisions and failing.

198. List four types of risk associated with adolescence, and describe two types of interventions that have been successful at decreasing the negative effects of these risks. (LG: 3)

Answer Guidelines:
Risks: delinquency, substance abuse, unprotected sex and adolescent pregnancy, school-related problems.

Interventions: Individualized programs; at-risk youth paired with responsible adults who pay attention to specific needs; providing counseling to adolescents and their families related to changing behaviors or considering alternative futures, such as going to college.

Community-wide programs; improving lives of youth requires treating problems beyond the individual level; community-wide health promotion, substance abuse prevention curriculum; neighborhood development programs.

199. Describe K. Warner Schaie's longitudinal study of intellectual abilities in adulthood, including main abilities tested and results. (LG: 4)

Answer Guidelines: Schaie used a longitudinal design beginning in 1956 to study the following abilities:

Vocabulary (ability to encode and understand ideas expressed in words)

Verbal memory (ability to encode and recall meaningful language units, such as a list of words)

Number (ability to perform simply mathematical computations such as arithmetic, subtraction, and multiplication)

Spatial orientation (ability to visualize and mentally rotate stimuli in two- and three-dimensional space)

Inductive reasoning (ability to recognize and understand patterns and relationships in a problem and use this understanding to solve other instances of the problem)

Perceptual speed (ability to quickly and accurately make simple discriminations in visual stimuli)

He has found in longitudinal studies that the highest level of functioning for four of the six intellectual abilities (vocabulary, verbal memory, inductive reasoning, and spatial orientation) occurred in middle adulthood. Two of the six abilities (numerical ability and perceptual speed) declined in middle age. Perceptual speed showed the earliest decline, beginning in early adulthood.

When he compared cross-sectional designs to longitudinal designs, he found a greater decline during middle-age in the cross-sectional assessment compared to the longitudinal design.

200. Describe four principles that have been documented to contribute to successful marriages, and common benefits and problems facing single adults. (LG: 4)

Answer Guidelines: Successful marriages include: (1) mutual fondness and admiration—praising the spouse; (2) seeing the spouse as a friend and a source of support in times of stress and difficulty; (3) sharing power; and (4) solving conflicts together, regulating emotions during conflicts and compromising.

Single adults have:

Benefits: independent decision making, developing personal resources to meet goals; freedom to pursue interests and make schedules; opportunities to explore new places; privacy.

Drawbacks: lack of intimate relationships with others, loneliness, feeling out of step with a marriage-oriented society.

Chapter 5: Sensation and Perception

Learning Goals

1. Discuss basic principles of sensation and perception.
2. Explain how the visual system enables us to see and, by communicating with the brain, to perceive the world.
3. Understand how the auditory system registers sound and how it connects with the brain to perceive it.
4. Know how the skin, chemical, and kinesthetic and vestibular senses work.
5. Describe what human factors psychologists do.

Multiple-Choice Items

Learning Goal 1: Discuss basic principles of sensation and perception.

1. When scientists have examined the effects of losing one channel of sensation, they have found all of the following *except* that
   a. blind individuals are more accurate at locating a sound.
   b. blind individuals have greater sensitivity to touch.
   c. the auditory cortex of deaf individuals is more responsive to touch compared to hearing individuals.
   d. the auditory cortex of deaf individuals is more responsive to sound compared to hearing individuals.
   Ans.: d   LG: 1   Page: 176   QT: C

2. The process of receiving stimulus energies from the external environment is known as
   a. perception.
   b. transduction.
   c. sensation.
   d. conception.
   Ans.: c   LG: 1   Page: 176   QT: F

3. Sensation refers to
   a. the process of receiving stimulus energies from the external environment.
   b. the process of transforming physical energy into electrochemical energy.
   c. the brain's process of organizing and interpreting sensory information to give it meaning.
   d. the minimum amount of stimulus energy that a person can detect.
   Ans.: a   LG: 1   Page: 176   QT: F

4. The process of transforming physical energy into electrochemical energy is known as
   a. perception.
   b. transduction.
   c. sensation.
   d. conception.
   Ans.: b   LG: 1   Page: 177   QT: F

5. Transduction refers to
   a. the process of receiving stimulus energies from the external environment.
   b. the process of transforming physical energy into electrochemical energy.
   c. the brain's process of organizing and interpreting sensory information to give it meaning.
   d. the minimum amount of stimulus energy that a person can detect.
   Ans.: b   LG: 1   Page: 177   QT: F

6. The brain's process of organizing and interpreting sensory information to give it meaning is called
   a. perception.
   b. transduction.
   c. sensation.
   d. conception.
   Ans.: a   LG: 1   Page: 177   QT: F

7. Perception refers to
   a. the process of receiving stimulus energies from the external environment.
   b. the process of transforming physical energy into electrochemical energy.
   c. the brain's process of organizing and interpreting sensory information to give it meaning.
   d. the minimum amount of stimulus energy that a person can detect.
   Ans.: c   LG: 1   Page: 177   QT: F

8. When receptor cells in the nose register a stimulus, they
   a. send the stimulus energy directly to the brain.
   b. convert the stimulus energy into a mechanical impulse.
   c. send the stimulus energy to the sense organs.
   d. convert the stimulus energy into an electrochemical impulse.
   Ans.: d   LG: 1   Page: 177   QT: C

9. After sensory information has been transduced,
   a. it travels through the nervous system to the brain.
   b. it travels from the brain to the sense organs.
   c. receptor cells convert it into mechanical impulses.
   d. it stimulates specialized receptors in sense organs.
   Ans.: a   LG: 1   Page: 177   QT: C

10. Bottom-up processing refers to
    a. perceptual processing that transforms physical energy into electrochemical energy.
    b. perceptual processing that begins with sensory receptors registering information then moving to integration and cognitive processing in the brain.
    c. perceptual processing that starts out with cognitive processing in the brain.
    d. perceptual processing of physical energy in specialized receptor cells.
    Ans.: b   LG: 1   Page: 177   QT: F

11. Top-down processing refers to
    a. perceptual processing that transforms physical energy into electrochemical energy.
    b. perceptual processing that begins with sensory receptors registering information then moving to integration and cognitive processing in the brain.
    c. perceptual processing that starts out with cognitive processing in the brain.
    d. perceptual processing of physical energy in specialized receptor cells.
    Ans.: c   LG: 1   Page: 177   QT: F

12. When putting together a jigsaw puzzle, you look at the picture on the box and use it to select the pieces that go in a particular section. In this example, you are relying on
    a. top-down processing.
    b. inside-out processing.
    c. fast-forward processing.
    d. bottom-up processing.
    Ans.: a   LG: 1   Page: 177   QT: A

13. When putting together a jigsaw puzzle, you find pieces that are similar in color and shape and try to piece them together, without looking at the final picture first. In this example, you are relying on
    a. top-down processing.
    b. inside-out processing.
    c. fast-forward processing.
    d. bottom-up processing.
    Ans.: d   LG: 1   Page: 177   QT: A

14. The purpose of perception is
    a. to send internal information out to the external world.
    b. to represent information from the outside world internally.
    c. to match information from internal and external worlds.
    d. to change sensory information into motor information.
    Ans.: b   LG: 1   Page: 177   QT: C

15. Which of the following is *not* an evolutionary purpose that sensation and perception might serve?
    a. sensing the approach of a predator
    b. responding quickly to the appearance of prey
    c. preventing the identification of food sources
    d. accurately detecting the appearance of a potential mate
    Ans.: c   LG: 1   Page: 178   QT: C

16. Specialized cells that detect and transmit stimulus information to afferent nerves and the brain are known as
    a. sensory receptors.
    b. sensory adaptors.
    c. sensory registers.
    d. sensory transducers.
    Ans.: a   LG: 1   Page: 178   QT: F

17. Sensory receptors
    a. are specialized to detect and transmit stimulus information to afferent nerves and the brain.
    b. are neurons in the brain that respond to particular lines or other features of a stimulus.
    c. produce a predisposition to perceive something in a particular way.
    d. produce apparent motion.
    Ans.: a   LG: 1   Page: 178   QT: C

18. Sensory nerves are also known as
    a. inter nerves.
    b. motor nerves.
    c. afferent nerves.
    d. perceptual nerves.
    Ans.: c   LG: 1   Page: 178   QT: C

19. When sensory receptors are stimulated,
    a. they receive action potentials from sensory neurons.
    b. they trigger action potentials in sensory neurons.
    c. they inhibit action potentials from sensory neurons.
    d. they receive action potentials from the brain.
    Ans.: b   LG: 1   Page: 178   QT: F

20. Which of the following is *not* a main class of sensory reception?
    a. photoreception
    b. microreception
    c. mechanoreception
    d. chemoreception
    Ans.: b   LG: 1   Page: 179   QT: C

21. Which of the following is *not* an example of mechanoreception?
    a. detection of chemical stimuli
    b. detection of vibration
    c. detection of pressure
    d. detection of movement
    Ans.: a   LG: 1   Page: 179   QT: C

22. Which of the following is an example of mechanoreception?
    a. detection of chemical stimuli
    b. detection of light
    c. detection of pressure
    d. detection of heat
    Ans.: c   LG: 1   Page: 179   QT: C

23. Nearly all sensory signals go through which part of the brain?
    a. cerebellum
    b. amygdala
    c. thalamus
    d. hippocampus
    Ans.: c   LG: 1   Page: 180   QT: F

24. Which of the following pairs is *least* correct?
    a. vision—occipital lobe
    b. hearing—temporal lobe
    c. pain—parietal lobe
    d. temperature—frontal lobe
    Ans.: d   LG: 1   Page: 180   QT: C

25. The absolute threshold refers to
    a. the ability to detect information below the level of conscious awareness.
    b. the minimum amount of energy a person can detect.
    c. the smallest difference in stimulation required to discriminate one stimulus from another 50 percent of the time.
    d. focusing on a specific aspect of experience while ignoring others.
    Ans.: b   LG: 1   Page: 180   QT: F

26. An absolute threshold refers to
    a. the smallest difference in stimulation required to discriminate one stimulus from another 50 percent of the time.
    b. the smallest difference in stimulate required to discriminate one stimulus from another 100 percent of the time.
    c. the smallest amount of energy a person can detect 50 percent of the time.
    d. the smallest amount of energy a person can detect 100 percent of the time.
    Ans.: c   LG: 1   Page: 180   QT: F

27. The smallest amount of energy a person can detect 50 percent of the time is known as the
    a. absolute threshold.
    b. perceptual threshold.
    c. discrimination threshold.
    d. sensory threshold.
    Ans.: a   LG: 1   Page: 180   QT: F

28. Noise refers to
    a. focusing attention on a specific aspect of an experience.
    b. the ability to detect information below the level of conscious awareness.
    c. irrelevant and competing stimuli.
    d. a predisposition to perceive something in a particular way.
    Ans.: c   LG: 1   Page: 181   QT: F

29. You are trying to locate a fly that's been bothering you in your room. Which of the following is *not* an example of noise in your search?
    a. smoke from your roommate's cigarette thatt keeps you from seeing
    b. the television in the background
    c. your roommate's blaring music
    d. the sound of the buzzing fly you are trying to locate
    Ans.: d   LG: 1   Page: 181   QT: A

30. The ability to detect sensations below the level of conscious awareness is known as
    a. sensory threshold.
    b. difference threshold.
    c. subliminal perception.
    d. signal detection.
    Ans.: c   LG: 1   Page: 181   QT: F

31. Research on subliminal perception has demonstrated that
    a. information processed below conscious awareness has a large effect on behavior.
    b. people can process some information below conscious awareness.
    c. rock songs contain messages from Satan.
    d. information cannot be processed below conscious awareness.
    Ans.: b   LG: 1   Page: 181   QT: C

32. When investigators examined claims that rock songs contain backwards recordings of messages from Satan, they found that
    a. people heard the message if they had been told the song did not contain a message.
    b. everyone heard the same message in the song.
    c. people heard the message if they had been told the song contained a message.
    d. no one heard any messages in the song.
    Ans.: c   LG: 1   Page: 182   QT: C

33. Difference threshold refers to
    a. the smallest difference in stimulation required to discriminate one stimulus from another 50 percent of the time.
    b. the smallest difference in stimulation required to discriminate one stimulus from another 100 percent of the time.
    c. the smallest amount of energy a person can detect 50 percent of the time.
    d. the smallest amount of energy a person can detect 100 percent of the time.
    Ans.: a   LG: 1   Page: 182   QT: F

34. The smallest difference in stimulation required to discriminate one stimulus from another 50 percent of the time is known as the
    a. absolute threshold.
    b. perceptual threshold.
    c. difference threshold.
    d. sensory threshold.
    Ans.: c   LG: 1   Page: 182   QT: F

35. Your roommate Ali likes to put 100-watt light bulbs in her overhead light, while your roommate Melissa prefers 40-watt bulbs. If you wanted to be able to see the illumination in the room change when you walked into Ali's room and Melissa's room with a flashlight, which of the following is most true?
    a. You would need a brighter flashlight in Melissa's room than in Ali's room.
    b. You would need a brighter flashlight in Ali's room than in Melissa's room.
    c. You wouldn't be able to see the illumination change in either room.
    d. It wouldn't matter how bright the overhead lights were, you could see the same amount of change in both rooms.
    Ans.: b   LG: 1   Page: 182   QT: A

36. According to Weber's law,
    a. to perceive two stimuli as different, they must differ by a constant minimum amount.
    b. to perceive two stimuli as different, they must differ by a constant minimum percentage.
    c. to perceive two stimuli as different, they must differ from the noise by 50 percent.
    d. to perceive two stimuli as different, they must differ from each other by 50 percent.
    Ans.: b   LG: 1   Page: 183   QT: F

37. According to signal detection theory, which of the following does *not* play a role in making decisions about stimuli?
    a. fatigue
    b. physical intensity of the stimulus
    c. sensory abilities of the observer
    d. presence of subliminal stimuli
    Ans.: d   LG: 1   Page: 183   QT: C

38. According to signal detection theory, a person reading a radar screen who fails to see a plane that appears on the screen is producing a
    a. hit.
    b. miss.
    c. false alarm.
    d. correct rejection.
    Ans.: b   LG: 1   Page: 183   QT: A

39. Selective attention refers to
    a. focusing on a specific aspect of experience while ignoring others.
    b. the ability to detect information below the level of conscious awareness.
    c. perceptual processing that begins with sensory receptors registering information then moving to integration and cognitive processing in the brain.
    d. perceptual processing that starts out with cognitive processing in the brain.
    Ans.: a   LG: 1   Page: 184   QT: F

40. Focusing on a specific aspect of experience while ignoring others is known as
    a. perceptual set.
    b. signal detection.
    c. subliminal perception.
    d. selective attention.
    Ans.: d   LG: 1   Page: 184   QT: F

41. The Stroop effect is an example of which of these?
    a. top-down processing
    b. selective attention
    c. signal detection theory
    d. just noticeable difference
    Ans.: b   LG: 1   Page: 184   QT: F

42. The predisposition to perceive something in a particular way is known as
    a. perceptual set.
    b. signal detection.
    c. subliminal perception.
    d. selective attention.
    Ans.: a   LG: 1   Page: 185   QT: F

43. A change in the responsiveness of your sensory systems based on the average level of surrounding stimulation is known as
    a. perceptual set.
    b. sensory adaptation.
    c. subliminal perception.
    d. selective attention.
    Ans.: b   LG: 1   Page: 186   QT: F

44. When you walk into a dark theater, you can't see anything. Eventually, though you begin to notice that you can see the other people sitting near you. This best illustrates which property?
    a. signal detection
    b. absolute threshold
    c. sensory adaptation
    d. subliminal perception
    Ans.: c   LG: 1   Page: 186   QT: C

Learning Goal 2: Explain how the visual system enables us to see and, by communicating with the brain, to perceive the world.

45. Wavelength refers to
    a. the distance betweens peaks in light.
    b. the height of the peaks in light.
    c. the mixture of levels of brightness of a light.
    d. the distance light must travel to reach the brain.
    Ans.: a   LG: 2   Page: 187   QT: F

46. Our perception of color is most closely related to
    a. amplitude.
    b. wavelength.
    c. cochlear displacement.
    d. pitch.
    Ans.: b   LG: 2   Page: 187   QT: C

47. Changes in the amplitude of light waves would be most likely perceived as
    a. changes in color.
    b. changes in saturation.
    c. changes in brightness.
    d. changes in hue.
    Ans.: c   LG: 2   Page: 187   QT: C

48. The perceived saturation or richness of a color is most closely related to
    a. the mixture of wavelengths in a light.
    b. the amount of infrared radiation in a light.
    c. the amplitude of the peaks in a light.
    d. the amount of ultraviolet light in a light.
    Ans.: a   LG: 2   Page: 187   QT: F

49. The sclera is
    a. the colored part of the eye.
    b. the opening in the center of the iris.
    c. the muscle that controls the size of the pupil.
    d. the white outer part that maintains the shape of the eye.
    Ans.: d   LG: 2   Page: 188   QT: F

50. The role of the pupil is to
    a. focus the light on the receptor cells.
    b. control the amount of light that gets into the eye.
    c. determine the color of the eye.
    d. transduce sensory information into electrochemical signals.
    Ans.: a   LG: 2   Page: 188   QT: F

51. If you increase the amount of light in the room,
    a. the sclera will increase in size.
    b. the iris will change from dark brown to blue.
    c. the pupil will decrease in size.
    d. the fovea will increase in size.
    Ans.: c   LG: 2   Page: 188   QT: C

52. Which of the following structures helps focus the image on the back of the eye?
    a. optic nerve
    b. pupil
    c. sclera
    d. cornea
    Ans.: d   LG: 2   Page: 189   QT: F

53. The light sensitive surface that converts light into neural impulses is called the
    a. optic nerve.
    b. pupil.
    c. retina.
    d. lens.
    Ans.: c   LG: 2   Page: 189   QT: F

54. Receptors which are used for color vision and are focused in the fovea are known as the
    a. rods.
    b. cones.
    c. pupils.
    d. iris.
    Ans.: b   LG: 2   Page: 190   QT: F

55. Receptors which are highly sensitive to light, but not color, are known as the
    a. rods,
    b. cones,
    c. pupils,
    d. iris,
    Ans.: a   LG: 2   Page: 190   QT: F

56. Fovea refers to
    a. receptors which are highly sensitive to light but not color.
    b. the area at the center of the retina at which vision is best.
    c. the bringing together and integration of what is processed through different pathways.
    d. focusing on a specific aspect of an experience.
    Ans.: b   LG: 2   Page: 190   QT: C

57. Which of the following is the direction that visual information travels?
    a. rods and cones—optic nerve—ganglion cells—bipolar cells
    b. rods and cone—visual cortex—ganglion cells—optic nerve
    c. rods and cones—bipolar cells—ganglion cells—optic nerve
    d. rods and cones—optic nerve—visual cortex—ganglion cells
    Ans.: c   LG: 2   Page:190   QT: C

58. The place in the retina which does not contain rods or cones is known as the
    a. fovea.
    b. blind spot.
    c. optic chiasm.
    d. detection threshold.
    Ans.: b   LG: 2   Page: 191   QT: F

59. Visual information from the right halves of both retinas
    a. is transmitted to the right side of the occipital lobe.
    b. is transmitted to both sides of the occipital lobe.
    c. is transmitted to the left side of the occipital lobe.
    d. is transmitted to the right side of the temporal lobe.
    Ans.: c   LG: 2   Page: 191   QT: C

60. At the optic chiasm,
    a. light is transduced into action potentials.
    b. cones are highly concentrated for the best vision.
    c. rods are highly concentrated for increased light sensitivity.
    d. the optic nerve fibers divide and cross over the midline of the brain.
    Ans.: d   LG: 2   Page: 191   QT: F

61. Feature detectors are neurons in the brain's visual system that
    a. distribute information across different neural pathways.
    b. bring together and integrate information processed through different pathways.
    c. respond to particular lines or other properties of a stimulus.
    d. transduce physical energy into electrochemical impulses.
    Ans.: c   LG: 2   Page: 192   QT: F

62. Parallel processing refers to
    a. distribution of information across different neural pathways.
    b. bringing together and integrating information processed through different pathways.
    c. responding to particular lines or other properties of a stimulus.
    d. transducing physical energy into electrochemical impulses.
    Ans.: a   LG: 2   Page: 192   QT: F

63. Which of the following properties is processed by the *what* visual pathway?
    a. location
    b. color
    c. movement
    d. depth
    Ans.: b   LG: 2   Page: 193   QT: C

64. Which of the following properties is processed by the *where* visual pathway?
    a. color
    b. form
    c. texture
    d. location
    Ans.: d   LG: 2   Page: 193   QT: C

65. Binding refers to
    a. distribution of information across different neural pathways.
    b. bringing together and integrating information processed through different pathways.
    c. responding to particular lines or other properties of a stimulus.
    d. transducing physical energy into electrochemical impulses.
    Ans.: b   LG: 2   Page: 193   QT: F

66. According to the trichromatic theory, color perception is produced by
    a. three types of visual cortical pathways.
    b. three types of bipolar cells.
    c. three types of retinal ganglion cells.
    d. three types of receptor cells.
    Ans.: d   LG: 2   Page: 194   QT: C

67. The theory that color perception is produced by three types of receptors is known as the
    a. feature detection theory.
    b. signal processing theory.
    c. trichromatic theory.
    d. opponent process theory.
    Ans.: c   LG: 2   Page: 194   QT: F

68. When people are asked to match any color by combining three wavelengths, they can do it. This result is support for which theory of color vision?
    a. feature detection theory
    b. signal processing theory
    c. trichromatic theory
    d. opponent-process theory
    Ans.: c   LG: 2   Page: 194   QT: C

69. A person who is missing the green cone system
    a. has trouble seeing any color.
    b. has trouble seeing in low levels of light.
    c. has trouble distinguishing red versus blue.
    d. has trouble distinguishing green versus blue and red.
    Ans.: d   LG: 2   Page: 195   QT: C

70. Afterimages refer to
    a. neurons in the brain's visual system that respond to particular features of a stimulus.
    b. sensations that remain after a stimulus is removed.
    c. irrelevant and competing stimuli.
    d. changes in the responsiveness of the visual system based on the average level of light.
    Ans.: b   LG: 2   Page: 195   QT: F

71. Which of the following theories of color vision is best able to explain the phenomenon of afterimages?
    a. feature detection theory
    b. signal processing theory
    c. trichromatic theory
    d. opponent-process theory
    Ans.: d   LG: 2   Page: 195   QT: C

72. According to the opponent-process theory of color vision, cells that are excited by red would be
    a. excited by blue.
    b. inhibited by green.
    c. inhibited by yellow.
    d. excited by green.
    Ans.: b   LG: 2   Page: 195   QT: C

73. If you stare at a red light, then look away, you are most likely to see
    a. a red afterimage.
    b. a blue afterimage.
    c. a green afterimage.
    d. a yellow afterimage.
    Ans.: c   LG: 2   Page: 195   QT: A

74. The principle by which we organize visual stimuli into those that stand out and those that are left over is known as
    a. similarity.
    b. closure.
    c. figure-ground relationship.
    d. continuity.
    Ans.: c   LG: 2   Page: 197   QT: F

75. The principle that states that when people see a disconnected figure, they fill in the spaces and see it as a complete figure is known as
    a. similarity.
    b. closure.
    c. figure-ground relationship.
    d. proximity.
    Ans.: b   LG: 2   Page: 197   QT: F

76. The principle that when a person sees objects close to each other they tend to group them together is known as
    a. similarity.
    b. closure.
    c. figure-ground relationship.
    d. proximity.
    Ans.: d   LG: 2   Page: 198   QT: F

77. The principle that the more similar objects are, the more likely we are to group them together is known as
    a. similarity.
    b. closure.
    c. figure-ground relationship.
    d. proximity.
    Ans.: a   LG: 2   Page: 198   QT: F

78. Which of the following is an example of a binocular depth cue?
    a. overlap
    b. familiar size
    c. disparity
    d. texture gradient
    Ans.: c   LG: 2   Page: 198   QT: C

79. Which of the following is *not* an example of a monocular depth cue?
    a. linear perspective
    b. height in the field of view
    c. familiar size
    d. disparity
    Ans.: d   LG: 2   Page: 198   QT: C

80. The monocular depth cue that involves changes in perception due to the position of the light and the position of the viewer is known as
    a. overlap.
    b. shading.
    c. disparity.
    d. texture gradient.
    Ans.: b   LG: 2   Page: 200   QT: C

81. The recognition that objects are constant and unchanging even though the sensory input about them is changing is known as
    a. subliminal perception.
    b. perceptual constancy.
    c. feature detection.
    d. parallel processing.
    Ans.: b   LG: 2   Page: 201   QT: F

82. Which of the following is *not* a type of perceptual constancy?
    a. size constancy
    b. shape constancy
    c. brightness constancy
    d. motion constancy
    Ans.: d   LG: 2   Page: 201   QT: C

83. A discrepancy between reality and the perceptional representation of it is known as a
    a. visual hallucination
    b. subliminal perception
    c. visual illusion
    d. false alarm
    Ans.: c   LG: 2   Page: 202   QT: F

Learning Goal 3: Understand how the auditory system registers sound and how it connects with the brain to perceive it.

84. The perceptual interpretation of the frequency of sound is known as
    a. pitch.
    b. timbre.
    c. amplitude.
    d. loudness.
    Ans.: a   LG: 3   Page: 205   QT: F

85. Pitch describes the perceptual interpretation of
    a. frequency.
    b. amplitude.
    c. decibels.
    d. timbre.
    Ans.: a   LG: 3   Page: 205   QT: F

86. The perception of the amplitude of a sound wave is known as
    a. pitch.
    b. timbre.
    c. frequency.
    d. loudness.
    Ans.: d   LG: 3   Page: 206   QT: F

87. The tonal saturation of a sound is known as its
    a. pitch.
    b. timbre.
    c. frequency.
    d. loudness.
    Ans.: b   LG: 3   Page: 206   QT: F

88. The function of the pinnae of the outer ear is to
    a. transduce sound waves into electrochemical impulses.
    b. collect sounds and channel them into the interior of the ear.
    c. send neural impulses on to the brain.
    d. transmit sound waves to the fluid-filled inner ear.
    Ans.: b   LG: 3   Page: 206   QT: F

89. Which of the following is *not* part of the middle ear?
    a. pinna
    b. eardrum
    c. hammer
    d. anvil
    Ans.: a   LG: 3   Page: 207   QT: C

90. The function of the middle ear is to
    a. transduce sound waves into electrochemical impulses.
    b. collect sounds and channel them into the interior of the ear.
    c. send neural impulses on to the brain.
    d. transmit sound waves to the fluid-filled inner ear.
    Ans.: d   LG: 3   Page: 207   QT: F

91. The function of the inner ear is to
    a. transduce sound waves into electrochemical impulses.
    b. collect sounds and channel them into the interior of the ear.
    c. send neural impulses on to the brain.
    d. transmit sound waves to the fluid-filled inner ear.
    Ans.: a   LG: 3   Page: 207   QT: F

92. Which of the following is *not* a structure of the inner ear?
    a. cochlea
    b. basilar membrane
    c. oval window
    d. eardrum
    Ans.: d   LG: 3   Page: 207   QT: F

93. Which of the following is a structure of the inner ear?
    a. eardrum
    b. pinna
    c. anvil
    d. cochlea
    Ans.: d   LG: 3   Page: 207   QT: F

94. The sensory receptors of the ear are known as
    a. hair cells.
    b. rods.
    c. cones.
    d. thermoreceptors.
    Ans.: a   LG: 3   Page: 207   QT: F

95. Hair cells are sensory receptors in the
    a. eye.
    b. mouth.
    c. ear.
    d. skin.
    Ans.: c   LG: 3   Page: 207   QT: F

96. Neural impulses in the ear are generated by movement of the
    a. hair cells against the basilar membrane.
    b. eardrum against the oval window.
    c. anvil against the eardrum.
    d. hair cells against the tectorial membrane.
    Ans.: d   LG: 3   Page: 207   QT: F

97. The fluid-filled, spiral structure of the inner ear is called the
    a. hair cell.
    b. eardrum.
    c. cochlea.
    d. oval window,
    Ans.: c   LG: 3   Page: 207   QT: F

98. According to the place theory of hearing, perception of a sound's frequency is related to
    a. vibrations produced at a particular spot on the basilar membrane.
    b. vibrations produced at a particular spot on the eardrum.
    c. the frequency of firing in the auditory nerve.
    d. clusters of neurons firing neural impulses in rapid succession.
    Ans.: a   LG: 3   Page: 208   QT: C

99. The theory of hearing which states that perception of a sound's frequency is related to vibrations produced at a particular spot on the basilar membrane is known as the
    a. volley theory.
    b. frequency theory.
    c. signal detection theory.
    d. place theory.
    Ans.: d   LG: 3   Page: 207   QT: F

100. According to the frequency theory of hearing, perception of a sound's frequency is related to
    a. vibrations produced at a particular spot on the basilar membrane.
    b. vibrations produced at a particular spot on the eardrum.
    c. the frequency of firing in the auditory nerve.
    d. clusters of neurons firing neural impulses in rapid succession.
    Ans.: c   LG: 3   Page: 208   QT: C

101. The theory of hearing which states that perception of a sound's frequency is related the frequency of firing in the auditory nerve is known as the
    a. volley theory.
    b. frequency theory.
    c. signal detection theory.
    d. place theory.
    Ans.: b   LG: 3   Page: 208   QT: F

102. The volley principle of hearing says that perception of a sound is related to
    a. vibrations produced at a particular spot on the basilar membrane.
    b. vibrations produced at a particular spot on the eardrum.
    c. the frequency of firing in the auditory nerve.
    d. clusters of neurons firing neural impulses in rapid succession.
    Ans.: d   LG: 3   Page: 209   QT: C

103. The theory of hearing which states that perception of a sound's frequency is related to clusters of neurons firing neural impulses in rapid succession is known as the
    a. volley theory.
    b. frequency theory.
    c. signal detection theory.
    d. place theory.
    Ans.: a   LG: 3   Page: 209   QT: F

104. The nerve that carries neural impulses to the brain's hearing areas is the
    a. optic nerve.
    b. basilar nerve.
    c. tectorial nerve.
    d. auditory nerve.
    Ans.: d   LG: 3   Page: 209   QT: F

105. Compared to processing of visual information, processing of auditory information
    a. is less complex.
    b. is more strictly lateralized.
    c. encounters more synapses before reaching the cortex.
    d. does not use parallel processing.
    Ans.: c   LG: 3   Page: 209   QT: C

106. The sound shadow influences our ability to
    a. detect the frequency of low-frequency noises.
    b. detect the location of a sound.
    c. eliminate noise pollution.
    d. determine the brightness of a white light.
    Ans.: b   LG: 3   Page: 209   QT: C

107. Which of the following sounds would be the easiest to localize?
    a. one directly in front of you
    b. one directly above your head
    c. one directly behind you
    d. one directly to your left
    Ans.: d   Learning Goal: 3   Page: 209/210   QT: C

108. Differences in the time that a sound arrives at each ear influence our ability to
    a. detect the frequency of low-frequency noises.
    b. detect the location of a sound.
    c. eliminate noise pollution.
    d. detect the frequency of high-frequency sounds.
    Ans.: b   LG: 3   Page: 209   QT: C

109. Which of the following contributes to differences in intensity of sounds reaching the two ears?
    a. One sound has traveled a shorter distance.
    b. One sound has a higher frequency.
    c. One sound is affected by the volley principle.
    d. One sound is affected by signal detection.
    Ans.: a   LG: 3   Page: 209   QT: C

110. Research on the effects of noise have demonstrated all of the following *except* that
    a. children's exposure to higher levels of noise is associated with poorer performance on reading tests.
    b. prolonged exposure to noises 80 decibels or greater can produce permanent hearing loss.
    c. children living in a high-noise airport corridor had higher blood pressure than children living in a low-noise neighborhood.
    d. children living in a low-noise neighborhood were more easily distracted than children living in a high-noise neighborhood.
    Ans.: d   LG: 3   Page: 210   QT: C

111. Exposure to loud music can lead to all of the following *except*
    a. damage to hair cells in the inner ear.
    b. buzzing in the ears.
    c. damage to bipolar cells.
    d. difficulty understanding speech.
    Ans.: c   LG: 3   Page: 212   QT: C

112. Which of the following is *not* a symptom of hearing loss following exposure to loud noise?
    a. buzzing in the ears
    b. muffling of sounds
    c. auditory hallucinations
    d. problems hearing conversations in groups of people
    Ans.: c   LG: 3   Page: 212   QT: C

Learning Goal 4: Know how the skin, chemical, and kinesthetic and vestibular senses work.

113. Which of the following is the most correct order for processing of touch information?
    a. sensory receptor—spinal cord—thalamus—parietal cortex
    b. spinal cord—parietal cortex—sensory receptor—thalamus
    c. parietal cortex—thalamus—sensory receptor—spinal cord
    d. thalamus—sensory receptor—spinal cord—parietal cortex
    Ans.: a   LG: 4   Page: 213   QT: C

114. The part of the cortex most involved in processing touch information is the
    a. occipital.
    b. visual.
    c. parietal.
    d. temporal.
    Ans.: c   LG: 4   Page: 213   QT: C

115. Which of the following areas has the biggest touch area in the brain?
    a. hands
    b. legs
    c. torso
    d. buttocks
    Ans.: a   LG: 4   Page: 213   QT: C

116. Which of the following is *not* an aspect of touch that we perceive?
    a. movement across the skin
    b. pressure
    c. temperature
    d. brightness
    Ans.: d   LG: 4   Page: 213   QT: C

117. When people had their fingertips covered, they were
    a. more able to detect whether there were two objects or one.
    b. more able to sense thin hairs, but not thick hairs.
    c. less able to sense thick hairs, but not thin hairs.
    d. less able to detect whether there were two objects or one.
    Ans.: d   LG: 4   Page: 213   QT: C

118. Which of the following sensory systems would be most sensitive in an infant?
    a. a boy's visual system
    b. a girl's touch system
    c. a girl's hearing system
    d. a boy's taste system
    Ans.: b   LG: 4   Page: 213   QT: C

119. Which of the following systems is most sensitive in newborn infants?
    a. vision
    b. taste
    c. touch
    d. hearing
    Ans.: c   LG: 4   Page: 213   QT: C

120. Thermoreceptors
    a. respond to vibrations on the skin.
    b. respond to changes in the length of hair cells.
    c. respond to increases and decreases in temperature.
    d. respond to changes in wavelength.
    Ans.: c   LG: 4   Page: 214   QT: F

121. Sensory cells that respond to increases and decreases in temperature are known as
    a. thermoreceptors.
    b. rods.
    c. motion detectors.
    d. signal detectors.
    Ans.: a   LG: 4   Page: 214   QT: F

122. When warm and cold receptors located close to each other on the skin are stimulated simultaneously,
    a. we experience the sensation of cold.
    b. we experience the sensation of hot.
    c. we do not perceive anything.
    d. we experience the sensation of movement.
    Ans.: b   LG: 4   Page: 214   QT: C

123. The sensation that warns us that damage to our bodies is occurring is
    a. vision.
    b. thermoreception.
    c. pain.
    d. taste.
    Ans.: c   LG: 4   Page: 214   QT: F

124. Which of the following receptors has the highest threshold for responding?
    a. temperature
    b. pain
    c. touch
    d. They're all equal.
    Ans.: b   LG: 4   Page: 214   QT: C

125. Prostaglandins are
    a. neurons in the visual pathway.
    b. attached to the tectorial membrane.
    c. rounded bumps on the tongue that contain taste buds.
    d. chemicals that stimulate pain receptors.
    Ans.: d   LG: 4   Page: 214   QT: F

126. Information about sharp, localized pain is transmitted
    a. by the slow pain pathway.
    b. by the fast pain pathway.
    c. by the hard pain pathway.
    d. by the soft pain pathway.
    Ans.: b   LG: 4   Page: 214   QT: C

127. Information about nagging pain is transmitted
    a. by the slow pain pathway.
    b. by the fast pain pathway.
    c. by the hard pain pathway.
    d. by the soft pain pathway.
    Ans.: a   LG: 4   Page: 214   QT: C

128. Information about sharp, localized pain travels
    a. directly to the motor and sensory areas of the cortex, then to the thalamus.
    b. directly to the thalamus, then the motor and sensory areas of cortex.
    c. through the thalamus, then to the motor areas of the cerebellum.
    d. through the limbic system, then to the motor and sensory areas of the cortex.
    Ans.: b   LG: 4   Page: 214   QT: C

129. The theory that the spinal column can either allow or block the perception of pain is known as the
    a. signal detection theory.
    b. gate control theory.
    c. subliminal perception theory.
    d. volley theory.
    Ans.: b   LG: 4   Page: 215   QT: F

130. Which of the following has been most implicated in control of pain?
    a. endorphins
    b. acetylcholine
    c. norepinephrine
    d. serotonin
    Ans.: a   LG: 4   Page: 215   QT: C

131. The effects of acupuncture on pain contributed to the development of which theory of pain control?
    a. gate control
    b. signal control
    c. brain control
    d. prostaglandin control
    Ans.: a   LG: 4   Page: 215   QT: C

132. Which of the following is *not* an effective method for reducing acute pain?
    a. distraction
    b. focused breathing
    c. counterstimulation
    d. focusing on the pain
    Ans.: d   LG: 4   Page: 216   QT: C

133. Papillae are
    a. neurons in the visual pathway.
    b. attached to the tectorial membrane.
    c. rounded bumps on the tongue that contain taste buds.
    d. chemicals that stimulate pain receptors.
    Ans.: c   LG: 4   Page: 217   QT: F

134. Rounded bumps on the tongue that contain taste buds are known as
    a. prostaglandins.
    b. cones.
    c. epithelium.
    d. papillae.
    Ans.: d   LG: 4   Page: 217   QT: F

135. The part of your mouth that responds most strongly to bitter tastes is
    a. the side of the tongue.
    b. the back of the tongue.
    c. the tip of the tongue.
    d. All parts of the tongue are equally sensitive.
    Ans.: b   LG: 4   Page: 217   QT: C

136. The side of your tongue has been very strongly activated by a taste, while the rest of your tongue has been only slightly stimulated. The taste is most likely
    a. sweet.
    b. sour.
    c. bitter.
    d. salty.
    Ans.: b   LG: 4   Page: 217   QT: C

137. The receptors for smell are located in
    a. the olfactory bulb.
    b. the olfactory cortex.
    c. the olfactory nerve.
    d. the olfactory epithelium.
    Ans.: d   LG: 4   Page: 218   QT: F

138. Which of the following types of receptor cells is most likely to replace itself after injury?
    a. hair cells in the ear
    b. rods
    c. cells in the olfactory epithelium
    d. cones
    Ans.: c   LG: 4   Page: 218   QT: C

139. Which of the following is the most accurate pathway for detecting smell?
    a. receptor—thalamus—sensory cortex
    b. receptor—sensory cortex—limbic system
    c. receptor—limbic system—thalamus—sensory cortex
    d. thalamus—cortex—limbic system—receptor
    Ans.: b   LG: 4   Page: 218   QT: C

140. Kinesthesic refers to our sense of
    a. pain.
    b. posture and orientation.
    c. temperature.
    d. touch.
    Ans.: b   LG: 4   Page: 219   QT: F

141. Our ability to detect information about balance and movement is related to our
    a. vestibular sense.
    b. sixth sense.
    c. subliminal perception.
    d. gate control sense.
    Ans.: a   LG: 4   Page: 219   QT: F

142. The sensory receptors for our kinesthetic senses
    a. are contained in the skin.
    b. are contained in the ears.
    c. are contained in muscles and joints.
    d. are contained in the brain.
    Ans.: c   LG: 4   Page: 219   QT: C

143. Proprioceptive feedback refers to information about
    a. the position of our body parts in relation to other body parts.
    b. the number of pain receptors that have been stimulated.
    c. the amount of damage to our olfactory receptors.
    d. the quantity of noise pollution in the environment.
    Ans.: a   LG: 4   Page: 219   QT: F

144. The sensory receptors for the motion of our head are contained in
    a. the semicircular canals.
    b. the olfactory epithelium.
    c. the perceptual set.
    d. papillae.
    Ans.: a   LG: 4   Page: 219   QT: F

145. The semicircular canals are involved in perception of
    a. taste.
    b. hearing.
    c. motion and tilt of our heads.
    d. movements of our fingers.
    Ans.: c   LG: 4   Page: 219   QT: C

146. Which of the following is the most correct pathway for transmitting vestibular information?
    a. auditory nerve—medulla—temporal cortex
    b. olfactory nerve—cerebellum—parietal cortex
    c. cochlear nerve—medulla—temporal cortex
    d. vestibular nerve—thalamus—occipital cortex
    Ans.: a   LG: 4   Page: 219   QT: C

147. The dizziness that accompanies motion sickness is most likely related to stimulation of
    a. cerebral cortex.
    b. cerebellum.
    c. cochlear nerve.
    d. medulla.
    Ans.: a   LG: 4   Page: 220   QT: C

Learning Goal 5: Describe what human factors psychologists do.

148. Which of the following would *not* be performed by a human factors psychologist?
    a. designing equipment to improve productivity
    b. arranging environments to make them safer
    c. producing more user-friendly software
    d. providing group therapy for depressed individuals
    Ans.: d   LG: 5   Page: 220   QT: C

149. A human factors psychologist would be least likely to be involved in
    a. reducing the impact of visual illusions.
    b. designing visual displays in a car.
    c. testing the effects of word order on memory.
    d. assessing the effects of fatigue on commercial pilots.
    Ans.: c   LG: 5   Page: 220   QT: C

150. The branch of psychology that deals with designing equipment and arranging environments to make them safer and more efficient is known as
    a. human factors.
    b. cognitive.
    c. social.
    d. educational.
    Ans.: a   LG: 5   Page: 220   QT: F

True/False Items

____ 151. The process of organizing and interpreting sensory information to give it meaning is known as transduction.

____ 152. All animals share the same sensory and perceptual systems.

____ 153. Perceptions of subliminal messages in rock songs are influenced by whether subjects are expecting to hear messages or not.

____ 154. Changes in the wavelength of light will be most likely perceived as changes in the brightness of the light.

____ 155. Rods are more sensitive to light than cones and cannot process color information.

____ 156. Motion, depth, and color are processed by the same pathway in the visual system.

____ 157. Both the trichromatic and opponent-process theories of color vision are correct.

____ 158. Overlap and shading are two common binocular depth cues.

____ 159. The function of the inner ear is to amplify sound waves before they reach the fluid-filled middle ear.

____ 160. The frequency theory of hearing describes our ability to hear high-frequency sounds better than the place theory.

____ 161. The same kind of physical energy can be perceived as sound and touch.

____ 162. Perception of pain is affected by cultural and ethnic contexts.

____ 163. Some parts of the tongue can only respond to one type of taste.

____ 164. The kinesthetic senses tell us about movement, posture and orientation.

____ 165. Human factors psychologists study the influence of childhood memories on dreams.

Answer Key for True/False Items

151.	Ans.: F	LG: 1	Page: 177	159.	Ans.: F	LG: 3	Page: 207
152.	Ans.: F	LG: 1	Page: 178	160.	Ans.: F	LG: 3	Page: 209
153.	Ans.: T	LG: 1	Page: 182	161.	Ans.: T	LG: 4	Page: 213
154.	Ans.: F	LG: 2	Page: 187	162.	Ans.: T	LG: 4	Page: 215
155.	Ans.: T	LG: 2	Page: 190	163.	Ans.: F	LG: 4	Page: 217
156.	Ans.: F	LG: 2	Page: 193	164.	Ans.: T	LG: 4	Page: 219
157.	Ans.: T	LG: 2	Page: 196	165.	Ans.: F	LG: 5	Page: 220
158.	Ans.: F	LG: 2	Page: 200				

Fill-in-the-Blank Items

166. The process of transforming physical energy into electrochemical energy is called _____.
167. Perceptual processing that begins with sensory receptors registering environmental information and moving to integration and cognitive processing in the brain is known as _____ processing.
168. The field that studies links between the physical properties of stimuli and a person's experience of them is known as _____.
169. The minimum amount of energy that a person can detect is known as _____.
170. The smallest difference in stimulation required to discriminate one stimulus from another 50 percent of the time is known as _____.
171. The part of the eye that contains muscles that control the amount of light that gets in is called the _____.
172. Neurons in the brain's visual system which respond to particular lines or other properties of a stimulus are known as _____.
173. The idea that color perception is based on the existence of three types of receptors is known as the _____.
174. Different parts of the _____ vibrate more intensely when exposed to different sound frequencies.
175. The theory that clusters of neurons fire in rapid succession to produce perception of a sound's frequency is known as the _____.
176. The two cues that help us localize sound are _____ and _____.
177. Drugs like aspirin reduce feelings of pain by reducing the body's production of _____.
178. Receptors for smell are located in the _____ and are covered with millions of _____.
179. The fluid-filled circular tubes that contain sensory receptors for detecting head motion are called _____.
180. Researchers who study the effects of pilot fatigue on flying performance are most likely _____ psychologists.

Answer Key for Fill-in-the-Blank Items

166.	Ans.: transduction	LG: 1	Page: 177
167.	Ans.: bottom-up	LG: 1	Page: 177
168.	Ans.: psychophysics	LG: 1	Page: 180
169.	Ans.: absolute threshold	LG: 1	Page: 180
170.	Ans.: difference threshold (or just noticeable difference)	LG: 1	Page: 182
171.	Ans.: sclera	LG: 2	Page: 188
172.	Ans.: feature detectors	LG: 2	Page: 192
173.	Ans.: trichromatic theory	LG: 2	Page: 194
174.	Ans.: basilar membrane	LG: 3	Page: 207
175.	Ans.: volley principle	LG: 3	Page: 209
176.	Ans.: timing; intensity	LG: 3	Page: 209
177.	Ans.: prostaglandins	LG: 4	Page: 214
178.	Ans.: olfactory epithelium; hairlike antennae	LG: 4	Page: 218
179.	Ans.: semicircular canals	LG: 4	Page: 219
180.	Ans.: human factors	LG: 5	Page: 221

Matching Items

___	181. photoreception	A.	green afterimage
___	182. mechanoreception	B.	pressure
___	183. pain	C.	eardrum
___	184. hearing	D.	temporal lobe
___	185. red	E.	papillae
___	186. blue afterimage	F.	semicircular canal
___	187. middle ear	G.	light
___	188. inner ear	H.	yellow
___	189. taste	I.	parietal lobe
___	190. kinesthesia	J.	cochlea

Answer Key for Matching Items

181.	Ans.: G	LG: 1	Page: 179		186.	Ans.: H	LG: 2	Page: 195
182.	Ans.: B	LG: 1	Page: 179		187.	Ans.: C	LG: 3	Page: 207
183.	Ans.: I	LG: 1	Page: 180		188.	Ans.: J	LG: 3	Page: 207
184.	Ans.: D	LG: 1	Page: 180		189.	Ans.: E	LG: 4	Page: 217
185.	Ans.: A	LG: 2	Page: 195		190.	Ans.: F	LG: 4	Page: 219

Essay Questions

191. Describe four possible outcomes of decision making about sensory stimuli according to signal detection theory and define the two main components of the decision-making process. (LG: 1)

> Answer Guidelines: Hit—signal is present and identified; miss—signal is present but not identified; false alarm—no signal is present, but one is identified; correct rejection—no signal is present, and none is identified.
> Components are: Information acquisition—what information is in the sensory signal; criterion—basis for making the judgment.

192. Describe the Stroop effect, and discuss how it is related to general characteristics of perception. (LG: 1)

> Answer Guidelines: In the Stroop effect, we are presented with the names of colors printed in different color inks. The task is to name the color of the ink, not the word which is printed. When the color of the ink and the printed word are not the same, our performance is impaired. This illustrates (1) automatic perception, (2) a failure of selective attention, and (3) bottom-up processing which is driven by the stimulus.

193. Describe the role of the cornea and lens in processing visual information and discuss the effects of aging on the lens. (LG: 2)

Answer Guidelines: The cornea and lens focus light on the back of the eye; the curved surface of the cornea bends the light and the lens fine-tunes the final image. The lens changes its curvature to adjust for the distance of objects; closer objects are focused with increased bending of the lens; as we age, the lens loses flexibility so we are less able to increase this bending and are more likely to require glasses to assist us in bending the light sufficiently.

194. You see a faint star in the sky off to the left side of your body. Describe the pathway that the light information would travel after it hits the retina on its way to the visual cortex. (LG: 2)

Answer Guidelines: Light would fall on the right half of the retina in both eyes, stimulating the rods; it would travel to bipolar cells and ganglion cells to the optic nerve; at the optic chiasm, fibers from the right eye would not cross the midline, but fibers from the left eye would; information from both eyes would thus eventually reach the right occipital lobe.

195. Describe the relationship between color blindness and the trichromatic theory of color vision. (LG: 2)

Answer Guidelines: The trichromatic theory states that color perception depends on input from three types of receptors; color blindness results from dysfunction in one of the three types of cones (red, green, and blue). Most common color blindness involves green cones, which makes green look like some combinations of blue and red; color matching experiments demonstrate that people with this kind of color blindness only require two wavelengths of light to match all other colors, while people with normal vision require three wavelengths of light.

196. Describe the structures of the middle ear, and explain their role in sound perception. (LG: 3)

Answer Guidelines: The middle ear consists of the eardrum, hammer, anvil, and stirrup. The eardrum is a membrane that vibrates in response to sound. The hammer, anvil, and stirrup are three bones connected in a chain which vibrate to transmit sound from the eardrum to the inner ear; because the sound must travel from air at the eardrum to fluid at the inner ear, the bones amplify the sound waves.

197. Describe one theory of how we perceive a sound's frequency, including a description of the weakness of that theory. (LG: 3)

Answer Guidelines: Place theory states that detection of frequency depends on maximum displacement of particular parts of the basilar membrane; high-frequency sounds maximally displace the basilar membrane near the oval window; low frequency sounds maximally displace the basilar membrane near the tip of the cochlea; place theory describes perception of high-frequency sounds better than low frequency sounds because high-frequency sounds have small areas of displacement, while low-frequency sounds have broad areas of displacement.

Frequency theory states that firing in the auditory nerve is related to the sound's frequency; higher frequency sounds cause higher frequency firing in the auditory nerve; limitation is that neurons can't fire more rapidly than 1,000 times a second, so higher frequencies can't be encoded by a single neuron.

198. Describe five methods that may be effective for treating pain. (LG: 4)

Answer Guidelines: (1) analgesic medications – aspirin; (2) distraction – think about something pleasant; (3) focused breathing – Lamaze breathing during childbirth; (4) counterstimulation – applying ice, or biting the inside of the cheek; (5) surgery – to repair the injury; (6) acupuncture – needle insertion to produce local anesthesia; (7) electrical stimulation; (8) massage; (9) exercise; (10) relaxation; (11) hypnosis.

199. You're riding on a very scary roller coaster, and you're starting to feel sick. Describe the pathways by which your sensory systems contribute to your detection of movement and motion sickness. (LG: 4)

Answer Guidelines: You would receive proprioceptive feedback from muscles and joints about where your body is. The semicircular canals in your inner ear would be stimulated by the movement and tilt of your head. The fluid inside each of the three canals would move, causing displacement of hair cells that are embedded in a gelatinous substance, and action potentials would be triggered in the auditory nerve. Signals would travel in the vestibular division of the auditory nerve to the medulla or the cerebellum. Then they would be transmitted to the temporal cortex. Cortical pathways would contribute to the dizziness, while the brainstem pathways contribute to motion sickness. Information from vision would also contribute to the perception of movement through the where pathway (rods and cones in retina; bipolar cells; ganglion cells; visual cortex).

200. Define human factors psychology and describe one example of what human factors psychologists do. (LG: 5)

Answer Guidelines: Human factors psychologists study equipment and environments to make them more easily used and safer. They might make dials and controls easier to read, easier to manipulate, less distracting; they might make displays visual, auditory or tactile; they might move controls to different place to make them easier to use; they might change the shapes of controls to make them usable without looking down; they might examine the effects of visual illusions; they might study the effects of fatigue, anxiety, and communication on performance.

Chapter 6: States of Consciousness

Learning Goals

1. Discuss the nature of consciousness.
2. Explain the nature of sleep and dreams.
3. Describe hypnosis.
4. Evaluate the uses and types of psychoactive drugs.

Multiple-Choice Items

Learning Goal 1: Discuss the nature of consciousness.

1. Awareness of external events and internal sensations, including awareness of the self and thoughts about one's experiences would be called
   a. behavior.
   b. memory.
   c. personality.
   d. consciousness.
   Ans.: d   LG: 1   Page: 228   QT: F

2. Which of the following would play the least important role in consciousness?
   a. internal and external sensations
   b. awareness of the self
   c. behavior
   d. thoughts about one's experiences
   Ans.: c   LG: 1   Page: 228   QT: C

3. Which of the following is *not* true about the study of consciousness?
   a. William James took great interest in the study of the conscious and unconscious mind.
   b. Conscious, by nature, is difficult to study scientifically.
   c. Skinner and Watson advanced the study of consciousness in the middle part of the twentieth century.
   d. Sigmund Freud was very interested in the conscious and unconscious mind.
   Ans.: c   LG: 1   Page: 228   QT: C

4. William James' concept that the mind is a continuous flow of sensations, images, thoughts, and feelings was called
   a. the collective unconscious.
   b. the unconscious.
   c. the stream of consciousness.
   d. consciousness in flux.
   Ans.: c   LG: 1   Page: 228   QT: F

5. Linda's mind seems to race from point to point, never staying in one place for long. She is checking cash receipts, while at the same time remembers that she has not shopped at a particular store in a while. She no sooner considers the store than she begins thinking about what she will be getting to eat. James would refer to this process as the
   a. collective unconscious.
   b. selective attention.
   c. consciousness in flux.
   d. the stream of consciousness.
   Ans.: d   LG: 1   Page: 228   QT: A

6. Individuals actively focus their efforts toward a goal while they are demonstrating
   a. higher level consciousness.
   b. controlled processes.
   c. automatic processes.
   d. both a and b
   Ans.: d   LG: 1   Page: 229   QT: C

7. Controlled processes are a part of
   a. higher level consciousness.
   b. lower level consciousness.
   c. daydreaming.
   d. subconscious awareness.
   Ans.: a   LG: 1   Page: 229   QT: F

8. Selective attention is most apparent in
   a. controlled processes.
   b. automatic processes.
   c. lower level awareness.
   d. subconscious awareness.
   Ans.: a   LG: 1   Page: 229   QT: F

9. Darlene is obviously daydreaming during her sociology class. Which of the levels of awareness would you use to describe her thought process?
   a. higher level awareness
   b. controlled processes
   c. lower level awareness
   d. no awareness
   Ans.: c   LG: 1   Page: 230   QT: A

10. Ketal is holding a conversation with his mother while he effortlessly plays a quick section of a song on the piano. For Ketal, playing this sequence of notes is a(n)
    a. controlled process.
    b. example of higher level awareness.
    c. automatic process.
    d. subconscious awareness.
    Ans.: c   LG: 1   Page: 230   QT: A

11. Which of the following is *not* true about daydreaming?
    a. Daydreaming takes place in lower level awareness.
    b. Daydreaming often involves making plans.
    c. Daydreaming is not like mind wandering.
    d. During daydreaming, we often solve problems.
    Ans.: c   LG: 1   Page: 230   QT: C

12. Your sociology professor becomes upset as you sit in the class daydreaming and accuses you of wasting a semester in another world. Which of the following would be a response that has research support?
    a. Daydreaming keeps our minds active while helping us to cope, create, and fantasize.
    b. Sociology is not an exciting class (unlike psychology, where no one daydreams).
    c. Daydreaming is actually a part of higher level consciousness.
    d. Daydreaming is a controlled process.
    Ans.: a   LG: 1   Page: 230   QT: A

13. Which of the following would not be considered a cause of an altered state of awareness?
    a. fatigue
    b. drugs
    c. trauma
    d. daydreaming
    Ans.: d   LG: 1   Page: 230   QT: C

14. When one speaks of altered levels of awareness, they are referring to
    a. lowered awareness brought on by drugs such as alcohol.
    b. heightened awareness brought on by drugs such as caffeine.
    c. mental states that are noticeably different from normal states.
    d. all of the above
    Ans.: d   LG: 1   Page: 230   QT: C

15. Sleep and dreams are best regarded as
    a. an absence of consciousness.
    b. a low level of consciousness.
    c. a level of awareness comparable to a daydream.
    d. all of the above
    Ans.: b   LG: 1   Page: 231   QT: C

16. Researchers have found that when people are asleep,
    a. they are unaware of what is happening around them.
    b. they remain aware of external stimuli to some degree.
    c. they have the same level of awareness as when they daydream.
    d. they are experiencing subconscious awareness.
    Ans.: b   LG: 1   Page: 231   QT: C

17. Which of the following is *not* true of the level of awareness known as "no awareness"?
    a. No awareness can be caused by an injury which has caused us to become unconscious.
    b. Freud's perspective of the unconscious was that most of our thoughts are unconscious.
    c. William James believed that the unconscious was a part of "no awareness" and it included many unacceptable wishes.
    d. No awareness can be brought about by anesthesia.
    Ans.: c   LG: 1   Page: 231   QT: F

18. Which of the following is *not* a perspective regarding consciousness and the brain?
    a. Using MRI's, researchers have located the source of consciousness in the brain.
    b. A number of separate distributed processing systems connect to produce consciousness.
    c. The cerebral cortex may be a key part of consciousness.
    d. Information from the senses, along with information about emotions and memories in the association areas creates consciousness.
    Ans.: a   LG: 1   Page: 232   QT: C

Learning Goal 2: Explain the nature of sleep and dreams.

19. What proportion of our lives do we spend sleeping?
    a. one tenth
    b. one fifth
    c. one third
    d. one half
    Ans.: c   LG: 2   Page: 232   QT: F

20. Periodic physiological fluctuations in the body are called
    a. physiological rhythms.
    b. biological rhythms.
    c. neurological sequences.
    d. anatomical sequences.
    Ans.: b   LG: 2   Page: 232   QT: F

21. An example of a biological rhythm would be a
    a. cycle of brain activity.
    b. change in body temperature.
    c. change of hormones in the blood stream.
    d. all of the above
    Ans.: d   LG: 2   Page: 232   QT: A

22. Which of the following would not be considered an example of a biological rhythm?
    a. hibernation of bears
    b. female menstrual cycle
    c. hunger
    d. sleep/wake cycle
    Ans.: c   LG: 2   Page: 233   QT: F

23. A. circadian rhythm is a
    a. physiological repeating event such as a heartbeat.
    b. sequence of brain events following a stimuli.
    c. monthly behavioral or physiological cycle.
    d. daily behavioral or physiological cycle.
    Ans.: d   LG: 2   Page: 233   QT: F

24. What role does the suprachiasmatic nucleus play in consciousness?
    a. The suprachiasmatic nucleus regulates subconscious level.
    b. The suprachiasmatic nucleus regulates sexual arousal.
    c. The suprachiasmatic nucleus controls the dream cycle.
    d. The suprachiasmatic nucleus works with the hypothalamus to regulate daily rhythms.
    Ans.: d   LG: 2   Page: 233   QT: F

25. Which of the following would not be regulated by the suprachiasmatic nucleus?
    a. fear
    b. temperature
    c. hunger
    d. wakefulness
    Ans.: a   LG: 2   Page: 233   QT: A

26. Which external stimuli is the suprachiasmatic nucleus sensitive to?
    a. temperature
    b. sound
    c. light
    d. smell
    Ans.: c   LG: 2   Page: 233   QT: F

27. Which of the following is *not* true about the effects of jet lag and shift work?
    a. Two or more body rhythms are out of sync.
    b. Jet lag and shift work affect individuals differently physiologically.
    c. Jet lag and shift work both disrupt circadian rhythms.
    d. Some individuals prefer shift work over a regular work schedule.
    Ans.: b   LG: 2   Page: 234   QT: C

28. Which of the following individuals would be least effected by being assigned to shift work?
    a. Bill, who is a morning person
    b. Joe, who needs at least nine hours of sleep
    c. Bernie, who is 57 years old
    d. Daryl, who is 31 years old
    Ans.: d   LG: 2   Page: 234   QT: A

29. Researchers have experimented with removing subjects from time devices so they could find out how close our biological clock was to the twenty-four-hour day that we exist in. Which of the following summarizes the research?
    a. We actually operate on a 22-hour circadian cycle.
    b. We operate on a 25-hour circadian cycle.
    c. It was believed for a long time that we operate on a 25-hour cycle, but recent research finds that we are very close to a 24-hour cycle.
    d. It was believed for a long time that we operate on a 25-hour cycle, but recent research has found that we are much closer to a 22-hour cycle.
    Ans.: c   LG: 2   Page: 234   QT: C

30. Strategies that have been successful in helping shift workers reset their biological clocks have included all but which of the following?
    a. brighter light in the workplace
    b. sleeping in complete darkness
    c. use of sedatives to realign the circadian mechanisms
    d. taking after-work late-morning naps and before-work late-afternoon naps
    Ans.: c   LG: 2   Page: 235   QT: C

31. Select the answer that best summarizes why we sleep.
    a. Sleep restores our brains and bodies.
    b. Animals needed to protect themselves in the dark hours.
    c. Sleep coincides with the release of growth hormone in children.
    d. Researchers have not yet found any one answer to explain why we sleep.
    Ans.: d   LG: 2   Page: 235   QT: C

32. Dr. Y has decided that the reason that we sleep is that many animals needed to protect themselves in the dark hours. Dr. Y's perspective is consistent with the
    a. restorative perspective of why we sleep.
    b. adaptive-evolutionary perspective of why we sleep.
    c. physiological perspective of why we sleep.
    d. psychodynamic perspective of why we sleep.
    Ans.: b   LG: 2   Page: 235   QT: A

33. In a study mentioned in the text, a subject went without sleep for 264 hours. When he finally went to sleep, approximately how long did he sleep?
    a. 35 hours
    b. 25 hours
    c. 15 hours
    d. 5 hours
    Ans.: c   LG: 2   Page: 236   QT: F

34. If you were to summarize American sleep habits, you would be *incorrect* in saying which of the following?
    a. Americans sleep too much.
    b. Americans' lack of sleep has a negative effect on their work productivity.
    c. At least 50 % of Americans are sleep deprived.
    d. Nearly 63 % of Americans surveyed get less than 8 hours of sleep a night.
    Ans.: a   LG: 2   Page: 236   QT: F

35. Which of the following was *not* mentioned in the text as a contributor to poor performance as a result of sleep deprivation?
    a. EEGs of individuals who experienced sleep deprivation for 24 hours revealed a decline in complexity of brain activity.
    b. Brain scans indicate that sleep deprivation decreases brain activity in the thalamus and prefrontal cortex.
    c. Sleep deprivation is linked with an inability to sustain attention.
    d. Sleep deprivation has been shown to cause long-term damage to the cerebral cortex.
    Ans.: d   LG: 2   Page: 237   QT: C

36. Which of the following is a contributing factor to American sleep deprivation?
    a. work pressures
    b. school pressures
    c. social obligations
    d. all of the above
    Ans.: d   LG: 2   Page: 237   QT:

37. How much more sleep does the text recommend for most Americans?
    a. 30 minutes
    b. 60–90 minutes
    c. 0 minutes
    d. 120 minutes
    Ans.: b   LG: 2   Page: 237   QT: F

38. Based on the sleep research discussed in the text, what would be a good strategy for preparing for a test?
    a. Stay up all night to cram for the test because your brain will have a fresh memory trace.
    b. Stay up all night to cram for a test because your brain normally processes information during the sleep period and the information will be better remembered.
    c. Be certain to get the correct amount of sleep the night before a test because research finds that poor sleep has a negative effect on memory.
    d. both a and b.
    Ans.: c   LG: 2   Page: 236   QT: C

39. Carskadon's study on adolescent sleep habits that was mentioned in the text found that
    a. adolescents today are lazier than previous generations and sleep too much.
    b. changes in adolescent sleep patterns are the result of changes in work patterns.
    c. adolescents' biological clocks undergo a hormonal change as they get older that pushes their time of wakefulness to an hour later.
    d. adolescent social lives are keeping them up too late at night and as a result they do not want to get out of bed in the morning.
    Ans.: c   LG: 2   Page: 237   QT: C

40. Recent research on adolescents suggests that the start of school should begin
    a. earlier each day.
    b. at the current time.
    c. later each day.
    d. at different times on different days.
    Ans.: c   LG: 2   Page: 237   QT: F

41. Which of the following is *not* true regarding the study mentioned in the text that involved changing a school starting time from 7:15 AM to 8:40 AM?
    a. There were fewer referrals for discipline problems.
    b. There were fewer illnesses.
    c. Test scores improved for both high school students and middle school students.
    d. Earlier school starting times were found to be more detrimental to older adolescents than younger adolescents.
    Ans.: c   LG: 2   Page: 237   QT: F

42. Which of the following is *not* true regarding developmental changes in sleep patterns?
    a. Beginning at age 60, adults report that they are less likely to sleep through the entire night than when they were younger.
    b. Middle-aged adults spend less time in the deepest sleep stage than when they were younger.
    c. Adolescents tend to stay up later than middle-aged adults.
    d. Almost one half of individuals in late adulthood report that they experience some degree of insomnia.
    Ans.: a   LG: 2   Page: 237   QT: C

43. Scientists monitor sleep stages with a(n)
    a. PET.
    b. MRI.
    c. EEG.
    d. Neuroemulsifier.
    Ans.: c   LG: 2   Page: 238   QT: F

44. Scientists monitor sleep stages by studying
    a. electrical brain activity.
    b. chemical brain activity.
    c. neurological firing.
    d. hemispherical brain differences.
    Ans.: a   LG: 2   Page: 238   QT: F

45. When people are awake, their EEG patterns may be _____ waves which reflect _____.
    a. beta; wakefulness
    b. alpha; relaxation
    c. beta; relaxation
    d. Both a and b are correct.
    Ans.: a   LG: 2   Page: 238   QT: F

46. Beta waves reflect _____ and are more _____ than other patterns.
    a. relaxation; desynchronous
    b. wakefulness; desynchronous
    c. relaxation; synchronous
    d. wakefulness; synchronous
    Ans.: b   LG: 2   Page: 238   QT: F

47. Not counting REM sleep, how many sleep stages are there?
    a. 2
    b. 3
    c. 4
    d. 5
    Ans.: c   LG: 2   Page: 238   QT: F

48. Which of the following is *not* correct regarding stage 1 sleep?
    a. Stage 1 sleep is characterized by theta waves.
    b. Theta waves are slower in frequency and greater in amplitude than alpha waves.
    c. The difference between just being relaxed and stage 1 sleep is gradual.
    d. Sleep spindles are a part of stage 1 sleep.
    Ans.: d   LG: 2   Page: 238   QT: C

49. Girard had obviously fallen asleep in class when the professor asked him a question that was ironically related to sleep stages. Girard said that he was not asleep at all. Girard was most likely in which of the following sleep stages?
    a. stage 1 or 2
    b. stage 3
    c. stage 4
    d. REM Sleep
    Ans.: a   LG: 2   Page: 238   QT: A

50. Which of the following is *not* true regarding stage 3 and stage 4 sleep?
    a. Both are characterized by slow- and high-amplitude brain waves.
    b. These two stages are often referred to as delta sleep.
    c. Distinguishing between stage 3 and stage 4 is difficult.
    d. In stage 3 and stage 4, our brain waves most resemble waking brain waves.
    Ans.: d   LG: 2   Page: 238   QT: F

51. Melanie returns to her dorm room to find her roommate Latrina taking a mid-afternoon nap. Melanie is going to get something to eat and wakes Latrina to see if she wants to join her. Latrina is dazed and confused when she wakes, not knowing where she is for a moment. Latrina was most likely in _____ sleep.
    a. REM
    b. stage 1
    c. stage 2
    d. stage 4
    Ans.: d   LG: 2   Page: 239   QT: A

52. The period of the sleep cycle when most dreaming occurs is
    a. stage 4 sleep.
    b. when the cerebral cortex is busy processing sensory inputs.
    c. REM sleep.
    d. dream sleep.
    Ans.: c   LG: 2   Page: 239   QT: F

148

53. REM sleep could also be called
    a. stage 1 sleep.
    b. stage 2 sleep.
    c. stage 4 sleep.
    d. stage 5 sleep.
    Ans.: d   LG: 2   Page: 239   QT: F

54. Freida is sound asleep when her little sister jumps on her to ask her what she is doing. Freida, being a patient older sister calmly explains to her sister, "I was dreaming." Her little sister, who has been watching a special on dreaming on educational television correctly says, "Aha, you were in _____ sleep."
    a. REM sleep
    b. stage 3
    c. stage 1
    d. stage 2
    Ans.: a   LG: 2   Page: 239   QT: A

55. Jessica hears her alarm go off at 6:00 AM, and once again, it has interrupted a good dream. Jessica was most likely in _____ sleep.
    a. REM
    b. stage 1
    c. stage 2
    d. stage 4
    Ans.: a   LG: 2   Page: 239   QT: A

56. During REM sleep, EEG patterns most closely resemble those of
    a. relaxed wakefulness.
    b. light sleep.
    c. sleep spindles.
    d. deep sleep.
    Ans.: a   LG: 2   Page: 239   QT: F

57. What does REM stand for?
    a. random eye movement
    b. residual electronic molecularization
    c. rapid eye movement
    d. rapid electron movement
    Ans.: c   LG: 2   Page: 239   QT: F

58. Your sister is asleep, but you seem to notice her eyes moving under her eyelids. If you were to wake her, she would most likely
    a. be dazed and confused.
    b. say that she had not been sleeping at all.
    c. report experiencing a sleep spindle.
    d. say that she was dreaming.
    Ans.: d   LG: 2   Page: 239   QT: C

59. Which of the following is *not* true regarding dreams?
    a. All dreams take place during REM sleep.
    b. Even people that do not usually remember dreaming report dreaming when awakened during REM sleep.
    c. The longer the REM period, the more likely the person will report dreaming.
    d. The duration of REM sleep increases during the sleep cycle.
    Ans.: a   LG: 2   Page: 239   QT: C

60. Which of the following subjects will have the largest proportion of REM sleep in their sleep cycles?
    a. Melissa, who is three months old
    b. Annie, who is 10 years old
    c. Bill, who is 40 years old
    d. Josephine, who is 80 years old
    Ans.: a   LG: 2   Page: 240   QT: A

61. Which of the following subjects would you expect to spend the least time sleeping each evening?
    a. Michael, who is 10 years old
    b. Dwayne, who is 20 years old
    c. Paul, who is 40 years old
    d. Martin, who is 70 years old
    Ans.: d   LG: 2   Page: 240   QT: A

62. If you were interested in the contents of your dreams, you could put a pad and a pencil next to your bed and then set your alarm to awaken you during a dream. When the alarm went off, you could write down on the paper whatever was on your mind at that time and then read it in the morning. If you were to go to bed at 11:00, which of the following alarm settings would most likely produce the desired result?
    a. 12:00
    b. 1:00
    c. 2:00
    d. 3:00
    Ans.: c   LG: 2   Page: 240   QT: C

63. Which of the following neurotransmitters are involved with sleep?
    a. serotonin
    b. epinephrine
    c. acytylcholine
    d. all of the above
    Ans.: d   LG: 2   Page: 241   QT: F

64. At which point in the sleep cycle do the neurotransmitters in the brain reach their lowest level?
    a. stage 1
    b. stage 2
    c. stage 4
    d. REM sleep
    Ans.: c   LG: 2   Page: 241   QT: F

65. _____ is initiated by a rise in acytylcholine, which activates the cerebral cortex while the rest of the brain remains relatively inactive.
    a. Waking up
    b. REM sleep
    c. Stage 4
    d. Stage 3
    Ans.: b   LG: 2   Page: 241   QT: F

66. You are most likely to wake up just after _____.
    a. stage 1 sleep
    b. stage 3 sleep
    c. stage 4 sleep
    d. REM sleep
    Ans.: d   LG: 2   Page: 241   QT: C

67. Which of the following is *not* true regarding sleep and disease?
    a. Stroke and asthma attacks are more common during the night.
    b. Infectious diseases interfere with our sleep.
    c. Cytokines are powerful sleep inducing chemicals.
    d. Sleep problems are common in Alzheimer's' disease and cancer.
    Ans.: b   LG: 2   Page: 241   QT: F

68. A sleep disorder that involves the inability to sleep is called
    a. insomnia.
    b. narcolepsy.
    c. sleep apnea.
    d. sleepwalking.
    Ans.: a   LG: 2   Page: 241   QT: F

69. Jeremy suffers from a sleep disorder in which he cannot fall asleep at night. Jeremy most likely suffers from
    a. insomnia.
    b. narcolepsy.
    c. sleep apnea.
    d. sleepwalking.
    Ans.: a   LG: 2   Page: 241   QT: A

70. Which of the following individuals is *least* likely to suffer from insomnia?
    a. Bailey, who is an older woman and is under a great deal of stress
    b. Karen, who is a thin, young woman
    c. Tyrone, who is a depressed younger male
    d. Fred, who is a healthy young male
    Ans.: d   LG: 2   Page: 241   QT: C

71. Which of the following is a drawback of using sleeping medications?
    a. Most sleeping pills stop working after several weeks of nightly use.
    b. Long-term use of sleeping pills can interfere with good sleep.
    c. Sleep medications are difficult to obtain.
    d. Both a and b are correct.
    Ans.: d   LG: 2   Page: 242   QT: C

72. Which of the following has been shown to be successful at helping subjects with mild insomnia?
    a. practicing good sleep habits
    b. eliminating daily naps
    c. setting an alarm to get up early rather than sleeping in
    d. all of the above
    Ans.: d   LG: 2   Page: 242   QT: C

73. Sleepwalking is also known as
    a. enuresis.
    b. sleep apnea.
    c. somnambulism.
    d. narcolepsy.
    Ans.: c   LG: 2   Page: 242   QT: F

74. Sleepwalking usually occurs
    a. early in the night in stage 1 or 2 sleep.
    b. late in the sleep cycle in stage 3 or 4.
    c. in REM sleep as subjects act out their dreams.
    d. early in the night in stage 3 or 4.
    Ans.: d   LG: 2   Page: 242   QT: F

75. You awaken to find that your roommate is sleepwalking out the door. You think that you should awaken her but you remember what you have heard about sleepwalkers. What should you do?
    a. Awaken her before she harms herself walking around in the dark.
    b. Do not awaken her. If you waken a sleepwalker, they will have a heart attack.
    c. Do not awaken her. If you waken a sleepwalker, they will attack you.
    d. Do not awaken her. Even though she is sleeping, she knows what she is doing.
    Ans.: a   LG: 2   Page: 242   QT: C

76. Mary has long suspected that Latrell has been cheating on her. One night she awakens to find that he is talking in his sleep. She asks him some questions about his affairs and it sounds to her like he has admitted guilt. If Mary asked your opinion on the validity of Latrell's responses, what could you tell her?
    a. He probably is cheating because when he is dreaming, his ego lets its guard down and the truth will come out.
    b. He probably is not cheating because his id is just acting upon unfulfilled wishes in giving responses.
    c. He probably is cheating because what comes out in sleep talking is usually the truth.
    d. There is really no way of telling because even though sleep talkers can give coherent responses, they are not always accurate.
    Ans.: d   LG: 2   Page: 243   QT: C

77. A frightening dream is called a
    a. night terror.
    b. nightmare.
    c. manifest content.
    d. all of the above
    Ans.: b   LG: 2   Page: 243   QT: F

78. A _____ takes place in REM sleep while a _____ takes place in non-REM sleep.
   a. night terror; nightmare
   b. night terror; bad dream
   c. nightmare; night terror
   d. somnambulism; nightmare
   Ans.: c   LG: 2   Page: 243   QT: C

79. _____ are accompanied by a number of physiological reactions.
   a. Bad dreams
   b. Night terrors
   c. Nightmares
   d. none of the above
   Ans.: b   LG: 2   Page: 243   QT: F

80. A sleep disorder in which a person will suddenly fall into REM sleep even though they were just awake is called
   a. sleep apnea.
   b. narcolepsy.
   c. somnambulism.
   d. none of the above
   Ans.: b   LG: 2   Page: 243   QT: F

81. Aaron is working with a new employee who is being trained to operate a bulldozer. He gives the person an instruction, turns his back for a moment, and when he looks at the employee again, the man is fast asleep. How could you explain this?
   a. The new employee may have somnambulism.
   b. The new employee may have night terrors.
   c. The new employee may have narcolepsy.
   d. The new employee may be bored.
   Ans.: c   LG: 2   Page: 243   QT: A

82. A sleep disorder in which individuals stop breathing because the windpipe fails to open or the brain processes involved in respiration fail to work properly is called
   a. narcolepsy.
   b. sleep apnea.
   c. somnambulism.
   d. enuresis.
   Ans.: b   LG: 2   Page: 243   QT: F

83. Which of the following is *not* true about sleep apnea?
   a. Sleep apnea is more common among the obese.
   b. Sleep apnea can cause high blood pressure and strokes.
   c. The daytime sleepiness caused by sleep apnea has been linked to accidents.
   d. Sleep apnea is most common among 35–45 year old males.
   Ans.: d   LG: 2   Page: 243   QT: C

84. Which of the following is *not* a theory of dreaming that is covered in the text?
   a. the behavioral theory
   b. the cognitive theory
   c. the Freudian theory
   d. the activation-synthesis theory
   Ans.: a   LG: 2   Page: 244-245 QT: F

85. Freud's concept that dreaming was an unconscious attempt to fulfill needs that cannot be expressed while awake was called
   a. Freudian dream analysis.
   b. wish fulfillment.
   c. Freud's cognitive theory of dreaming.
   d. Freud's activation-synthesis theory.
   Ans.: b   LG: 2   Page: 244   QT: F

86. From Freud's perspective, the dream's surface content is called _____ content, while the hidden content or unconscious meaning would be called the _____ content.
   a. latent; manifest
   b. manifest; latent
   c. open; hidden
   d. manifest; hidden
   Ans.: b   LG: 2   Page: 244   QT: C

87. Ally has a dream that she is continually walking through doorways. She decides to look in a dream interpretation book to see what this means. It turns out that it has a sexual meaning. In this example, Ally's walking through doorways was the _____ and the dream interpretation book's explanation was the _____.
   a. latent content; manifest content
   b. wish fulfillment; manifest content
   c. manifest content; latent content
   d. latent content; wish fulfillment
   Ans.: c   LG: 2   Page: 244   QT: A

88. The emphasis of Freud's dream analysis was on _____ and _____.
   a. males; females
   b. sex; females
   c. males; aggression
   d. sex; aggression
   Ans.: d   LG: 2   Page: 244   QT: F

89. Which of the following is the major problem with Freud's theory of dreaming?
   a. It is not interesting.
   b. It has not had much effect on the field of psychology.
   c. He believed that our dreams are influenced by our daily lives.
   d. His theories are difficult to support scientifically.
   Ans.: d   LG: 2   Page: 244   QT: C

90. The theory of dreaming that proposes that dreaming can be understood by studying the same processes that are used in the waking mind is called the
   a. the behavioral theory.
   b. the cognitive theory.
   c. the Freudian theory.
   d. the activation-synthesis theory.
   Ans.: b   LG: 2   Page: 244   QT: F

91. From the cognitive theory , which of the following is *not* of interest?
   a. information processing
   b. hidden meanings
   c. memory
   d. problem solving
   Ans.: b   LG: 2   Page: 245   QT: F

92. Jerome went to bed having exhausted every possible solution to a problem he was dealing with. He gave up, deciding to "sleep on it," and try again in the morning. In the middle of the night, he woke with the answer. Which of the following theories of dreaming could explain this?
   a. the behavioral theory
   b. the activation-synthesis theory
   c. the Freudian theory
   d. the cognitive theory
   Ans.: d   LG: 2   Page: 245   QT: A

93. The theory that states that dreaming occurs when the cerebral cortex processes neural signals emanating from activity in the lower part of the brain is the
   a. the behavioral theory.
   b. the cognitive theory.
   c. the Freudian theory.
   d. the activation-synthesis theory.
   Ans.: d   LG: 2   Page: 245   QT: F

94. Lionel says that dreams are the brain's attempt to make sense of random neural activity that takes place during sleep. Lionel agrees with which of the following theories?
   a. the behavioral theory
   b. the activation-synthesis theory
   c. the Freudian theory
   d. the cognitive theory
   Ans.: b   LG: 2   Page: 245   QT: C

95. Which of the theories of dreaming mentioned in the text is the most recently developed?
   a. the behavioral theory
   b. the activation-synthesis theory
   c. the Freudian theory
   d. the cognitive theory
   Ans.: b   LG: 2   Page: 246   QT: F

155

Learning Goal 3: Describe hypnosis.

96. A psychological state of possibly altered attention and awareness in which the individual is unusually responsive to suggestions is called
    a. narcolepsy.
    b. somnambulism.
    c. activation-synthesis.
    d. hypnosis.
    Ans.: d   LG: 3   Page: 247   QT: F

97. Which of the following is *not* true regarding hypnosis?
    a. Hypnosis is a psychological state.
    b. All humans can be hypnotized.
    c. Hypnosis involves altered attention and awareness.
    d. A hypnotized individual is unusually receptive to suggestions.
    Ans.: b   LG: 3   Page: 247   QT: C

98. Friedrich Anton Mesmer was famous for
    a. inventing hypnosis.
    b. developing "mesmerism" which led to the term "mesmerized."
    c. his developments in electromagnetics.
    d. all of the above
    Ans.: b   LG: 3   Page: 247   QT: F

99. Which of the following statements about hypnotic susceptibility is *not* true?
    a. Some people are more easily hypnotized than others.
    b. About 10 to 20 percent of people are very susceptible to hypnosis.
    c. 50 percent of people cannot be hypnotized at all.
    d. 10 percent or less cannot be hypnotized at all.
    Ans.: c   LG: 3   Page: 247   QT: C

100. Hilgard's experiment in which participants placed one arm in ice cold water provided support for the _____ view of hypnosis.
    a. behavioral
    b. divided state of consciousness
    c. social cognitive
    d. humanistic
    Ans.: b   LG: 3   Page: 248   QT: C

101. The perspective that hypnosis works because the hypnotized person behaves the way he or she believes a hypnotized person should behave is called the _____ behavior view of hypnosis.
    a. social cognitive
    b. behavioral
    c. divided state of consciousness
    d. humanistic
    Ans.: a   LG: 3   Page: 248   QT: C

102. In the social cognitive behavior view of hypnosis, which of the following would be *least* significant?
    a. subject's attitudes
    b. subject's expectations and beliefs
    c. social context
    d. subject's subliminal perception
    Ans.: d   LG: 3   Page: 248   QT: C

103. Which of the following outcomes of hypnosis is *true*?
    a. Hypnosis has often been used with psychotherapy to treat alcoholism.
    b. Hypnosis has often been used to successfully stop smoking.
    c. Hypnosis has often been used to successfully increase muscle strength.
    d. Hypnosis has often been used to successfully increase endurance.
    Ans.: a   LG: 3   Page: 248   QT: F

104. Which of the following is *not* true regarding hypnosis and recovered memory?
    a. Non-hypnotic instructions have shown success in recovered memory cases.
    b. Hypnotists need to be aware of leading questions.
    c. Hypnotism has never led to a recovered memory that is accurate.
    d. Highly hypnotizable subjects remember both more correct and more incorrect information than low-hypnotizable subjects.
    Ans.: c   LG: 3   Page: 250   QT: C

105. Hypnotic testimony is banned in some states because it
    a. is relatively new.
    b. has questionable reliability.
    c. requires corroborating evidence which is impossible to find.
    d. never works.
    Ans.: b   LG: 3   Page: 250   QT: C

Learning Goal 4: Evaluate the uses and types of psychoactive drugs.

106. Substances that act on the nervous system to alter states of consciousness, modify perceptions, and change moods are called
    a. psychological drugs.
    b. pharmaceuticals.
    c. psychoactive drugs.
    d. chemical inertiates.
    Ans.: c   LG: 4   Page: 251   QT: F

107. Which of the following is a way that psychoactive drugs act upon the nervous system?
    a. alter states of consciousness
    b. modify perceptions
    c. change moods
    d. all of the above
    Ans.: d   LG: 4   Page: 251   QT: F

108. People use psychoactive drugs for all but which of the following reasons?
    a. reduce tension
    b. develop a dependence
    c. relieve boredom
    d. relieve fatigue
    Ans.: b   LG: 4   Page: 251   QT: F

109. The need to take increasing amounts of a drug to produce the same effect is called
    a. resistance.
    b. adaptation.
    c. adjustment.
    d. tolerance.
    Ans.: d   LG: 4   Page: 251   QT: F

110. Which of the following is *true* regarding patterns of drug use by U.S. high school seniors?
    a. Drug use peaked in the early nineties and has been on the decline since.
    b. Drug use is at the highest point ever today.
    c. Drug use peaked in the late seventies, declined until the early nineties, and then began to increase again.
    d. Drug use has never been lower than it is today.
    Ans.: c   LG: 4   Page: 251   QT: F

111. Darius has been taking a prescription drug for the past six months. When he first started taking the drug, his prescription called for 5 milligrams. Now his doctor has him taking 10 milligrams to get the same effect. It would appear that Darius has develop a(n)
    a. addiction.
    b. tolerance.
    c. adjustment.
    d. reaction.
    Ans.: b   LG: 4   Page: 251   QT: A

112. A physical need for a drug, accompanied by unpleasant withdrawal symptoms when the drug is discontinued, is called
    a. psychological dependence.
    b. physical dependence.
    c. anatomical dependence.
    d. neurological dependence.
    Ans.: b   LG: 4   Page: 251   QT: F

113. The strong desire and craving to repeat the use of a drug for emotional reasons is called
    a. psychological dependence.
    b. physical dependence.
    c. anatomical dependence.
    d. neurological dependence.
    Ans.: a   LG: 4   Page: 251   QT: F

114. Experts on drugs use the term *addiction* to describe
    a. psychological dependence.
    b. physical dependence.
    c. a combination of psychological and physical dependence.
    d. all of the above
    Ans.: d   LG: 4   Page: 251   QT: C

115. A subject who is trying to quit using a drug and is suffering from withdrawal would be dealing with _____ dependence.
    a. emotional
    b. psychological
    c. physical
    d. social
    Ans.: c   LG: 4   Page: 251   QT: C

116. Beatrice has been taking a drug to make her feel more relaxed but she has decided to stop because of potential side effects. She thinks about not taking the drug a great deal and fights a craving for the drug. Beatrice is showing signs of _____ dependence.
    a. psychological
    b. physical
    c. anatomical
    d. quasi-addictive
    Ans.: a   LG: 4   Page: 251   QT: A

117. From a neurobiological perspective, how do psychoactive drugs affect the brain?
    a. Psychoactive drugs increase dopamine levels in the brain's reward pathways.
    b. Psychoactive drugs block reuptake.
    c. Psychoactive drugs mimic neurotransmitters.
    d. all of the above
    Ans.: d   LG: 4   Page: 252   QT: C

118. Which of the following pairs of words go together correctly?
    a. block reuptake-agonist
    b. reuptake-agonist
    c. reuptake-antagonist
    d. mimic neurotransmitter-antagonist
    Ans.: a   LG: 4   Page: 252   QT: C

119. Which of the following is *not* considered a type of psychoactive drug?
    a. antagonist
    b. depressants
    c. stimulants
    d. hallucinogens
    Ans.: a   LG: 4   Page: 252   QT: F

120. Psychoactive drugs that slow down mental and physical activity are called
    a. stimulants.
    b. depressants.
    c. hallucinogens.
    d. agonists.
    Ans.: b   LG: 4   Page: 252   QT: F

121. Which of the following drugs would not be considered a depressant?
    a. alcohol
    b. barbiturates
    c. MDMA
    d. opiates
    Ans.: c   LG: 4   Page: 252   QT: F

122. What is the most widely used drug in America?
    a. alcohol
    b. caffeine
    c. marijuana
    d. MDMA
    Ans.: b   LG: 4   Page: 253   QT: F

123. Which of the following statistics regarding alcohol abuse is true?
    a. Nearly 2/3 of homicides involve the use of alcohol by either the offender or the victim.
    b. Nearly 2/3 of aggressive sexual acts against women involve the use of alcohol by the offender.
    c. Approximately 1.5 million people are injured by drunk drivers each year.
    d. all of the above
    Ans.: d   LG: 4   Page: 253   QT: C

124. Binge drinking is defined as
    a. drinking at least 2 drinks every night for two weeks.
    b. drinking five or more drinks in a row at least once in a two-week period.
    c. drinking two six-packs of beer in one evening.
    d. drinking at least six mixed drinks for two nights in a row.
    Ans.: b   LG: 4   Page: 254   QT: F

125. Bluto is a binge drinker who is also a college student. Which of the following is *least* likely to be true about Bluto?
    a. He is 11 times more likely to fall behind in school.
    b. He is 10 times more likely to drive after drinking.
    c. He is not likely to miss classes.
    d. He is away from home.
    Ans.: c   LG: 4   Page: 254   QT: C

126. Which of the following is a characteristic associated with alcohol abuse on college campuses?
    a. unprotected sex
    b. injuries
    c. poor academics
    d. all of the above
    Ans.: d   LG: 4   Page: 254   QT: F

127. Which of the following is *not* true regarding alcoholism?
    a. One in nine individuals who drinks continues on the path to alcoholism.
    b. Alcoholism is influenced by both genetics and the environment.
    c. Family studies find a high frequency of alcoholism in first-degree relatives of alcoholics.
    d. About two-thirds of alcoholics recover.
    Ans.: d   LG: 4   Page: 254   QT: C

128. What is the "One-third rule" for alcoholism?
    a. One third of alcoholics do not recover.
    b. By age 65, one third of alcoholics are dead or in bad shape, one third of alcoholics are abstinent or drinking socially, and one third are still trying to beat their addiction.
    c. One third of alcoholics need professional help, one third of alcoholics can recover on their own, and one third of alcoholics never need help.
    d. none of the above
    Ans.: b   LG: 4   Page: 255   QT: F

129. Vaillant found that which of the following predicted a positive outcome and recovery from alcoholism?
    a. a strong negative experience with drinking, such as a medical emergency
    b. developing new, positive relationships with others
    c. joining a support group
    d. all of the above
    Ans.: d   LG: 4   Page: 255   QT: C

130. Depressant drugs that are used to decrease the activity of the central nervous system are called
    a. barbiturates.
    b. tranquilizers.
    c. opiates.
    d. antianxiety drugs.
    Ans.: a   LG: 4   Page: 255   QT: F

131. Depressant drugs that reduce anxiety and induce relaxation are called
    a. barbiturates.
    b. tranquilizers.
    c. opiates.
    d. morphines.
    Ans.: b   LG: 4   Page: 255   QT: F

132. At one time, _____ were the most widely prescribed sleep aids. Because of addictive potential and relative ease of toxic overdose, they have been largely replaced by _____ in the treatment of insomnia.
    a. opiates; barbiturates
    b. tranquilizers; opiates
    c. barbiturates; tranquilizers
    d. barbiturates; opiates
    Ans.: c   LG: 4   Page: 255   QT: F

133. Which of the following drugs is not considered an opiate?
    a. opium
    b. morphine
    c. valium
    d. heroin
    Ans.: c   LG: 4   Page: 255   QT: F

134. Which of the following is a drawback of opiate use?
    a. highly addictive
    b. because of intravenous use, risk of AIDS
    c. painful withdrawal
    d. all of the above
    Ans.: d   LG: 4   Page: 255   QT: C

135. Psychoactive drugs that increase the central nervous system's activity are called
    a. stimulants.
    b. barbiturates.
    c. opiates.
    d. tranquilizers.
    Ans.: a   LG: 4   Page: 256   QT: F

136. Which of the following would not be an example of a stimulant?
    a. cocaine
    b. alcohol
    c. nicotine
    d. caffeine
    Ans.: b   LG: 4   Page: 256   QT: F

137. Amphetamines are stimulants that are used to do all of the following *except*
    a. boost energy.
    b. improve memory.
    c. lose weight.
    d. stay awake.
    Ans.: b   LG: 4   Page: 256   QT: F

138. Which of the following is *not* true regarding cocaine?
    a. Cocaine works by preventing the uptake pumps from removing the neurotransmitter dopamine from the synapse
    b. More than one half of cocaine abusers return to the drug within six months of treatment.
    c. Crack is a form of cocaine that is one of the most addictive substances known.
    d. Cocaine works by mimicking a neurotransmitter.
    Ans.: d   LG: 4   Page: 256   QT: C

139. Which of the following is potentially a negative outcome of cocaine ingestion?
    a. heart attack or stroke
    b. brain seizure
    c. addiction
    d. all of the above
    Ans.: d   LG: 4   Page: 256   QT: F

140. Ecstasy is a street name for
    a. crack.
    b. cocaine.
    c. MDMA.
    d. heroin.
    Ans.: c   LG: 4   Page: 256   QT: F

141. Which of the following is *true* regarding use of MDMA?
    a. MDMA use is on the decline among secondary school students.
    b. Use of MDMA for as little as 4 days can cause brain damage that is still evident 6–7 years later.
    c. MDMA has just stimulant properties.
    d. MDMA has just hallucinogenic properties.
    Ans.: b   LG: 4   Page: 257   QT: F

142. Which of the following is *not* true regarding use of caffeine?
    a. Withdrawal from caffeine can last for weeks.
    b. Caffeine is the most widely used psychoactive drug in the world.
    c. Caffeine is found is coffee, tea, soft drinks, and other sources.
    d. Caffeine affects the brain's pleasure centers.
    Ans.: a   LG: 4   Page: 257   QT: F

143. Louanne has been told that she has been affected by caffeinism. Which of the following would *not* apply to Louanne?
    a. She is in for a long and agonizing withdrawal.
    b. She drinks five or more cups of coffee a day (500 milligrams of caffeine or more).
    c. She is irritable.
    d. She has been experiencing headaches.
    Ans.: a   LG: 4   Page: 257   QT: C

144. Which of the following is *not* true regarding the effects of nicotine?
    a. Tolerance develops for nicotine in the short term so that cigarettes smoked later in the day have less effect than cigarettes smoked earlier in the day.
    b. Withdrawal symptoms from nicotine can last for a month or more.
    c. Nicotine decreases alertness.
    d. Tolerance for nicotine develops over long period of time.
    Ans.: c   LG: 4   Page: 257   QT: F

145. Psychoactive drugs that modify a person's perceptual experiences and produce visual images that are not real are called
    a. stimulants.
    b. hallucinogens.
    c. depressants.
    d. amphetamines.
    Ans.: b   LG: 4   Page: 258   QT: F

146. Which of the following is *not* true regarding marijuana?
    a. The active ingredient in marijuana is THC.
    b. Marijuana affects a specific neurotransmitter.
    c. Marijuana disrupts the membranes of neurons.
    d. Because of diverse physical effects, it is difficult to classify it as a type of drug.
    Ans.: b   LG: 4   Page: 258   QT: F

147. A hallucinogen that even in low doses produces striking perceptual changes is
    a. marijuana.
    b. ecstasy.
    c. LSD.
    d. hashish.
    Ans.: c   LG: 4   Page: 259   QT: F

148. Which of the following is *not* true of LSD?
    a. LSD can cause dizziness, nausea, and tremors.
    b. LSD has no beneficial effects.
    c. LSD can influence the user's sense of time.
    d. LSD use reached a peak in the 60's and 70's and has rarely been used since.
    Ans.: d   LG: 4   Page: 261   QT: F

149. A pattern of behavior characterized by an overwhelming need to use the drug and secure its supply is called
    a. withdrawal.
    b. craving.
    c. physiological need.
    d. addiction.
    Ans.: d   LG: 4   Page: 261   QT: F

150. A model of addiction that describes addiction as a biologically based, lifelong disease that involves loss of control over behavior and requires medical and/or spiritual treatment for recovery is called the
    a. medical model.
    b. disease model.
    c. psychoactive model.
    d. sociocultural model.
    Ans.: b   LG: 4   Page: 261   QT: F

True/False Items

____ 151.   William James described the mind as a stream of consciousness.
____ 152.   "No awareness" is comparable to Freud's concept of unconscious thought.
____ 153.   An example of circadian rhythms would be a woman's menstrual cycle.
____ 154.   Americans do not get enough sleep.
____ 155.   Insomnia is also called somnambulism.
____ 156.   Sleep stages are monitored with an EEG.
____ 157.   Dreaming occurs primarily in stage 5 sleep.
____ 158.   The cognitive theory of dreaming attempts to explain dreaming in terms of the same cognitive concepts that are used in studying the waking mind.

___ 159. There have been no cultural differences found in human dreaming.
___ 160. Anyone can be hypnotized.
___ 161. Individuals who have been hypnotized have no free will and do whatever the hypnotist suggests.
___ 162. Humans are attracted to psychoactive drugs because they help them adapt to change.
___ 163. Alcohol is the most widely used psychoactive drug in America.
___ 164. Marijuana is a mild hallucinogen.
___ 165. The disease model of addiction emphasizes social and cognitive factors.

Answer Key for True/False Items

151.	Ans.: T	LG: 1	Page: 228	159.	Ans.: F	LG: 2	Page: 244
152.	Ans.: T	LG: 1	Page: 231	160.	Ans.: F	LG: 3	Page: 247
153.	Ans.: F	LG: 2	Page: 233	161.	Ans.: F	LG: 3	Page: 248
154.	Ans.: T	LG: 2	Page: 236	162.	Ans.: T	LG: 4	Page: 251
155.	Ans.: F	LG: 2	Page: 241	163.	Ans.: F	LG: 4	Page: 253
156.	Ans.: T	LG: 2	Page: 238	164.	Ans.: T	LG: 4	Page: 258
157.	Ans.: T	LG: 2	Page: 239	165.	Ans.: F	LG: 4	Page: 261
158.	Ans.: T	LG: 2	Page: 244				

Fill-in-the-Blank Items

166. _____ is the awareness of external events and internal sensations, including awareness of the self and thoughts about experiences.
167. _____ consciousness includes controlled processes and selective attention.
168. _____ consciousness includes automatic processes and daydreaming.
169. The _____ that regulates the daily sleep/wake cycle is a circadian rhythm.
170. The part of our brain that keeps the biological clock synchronized is the _____.
171. Humans go through _____ stages of non-REM sleep and one stage of REM sleep.
172. Most dreaming occurs during _____ sleep.
173. Somnambulism takes place during _____ sleep.
174. _____ believed that the reason people dream is wish fulfillment.
175. The _____ infers that dreaming occurs when the cerebral cortex synthesizes neural signals emanating from activity in the lower part of the brain.
176. In Hilgard's _____ view, hypnosis involves a splitting of consciousness into separate components.
177. In the _____ view of hypnosis, the hypnotized individual acts the way he or she believes a hypnotized person is supposed to act.
178. _____ drugs act on the nervous system to alter consciousness, modify perceptions, and change moods.
179. _____ dependence is accompanied by unpleasant withdrawal symptoms when the drug is discontinued.
180. _____ dependence brings about the craving of a drug for emotional reasons.

Answer Key for Fill-in-the-Blank Items

166.	Ans.: Consciousness	LG: 1	Page: 228
167.	Ans.: Higher level	LG: 1	Page: 229
168.	Ans.: Lower level	LG: 1	Page: 229
169.	Ans.: biological rhythm	LG: 2	Page: 233
170.	Ans.: suprachiasmatic nucleus	LG: 2	Page: 233
171.	Ans.: four	LG: 2	Page: 238
172.	Ans.: REM	LG: 2	Page: 239
173.	Ans.: stage 3 and 4	LG: 2	Page: 242
174.	Ans.: Freud	LG: 2	Page: 244
175.	Ans.: activation-synthesis theory	LG: 2	Page: 245
176.	Ans.: divided state of consciousness	LG: 3	Page: 248
177.	Ans.: social cognitive behavior	LG: 3	Page: 248
178.	Ans.: Psychoactive	LG: 4	Page: 251
179.	Ans.: Physical	LG: 4	Page: 251
180.	Ans.: Psychological	LG: 4	Page: 251

Matching Items

___	181. Circadian rhythm	A.	preoccupation
___	182. Deep sleep	B.	adaptation
___	183. Dream sleep	C.	what you remember
___	184. Manifest content	D.	slows down
___	185. Hypnosis	E.	heightened suggestibility
___	186. Tolerance	F.	distortion
___	187. Depressant	G.	REM
___	188. Stimulant	H.	increase activity
___	189. Hallucinogen	I.	stage 4
___	190. Addiction	J.	body temperature changes

Answer Key for Matching Items

181.	Ans.: J	LG: 2	Page: 233		186.	Ans.: B	LG: 4	Page: 251
182.	Ans.: I	LG: 2	Page: 238		187.	Ans.: D	LG: 4	Page: 252
183.	Ans.: G	LG: 2	Page: 239		188.	Ans.: H	LG: 4	Page: 256
184.	Ans.: C	LG: 2	Page: 244		189.	Ans.: F	LG: 4	Page: 258
185.	Ans.: E	LG: 3	Page: 247		190.	Ans.: A	LG: 4	Page: 261

Essay Questions

191. What is the difference between higher level awareness and lower level awareness? Include controlled processes and automatic processes in your answer and give an example of each. (LG: 1)

    Answer Guidelines: Higher level awareness includes controlled processes and selective attention. Lower level awareness includes automatic processes and daydreaming. Controlled processes are the most alert levels of human consciousness, when individuals actively focus their efforts on a goal. Automatic processes require little attention and do not interfere with other ongoing activities.

192. Explain the concept of biological rhythms. Include circadian rhythms in your answer. (LG: 2)

    Answer Guidelines: Biological rhythms are periodic physiological fluctuations in the body. Circadian rhythms are daily behavioral or physiological cycles.

193. What does research say about the reasons why human beings sleep? (LG: 2)

    Answer Guidelines: There are a number of ideas about why we sleep. Included in the text are physical restoration, adaptation, growth, and information processing.

194. List and briefly describe the stages of sleep. (LG: 2)

    Answer Guidelines: Possible options include mentioning the following: stage1—irregular, light sleep, about 10 minutes; stage 2—sleep spindles, about 20 minutes; stage 3—transition stage to deep sleep, lasts up to 30 minutes; stage 4—deep sleep, large, slow delta waves; and stage 5—REM sleep where most dreaming takes place.

195. Explain the three theories of dreaming that are mentioned in the text. (LG: 2)

    Answer Guidelines: Freud viewed dreams as wish fulfillment and believed in the importance of dream interpretation. The cognitive theory about dreams states that dreaming involves information processing, memory, and problem-solving. The activation-synthesis theory states that dreams represent the brain's attempt to make sense of random neural activity.

196. Describe hypnosis and explain two different theories of the hypnosis. (LG: 3)

    Answer Guidelines: Hypnosis can be defined as a psychological state of possibly altered attention and awareness in which the individual is unusually receptive to suggestions. Hilgard's view is that hypnosis involves a divided state of consciousness. In the social cognitive behavior view, the hypnotized individual behaves the way he or she believes a hypnotized person is expected to behave.

197. Explain the following terms as they apply to drugs and consciousness: psychological dependence, physical dependence, tolerance, and addiction. (LG: 4)

Answer Guidelines: Psychological dependence involves a craving for the drug. Physical dependence is the body's need for the drug to function normally. Tolerance is when the subject needs to take greater amounts of a drug to get the same effect. Addiction is a pattern of behavior characterized by a preoccupation with the use of a drug and securing its supply.

198. Explain how depressants affect the nervous system. In your answer, include two examples of negative side effects of depressants. (LG: 4)

Answer Guidelines: Depressants slow down mental and physical activity of the individual who ingests them. They cause drowsiness, slow reaction time, impair concentration, and impair judgment. They can lead to accidents, brain damage, coma, organic damage, and other problems.

199. Explain how stimulants affect the nervous system. In your answer, include two examples of negative side effects of stimulants. (LG: 4)

Answer Guidelines: Stimulants increase the central nervous system's activity. They can cause insomnia, hypertension, cardiovascular problems, irritability, and brain damage.

200. Explain how hallucinogens affect the nervous system. In your answer, include two examples of negative side effects of hallucinogens.

Answer Guidelines: Hallucinogens are psychoactive drugs that modify a person's perceptual experiences and produce visual images that are not real. They are also called "mind altering" drugs. They can cause fatigue, accidents, and respiratory disease.

Chapter 7: Learning

Learning Goals

1. Explain what learning is.
2. Describe classical conditioning.
3. Discuss operant conditioning.
4. Understand observational learning.
5. Know about the role of cognition in learning.
6. Identify biological and cultural factors in learning.

Multiple-Choice Items

Learning Goal 1: Explain what learning is.

1. Learning is defined as the
   a. relatively permanent influence on behavior that occurs through experience
   b. retention of information over time
   c. retrieval of information from storage
   d. activation of information from storage to help acquisition of additional information
   Ans.: a   LG: 1   Page: 269   QT: F

2. A relatively permanent influence on behavior that occurs through experience is called
   a. memory.
   b. learning.
   c. storage.
   d. encoding.
   Ans.: b   LG: 1   Page: 269   QT: F

3. Which of the following is *not* a type of learning studied by psychologists?
   a. observational learning
   b. associative learning
   c. imaginative learning
   d. operant conditioning
   Ans.: c   LG: 1   Page: 269   QT: C

4. Learning by watching what other people do and say is known as
   a. observational learning.
   b. associative learning.
   c. imaginative learning.
   d. operant conditioning.
   Ans.: a   LG: 1   Page: 269   QT: F

5. Types of learning in which a connection is made between two events are known as
   a. observational learning.
   b. associative learning.
   c. imaginative learning.
   d. connectionist learning.
   Ans.: b   LG: 1   Page: 269   QT: F

6. Research on learning in lower animals and humans has demonstrated that
   a. principles of learning in humans are dissimilar to those in lower animals.
   b. lower animals use more complex learning mechanisms than humans.
   c. humans and lower animals share many properties of learning.
   d. researchers have more control in studies of learning in humans.
   Ans.: c   LG: 1   Page: 269   QT: C

Learning Goal 2: Describe classical conditioning

7. When a neutral stimulus becomes associated with a meaningful stimulus and acquires the capacity to elicit a response, this is known as
   a. classical conditioning.
   b. operant conditioning.
   c. observational conditioning.
   d. connectionist conditioning.
   Ans.: a   LG: 2   Page: 270   QT: F

8. Classical conditioning is a form of learning in which
   a. the consequences of a behavior change the probability of the behavior's occurrence.
   b. a person observes and imitates someone's behavior.
   c. an organism develops a sudden understanding of the solution to a problem.
   d. a neutral stimulus becomes associated with a meaningful stimulus and acquires the capacity to elicit a response.
   Ans.: d   LG: 2   Page: 270   QT: F

9. In Pavlov's studies of classical conditioning, which of the following did *not* cause dogs to salivate?
   a. sight of the food dish
   b. sound of the door closing
   c. placing meat powder into the dog's mouth
   d. shock
   Ans.: d   LG: 2   Page: 270   QT: C

10. An unconditioned stimulus is a
   a. stimulus that produces a response without prior learning.
   b. response that is automatically elicited.
   c. response that is learned.
   d. previously neutral stimulus that elicits a response after learning.
   Ans.: a   LG: 2   Page: 270   QT: F

11. A stimulus that produces a response without prior learning is called a(n)
    a. unconditioned stimulus.
    b. conditioned stimulus.
    c. unconditioned response.
    d. conditioned response.
    Ans.: a   LG: 2   Page: 271   QT: F

12. An unconditioned response is a
    a. stimulus that produces a response without prior learning.
    b. response that is automatically elicited.
    c. response that is learned.
    d. previously neutral stimulus that elicits a response after learning.
    Ans.: b   LG: 2   Page: 271   QT: F

13. A response that is automatically elicited without prior learning is called a(n)
    a. unconditioned stimulus.
    b. conditioned stimulus.
    c. unconditioned response.
    d. conditioned response.
    Ans.: c   LG: 2   Page: 271   QT: F

14. A conditioned stimulus is a
    a. stimulus that produces a response without prior learning.
    b. response that is automatically elicited.
    c. response that is learned.
    d. previously neutral stimulus that elicits a response after learning.
    Ans.: d   LG: 2   Page: 271   QT: F

15. A previously neutral stimulus that elicits a response after learning is called a(n)
    a. unconditioned stimulus.
    b. conditioned stimulus.
    c. unconditioned response.
    d. conditioned response.
    Ans.: b   LG: 2   Page: 271   QT: F

16. A conditioned response is a
    a. stimulus that produces a response without prior learning.
    b. response that is automatically elicited.
    c. response that is learned.
    d. previously neutral stimulus that elicits a response after learning.
    Ans.: c   LG: 2   Page: 271   QT: F

17. A response that is learned is called a(n)
    a. unconditioned stimulus.
    b. conditioned stimulus.
    c. unconditioned response.
    d. conditioned response.
    Ans.: d   LG: 2   Page: 271   QT: F

18. While sitting in a chair in class, you hear a high-pitched noise you've never heard before, then the person next to you taps you on the shoulder, startling you, and you jump in surprise. The next time you hear the same high-pitched noise, you jump in surprise, even though no one has touched you. In this example, the high-pitched noise represents the
    a. unconditioned stimulus.
    b. unconditioned response.
    c. conditioned stimulus.
    d. conditioned response.
    Ans.: c   LG: 2   Page: 271   QT: A

19. While sitting in a chair in class, you hear a high-pitched noise you've never heard before, then the person next to you taps you on the shoulder, startling you, and you jump in surprise. The next time you hear the same high-pitched noise, you jump in surprise, even though no one has touched you. In this example, the tap on the shoulder represents the
    a. unconditioned stimulus.
    b. unconditioned response.
    c. conditioned stimulus.
    d. conditioned response.
    Ans.: a   LG: 2   Page: 271   QT: A

20. While sitting in a chair in class, you hear a high-pitched noise you've never heard before, then the person next to you taps you on the shoulder, startling you, and you jump in surprise. The next time you hear the same high-pitched noise, you jump in surprise, even though no one has touched you. In this example, your jumping when tapped on the shoulder represents the
    a. unconditioned stimulus.
    b. unconditioned response.
    c. conditioned stimulus.
    d. conditioned response.
    Ans.: b   LG: 2   Page: 271   QT: A

21. While sitting in a chair in class, you hear a high-pitched noise you've never heard before, then the person next to you taps you on the shoulder, startling you, and you jump in surprise. The next time you hear the same high-pitched noise, you jump in surprise, even though no one has touched you. In this example, your jumping when hearing the high-pitched noise the second time represents the
    a. unconditioned stimulus.
    b. unconditioned response.
    c. conditioned stimulus.
    d. conditioned response.
    Ans.: d   LG: 2   Page: 271   QT: A

22. Your roommate has a new boyfriend who at first seems very nice. However, every time he comes over to your apartment, he smokes like a chimney and the smell gives you a really bad headache. Now, whenever you see him, you start to get a headache, even if he isn't smoking. In this example, the sight of your roommate's boyfriend that gives you a headache represents the
    a. unconditioned stimulus.
    b. unconditioned response.
    c. conditioned stimulus.
    d. conditioned response.
    Ans.: c   LG: 2   Page: 271   QT: A

23. Your roommate has a new boyfriend who at first seems very nice. However, every time he comes over to your apartment, he smokes like a chimney and the smell gives you a really bad headache. Now, whenever you see him, you start to get a headache, even if he isn't smoking. In this example, the headache you get when you see your roommate's boyfriend represents the
    a. unconditioned stimulus.
    b. unconditioned response.
    c. conditioned stimulus.
    d. conditioned response.
    Ans.: d   LG: 2   Page: 271   QT: A

24. Your roommate has a new boyfriend who at first seems very nice. However, every time he comes over to your apartment, he smokes like a chimney and the smell gives you a really bad headache. Now, whenever you see him, you start to get a headache, even if he isn't smoking. In this example, the smell of cigarette smoke that gives you a headache represents the
    a. unconditioned stimulus.
    b. unconditioned response.
    c. conditioned stimulus.
    d. conditioned response.
    Ans.: a   LG: 2   Page: 271   QT: A

25. Your roommate has a new boyfriend who at first seems very nice. However, every time he comes over to your apartment, he smokes like a chimney and the smell gives you a really bad headache. Now, whenever you see him, you start to get a headache, even if he isn't smoking. In this example, the headache you get when you smell cigarette smoke represents the
    a. unconditioned stimulus.
    b. unconditioned response.
    c. conditioned stimulus.
    d. conditioned response.
    Ans.: b   LG: 2   Page: 271   QT: A

26. Your roommate has a new boyfriend who at first seems very nice. However, every time he comes over to your apartment, he smokes like a chimney and the smell gives you a really bad headache. Now, whenever you see him, you start to get a headache, even if he isn't smoking. This is an example of
    a. operant conditioning.
    b. observational learning.
    c. imitation.
    d. classical conditioning.
    Ans.: d   LG: 2   Page: 271   QT: A

27. You decide to start feeding your dog canned dog food. The first time you turn on the electric can opener, the dog pays no attention to the noise it makes but runs over when it smells the yummy odors coming from the open can. Eventually, the dog learns that the noise is related to the yummy smell and comes running as soon as he hears the can opener. In this example, the noise of the can opener represents the
    a. unconditioned stimulus.
    b. conditioned stimulus.
    c. unconditioned response.
    d. conditioned response.
    Ans.: b   LG: 2   Page: 271   QT: A

28. You decide to start feeding your dog canned dog food. The first time you turn on the electric can opener, the dog pays no attention to the noise it makes but runs over when it smells the yummy odors coming from the open can. Eventually, the dog learns that the noise is related to the yummy smell and comes running as soon as he hears the can opener. In this example, the smell of the yummy food represents the
   a. unconditioned stimulus.
   b. conditioned stimulus.
   c. unconditioned response.
   d. conditioned response.
   Ans.: a   LG: 2   Page: 271   QT: A

29. You decide to start feeding your dog canned dog food. The first time you turn on the electric can opener, the dog pays no attention to the noise it makes but runs over when it smells the yummy odors coming from the open can. Eventually, the dog learns that the noise is related to the yummy smell and comes running as soon as he hears the can opener. In this example, your dog running over when he smells the yummy food represents the
   a. unconditioned stimulus.
   b. conditioned stimulus.
   c. unconditioned response.
   d. conditioned response.
   Ans.: c   LG: 2   Page: 271   QT: A

30. You decide to start feeding your dog canned dog food. The first time you turn on the electric can opener, the dog pays no attention to the noise it makes but runs over when it smells the yummy odors coming from the open can. Eventually, the dog learns that the noise is related to the yummy smell and comes running as soon as he hears the can opener. In this example, your dog running over when he hears the can opener represents the
   a. unconditioned stimulus.
   b. conditioned stimulus.
   c. unconditioned response.
   d. conditioned response.
   Ans.: d   LG: 2   Page: 271   QT: A

31. You decide to start feeding your dog canned dog food. The first time you turn on the electric can opener, the dog pays no attention to the noise it makes but runs over when it smells the yummy odors coming from the open can. Eventually, the dog learns that the noise is related to the yummy smell and comes running as soon as he hears the can opener. In this example, the unconditioned stimulus is
   a. the sound of the can opener.
   b. the smell of the yummy food.
   c. your dog running over when he hears the can opener.
   d. your dog running over when he smells the yummy food.
   Ans.: b   LG: 2   Page: 271   QT: A

32. You decide to start feeding your dog canned dog food. The first time you turn on the electric can opener, the dog pays no attention to the noise it makes but runs over when it smells the yummy odors coming from the open can. Eventually, the dog learns that the noise is related to the yummy smell and comes running as soon as he hears the can opener. In this example, the conditioned stimulus is
    a. the sound of the can opener.
    b. the smell of the yummy food.
    c. your dog running over when he hears the can opener.
    d. your dog running over when he smells the yummy food.
    Ans.: a   LG: 2   Page: 271   QT: A

33. You decide to start feeding your dog canned dog food. The first time you turn on the electric can opener, the dog pays no attention to the noise it makes but runs over when it smells the yummy odors coming from the open can. Eventually, the dog learns that the noise is related to the yummy smell and comes running as soon as he hears the can opener. In this example, the unconditioned response is
    a. the sound of the can opener.
    b. the smell of the yummy food.
    c. your dog running over when he hears the can opener.
    d. your dog running over when he smells the yummy food.
    Ans.: d   LG: 2   Page: 271   QT: A

34. You decide to start feeding your dog canned dog food. The first time you turn on the electric can opener, the dog pays no attention to the noise it makes but runs over when it smells the yummy odors coming from the open can. Eventually, the dog learns that the noise is related to the yummy smell and comes running as soon as he hears the can opener. In this example, the conditioned response is
    a. the sound of the can opener.
    b. the smell of the yummy food.
    c. your dog running over when he hears the can opener.
    d. your dog running over when he smells the yummy food.
    Ans.: c   LG: 2   Page: 271   QT: A

35. In classical conditioning, acquisition refers to
    a. the tendency of a new stimulus that is similar to the original stimulus to elicit a response similar to the conditioned response.
    b. the process of learning to respond to certain stimuli and not to others.
    c. the weakening of the conditioned response in the absence of the unconditioned stimulus.
    d. the initial learning of the stimulus-response link.
    Ans.: d   LG: 2   Page: 272   QT: C

36. In classical conditioning, generalization refers to
    a. the tendency of a new stimulus that is similar to the original stimulus to elicit a response similar to the conditioned response.
    b. the process of learning to respond to certain stimuli and not to others.
    c. the weakening of the conditioned response in the absence of the unconditioned stimulus.
    d. the initial learning of the stimulus-response link.
    Ans.: a   LG: 2   Page: 272   QT: C

175

37. In classical conditioning, discrimination refers to the
    a. tendency of a new stimulus that is similar to the original stimulus to elicit a response similar to the conditioned response.
    b. process of learning to respond to certain stimuli and not to others.
    c. weakening of the conditioned response in the absence of the unconditioned stimulus.
    d. initial learning of the stimulus-response link.
    Ans.: b   LG: 2   Page: 272   QT: C

38. In classical conditioning, extinction refers to the
    a. process of learning to respond to certain stimuli and not to others.
    b. weakening of the conditioned response in the absence of the unconditioned stimulus.
    c. initial learning of the stimulus-response link.
    d. recurrence of a conditioned response after a time delay without further conditioning.
    Ans.: b   LG: 2   Page: 272   QT: C

39. In classical conditioning, spontaneous recovery refers to the
    a. process of learning to respond to certain stimuli and not to others.
    b. weakening of the conditioned response in the absence of the unconditioned stimulus.
    c. initial learning of the stimulus-response link.
    d. recurrence of a conditioned response after a time delay without further conditioning.
    Ans.: d   LG: 2   Page: 272   QT: C

40. Your roommate has a new boyfriend who at first seems very nice. However, every time he comes over to your apartment, he smokes like a chimney and the smell gives you a really bad headache. Eventually, whenever you see him, you start to get a headache, even if he isn't smoking. He stops smoking, and you notice that the sight of him becomes less likely to give you a headache. This decrease in your headaches when you seem him represents
    a. spontaneous recovery.
    b. discrimination.
    c. generalization.
    d. extinction.
    Ans.: d   LG: 2   Page: 272   QT: C

41. Your roommate has a new boyfriend who at first seems very nice. However, every time he comes over to your apartment, he smokes like a chimney and the smell gives you a really bad headache. Eventually, whenever you see him, you start to get a headache, even if he isn't smoking. He stops smoking, and you notice that the sight of him becomes less likely to give you a headache. Then they break up and you don't see him for a while. The next time you do see him, you get a headache. This recurrence of headaches is an example of
    a. spontaneous recovery.
    b. discrimination.
    c. generalization.
    d. extinction.
    Ans.: a   LG: 2   Page: 272   QT: C

42. In humans, classical conditioning explanations have been used for all of the following *except* explaining
    a. fears.
    b. pleasant emotions.
    c. health problems.
    d. the role of the superego.
    Ans.: d   LG: 2   Page: 274/275 QT: C

43. Counterconditioning refers to
    a. a way to produce phobias.
    b. weakening a conditioned response by associating a fear-provoking stimulus with a new response incompatible with fear.
    c. the tendency of a new stimulus that is similar to the original stimulus to elicit a response that is similar to the conditioned response
    d. a form of learning in which the consequences of behavior produce changes in the probability of the behavior's occurrence
    Ans.: b   LG: 2   Page: 274   QT: F

44. The process of weakening a conditioned response by associating a fear-provoking stimulus with a new response incompatible with fear is known as
    a. operant conditioning.
    b. discrimination.
    c. counterconditioning.
    d. punishment.
    Ans.: c   LG: 2   Page: 274   QT: F

45. Counterconditioning is a procedure that has been used to
    a. explain positive emotions.
    b. eliminate fears.
    c. explain health problems.
    d. eliminate gambling.
    Ans.: b   LG: 2   Page: 274   QT: C

46. According to theories of classical conditioning, drug overdoses are more likely to occur if a person takes a drug
    a. in a familiar place.
    b. with familiar people.
    c. at regular time intervals.
    d. in new situations.
    Ans.: d   LG: 2   Page: 275   QT: F

Learning Goal 3: Discuss operant conditioning.

47. Which of the following types of learning is best at explaining voluntary behaviors?
    a. classical conditioning
    b. counter conditioning
    c. imaginative conditioning
    d. operant conditioning
    Ans.: d   LG: 3   Page: 277   QT: C

48. A form of associative learning in which the consequences of a behavior produce changes in the probability of the behavior's occurrence is known as
    a. classical conditioning.
    b. counter conditioning.
    c. observational conditioning.
    d. operant conditioning.
    Ans.: d   LG: 3   Page: 277   QT: F

49. Operant conditioning refers to a type of learning in which
    a. the consequences of a behavior change the probability of the behavior's occurrence.
    b. a person observes and imitates someone's behavior.
    c. an organism develops a sudden understanding of the solution to a problem.
    d. a neutral stimulus becomes associated with a meaningful stimulus and acquires the capacity to elicit a response.
    Ans.: a   LG: 3   Page: 277   QT: F

50. In associative learning, contingency refers to
    a. whether the occurrence of one stimulus can be predicted from the presence of another one.
    b. the learned response that occurs after CS-US pairing.
    c. the weakening of a conditioned behavior in the absence of reward.
    d. the process of rewarding approximations of desired behavior.
    Ans.: a   LG: 3   Page: 277   QT: F

51. The ability of one stimulus to predict the presence of another stimulus is known as
    a. generalization.
    b. insight.
    c. contingency.
    d. shaping.
    Ans.: c   LG: 3   Page: 277   QT: F

52. Thorndike's law of effect says that
    a. behaviors that are followed by negative outcomes are strengthened.
    b. unconditioned stimuli that are associated with pleasant events occur more frequently than those that are associated with unpleasant events.
    c. conditioned stimuli that are associated with negative outcomes are weakened.
    d. behaviors that are followed by positive outcomes are strengthened.
    Ans.: d   LG: 3   Page: 278   QT: F

53. The idea that behaviors that are followed by positive outcomes are strengthened is known as
    a. law of latent learning.
    b. law of insight.
    c. law of effect.
    d. law of shaping.
    Ans.: c   LG: 3   Page: 278   QT: F

54. According to Thorndike's view, an organism's behavior is related to a connection between
    a. observation and insight.
    b. stimulus and response.
    c. punishment and reward.
    d. generalization and extinction.
    Ans.: b   LG: 3   Page: 278   QT: C

55. Skinner's experiment with pigeon-guided missiles demonstrated that
    a. classical conditioning could be used to control human behavior.
    b. operant conditioning was ineffective at manipulating human behavior.
    c. classical conditioning was an effective way to alter animal behavior.
    d. animal's could be trained to behave in new ways using operant conditioning.
    Ans.: d   LG: 3   Page: 278   QT: C

56. Skinner's novel *Walden Two* advocated a utopian society based on
    a. classical conditioning.
    b. observational learning.
    c. operant conditioning.
    d. insight learning.
    Ans.: c   LG: 3   Page: 278   QT: C

57. The process of rewarding approximations of desired behavior is known as
    a. priming.
    b. insight learning.
    c. shaping.
    d. latent learning.
    Ans.: c   LG: 3   Page: 279   QT: F

58. In operant conditioning, shaping refers to
    a. the process of rewarding approximations of desired behavior.
    b. recurrence of a conditioned response after a time delay without further conditioning.
    c. the process by which a stimulus or event increases the probability of an event that it follows.
    d. a procedure for weakening a conditioned response by associating a stimulus with a new response
       that is incompatible with fear.
    Ans.: a   LG: 3   Page: 279   QT: F

59. The process by which a stimulus increases the probability of a behavior that it follows is known as
    a. punishment.
    b. operant conditioning.
    c. classical conditioning.
    d. reinforcement.
    Ans.: d   LG: 3   Page: 280   QT: F

60. Reinforcement refers to
    a. the process of rewarding approximations of desired behavior.
    b. recurrence of a conditioned response after a time delay without further conditioning.
    c. the process by which a stimulus or event increases the probability of an event that it follows.
    d. a procedure for weakening a conditioned response by associating a stimulus with a new response
       that is incompatible with fear.
    Ans.: c   LG: 3   Page: 280   QT: F

61. During positive reinforcement, the frequency of an event
    a. increases because it is followed by the removal of a pleasant stimulus.
    b. increases because it is followed by the removal of an unpleasant stimulus.
    c. increases because it its followed by a pleasant stimulus.
    d. decreases because it is followed by an unpleasant stimulus.
    Ans.: c   LG: 3   Page: 281   QT: F

62. When the frequency of an event increases because it is followed by a pleasant stimulus, it is called
    a. positive reinforcement.
    b. negative reinforcement.
    c. positive punishment.
    d. negative punishment.
    Ans.: a   LG: 3   Page: 281   QT: F

63. Four-year-old Alexis clears her plate from the table and gets lots of praise from her mother. Now Alexis clears her plate from the table after every meal. This is an example of
    a. positive reinforcement.
    b. negative reinforcement.
    c. positive punishment.
    d. negative punishment.
    Ans.: a   LG: 3   Page: 281   QT: C

64. Mark used to clean his room once a week. Mark's mother begins giving him 30 minutes of computer time every time he cleans his room. Now Mark cleans his room every day. Mark's mother has used which of the following to change his behavior?
    a. positive reinforcement
    b. negative reinforcement
    c. positive punishment
    d. negative punishment
    Ans.: a   LG: 3   Page: 281   QT: C

65. My alarm clock emits a really obnoxious noise. If I hit the snooze alarm button, the obnoxious noise stops. Now, I hit the snooze alarm button a lot more frequently than I used to. This is an example of
    a. positive reinforcement.
    b. negative reinforcement.
    c. positive punishment.
    d. negative punishment.
    Ans.: b   LG: 3   Page: 281   QT: C

66. Fred cries loudly when his mom won't buy him candy. Fred's mom buys him some candy and he stops crying. As a result, Fred's mom buys him candy more frequently. The change in Fred's mom's behavior is a result of
    a. positive reinforcement.
    b. negative reinforcement.
    c. positive punishment.
    d. negative punishment.
    Ans.: b   LG: 3   Page: 281   QT: C

67. During negative reinforcement, the frequency of an event
    a. increases because it is followed by the removal of a pleasant stimulus.
    b. increases because it is followed by the removal of an unpleasant stimulus.
    c. increases because it its followed by a pleasant stimulus.
    d. decreases because it is followed by an unpleasant stimulus.
    Ans.: b   LG: 3   Page: 281   QT: C

68. When the frequency of an event increases because it is followed by the removal of an unpleasant stimulus, it is called
    a. positive reinforcement.
    b. negative reinforcement.
    c. positive punishment.
    d. negative punishment.
    Ans.: b   LG: 3   Page: 281   QT: F

69. Which of the following is *not* an example of a primary reinforcer?
    a. money
    b. food
    c. water
    d. sex
    Ans.: a   LG: 3   Page: 281   QT: C

70. A primary reinforcer is a stimulus that
    a. has acquired positive value through experience.
    b. is pleasurable in the absence of prior learning.
    c. has no effect on positive behavior but large effects on negative behavior.
    d. affects classical conditioning but not operant conditioning.
    Ans.: b   LG: 3   Page: 281   QT: F

71. A stimulus that is pleasurable in the absence of prior learning is known as a
    a. negative reinforcer.
    b. secondary reinforcer.
    c. classical conditioner.
    d. primary reinforcer.
    Ans.: d   LG: 3   Page: 281   QT: F

72. A secondary reinforcer is a stimulus that
    a. has acquired positive value through experience.
    b. is pleasurable in the absence of prior learning.
    c. has no effect on positive behavior but large effects on negative behavior.
    d. affects classical conditioning but not operant conditioning.
    Ans.: a   LG: 3   Page: 281   QT: F

73. Which of the following is a secondary reinforcer?
    a. food
    b. sex
    c. poker chips
    d. water
    Ans.: c   LG: 3   Page: 281   QT: C

74. The timetables that determine when a behavior will be reinforced are known as
    a. schedules of reinforcement.
    b. behavior modifications.
    c. token economies.
    d. instinctive drifts.
    Ans.: a   LG: 3   Page: 282   QT: F

75. During continuous reinforcement, a behavior is reinforced
    a. only after it has been performed a certain fixed number of times.
    b. only after a certain fixed amount of time has elapsed.
    c. every time it occurs.
    d. after a variable amount of time has elapsed.
    Ans.: c   LG: 3   Page: 282   QT: C

76. During a fixed-ratio schedule of reinforcement, a behavior is reinforced
    a. only after it has been performed a certain fixed number of times.
    b. only after a certain fixed amount of time has elapsed.
    c. every time it occurs.
    d. after a variable amount of time has elapsed.
    Ans.: a   LG: 3   Page: 282   QT: C

77. If a behavior is reinforced after it has been performed an unpredictable number of times, which
    schedule of reinforcement is being followed?
    a. fixed interval
    b. fixed ratio
    c. variable interval
    d. variable ratio
    Ans.: d   LG: 3   Page: 282   QT: C

78. If a behavior is reinforced after every 10-minute period has elapsed, which schedule of
    reinforcement is being followed?
    a. fixed interval
    b. fixed ratio
    c. variable interval
    d. variable ratio
    Ans.: a   LG: 3   Page: 282   QT: C

79. During a variable-ratio schedule, reinforcement is delivered
    a. only after it has been performed an unpredictable number of times.
    b. only after a certain fixed amount of time has elapsed.
    c. every time it occurs.
    d. after a variable amount of time has elapsed.
    Ans.: a   LG: 3   Page: 282   QT: C

80. The schedule that produces high, steady rates of behavior that are most resistant to extinction is
    a. continuous reinforcement.
    b. variable ratio.
    c. fixed interval.
    d. variable interval.
    Ans.: b   LG: 3   Page: 282   QT: C

81. The reinforcement schedule that produces rapid learning and rapid extinction is
    a. continuous reinforcement.
    b. variable ratio.
    c. fixed interval.
    d. variable interval.
    Ans.: a   LG: 3   Page: 282   QT: C

82. Which reinforcement schedule is most likely to produce slow, consistent levels of behavior?
    a. variable ratio
    b. fixed ratio
    c. variable interval
    d. fixed interval
    Ans.: c   LG: 3   Page: 283   QT: C

83. Robert is a painter who is paid for every room that he paints. The money that Robert receives is being given on which of the following schedules?
    a. variable ratio
    b. fixed ratio
    c. variable interval
    d. fixed interval
    Ans.: b   LG: 3   Page: 282   QT: C

84. Betty is fishing, and sometimes catches a fish after ten minutes, sometimes after two hours, sometimes after one minute; she can't predict how much time will elapse until she catches her next fish. In this example, Betty is being reinforced on which of the following schedules?
    a. variable ratio
    b. fixed ratio
    c. variable interval
    d. fixed interval
    Ans.: c   LG: 3   Page: 283   QT: C

85. In operant conditioning, generalization means
    a. giving the same response to similar stimuli.
    b. responding to stimuli which signal that a behavior will or will not be reinforced.
    c. a decreased tendency to perform a behavior that is no longer reinforced.
    d. learning in the absence of reinforcement.
    Ans.: a   LG: 3   Page: 283   QT: F

86. In operant conditioning, giving the same response to similar stimuli is known as
    a. latent learning.
    b. discrimination.
    c. generalization.
    d. extinction.
    Ans.: c   LG: 3   Page: 283   QT: F

87. In operant conditioning, discrimination means
    a. giving the same response to similar stimuli.
    b. responding to stimuli which signal that a behavior will or will not be reinforced.
    c. a decreased tendency to perform a behavior that is no longer reinforced.
    d. learning in the absence of reinforcement.
    Ans.: b   LG: 3   Page: 284   QT: F

88. In operant conditioning, responding to stimuli which signal that a behavior will or will not be reinforced is known as
    a. latent learning.
    b. discrimination.
    c. generalization.
    d. extinction.
    Ans.: b   LG: 3   Page: 284   QT: F

89. In operant conditioning, extinction means
    a. giving the same response to similar stimuli.
    b. responding to stimuli which signal that a behavior will or will not be reinforced.
    c. a decreased tendency to perform a behavior that is no longer reinforced.
    d. learning in the absence of reinforcement.
    Ans.: c   LG: 3   Page: 284   QT: F

90. In operant conditioning, a decreased tendency to perform a behavior that is no longer reinforced is known as
    a. latent learning.
    b. discrimination.
    c. generalization.
    d. extinction.
    Ans.: d   LG: 3   Page: 284   QT: F

91. When you first started dating your girlfriend, she complimented the way you dressed, so you made a special effort to look good. Now she never says anything about your appearance, so you no longer make an effort to look good. In this example, the decrease in your efforts to look good is an example of
    a. generalization.
    b. latent learning.
    c. extinction.
    d. discrimination.
    Ans.: c   LG: 3   Page: 284   QT: A

92. A consequence that decreases the likelihood that a behavior will occur is known as
    a. a negative reinforcer.
    b. punishment.
    c. shaping.
    d. instinctive drift.
    Ans.: b   LG: 3   Page: 284   QT: F

93. During punishment, the frequency of a behavior
    a. increases because it is followed by the removal of a pleasant stimulus.
    b. increases because it is followed by the removal of an unpleasant stimulus.
    c. increases because it its followed by a pleasant stimulus.
    d. decreases because it is followed by an unpleasant stimulus.
    Ans.: d   LG: 3   Page: 284   QT: C

94. During positive punishment, the frequency of a behavior
    a. increases because it is followed by the removal of a pleasant stimulus.
    b. decreases because it is followed by the removal of an unpleasant stimulus.
    c. decreases because it its followed by a pleasant stimulus.
    d. decreases because it is followed by an unpleasant stimulus.
    Ans.: d   LG: 3   Page: 284   QT: C

95. During negative punishment, the frequency of a behavior
    a. decreases because it is followed by the removal of a pleasant stimulus.
    b. decreases because it is followed by the removal of an unpleasant stimulus.
    c. decreases because it its followed by a pleasant stimulus.
    d. decreases because it is followed by an unpleasant stimulus.
    Ans.: a   LG: 3   Page: 284   QT: C

96. When behavior decreases in frequency because it is followed by the removal of a pleasant stimulus, it is called
    a. positive punishment.
    b. positive reinforcement.
    c. negative punishment.
    d. negative reinforcement.
    Ans.: c   LG: 3   Page: 284   QT: C

97. Amanda is playing with her dolls when she hits her sister. Amanda's mom takes away the doll and Amanda stops hitting her sister. The removal of the doll is an example of
    a. positive punishment.
    b. positive reinforcement.
    c. negative punishment.
    d. negative reinforcement.
    Ans.: c   LG: 3   Page: 284   QT: C

98. When Vanessa used to scream at her top of the lungs, her parents always used to pay attention to her. Now, they ignore Vanessa when she screams and she does it much less frequently. The change in Vanessa's behavior resulted from
    a. positive punishment.
    b. positive reinforcement.
    c. negative punishment.
    d. negative reinforcement.
    Ans.: c   LG: 3   Page: 284   QT: C

99. Harold frequently used to forget to return his library books on time. Then his mother started making him clean the toilets (which he hates doing) every time he returned a book late. As a result, Harold almost never returns a book late anymore. The change in Harold's behavior resulted from
    a. positive punishment.
    b. positive reinforcement.
    c. negative punishment.
    d. negative reinforcement.
    Ans.: a   LG: 3   Page: 284   QT: C

100. Time-out is a form of
    a. positive punishment.
    b. positive reinforcement.
    c. negative punishment.
    d. negative reinforcement.
    Ans.: c   LG: 3   Page: 284   QT: C

101. During operant conditioning, learning is most efficient when the delay between a behavior and its reinforcement is
    a. a few seconds.
    b. a few minutes.
    c. a few hours.
    d. It doesn't matter.
    Ans.: a   LG: 3   Page: 286   QT: C

102. Compared to rats, humans are better able to respond to
    a. food reinforcers.
    b. punishments.
    c. primary reinforcers.
    d. delayed reinforcers.
    Ans.: d   LG: 3   Page: 286   QT: C

103. The high level of obesity in the U.S. may be related to the finding that
    a. immediate negative consequences are more important than delayed positive consequences.
    b. immediate positive consequences are more important than delayed negative consequences.
    c. immediate positive consequences are more important than delayed positive consequences.
    d. immediate negative consequences are more important than delayed negative consequences.
    Ans.: b   LG: 3   Page: 286   QT: C

104. Behavior modification refers to
    a. the application of operant conditioning principles to change human behavior.
    b. a form of learning in which the consequences of behavior produce changes in the probability of the behavior's occurrence.
    c. the process by which a stimulus strengthens the probability of an event that it follows.
    d. the form of learning that occurs when a person observes and imitates someone's behavior.
    Ans.: a   LG: 3   Page: 288   QT: F

105. The application of operant conditioning principles to change human behavior is known as
    a. shaping.
    b. operant conditioning.
    c. behavior modification.
    d. counterconditioning.
    Ans.: c   LG: 3   Page: 288   QT: F

106. Applied behavior analysis refers to
    a. the application of operant conditioning principles to change human behavior.
    b. a form of learning in which the consequences of behavior produce changes in the probability of the behavior's occurrence.
    c. the process by which a stimulus strengthens the probability of an event that it follows.
    d. the form of learning that occurs when a person observes and imitates someone's behavior.
    Ans.: a   LG: 3   Page: 288   QT: F

107. The application of operant conditioning principles to change human behavior is known as
    a. shaping.
    b. operant conditioning.
    c. applied behavior analysis.
    d. counterconditioning.
    Ans.: c   LG: 3   Page: 288   QT: F

108. Which of the following is *not* one of the steps to self-control in a behavior modification program?
    a. defining the behavior.
    b. designing a self-control program.
    c. having someone else observe your behavior.
    d. making a commitment to change.
    Ans.: c   LG: 3   Page: 289   QT: C

109. In a behavior modification program to improve self-control, which of the following definitions of a problem would be most useful?
    a. being depressed
    b. worrying too much
    c. being bored
    d. quitting smoking by the end of the month
    Ans.: d   LG: 3   Page: 289   QT: C

110. In a behavior modification program aimed at improving self-control, one step is to make a commitment to change. Commitment strategies that contribute to success include all of the following *except*
    a. keeping the goals to yourself.
    b. providing yourself with frequent reminders of your goal.
    c. putting effort into planning your project.
    d. planning ahead to deal with temptation.
    Ans.: a   LG: 3   Page: 289   QT: C

111. Good self-control programs include all of the following *except*
    a. self-talk.
    b. self-instruction.
    c. self-reinforcement.
    d. self-punishment.
    Ans.: d   LG: 3   Page: 290   QT: C

112. Establishing a buddy system by finding a friend with a similar problem is one method of accomplishing which step of a self-control program?
    a. defining the problem
    b. collecting data about yourself
    c. designing a self-control program
    d. making the program last
    Ans.: d   LG: 3   Page: 290   QT: C

113. Skinner's teaching machine did all of the following *except*
    a. pace material at the student's rate.
    b. test the student's knowledge of the material.
    c. revolutionize learning in schools.
    d. provide immediate feedback about correct and incorrect answers.
    Ans.: c   LG: 3   Page: 290   QT: C

114. Computer-assisted instruction has produced superior results in which of the following areas?
    a. drill and practice on math problems
    b. designing scientific studies
    c. learning to write poetry
    d. speaking a second language
    Ans.: a   LG: 3   Page: 290   QT: C

115. The Premack principle says that
    a. behaviors followed by positive outcomes are strengthened, while behaviors followed by negative outcomes are weakened.
    b. high-probability activities can be used to reinforce low-probability activities.
    c. learning can occur in the absence of reinforcement.
    d. animals tend to revert to instinctive behavior that interferes with learning.
    Ans.: b   LG: 3   Page: 290   QT: C

Learning Goal 4: Understand observational learning.

116. Which of the following is *not* a term used to describe learning that occurs when someone watches someone else's behavior?
    a. observational learning
    b. imitation
    c. modeling
    d. associative learning
    Ans.: d   LG: 4   Page: 291   QT: C

117. Observational learning is also known as
    a. modeling.
    b. shaping.
    c. forming.
    d. molding.
    Ans.: a   LG: 4   Page: 291   QT: F

118. Imitation is also known as
    a. observational learning.
    b. classical conditioning.
    c. shaping.
    d. reinforcement.
    Ans.: a   LG: 4   Page: 291   QT: F

119. Which of the following types of learning would be the best way to teach someone to drive?
    a. operant conditioning
    b. trial-and-error
    c. classical conditioning
    d. observational learning
    Ans.: d   LG: 4   Page: 291   QT: C

120. Which of the following is *not* a main process involved in observational learning?
    a. attention
    b. reinforcement
    c. retention
    d. shaping
    Ans.: d   LG: 4   Page: 291   QT: C

121. Which of the following is a main process involved in observational learning?
    a. motor reproduction
    b. punishment
    c. shaping
    d. stimulus-response contingency
    Ans.: a   LG: 4   Page: 291   QT: C

122. In observational learning, a model who displayed which of the following characteristics would command the most attention?
    a. powerful
    b. weak
    c. typical
    d. cold
    Ans.: a   LG: 4   Page: 291   QT: C

123. In observational learning, a model who is powerful, warm, and atypical influences which component?
    a. retention
    b. production
    c. attention
    d. reinforcement
    Ans.: c   LG: 4   Page: 291   QT: C

124. In observational learning, the process of imitating a model's actions is known as
    a. reinforcement.
    b. production.
    c. retention.
    d. attention.
    Ans.: b   LG: 4   Page: 292   QT: F

125. In observational learning, the process of coding information and keeping it in memory is known as
    a. reinforcement.
    b. production.
    c. retention.
    d. attention.
    Ans.: c   LG: 4   Page: 292   QT: F

126. In observational learning, the process of offering incentives for performing a behavior is known as
    a. reinforcement.
    b. production.
    c. retention.
    d. attention.
    Ans.: a   LG: 4   Page: 292   QT: F

Learning Goal 5: Know about the role of cognition in learning.

127. Which of the following types of learning most emphasizes the role of cognitive processes?
    a. operant conditioning
    b. classical conditioning
    c. behaviorism
    d. observational learning
    Ans.: d   LG: 5   Page: 292   QT: C

128. Tolman's view of the purposiveness of behavior emphasizes the fact that behavior is
    a. affected by immediate rewards.
    b. goal directed.
    c. a result of imitation.
    d. directed by stimulus-response relationships.
    Ans.: b   LG: 5   Page: 293   QT: C

129. Tolman's view that most behavior is goal directed is known as
    a. generalization.
    b. discrimination.
    c. purposiveness.
    d. law of effect.
    Ans.: c   LG: 5   Page: 293   QT: C

130. The learning goals in each chapter are most related to which perspective on learning?
    a. Tolman's purposive behavior
    b. Skinner's operant behavior
    c. Thorndike's law of effect
    d. Pavlov's classical conditioning
    Ans.: a   LG: 5   Page: 294   QT: C

131. According to Tolman, the critical feature of classical conditioning is
    a. the unconditioned stimulus.
    b. expectancies.
    c. the conditioned response.
    d. shaping.
    Ans.: b   LG: 5   Page: 294   QT: C

132. Expectancy learning refers to
    a. the process by which an event increases the probability of an event that it follows.
    b. the relationship between a stimulus and the result that the organism expects.
    c. the use of reinforcers that an organism doesn't expect.
    d. using reinforcers that have acquired their positive value through experience.
    Ans.: b   LG: 5   Page: 294   QT: C

133. In Leon Kamin's classic experiment, he repeatedly presented a rat with a tone followed by a shock until the tone by itself produced fear. Then, while he continued to present the tone, he also repeatedly presented a light with the shock. What were the effects of the light on the rat's behavior?
    a. The rat learned to fear the light more than the shock.
    b. The rat learned to fear the light and forgot to fear the shock.
    c. The rat continued to fear the shock, but did not fear the light.
    d. The rat learned to fear the light and shock equally.
    Ans.: c   LG: 5   Page: 294   QT: C

134. In Leon Kamin's classic experiment, he repeatedly presented a rat with a tone followed by a shock until the tone by itself produced fear. Then, while he continued to present the tone, he also repeatedly presented a light with the shock. The results of this experiment demonstrated that
    a. operant conditioning is controlled by the contiguity of the CS and the UCS.
    b. classical conditioning is controlled by the contiguity of the CS and the UCS.
    c. operant conditioning is affected by the rat's history.
    d. classical conditioning is affected by the rat's history.
    Ans.: d   LG: 5   Page: 294   QT: C

135. An organism's mental representation of a physical space is known as a cognitive
    a. map.
    b. stream.
    c. image.
    d. shape.
    Ans.: a   LG: 5   Page: 294   QT: F

136. Latent learning refers to learning
    a. in which the organism develops a sudden understanding of the solution to a problem.
    b. that is strengthened by cognitive maps.
    c. in which behaviors that are reinforced are strengthened.
    d. in the absence of reinforcement that is not immediately reflected in behavior.
    Ans.: d   LG: 5   Page: 295   QT: F

137. Learning that is unreinforced and not immediately reflected in behavior is called
    a. insight learning.
    b. observational learning.
    c. latent learning.
    d. primary learning.
    Ans.: c   LG: 5   Page: 295   QT: F

138. A form of learning in which an organism suddenly develops an understanding of the solution to a problem is known as
    a. insight learning.
    b. observational learning.
    c. latent learning.
    d. primary learning.
    Ans.: a   LG: 5   Page: 296   QT: F

139. Insight learning refers to learning
    a. in which the organism develops a sudden understanding of the solution to a problem.
    b. that is strengthened by cognitive maps.
    c. in which behaviors that are reinforced are strengthened.
    d. in the absence of reinforcement that is not immediately reflected in behavior.
    Ans.: a   LG: 5   Page: 296   QT: F

Learning Goal 6: Identify biological and cultural factors in learning.

140. The tendency of animals to revert to instinctive behavior that interferes with learning is known as
    a. law of effect.
    b. shaping.
    c. latent learning.
    d. instinctive drift.
    Ans.: d   LG: 6   Page: 296   QT: F

141. Instinctive drift refers to
    a. the application of operant conditioning principles to change human behavior.
    b. a form of learning in which the consequences of behavior produce changes in the probability of the behavior's occurrence.
    c. the tendency of animals to revert to instinctive behavior that interferes with learning.
    d. the form of learning that occurs when a person observes and imitates someone's behavior.
    Ans.: c   LG: 6   Page: 296   QT: F

142. The Breland's trained raccoons to place a coin in a metal tray. They discovered that when the raccoons were given two coins, they would rub them together, even though they had never been reinforced for rubbing coins together. The raccoons' behavior is an example of
    a. law of effect.
    b. shaping.
    c. insight earning.
    d. instinctive drift.
    Ans.: d   LG: 6   Page: 297   QT: F

143. Pigs that had been trained to drop nickels into piggy banks eventually began to repeatedly shove the nickels with their snouts and toss them in the air even though they had not be taught to do so. Their shoving and tossing behavior is an example of
    a. preparedness.
    b. shaping.
    c. insight learning.
    d. instinctive drift.
    Ans.: d   LG: 6   Page: 297   QT: F

144. Preparedness refers to
    a. the application of operant conditioning principles to change human behavior.
    b. a species-specific biological disposition to learn in certain ways and not others.
    c. the tendency of animals to revert to instinctive behavior that interferes with learning.
    d. the form of learning that occurs when a person observes and imitates someone's behavior.
    Ans.: b   LG: 6   Page: 297   QT: F

145. A species-specific biological disposition to learn in certain ways and not others is known as
    a. preparedness.
    b. shaping.
    c. latent learning.
    d. instinctive drift.
    Ans.: a   LG: 6   Page: 297   QT: F

146. Taste aversion refers to
    a. a distaste for a substance that has previously produced illness.
    b. learning in the absence of reinforcement.
    c. the tendency of animals to revert to instinctive behavior.
    d. the process by which behaviors that are followed by negative outcomes are strengthened.
    Ans.: a   LG: 6   Page: 297   QT: F

147. An animal develops a distaste for a substance that has previously made it sick; this distaste is known as
    a. preparedness.
    b. instinctive drift.
    c. taste aversion.
    d. latent learning.
    Ans.: c   LG: 6   Page: 297   QT: F

148. One night, you drink way too much tequila, and become violently ill. The next time someone offers you a margarita, you feel sick because of the tequila in the drink. In this example, you are experiencing
   a. taste aversion.
   b. preparedness.
   c. instinctive drift.
   d. shaping.
   Ans.: a   LG: 6   Page: 297   QT: A

149. People who are undergoing chemotherapy which makes them sick often develop distaste for the flavor of the solution that contains the drug. This distaste is called
   a. taste aversion.
   b. preparedness.
   c. instinctive drift.
   d. shaping.
   Ans.: a   LG: 6   Page: 297   QT: C

150. A 4-year-old growing up among the Bushmen of the Kalahari Desert is more likely to learn about tracking animals than pouring water from one glass into another. This is an example of
   a. instinctive drift.
   b. cultural influences on learning.
   c. law of effect.
   d. negative reinforcement.
   Ans.: b   LG: 6   Page: 299   QT: C

True/False Items

____ 151. Learning refers to a relatively permanent change in behavior that occurs as a result of experience.

____ 152. Learning that occurs by watching what other people say and do is known as associative learning.

____ 153. Operant conditioning is an example of observational learning.

____ 154. In classical conditioning, the unconditioned stimulus is a stimulus that automatically elicits a response in the absence of learning.

____ 155. In classical conditioning, extinction refers to the process of learning to respond to certain stimuli and not respond to other stimuli.

____ 156. Positive reinforcement occurs when the frequency of a behavior increases because it is followed by a positive stimulus.

____ 157. A primary reinforcer is a stimulus that is pleasurable in the absence of prior learning.

____ 158. On a fixed-ratio schedule of reinforcement, a behavior is rewarded after it has occurred a set number of times.

____ 159. Variable interval schedules produce high, steady rates of behavior that are more resistant to extinction than other schedules.

____ 160. According to the Premack principle, one effective reinforcement strategy would be for a teacher to tell a class, "If all of the class finishes their homework by Friday, we will go on a field trip."

____ 161. In observational learning, models who are cold, powerful, and typical attract the most attention.

___ 162. In observational learning, retention refers to the process of imitating the model's actions.
___ 163. Latent learning refers to learning that takes place in the absence of reinforcement and is not immediately observable in behavior.
___ 164. Instinctive drift refers to the tendency of animals to follow instinctive behavior that interferes with learning.
___ 165. Taste aversions have been used to discourage wolves and coyotes from attacking livestock.

Answer Key for True/False Items

151.	Ans.: T	LG: 1	Page: 269	159.	Ans.: F	LG: 3	Page: 283
152.	Ans.: F	LG: 1	Page: 269	160.	Ans.: T	LG: 3	Page: 290
153.	Ans.: F	LG: 1	Page: 269	161.	Ans.: F	LG: 4	Page: 291
154.	Ans.: T	LG: 2	Page: 271	162.	Ans.: F	LG: 4	Page: 292
155.	Ans.: F	LG: 2	Page: 272	163.	Ans.: T	LG: 5	Page: 295
156.	Ans.: T	LG: 3	Page: 281	164.	Ans.: T	LG: 6	Page: 297
157.	Ans.: F	LG: 3	Page: 281	165.	Ans.: T	LG: 6	Page: 298
158.	Ans.: T	LG: 3	Page: 282				

Fill-in-the-Blank Items

166. Learning that occurs as a result of watching what others say and do is known as _____ learning.
167. When we make connections between two events, this is known as _____ learning.
168. A stimulus that produces a response without prior learning is known as a(n) _____.
169. In classical conditioning, the process of learning to respond to certain stimuli and not respond to others is known as _____.
170. A classical conditioning procedure for weakening a fear by associating a fear-provoking stimulus with a new response that is incompatible with fear is known as _____.
171. When the frequency of a behavior increases because it is followed by the removal of an unpleasant stimulus, it is known as _____.
172. Reinforcers that acquire their positive value through experience are known as _____ reinforcers.
173. The schedule of reinforcement which produces rapid learning and rapid extinction is called a _____ schedule.
174. A schedule which produces high, steady rates of reinforcement that are resistant to extinction is most likely a _____ schedule.
175. In observational learning, the process of imitating the model's actions is known as _____.
176. Learning that occurs in the absence of reinforcement and that is not immediately reflected in behavior is known as _____ learning.
177. A form of problem solving in which the organism develops a sudden understanding of the solution is called _____ learning.
178. The tendency of animals to revert to instinctive behavior that interferes with learning is known as _____.
179. The species-specific biological disposition to learn in certain ways and not others is called _____.
180. An organism that eats a substance that poisons but does not kill it subsequently shows distaste for that substance. This distaste is called a _____.

Answer Key for Fill-in-the-Blank Items

166.	Ans.: observational	LG: 1	Page: 269
167.	Ans.: associative	LG: 1	Page: 269
168.	Ans.: unconditioned stimulus	LG: 2	Page: 271
169.	Ans.: discrimination	LG: 2	Page: 272
170.	Ans.: counterconditioning	LG: 2	Page: 274
171.	Ans.: negative reinforcement	LG: 3	Page: 281
172.	Ans.: secondary	LG: 3	Page: 281
173.	Ans.: continuous reinforcement	LG: 3	Page: 282
174.	Ans.: variable-ratio	LG: 3	Page: 282
175.	Ans.: motor reproduction (or production)	LG: 4	Page: 292
176.	Ans.: latent	LG: 5	Page: 295
177.	Ans.: insight	LG: 5	Page: 296
178.	Ans.: instinctive drift	LG: 6	Page: 296
179.	Ans.: preparedness	LG: 6	Page: 297
180.	Ans.: taste aversion	LG: 6	Page: 297

Matching Items

___	181. acquisition	A.	reinforcement
___	182. extinction	B.	slow, consistent responding
___	183. phobias	C.	initial learning
___	184. increased frequency	D.	sudden understanding of the solution
___	185. decreased frequency	E.	unreinforced
___	186. variable interval	F.	counterconditioning
___	187. variable ratio	G.	taste aversion
___	188. insight learning	H.	high, steady rates of responding
___	189. latent learning	I.	punishment
___	190. biological constraint	J.	weakening of response

Answer Key for Matching Items

181.	Ans.: C	LG: 2	Page: 272		186.	Ans.: B	LG: 3	Page: 283
182.	Ans.: J	LG: 2	Page: 272		187.	Ans.: H	LG: 3	Page: 283
183.	Ans.: F	LG: 2	Page: 274		188.	Ans.: D	LG: 5	Page: 296
184.	Ans.: A	LG: 3	Page: 281		189.	Ans.: E	LG: 5	Page: 295
185.	Ans.: I	LG: 3	Page: 284		190.	Ans.: G	LG: 6	Page: 298

Essay Questions

191: Define unconditioned stimulus, conditioned stimulus, unconditioned response, and conditioned response, and provide an example. Identify each term in the example. (LG: 2)

Answer Guidelines: (1) Unconditioned stimulus is a stimulus that produces a response without prior learning; examples might include food, sex, painful stimuli. (2) Conditioned stimulus is a stimulus that starts out neutral (doesn't cause a response) but that acquires the ability to produce a response through experience (examples could be sounds, lights, touch). (3) Unconditioned response is the reaction automatically elicited by the unconditioned stimulus; the example should be related to the unconditioned stimulus example (foods elicit salivating, sex elicits arousal, painful stimui elicit withdrawal). (4) Conditioned response is the reaction elicited by the conditioned stimulus after learning; the example should be related to the unconditioned response (can be opposite of conditioned response, as in drug overdose).

192. Describe the processes of acquisition, generalization, discrimination and extinction in classical conditioning, giving an example of each. (LG: 2)

Answer Guidelines: Acquisition: the initial learning that a neutral stimulus is associated with an unconditioned stimulus so that the neutral stimulus eventually elicits a conditioned response. Generalization: the tendency for new stimuli that are similar to previously learned stimuli to produce responses similar to the conditioned responses. Discrimination: the process of learning to respond to certain stimuli and not to others. Extinction: the weakening of the conditioned response in the absence of the unconditioned stimulus.

193. Describe three applications of the principles of classical conditioning to human behavior. (LG: 2)

Answer Guidelines: (1) Explaining and eliminating fears (phobias and counter conditioning); (2) pleasant emotions associated with sexual encounters may explain positive responses to places, music, clothing, etc.; (3) sexual arousal associated with objects that deviate from the norm may lead to fetishes; (4) behaviors associated with health problems like headaches, ulcers, high blood pressure may result from associations between chronic stimuli (boss's attitude or wife's threats of divorce) and their consequences; the persistent relationship may result in generalization to other stimuli associated with the chronic stimulus, leading to health problems; (5) drug overdoses have been associated with drug taking in particular contexts which lead to anticipatory responses; if drugs are taken in novel contexts, overdoses can occur; (6) immunosuppression—drugs that suppress the immune system can be associated with tastes; the tastes then can come to suppress the immune system on their own; (7) advertising—attractive people lead to an unconditioned sexual response; an attractive person is associated with a product; the product comes to produce a conditioned emotional response.

194. Explain positive and negative reinforcement and positive and negative punishment and give an example of each. (LG: 3)

Answer Guidelines: Positive reinforcement—the frequency of a behavior increases because it is followed by a pleasant stimulus. Negative reinforcement—the frequency of a behavior increases because it is followed by the removal of an unpleasant stimulus. Positive punishment—the frequency of a behavior decreases because it is followed by an unpleasant stimulus. Negative punishment—the frequency of a behavior decreases because it is followed by the removal of a pleasant stimulus

195. Describe the four schedules of partial reinforcement and indicate the pattern of behavior produced by each. (LG: 3)

Answer Guidelines: Fixed ratio: behavior is reinforced after it has occurred a set number of times; produces patterns of behavior where the frequency of the behavior decreases just after reinforcement. Variable ratio: behavior is reinforced after it has occurred a variable, unpredictable number of times; produces high, steady rates of reinforcement that are highly resistant to extinction. Fixed interval: behavior is reinforced after a set amount of time has elapsed; produces low levels of activity until it is close to the time of the next reinforcer. Variable interval: behavior is reinforced after a variable amount of time has elapsed; produces slow, consistent levels of responding

196. Describe the four components of observational learning, giving an example of each. (LG: 4)

Answer Guidelines: (1) Attention: to be able to imitate a model's actions, you have to devote attention to what they are; attention to models is influenced by characteristics of the model; models who are weak, typical or cold receive less attention than models who are powerful, warm or atypical. (2) Retention: to reproduce the actions, you must code the information and store it in memory so it can be retrieved. (3) Motor Reproduction: the actual process of imitating the actions that have been observed and stored. (4) Reinforcement or incentives: production of the behavior must result in a positive consequence or be accompanied by an incentive to reproduce the behavior

197. Define latent learning and insight learning, and compare them to operant conditioning. (LG: 5)

Answer Guidelines: Latent learning refers to learning that occurs in the absence of reinforcement and is not observable immediately in behavior. Insight learning refers to the development of a sudden understanding of how to solve a problem. They differ from operant conditioning in that there is no straightforward relationship between a reinforcer or punisher and the frequency of a behavior. In latent learning, the learning occurs without reinforcement, and in insight learning, the behavior has not been previously performed, although solving the problem may serve as a reinforcer to increase the frequency of performing the behavior that solved the problem. Insight learning and latent learning emphasize the role of cognition in learning, whereas operant learning ignores cognition.

198. Define cognitive maps and explain how they are related to expectancies. (LG: 5)

Answer Guidelines: Cognitive maps are internal, mental representations of the structure of a physical space. They are made up of expectancies of which actions will be needed to attain a goal. We develop them as we move around our environments, and they are on multiple scales from maps of the locations of the rooms in our apartment to maps of the location of our state in the United States. The size and shapes of our mental maps are not directly related to the actual, physical size and shape of the space.

199. Define instinctive drift and preparedness and give examples of each. (LG: 6)

Answer Guidelines: Instinctive drift refers to the tendency of animals to revert to instinctive behaviors that interfere with learning. Examples include pigs trained to drop wooden nickels into piggy banks and raccoons given coins to place in a tray. The pigs eventually began to shove the coins with their snouts and toss them in the air repeatedly; the raccoons, when given two coins, eventually began to rub the coins together. Both of these responses represented behaviors typically associated with food in each species.

Preparedness refers to the species-specific disposition to learn in certain ways and not others. An example is taste aversion; certain species (including humans) are able to learn that a food that makes them ill should be avoided. This learning can occur with only one experience, can last a long time, and can happen even though there is a long delay between the taste and its unpleasant consequences.

200. Discuss the effects of behaviorism on parenting practices and describe how this view differs from current theories of effective parenting. (LG: 6)

Answer Guidelines: Behaviorists stressed the importance of punishing unacceptable behavior and reinforcing desired behavior. They advocated practices like never letting the child suck its thumb, and never picking up a crying child because the behavior would be reinforced. Child rearing was supposed to be a highly controlled and structured conditioning environment.

Current theories stress the importance of parental love and responsiveness to needs, setting limits and making authoritative decisions in areas where the child is not capable of reasonable judgments. They also discourage punishment as a discipline since it teaches what not to do, but doesn't provide examples of what the child should do.

Chapter 8: Memory

Learning Goals

1. Identify three domains of memory.
2. Explain how memories are encoded.
3. Discuss how memories are stored.
4. Summarize how memories are retrieved.
5. Describe how encoding and retrieval failure are involved in forgetting.
6. Evaluate study strategies based on an understanding of memory.

Multiple-Choice Items

Learning Goal 1: Identify three domains of memory.

1. A researcher who is interested in the retention of information over time would most likely study which of the following?
   a. operants
   b. classical conditioning
   c. memory
   d. the S-O-R model
   Ans.: c   LG: 1   Page: 306   QT: C

2. Which of the following is the correct definition of memory?
   a. the retention of information over time
   b. the retention of time through conditioning
   c. the conditioning of thoughts via observation
   d. the neural processing of subconscious material
   Ans.: a   LG: 1   Page: 306   QT: F

3. Which of the following is *not* a domain of memory?
   a. encoding
   b. recoding
   c. retrieval
   d. storage
   Ans.: b   LG: 1   Page: 307   QT: C

4. Encoding, storage and retrieval are domains of
   a. learning
   b. emotional
   c. information processing
   d. memory
   Ans.: d   LG: 1   Page: 307   QT: C

5. In the study of memory, encoding refers to
   a. getting information into memory.
   b. retaining information over time.
   c. taking information out of storage.
   d. removing information from memory.
   Ans.: a   LG: 1   Page: 307   QT: F

6. In the study of memory, storage refers to
   a. getting information into memory.
   b. retaining information over time.
   c. taking information out of storage.
   d. removing information from memory.
   Ans.: b   LG: 1   Page: 307   QT: F

7. When you are trying to commit some new information to memory, you would first do which of the following?
   a. retrieve the information
   b. store the information
   c. save the information
   d. encode the information
   Ans.: d   LG: 1   Page: 307   QT: C

8. You and your friend are at a party. In order to introduce your friend to a person you have met recently, you must
   a. encode that person's name.
   b. retrieve that person's name.
   c. store that person's name.
   d. recode that person's name.
   Ans.: b   LG: 1   Page: 307   QT: C

Learning Goal 2: Explain how memories are encoded.

9. The process of attending to several things simultaneously is known as
   a. selective attention.
   b. multiple attention.
   c. divided attention.
   d. semantic attention.
   Ans.: c   LG: 2   Page: 308   QT: F

10. Divided attention refers to
    a. the process of focusing on a specific aspect of experience while ignoring others.
    b. the process of attending to several things simultaneously.
    c. the process of temporarily holding information as we perform tasks.
    d. the process of consciously recalling information.
    Ans.: b   LG: 2   Page: 308   QT: F

11. Which of the following is *not* a feature of the levels of processing theory?
    a. intermediate processing
    b. deep processing
    c. shallow processing
    d. explicit processing
    Ans.: d   LG: 2   Page: 309   QT: C

12. Which of the following encoding strategies results in the best memory?
    a. intermediate processing
    b. deep processing
    c. shallow processing
    d. explicit processing
    Ans.: b   LG: 2   Page: 309   QT: C

13. While studying for a test, you process the information in terms of its meaning, and you associate the new information with information that you have learned in other classes. This is an example of which level of processing?
    a. intermediate processing
    b. deep processing
    c. shallow processing
    d. explicit processing
    Ans.: b   LG: 2   Page: 309   QT: C

14. What is the main difference between shallow processing and deep processing?
    a. Deep processing involves imparting meaning.
    b. Shallow processing is more active.
    c. Shallow processing is less automatic.
    d. Deep processing requires less effort.
    Ans.: a   LG: 2   Page: 309   QT: C

15. You are studying the term *encoding*. In order to elaborate on this term, you would do which of the following?
    a. Repeat the term at least ten times in a row.
    b. Think of examples of encoding strategies.
    c. Memorize the definition of the term.
    d. Create a mental picture of the word.
    Ans.: b   LG: 2   Page: 309   QT: C

16. Elaboration improves memory because it
    a. provides practice through repetition.
    b. imparts order to the information to be remembered.
    c. groups individual pieces of information into larger units.
    d. creates more distinctive memory codes.
    Ans.: d   LG: 2   Page: 310   QT: C

17. For many of the concepts covered in this course, your textbook provides flow-charts or pictures. The students who will benefit most from these illustrations probably encode which characteristics of the illustrations?
    a. self-referent
    b. physical
    c. acoustic
    d. semantic
    Ans.: a   LG: 2   Page: 310   QT: C

18. You are studying cell division in biology. If you wanted to use imagery to help you remember this process, you would do which of the following?
    a. Form a mental picture of dividing cells.
    b. List the purposes of cell division.
    c. Memorize the definition of the term.
    d. Organize the information alphabetically.
    Ans.: a   LG: 2   Page: 310   QT: C

19. According to the dual-code hypothesis of memory, memory for images is
    a. better than memory for words.
    b. worse then memory for words.
    c. the same as memory for words.
    d. unrelated to memory for words.
    Ans.: a   LG: 2   Page: 311   QT: C

Learning Goal 3: Discuss how memories are stored.

20. Which of the following is *not* a memory stage included in the Atkinson-Shiffrin theory of memory?
    a. long-term memory
    b. short-term memory
    c. pseudo memory
    d. sensory memory
    Ans.: c   LG: 3   Page: 312   QT: C

21. Virtually all of the information being taken in by our senses appears to be held for a moment in a type of memory known as
    a. cognitive memory.
    b. sensory memory.
    c. neural storage.
    d. receptor memory.
    Ans.: b   LG: 3   Page: 312   QT: C

22. According to your text, the most temporary stage of memory is
    a. semantic memory.
    b. working memory.
    c. sensory memory.
    d. virtual memory.
    Ans.: c   LG: 3   Page: 312   QT: C

23. Which of the following statements about sensory memory is incorrect?
    a. Information does not stay in sensory memory for very long.
    b. Sensory memory processes more information than we may realize.
    c. Sensory memory retains information from our senses.
    d. Information in sensory memory is resistant to decay.
    Ans.: d   LG: 3   Page: 312   QT: C

24. You are reading a book and your friend Rachel asks you a question. By the time you say, "Sorry, what did you say?" you "hear" her question in your head. This is due to
    a. echoic memory.
    b. long-term sensory memory.
    c. working memory.
    d. iconic memory.
    Ans.: a   LG: 3   Page: 312   QT: C

25. Which stimulus is most likely to activate your iconic memory?
    a. a song on the radio
    b. a billboard along the highway
    c. your teacher's lecture
    d. a salesclerk's question
    Ans.: b   LG: 3   Page: 312   QT: C

26. Name That Tune" was a television game show in which people would listen to several musical notes and then try to identify a song more quickly than their rivals. The form of sensory memory in which the musical notes are first held is
    a. working memory.
    b. iconic memory.
    c. echoic memory.
    d. LTM.
    Ans.: c   LG: 3   Page: 312   QT: C

27. Echoic memory is formed from
    a. visual stimuli.
    b. tactile stimuli.
    c. olfactory stimuli.
    d. auditory stimuli.
    Ans.: d   LG: 3   Page: 312   QT: C

28. Iconic memory is retained for
    a. a lifetime.
    b. 30 seconds.
    c. 1 second.
    d. ¼ of a second.
    Ans.: d   LG: 3   Page: 312   QT: C

29. Iconic memory and echoic memory can be contrasted in all of the following ways except which one?
    a. They belong to different memory stages.
    b. They have different duration.
    c. They retain different types of information.
    d. They are formed from different stimuli.
    Ans.: a   LG: 3   Page: 312   QT: C

30. Echoic memory is retained for
    a. ¼ of a second.
    b. several seconds.
    c. long-term use.
    d. a lifetime.
    Ans.: b   LG: 3   Page: 312   QT: C

31. In comparing echoic and iconic memory, which lasts longer?
    a. echoic memory
    b. iconic memory
    c. both last about 1 second
    d. both last less than ½ second
    Ans.: a   LG: 3   Page: 312   QT: C

32. Which is another term commonly used for short-term memory?
    a. retroactive memory
    b. cognitive memory
    c. virtual memory
    d. working memory
    Ans.: d   LG: 3   Page: 314   QT: C

33. Suppose that you call the telephone operator to get a friend's phone number. When you dial your friend's number, you get a busy signal. A few moments later, when you start to dial the number again, you realize that you have forgotten it. This experience probably occurred because the phone number was only temporarily stored in your
    a. working memory.
    b. long-term memory.
    c. semantic memory.
    d. declarative memory.
    Ans.: a   LG: 3   Page: 314   QT: C

34. Air traffic controllers must monitor several airplanes taking off and landing by observing their location on a radar screen. What would be a safe number of airplanes for the typical controller to track in working memory?
    a. no more than five
    b. about seven
    c. at least 10
    d. as many as 20
    Ans.: b   LG: 3   Page: 313   QT: C

35. Without rehearsal, information remains in working memory for about
    a. ¼ second.
    b. 10 seconds.
    c. 30 seconds.
    d. 1 minute.
    Ans.: c   LG: 3   Page: 313   QT: C

36. When making a phone call, you must consciously think about the number being dialed. During this time, the number is being held in
    a. sensory memory.
    b. working memory.
    c. long-term memory.
    d. iconic memory.
    Ans.: b   LG: 3   Page: 313   QT: C

37. You have just looked up a phone number in a phone book. Which of the following strategies would be the most effective for remembering this phone number longer than 30 seconds?
    a. transferring the phone number to short-term memory
    b. processing the phone number in sensory memory
    c. thinking of as many phone numbers as possible
    d. rehearsing the phone number
    Ans.: d   LG: 3   Page: 313   QT: C

38. Which of the following statements is true concerning working memory?
    a. The capacity of working memory is essentially the same as that of long-term memory.
    b. Working memory is rarely able to hold more than 5-9 units of information.
    c. Information remains in working memory for extended periods of time.
    d. The capacity of working memory is infinite.
    Ans.: b   LG: 3   Page: 313   QT: C

39. What is the main advantage of chunking?
    a. It encourages repetition of the information.
    b. It helps us manage large amounts of information.
    c. It provides mental pictures of the information.
    d. It uses associations with familiar concepts.
    Ans.: b   LG: 3   Page: 313   QT: C

40. What would be the best way to chunk the letters CATPUPPYBIRD?
    a. CA TPU P PYB IRD
    b. CAT PUPPY BIRD
    c. ABCDIPPPRTUY
    d. YUTRPPPIDCBA
    Ans.: b   LG: 3   Page: 313   QT: C

41. What is the relationship between chunking and elaboration?
    a. Elaboration usually involves chunking.
    b. Chunking is basically the same as elaboration.
    c. Elaboration is a less complex form of chunking.
    d. Chunking is a form of elaboration.
    Ans.: d   LG: 3   Page: 313   QT: C

42. Rehearsal refers to
    a. conscious repetition of information.
    b. transfer of memory into long-term storage.
    c. the conscious recollection of information.
    d. retrieval of information from storage.
    Ans.: a   LG: 3   Page: 313   QT: C

43. Contemporary memory experts criticize the Atkinson-Shiffrin theory of memory primarily on which count?
    a. its sequence
    b. its simplicity
    c. its time frames
    d. its components
    Ans.: b   LG: 3   Page: 314   QT: C

44. How does Baddeley's view of working memory compare to that of Atkinson and Shiffrin?
    a. Baddeley views working memory as more complex than do Atkinson and Shiffrin.
    b. Baddeley believes that working memory's capacity is larger than 9 items.
    c. Baddeley views working memory as essentially the same as long-term memory.
    d. Baddeley believes that working memory has a greater duration than 30 seconds.
    Ans.: a   LG: 3   Page: 314   QT: C

45. According to Baddeley, working memory consists of which three components?
    a. iconic memory, main executive, and echoic memory
    b. semantic memory, procedural memory, and executive director
    c. declarative memory, visual memory, and general manager
    d. central executive, visuospatial scratch pad, and phonological loop
    Ans.: d   LG: 3   Page: 314   QT: C

46. According to Baddeley's theory, patients with brain damage who have normal long-term memories but have a working memory span of only two digits most likely have damage to the
    a. phonological loop.
    b. visuospatial working memory.
    c. central executive.
    d. scratch pad.
    Ans.: a   LG: 3   Page: 315   QT: C

47. In Alan Baddeley's theory of working memory, the component that is specialized to briefly store speech-based information is the
    a. phonological loop.
    b. visuospatial working memory.
    c. central executive.
    d. scratch pad.
    Ans.: a   LG: 3   Page: 315   QT: F

48. In Alan Baddeley's theory of working memory, the component that is specialized to integrate information is the
   a. phonological loop
   b. visuospatial working memory
   c. central executive
   d. scratch pad
   Ans.: c   LG: 3   Page: 315   QT: F

49. A recent study of the influence of emotion on working memory demonstrated that college students who wrote about a negative emotional event showed
   a. increases in working memory compared to a control group and a group that wrote about a positive event.
   b. decreases in working memory compared to a group that wrote about a positive event.
   c. decreases in working memory compared a group that wrote about a positive event, but increases in working memory compared a control group.
   d. increases in working memory compared to a control group, but decreases compared to a group that wrote about a positive event.
   Ans.: a   LG: 3   Page: 315   QT: C

50. How long does information remain in long-term memory?
   a. forever
   b. only as long as we see it
   c. a few minutes
   d. 30 seconds
   Ans.: a   LG: 3   Page: 315   QT: C

51. Long-term memory is divided into which two subtypes?
   a. episodic and semantic memory
   b. echoic and iconic memory
   c. procedural and semantic memory
   d. declarative and nondeclarative memory
   Ans.: d   LG: 3   Page: 316   QT: C

52. Declarative memory is to explicit memory as nondeclarative memory is to
   a. implicit memory.
   b. semantic memory.
   c. procedural memory.
   d. episodic memory.
   Ans.: a   LG: 3   Page: 316   QT: C

53. Declarative memory is subdivided into
   a. procedural and virtual memory.
   b. episodic and semantic memory.
   c. echoic and iconic memory.
   d. automatic and deliberate memory.
   Ans.: b   LG: 3   Page: 316   QT: C

54. Raymond remembers, "When I was a sophomore, I took the hardest physics test of my life, and I was happy with my C." This memory represents a(n)
    a. implicit memory.
    b. procedural memory.
    c. explicit memory.
    d. prime memory.
    Ans.: c   LG: 3   Page: 316   QT: C

55. Remembering your last birthday is an example of a(n)
    a. semantic memory.
    b. episodic memory.
    c. procedural memory.
    d. iconic memory.
    Ans.: b   LG: 3   Page: 316   QT: C

56. If I describe an event in detail, including descriptions of the setting, objects, colors, smells, and sounds, I am probably using which kind of long-term memory?
    a. kinetic
    b. semantic
    c. episodic
    d. descriptive
    Ans.: c   LG: 3   Page: 316   QT: C

57. Remembering the three stages of memory is an example of
    a. procedural memory.
    b. nondeclarative memory.
    c. semantic memory.
    d. episodic memory.
    Ans.: c   LG: 3   Page: 316   QT: C

58. Which of the following is a common criticism of the episodic/semantic distinction in memory?
    a. many cases of implicit memory are both episodic or semantic
    b. many cases of declarative memory are both episodic and semantic
    c. many cases of procedural memory are both episodic and semantic
    d. many cases of priming are both episodic and semantic
    Ans.: b   LG: 3   Page: 317   QT: C

59. Prospective memory refers to
    a. remembering information about the past.
    b. remembering information about the world.
    c. the conscious recollection of specific facts.
    d. remembering information about doing something in the future.
    Ans.: d   LG: 3   Page: 318   QT: F

60. Research on prospective memory focuses on all of the following *except*
    a. timing.
    b. content.
    c. future events.
    d. memory of the past.
    Ans.: d   LG: 3   Page: 318   QT: C

61. "Absentmindedness" is another term for failures of
    a. procedural memory.
    b. prospective memory.
    c. priming.
    d. classical conditioning.
    Ans.: b   LG: 3   Page: 318   QT: C

62. Remembering how to ride a bicycle is an example of
    a. explicit memory.
    b. semantic memory.
    c. priming.
    d. implicit memory.
    Ans.: d   LG: 3   Page: 318   QT: C

63. Which of the following is the best example of a procedural memory?
    a. touch typing a term paper
    b. explaining to your mother what you're going to do after graduation
    c. remembering what you had for dinner last night
    d. after a bad experience involving too much tequila, feeling sick at the smell of a margarita
    Ans.: a   LG: 3   Page: 318   QT: C

64. Priming refers to
    a. personal knowledge about the world.
    b. activation of information already in storage to help remember new information better.
    c. retention of information about the past.
    d. remembering information about the future.
    Ans.: b   LG: 3   Page: 319   QT: F

65. A memory system in which items are organized from general to specific classes is known as a
    a. hierarchy.
    b. schema.
    c. connectionist.
    d. script.
    Ans.: a   LG: 3   Page: 320   QT: C

66. The memory theory that suggests memories are organized into nodes that stand for labels or concepts is known as the
    a. semantic network model.
    b. connectionist network model.
    c. schema network model.
    d. script network model.
    Ans.: a   LG: 3   Page: 320   QT: F

67. Early hierarchical network theories of memory were primarily criticized for
    a. underestimating the complexity of human memory.
    b. being too abstract.
    c. including too many hierarchical levels.
    d. focusing exclusively on semantic memory.
    Ans.: a   LG: 3   Page: 320   QT: C

68. A preexisting mental concept or framework that helps people organize and interpret information is known as a
    a. schema.
    b. hierarchy.
    c. semantic.
    d. node.
    Ans.: a   LG: 3   Page: 321   QT: F

69. Schemas are
    a. limited-capacity memory systems that holds information for less than 30 seconds.
    b. preexisting mental concepts or frameworks that help people organize and interpret information.
    c. memories in which behavior is affected by prior experience without conscious recollection.
    d. tendencies to remember information at the beginning of a list.
    Ans.: b   LG: 3   Page: 321   QT: F

70. Bartlett's studies of how people remember stories led to the development of which theory of memory?
    a. semantic network
    b. levels of processing
    c. parallel distributed processing
    d. schema
    Ans.: d   LG: 3   Page: 322   QT: C

71. When discussing memory, scripts refer to
    a. limited-capacity memory systems that holds information for less than 30 seconds.
    b. preexisting mental concepts about events that help people organize and interpret information.
    c. memories in which behavior is affected by prior experience without conscious recollection.
    d. tendencies to remember information at the beginning of a list.
    Ans.: b   LG: 3   Page: 322   QT: F

72. Schemas about events are also known as
    a. primes.
    b. storage.
    c. scripts.
    d. episodic memories.
    Ans.: c   LG: 3   Page: 322   QT: F

73. Which theory suggests that memory is stored throughout the brain in connections between neurons?
    a. semantic network
    b. connectionism
    c. schema
    d. behavioral
    Ans.: b   LG: 3   Page: 323   QT: F

74. Which theory suggests that memory is stored throughout the brain in connections between neurons?
    a. semantic network
    b. parallel distributed processing
    c. schema
    d. hierarchy
    Ans.: b   LG: 3   Page: 323   QT: F

75. In connectionist theories of memory, memories are
    a. abstract concepts.
    b. large knowledge structures.
    c. small units of interrelated neurons.
    d. phonological loops.
    Ans.: c   LG: 3   Page: 323   QT: F

76. The concept of nodes is a key feature of which network theory of memory?
    a. semantic network
    b. connectionism
    c. schema
    d. behavioral
    Ans.: b   LG: 3   Page: 323   QT: C

77. After many experiments with rats, Lashley and other researchers have come to the conclusion that
    a. memories are not stored in a specific location in the brain.
    b. memories for maze pathways can never be established in rats.
    c. memories are bundled in specific neuron circuits of the brain.
    d. working memory is the same as procedural memory.
    Ans.: a   LG: 3   Page: 324   QT: C

78. Why did Kandel and Schwartz use the sea slug in their memory research?
    a. Its brain makes the same decisions humans do.
    b. Its brain has only 10,000 neurons.
    c. Its neurons are smaller than human neurons.
    d. Its brain is very similar to the human brain.
    Ans.: b   LG: 3   Page: 324   QT: C

79. Experiments with sea slugs led to the speculation that memories are related to activity of
    a. the hippocampus.
    b. the amygdala.
    c. brain chemicals.
    d. the cell nucleus.
    Ans.: c   LG: 3   Page: 324   QT: C

80. Long-term potentiation refers to the concept that
    a. if two neurons are activated at the same time, the connection between them may be strengthened.
    b. memory is affected by prior experience that is not consciously recalled.
    c. information that is already in storage can be activated to help remember new information.
    d. information processed at deeper levels is remembered longer.
    Ans.: a   LG: 3   Page: 324   QT: F

81. The concept that when two neurons are activated at the same time, the connections between them are strengthened is known as
    a. priming.
    b. interference.
    c. decay.
    d. long-term potentiation.
    Ans.: d   LG: 3   Page: 324   QT: F

82. According to research findings, which brain structures are involved in explicit memory?
    a. hippocampus and frontal lobes
    b. hippocampus and temporal lobes
    c. amygdala and cerebellum
    d. cerebellum and thalamus
    Ans.: a   LG: 3   Page: 325   QT: C

83. Studies using MRI scans during cognitive tasks have supported the role of which of the following structures in memory for scenic photographs?
    a. cerebellum and amygdala
    b. temporal lobes and limbic system
    c. hippocampus and prefrontal lobes
    d. hypothalamus and frontal lobes
    Ans.: c   LG: 3   Page: 325   QT: C

Learning Goal 4: Summarize how memories are retrieved.

84. Which of the following is *not* an example of reconstructive memory?
    a. recall of stories
    b. remembering the past
    c. giving eyewitness testimony
    d. planning a party
    Ans.: d   LG: 4   Page: 326   QT: C

85. Your brother gives you a list of items he wants you to pick up at the grocery store on your way home from work. You glanced over the list during your lunch hour but inadvertently left the list on your desk when you left work. When you get to the grocery store, which items on the list are you most likely to remember?
    a. the items at the beginning of the list
    b. the items at the end of the list
    c. the items in the middle of the list
    d. the items at the beginning and end of the list
    Ans.: d   LG: 4   Page: 327   QT: C

86. The manager at a fast-food restaurant loves to call out orders as fast as she can speak. When she does this, the food preparation crew is most likely to make mistakes preparing food for people whose orders were spoken
    a. at the beginning of the list.
    b. in the middle of the list.
    c. at the end of the list.
    d. after the workers were already anxious.
    Ans.: b   LG: 4   Page: 327   QT: C

87. You are studying for a test. At the end of one hour, you are getting ready to review the information you have just studied. According to the findings regarding the serial position effect, you should focus your review mostly on which material?
    a. the material studied at the beginning of the hour
    b. the material coming up for the next study session
    c. the material studied in the middle of the hour
    d. the material studied at the end of the hour
    Ans.: c   LG: 4   Page: 327   QT: C

88. Mr. Garcia teaches a 2-hour history class. Since there is a lot of information to cover, Mr. Garcia always lectures at a steady pace for the entire 2 hours. His students complain that they can't keep up with all the information he is presenting. Mr. Garcia wonders, "How can I help my students better cope with the information I present in class?" Given your knowledge about the serial position effect, what advice would you give Mr. Garcia?
    a. He should give the students a quiz at the end of each class.
    b. He should allow students to drink coffee during the class.
    c. He should emphasize key concepts and names during his lecture.
    d. He should give his students a 10-minute break after the first 55 minutes of lecture.
    Ans.: d   LG: 4   Page: 327   QT: C

89. At the beginning of class, Sean's anatomy teacher required the students to memorize the twelve cranial nerves. When Sean tried to recall them at the end of class, what was the most likely result?
    a. He could remember the first few, but had trouble with the rest.
    b. He remembered the last few easily, but had trouble with the rest.
    c. He remembered the ones in the middle best.
    d. He remembered the first few and the last few better than the ones in the middle.
    Ans.: d   LG: 4   Page: 327   QT: C

90. When you remember the names of people you met at the end of a party better than the names of the first few people you met when you arrived, you are experiencing
    a. retroactive interference.
    b. the primacy effect.
    c. the recency effect.
    d. consolidation.
    Ans.: c   LG: 4   Page: 327   QT: C

91. The primacy effect appears to be due to
    a. novelty of information.
    b. longer rehearsal time.
    c. distinctiveness of information.
    d. strong iconic memories.
    Ans.: b   LG: 4   Page: 327   QT: C

92. The view that associations formed at the time of learning serve as effective retrieval cues is known as the
    a. encoding specificity principle.
    b. levels of processing theory.
    c. matching hypothesis.
    d. conditioning theory.
    Ans.: a   LG: 4   Page: 328   QT: F

93. According to the encoding specificity principle, which are the best retrieval cues?
    a. those formed after learning has occurred
    b. those formed prior to learning
    c. those formed at the time of learning
    d. those formed a long time ago
    Ans.: c   LG: 4   Page: 328   QT: C

94. You are studying a new chapter in your psychology text. According to the encoding specificity principle, you should do which of the following in order to maximize your later recall of the information?
    a. Repeat the new information over and over again.
    b. Form associations between the new material and already familiar concepts while studying.
    c. Copy all of the new information from the text into a notebook.
    d. Study primarily the first and the last section of the chapter in the textbook.
    Ans.: b   LG: 4   Page: 328   QT: C

95. When forming associations during the encoding of new material, you are performing a cognitive activity most closely related to
    a. organizing.
    b. memorizing.
    c. rehearsal.
    d. elaboration.
    Ans.: d   LG: 4   Page: 328   QT: C

96. A psychology professor meets one of her new students at the grocery store. As she is trying to recall the student's name, she thinks to herself, "This student sits on the right-hand side of the front row in my 8:00 a.m. General Psychology class. On the first day of class she shared that her hobby is horseback riding." These specific retrieval cues then enable the professor to recall the student's name. This situation best illustrates which of the following?
    a. encoding specificity
    b. retroactive recall
    c. serial position effect
    d. proactive recall
    Ans.: a   LG: 4   Page: 328   QT: C

97. Which type of test requires mostly recall?
    a. matching
    b. true/false test
    c. multiple-choice
    d. essay
    Ans.: d   LG: 4   Page: 328   QT: C

98. An essay examination is to recall as a multiple-choice test is to
    a. recognition.
    b. reconstruction.
    c. reorganization.
    d. restructuring.
    Ans.: a   LG: 4   Page: 328   QT: C

99. A recall test requires a person to do which of the following?
    a. recognize information
    b. retrieve information
    c. identify information
    d. encode information
    Ans.: b   LG: 4   Page: 328   QT: C

100. If Alicia is working on a multiple-choice test in General Psychology, what kind of memory is she using?
    a. recall
    b. procedural
    c. recognition
    d. episodic
    Ans.: c   LG: 4   Page: 328   QT: C

101. Brian has to write two essays for his Western Civilization exam. What type of memory will he be using?
    a. recognition
    b. procedural
    c. recall
    d. identification
    Ans.: c   LG: 4   Page: 328   QT: C

102. Many students experience more difficulty with essay tests than with multiple-choice tests because essay tests
    a. take longer to complete.
    b. do not provide very good retrieval cues.
    c. are usually unannounced.
    d. require too much identification.
    Ans.: b   LG: 4   Page: 328   QT: C

103. Based on what you have learned about the difference between recall and recognition, what would be your best strategy for studying for an essay exam?
    a. Focus on the main concepts, the connections among those ideas, and the "big" picture.
    b. Focus on remembering the verbatim definitions of all the key words.
    c. Focus on the details and the bold-faced words in the textbook.
    d. Focus on the names and the facts that are associated with the key concepts.
    Ans.: a   LG: 4   Page: 328   QT: C

104. Which pair of terms most accurately describes the types of retrieval cues associated with recall tests versus recognition tests?
    a. poor; poor
    b. good; poor
    c. poor; good
    d. good; good
    Ans.: c   LG: 4   Page: 328   QT: C

105. Unintentional acts of plagiarism have been linked to which cognitive process?
   a. amnesia
   b. priming
   c. elaboration
   d. semantic memory
   Ans.: b   LG: 4   Page: 329   QT: C

106. Vera is taking a psychology test. She is supposed to write an essay discussing the two types of declarative memory. She is frustrated because she is sure she knows the information, and she can even picture the diagram in her text, but no matter how much she tries, she cannot retrieve the name for the second type of declarative memory. Vera is most likely experiencing
   a. proactive interference.
   b. retroactive interference.
   c. habituation.
   d. the tip-of-the-tongue phenomenon.
   Ans.: d   LG: 4   Page: 329   QT: C

107. Research on the "tip-of-the-tongue" phenomenon indicates that when people cannot remember something, it is often because
   a. proactive interference prevents the memory.
   b. the memory has been distorted.
   c. the memory trace has faded.
   d. they merely have trouble retrieving the memory.
   Ans.: d   LG: 4   Page: 329   QT: C

108. All of your studying for your test was done in a loud, smoky bar filled with people. According to the theory of context-dependent memory, in which of the following places would your performance on the test be best?
   a. a quiet room by yourself
   b. a quiet examination room filled with other students
   c. the same crowded, loud, smoky bar
   d. under water
   Ans.: c   LG: 4   Page: 329   QT: C

109. According to the idea of state-dependent memory, if you were upset and angry when you studied for a test, you would recall the information best if you took the test while you were
   a. in a calm, neutral mood.
   b. upset and angry.
   c. happy and relaxed.
   d. anxious and depressed.
   Ans.: b   LG: 4   Page: 330   QT: C

110. If you wanted to form happy memories about your vacation, you should try to do which of the following?
   a. maintain a good mood during the vacation
   b. worry about spending too much money
   c. dread the end of the vacation
   d. anticipate a lot of stress at work upon your return
   Ans.: a   LG: 4   Page: 330   QT: A

111. Which of the following is *not* a level of autobiographical memory?
    a. life time periods
    b. general events
    c. event-specific knowledge
    d. priming
    Ans.: d   LG: 4   Page: 330   QT: C

112. Eric remembers very vividly where he was, who was with him, and how he felt when he found out that his father had suffered a heart attack. This type of memory is known as a
    a. repressed memory.
    b. reconstructed memory.
    c. state dependent memory.
    d. flashbulb memory.
    Ans.: d   LG: 4   Page: 331   QT: C

113. Rubin and Kozin's study on flashbulb memories showed all of the following *except* which one?
    a. Flashbulb memories tend to involve significant events.
    b. Flashbulb memories tend to involve highly accurate memories.
    c. Flashbulb memories tend to involve personal events.
    d. Flashbulb memories tend to involve emotional events.
    Ans.: b   LG: 4   Page: 331   QT: C

114. An individual would most likely repress which of the following memories?
    a. the night of her high school graduation
    b. a traumatic car accident that resulted in the death of a parent
    c. a blind date with a person who turned out to be very nice
    d. the breakup of a friendship after a serious argument
    Ans.: b   LG: 4   Page: 332   QT: C

115. Which of the following is *not* true of repressed memories?
    a. They may emerge in consciousness at a later point.
    b. They tend to involve traumatic events.
    c. They normally are difficult to remember consciously.
    d. They remain in the unconscious forever.
    Ans.: d   LG: 4   Page: 332   QT: C

116. What do repressed memories and state-dependent memories have in common?
    a. Both are usually distorted.
    b. Both are usually negative.
    c. Both are related to emotions.
    d. Both are in the unconscious.
    Ans.: c   LG: 4   Page: 330/332 QT: C

117. Research on eyewitness testimony has demonstrated that
    a. people of one ethnic group are more likely to recognize individual differences among people of another ethnic group.
    b. the accuracy of eyewitness testimony increases as the amount of time after the event increases.
    c. new information can be incorporated into existing memories.
    d. eyewitness memories are accurate representations of what actually occurs.
    Ans.: c   LG: 4   Page: 334   QT: C

Learning Goal 5: Describe how encoding and retrieval failure are involved in forgetting.

118. Encoding failure refers to
    a. information that was never entered into long-term memory.
    b. when material that was learned earlier disrupts the recall of material learned later.
    c. when material learned later disrupts the recall of material learned earlier.
    d. a memory disorder that affects the retention of new information or events.
    Ans.: a   LG: 5   Page: 336   QT: F

119. Forgetting your old telephone number just a few weeks after you get a new number is an example of
    a. engram decay.
    b. proactive interference.
    c. retroactive interference.
    d. retroactive decay.
    Ans.: c   LG: 5   Page: 337   QT: C

120. Justin's new telephone number is 663-7589. He frequently tells people that it is 633-7589. He is puzzled as to why he keeps doing that until he realizes that the first three digits of his social security number are 633. Justin realizes that his problem is caused by
    a. decay.
    b. interference.
    c. reconstruction.
    d. serial positioning.
    Ans.: b   LG: 5   Page: 337   QT: C

121. Suppose that you train a rat to run through Maze A. After the rat has learned this maze, you train it to run through Maze B. You find that the rat has more trouble remembering the way through Maze B than it did in Maze A. This situation best illustrates
    a. retroactive facilitation.
    b. retroactive interference.
    c. proactive facilitation.
    d. proactive interference.
    Ans.: d   LG: 5   Page: 337   QT: C

122. You studied French last semester. This semester, you are studying Spanish. When your Spanish teacher asks a question, you often find yourself answering in French. Your problem reflects
    a. retroactive interference.
    b. decay.
    c. proactive interference.
    d. retrograde amnesia.
    Ans.: c   LG: 5   Page: 337   QT: C

123. When something you learned today makes it harder to retrieve what you learned last week, you are experiencing
    a. proactive interference.
    b. cue-dependence.
    c. decay.
    d. retroactive interference.
    Ans.: d   LG: 5   Page: 337   QT: C

124. Which term refers to the phenomenon that old memories can work in a forward direction to interfere with new memories?
    a. retroactive trace decay
    b. temporal interference
    c. proactive interference
    d. retroactive interference
    Ans.: c   LG: 5   Page: 337   QT: F

125. You cram for several days for your final in psychology. When you begin to study for your final in sociology, you find that you keep recalling the psychology concepts you learned earlier but cannot remember the sociology material. This is an example of
    a. emotional fatigue.
    b. retroactive interference.
    c. proactive interference.
    d. long-term memory decay.
    Ans.: c   LG: 5   Page: 337   QT: C

126. Which theory suggests that forgetting is caused by a fading memory trace?
    a. reconstruction theory
    b. repression
    c. decay theory
    d. interference theory
    Ans.: c   LG: 5   Page: 337   QT: F

127. While Tom's five-speed sports car was in the shop for repairs, he borrowed a car with an automatic transmission. While driving the borrowed car, Tom kept trying to shift gears as he would have with his "stick shift." This situation illustrates
    a. proactive interference.
    b. retroactive interference.
    c. decay.
    d. positive transfer.
    Ans.: a   LG: 5   Page: 337   QT: C

128. Forgetting that occurs with the passage of time is also known as
    a. motivated forgetting.
    b. repressed memory.
    c. transience.
    d. amnesia.
    Ans.: c   LG: 5   Page: 338   QT: F

129. When people forget something because it is so painful or anxiety laden that remembering is intolerable, it is known as
    a. motivated forgetting.
    b. false memory.
    c. transience.
    d. amnesia.
    Ans.: a   LG: 5   Page: 338   QT: F

130. Repression is a form of
    a. motivated forgetting.
    b. false memory.
    c. transience.
    d. amnesia.
    Ans.: a   LG: 5   Page: 338   QT: C

131. A memory disorder in which the individual cannot recall information acquired before sustaining an injury to the brain is known as
    a. retrograde amnesia.
    b. anterograde amnesia.
    c. psychogenic amnesia.
    d. traumatic memory degeneration.
    Ans.: a   LG: 5   Page: 339   QT: F

132. Suppose a person was injected with a drug that destroyed old memories but did not interfere with the person's ability to learn new information. This drug produced
    a. anterograde amnesia.
    b. decay with the passage of time.
    c. retroactive amnesia.
    d. retrograde amnesia.
    Ans.: d   LG: 5   Page: 338   QT: C

133. An inability to store new information is called
    a. retrograde amnesia.
    b. Korsakoff's amnesia.
    c. anterograde amnesia.
    d. degenerative amnesia.
    Ans.: c   LG: 5   Page: 338   QT: F

134. In the famous case of H.M., the man who could not form new memories after a drastic surgical procedure to help his epilepsy, H.M. suffered from
    a. anterograde amnesia.
    b. retrograde amnesia.
    c. script loss.
    d. schema imbalance.
    Ans.: a   LG: 5   Page: 338   QT: C

135. Retrograde amnesia differs from anterograde amnesia in all of the following ways except which one?
    a. Retrograde amnesia is more common than anterograde amnesia.
    b. Retrograde amnesia involves forgetting of information acquired prior to the memory loss.
    c. Retrograde amnesia does not affect the ability to form new memories.
    d. Retrograde amnesia does not affect short-term memory.
    Ans.: d   LG: 5   Page: 339   QT: C

Learning Goal 6: Evaluate study strategies based on an understanding of memory.

136. Which of the following memory strategies would *not* be considered an encoding strategy?
    a. spreading out and consolidating your learning
    b. asking yourself questions
    c. paying attention and minimizing distractions
    d. understanding the material rather than rotely memorizing it
    Ans.: a   LG: 6   Page: 340   QT: C

137. Which of the following memory strategies would be considered an encoding strategy?
    a. using good retrieval cues
    b. keyword method
    c. organizing your memory
    d. taking good notes
    Ans.: d   LG: 6   Page: 340   QT: C

138. Wesley has 12 hours of class per week. In order to give himself the best chance at making good grades this semester, he should manage his time to study how many hours outside of class each week?
    a. 24-36
    b. 12-24
    c. 6-12
    d. 3-6
    Ans.: a   LG: 6   Page: 340   QT: C

139. Asking yourself questions about the material you are studying primarily helps you accomplish which the following?
    a. memorizing information
    b. inhibiting learning
    c. shallow processing
    d. forming associations
    Ans.: d   LG: 6   Page: 340   QT: C

140. Which main benefit will you derive from reviewing your class notes on a regular basis?
    a. organized learning
    b. forming associations
    c. minimizing distractions
    d. consolidated learning
    Ans.: d   LG: 6   Page: 341   QT: C

141. Which of the following is *not* a good note-taking strategy?
    a. outlining
    b. summarizing
    c. doodling
    d. the Cornell method
    Ans.: c   LG: 6   Page: 341   QT: C

142. If you had five items to buy at the grocery, and you associated each item with a geographical location between your house and the grocery, you would be using a popular mnemonic called
    a. the peg method.
    b. the one-is-a-bun system.
    c. the method of loci.
    d. systematic recall.
    Ans.: c   LG: 6   Page: 341   QT: C

143. Which of the following is an example of a mnemonic device?
    a. summarizing
    b. outlining
    c. keyword method
    d. concept maps
    Ans.: c   LG: 6   Page: 341   QT: C

144. Erin is taking a general psychology course. The first chapter in the textbook discusses the different approaches to psychology, such as psychoanalysis, behaviorism, etc. Which of the following study strategies is least likely to help Erin gain a true understanding of these different approaches?
    a. using elaboration
    b. asking herself questions
    c. giving the material meaning
    d. using mnemonic devices
    Ans.: d   LG: 6   Page: 341   QT: C

145. In your textbook, the phrase "Roy G. Biv" was presented as a technique for remembering the colors of the electromagnetic spectrum (red, orange, yellow, green, blue, indigo, and violet). This memory strategy is an example of
    a. a primacy aid.
    b. cultural specificity.
    c. a recency cue.
    d. a mnemonic device.
    Ans.: d   LG: 6   Page: 341   QT: C

146. According to the text, which of the following does *not* contribute to promoting effective memory storage?
    a. being well rested
    b. being well nourished
    c. being free of mind-altering substances
    d. being well satisfied
    Ans.: d   LG: 6   Page: 341   QT: C

147. The key word method and the method of loci are examples of
    a. mnemonic devices.
    b. schematic devices.
    c. amnesic techniques.
    d. hierarchical techniques.
    Ans.: a   LG: 6   Page: 341   QT: F

148. Your psychology final is in two weeks. Which of the following study strategies would you choose to give yourself the best chance at optimal preparation?
    a. cramming for the test on the two nights before the final
    b. studying intensively at the beginning and at the end of the two weeks
    c. cramming for the test in the middle of the two weeks before the exam
    d. studying regularly over the next two weeks and consolidating before the exam
    Ans.: d   LG: 6   Page: 342   QT: C

149. Which of the following memory strategies would be considered a storage strategy?
    a. asking yourself questions
    b. organizing your memory
    c. understanding material rather than rotely memorizing it
    d. using good retrieval cues
    Ans.: b   LG: 6   Page: 342   QT: C

150. The abbreviation PQ4R stands for which of the following?
    a. Preview, Question, Reflect, Read, Recite, and Review
    b. Preview, Question, Read, Reflect, Review, and Recite
    c. Preview, Question, Read, Reflect, Recite, and Review
    d. Preview, Question, Reflect, Read, Review, and Recite
    Ans.: c   LG: 6   Page: 343   QT: F

True/False Items

___ 151.   Researchers who study memory are only interested in examining the encoding of information.
___ 152.   Storage involves the encoding of information.
___ 153.   Information processed at the deep level produces the most enduring memory.
___ 154.   Sensory memory has a large capacity but a short duration.
___ 155.   Without rehearsal, information stays in short-term memory for less than 30 seconds.
___ 156.   Long-term memory is believed to be relatively permanent.
___ 157.   Another name for nondeclarative memory is explicit memory.
___ 158.   Memory researchers have largely abandoned the notion that memories are organized in a complex network of nodes.
___ 159.   Associations that are formed during encoding can serve as useful retrieval cues.
___ 160.   An essay test requires recognition memory.
___ 161.   Emotionally significant events can produce flashbulb memories.
___ 162.   The interference theory and decay theory are essentially the same.
___ 163.   The decay theory predicts that the passage of time always increases forgetting.
___ 164.   Anterograde amnesia is much more common than retrograde amnesia.
___ 165.   Cognitive monitoring is an aspect of effective encoding strategy.

Answer Key for True/False Items

151.	Ans.: F	LG: 1	Page: 307	159.	Ans.: T	LG: 4	Page: 328
152.	Ans.: F	LG: 1	Page: 307	160.	Ans.: F	LG: 4	Page: 328
153.	Ans.: T	LG: 2	Page: 309	161.	Ans.: T	LG: 4	Page: 331
154.	Ans.: T	LG: 3	Page: 312	162.	Ans.: F	LG: 5	Page: 337
155.	Ans.: T	LG: 3	Page: 313	163.	Ans.: T	LG: 5	Page: 337
156.	Ans.: T	LG: 3	Page: 315	164.	Ans.: F	LG: 5	Page: 338
157.	Ans.: F	LG: 3	Page: 318	165.	Ans.: T	LG: 6	Page: 340
158.	Ans.: F	LG: 3	Page: 323				

Fill-in-the-Blank Items

166. The retention of information over time is known as _____.
167. In order to retrieve information, you have to take it out of _____.
168. You are more likely to remember information when you process the information at a(n) _____ level.
169. The idea that memory for images is better than memory for words because memory for images is stored as both an image code and a verbal code is known as the _____ hypothesis.
170. According to Atkinson and Shiffrin, human memory can be divided into _____ memory, working memory, and long-term memory.
171. _____ memory can be subdivided into episodic and semantic memory.
172. "Absentmindedness" is another term for failures of _____ memory.
173. The theories of long-term memory which have paid the most attention to actual brain function are _____ theories.
174. Superior recall for items at the end of a list is known as the _____ effect.
175. The finding that people remember information better when their mood is similar at encoding and retrieval is known as _____ memory.
176. Although _____ memories sometimes involve nationally significant events, they are more often of a personal nature.
177 According to the _____ theory of forgetting, retrieval failure is due to the disintegration of memory traces over time.
178. _____ interference is essentially interference that works forward in time.
179. A person who cannot form any new memories after a brain trauma most likely is suffering from _____ amnesia.
180. While learning new terms, you associate vivid images with important terms. This activity is known as the _____ method.

Answer Key for Fill-in-the-Blank Items

166.	Ans.: memory	LG: 1	Page: 306
167.	Ans.: storage	LG: 1	Page: 307
168.	Ans.: deep	LG: 2	Page: 309
169.	Ans.: dual-code	LG: 2	Page: 311
170.	Ans.: sensory	LG: 3	Page: 312
171.	Ans.: Explicit	LG: 3	Page: 316
172.	Ans.: prospective	LG: 3	Page: 318
173.	Ans.: connectionist	LG: 3	Page: 323
174.	Ans.: recency	LG: 4	Page: 327
175.	Ans.: state-dependent	LG: 4	Page: 330
176.	Ans.: flashbulb	LG: 4	Page: 331
177.	Ans.: decay	LG: 5	Page: 337
178.	Ans.: Proactive	LG: 5	Page: 337
179.	Ans.: anterograde	LG: 5	Page: 338
180.	Ans.: keyword	LG: 6	Page: 341

Matching Items

___	181. shallow processing	A.	chunking
___	182. deep processing	B.	implicit memory
___	183. sensory memory	C.	physical and perceptual features
___	184. short-term memory	D.	script
___	185. long-term memory	E.	iconic memory
___	186. procedural memory	F.	recency
___	187. schema	G.	transience
___	188. serial position	H.	meaning and associations
___	189. decay theory	I.	mnemonics
___	190. encoding strategy	J.	explicit memory

Answer Key for Matching Items

181.	Ans.: C	LG: 2	Page: 309		186.	Ans.: B	LG: 3	Page: 318
182.	Ans.: H	LG: 2	Page: 309		187.	Ans.: D	LG: 3	Page: 322
183.	Ans.: E	LG: 3	Page: 312		188.	Ans.: F	LG: 4	Page: 327
184.	Ans.: A	LG: 3	Page: 313		189.	Ans.: G	LG: 5	Page: 337/338
185.	Ans.: J	LG: 3	Page: 316		190.	Ans.: I	LG: 6	Page: 341

Essay Questions

191. Briefly explain the memory processes of encoding, storage, and retrieval. (LG: 1)

Answer Guidelines: Possible options include mentioning that encoding involves placing information into memory. Rehearsal, deep encoding, elaboration, imagery, organization, and chunking are helpful encoding techniques. Storage involves retaining information in memory over time. Information is retained longer, the better it is encoded into long-term memory. Retrieval involves taking information out of memory storage, i.e., bringing information from long-term memory back into short-term memory. The tip-of-the-tongue phenomenon, the serial position effect, the lack of appropriate retrieval cues, the nature of the retrieval task, the nature of the information to be retrieved, and interference from other information can affect retrieval.

192. Describe the three levels of processing during encoding, and discuss the way elaboration can enhance memory. (LG: 2)

Answer Guidelines: Shallow processing refers to the level at which the sensory or physical features are analyzed, includes noticing the color of something, its shape, loudness, frequency.

Intermediate processing refers to recognizing and labeling information; a large round, orange object is called a basketball.

Deep processing refers to processing the information in terms of its meaning, and forming associations between the information and previously acquired information.

Elaboration is one strategy for ensuring deep processing; it involves increasing the distinctiveness of memory codes by including physical, acoustic, semantic and most importantly self-referent information. Increasing the uniqueness of the memory code makes it more likely to be retrieved from storage.

193. Distinguish between echoic and iconic sensory memories. How are these memories formed and how long do they last? (LG: 3)

Answer Guidelines: Possible options include mentioning that iconic memories are visual sensory images that last for about ¼ of a second. Echoic memories are the auditory sensory signals that last for several seconds.

194. Describe Alan Baddely's concept of working memory and discuss its three main components. (LG: 3)

Answer Guidelines: Working memory is a three-part system that temporarily holds information as people perform cognitive tasks; it is an active memory system.

The components are: (1) the phonological loop stores speech-based information about the sounds of language; contains two separate components, acoustic code which decays in a few seconds and rehearsal which allow individuals to repeat the words in phonological storage; limited capacity; (2) visuospatial working memory (or scratch pad) processes spatial and visual information; functions independently from the phonological loop; limited capacity; and (3) the central executive integrates information from phonological loop, visuospatial working memory, and long-term memory; plays an important role in planning, attention, and organizing; limited capacity.

195. Contrast working memory and long-term memory in terms of their duration and capacity. (LG: 3)

Answer Guidelines: Possible options include mentioning that working memory, or short-term memory, lasts for about 30 seconds without rehearsal; its capacity is 7 ± 2 items. Rehearsal can increase STM duration; chunking can increase STM capacity. Long-term memory can last forever and its capacity is infinite.

196. Distinguish between the recency and the primacy effect. Explain what these effects imply about the ideal study schedule. (LG: 4)

Answer Guidelines: Possible options include mentioning that recall tends to be superior for items at the beginning (primacy effect) and items at the end (recency effect) of a list, or sequence, of information. Recall for items from the middle of a list, or sequence, tends to be low. With regard to the ideal study schedule, these findings imply that frequent short study sessions, rather than long cramming sessions, will result in better recall of information. Numerous short study sessions provide multiple primacy and recency opportunities.

197. Recognition and recall are two different, yet related processes in retrieving memories. State what these two processes have in common and how they are different. Give an example of a recognition task; give an example of a recall task. (LG: 4)

Answer Guidelines: Possible options include mentioning that recall involves the retrieval of previously learned information; recognition involves the ability to identify the correct answer or solution from presented information. Although they represent different decision tasks, they are similar in that prior memories must be tapped into in order to make an accurate decision about a prior event.

198. Compare and contrast the interference theory of forgetting and the decay theory of forgetting. (LG: 5)

Answer Guidelines: Possible options include mentioning that the interference theory suggests that we forget because other information gets in the way of what we want to remember. Memory specialists have identified two types of interference. Proactive interference occurs when previously learned material interferes with, or disrupts, the recall of information that was learned later. Retroactive interference occurs when recently learned information interferes with, or disrupts, the recall of information that was learned previously. The decay theory suggests that forgetting, or retrieval failure, is due to the fading of memory traces over time.

199. Explain anterograde and retrograde amnesia in terms of proactive and retroactive interference. (LG: 5)

Answer Guidelines: Possible options include mentioning that proactive interference involves trying to remember new information, but previously learned information gets in the way. With anterograde amnesia, new information cannot be retained; all that can be remembered is the "old" information that was encoded before some sort of accident or injury caused the anterograde amnesia. Retroactive interference involves trying to remember "old" information, but new information gets in the way. In retrograde amnesia, "old" event memories, i.e., those that were encoded prior to the accident or injury that caused the retrograde amnesia, are lost; memories of new events can be formed without problems.

200. Your text discusses a number of memory and study strategies. List and describe at least three strategies mentioned in your text and give an example of how each method would be used. (LG: 6)

Answer Guidelines: Possible options include mentioning any three of the following: paying attention, understanding the material, using mnemonic devices, spreading out and consolidating learning, asking oneself questions, monitoring one's progress, managing one's time, and using PQ4R.

Chapter 9: Thinking and Language

Learning Goals

1. Characterize the "cognitive revolution" in psychology.
2. Explain concept formation.
3. Describe the requirements for solving problems.
4. Discuss the main factors in thinking critically, reasoning, and making decisions.
5. Identify the possible connections between language and thought.
6. Summarize how language is acquired and develops.

Multiple-Choice Items

Learning Goal 1: Characterize the "cognitive revolution" in psychology.

1. Which of the following is true about the development of the cognitive revolution?
   a. Cognitive psychology was the dominant force in American psychology during the first half of the twentieth century.
   b. The cognitive perspective explains all of human behavior.
   c. Cognitive psychology developed when researchers realized that to fully understand human behavior, they must learn more about mental processes.
   d. The cognitive perspective developed as a result of the need to combine the behaviorist and psychodynamic perspectives into one.
   Ans.: c   LG: 1   Page: 351   QT: F

2. Cognitive psychology seeks to explain behavior by
   a. observing behavior.
   b. investigating mental processes.
   c. investigating the unconscious.
   d. both a and b
   Ans.: d   LG: 1   Page: 351   QT: F

3. Which of the following would a cognitive psychologist be *least* interested in?
   a. problem solving
   b. language
   c. decision making
   d. reflexive responses
   Ans.: d   LG: 1   Page: 351   QT: C

4. Dwayne is watching a game show on television with friends. They watch in disbelief as a contestant makes a blatantly wrong decision on an easy question, which would have been worth ten million dollars. If Dwayne takes a cognitive perspective, which of the following statements would you attribute to him?
   a. "What a fool!"
   b. "What was he thinking?"
   c. "The poor guy."
   d. "He deserves to lose for giving an answer like that."
   Ans.: b   LG: 1   Page: 351   QT: A

5. Which of the following is not directly related to cognition?
   a. remembering
   b. knowing
   c. doing
   d. thinking
   Ans.: c   LG: 1   Page: 351   QT: F

6. Which of the following is *not* a similarity between the computer and the human brain?
   a. They both can think and develop goals.
   b. They both can convert information.
   c. They both perform processes that cannot be observed directly.
   d. They both can perform logical operations.
   Ans.: a   LG: 1   Page: 352   QT: C

7. When comparing the computer to the human brain, which statement is incorrect?
   a. Computers can represent complex mathematical patterns better than the human brain.
   b. Computers perform complex numerical calculations faster than the human brain.
   c. Computers apply rules more consistently than the human brain.
   d. Computers can develop more sophisticated learning goals than the human brain.
   Ans.: d   LG: 1   Page: 352   QT: C

8. According to the computer analogy, the computer's software is to cognition as the computer's hardware is to
   a. the senses.
   b. the brain.
   c. the neurons.
   d. the cerebellum.
   Ans.: b   LG: 1   Page: 351   QT: A

9. When compared to the computer, the human brain is superior in the ability to
   a. learn and generalize information.
   b. perform complex numerical calculations.
   c. apply rules consistently.
   d. represent complex mathematical patterns.
   Ans.: a   LG: 1   Page: 352   QT: C

10. Joanne is trying to develop a computer program that can evaluate and rank the potential of race horses. Joanne will then use this program to place recreational wagers on races. Joanne is working in which of the following areas?
    a. intelligence simulation
    b. artificial intelligence
    c. synthetic intelligence
    d. computer engineering
    Ans.: b   LG: 1   Page: 352   QT: A

11. Artificial intelligence systems tend to fall short in which of the following areas?
    a. speed
    b. generalization
    c. vast memory
    d. persistence
    Ans.: b   LG: 1   Page: 352   QT: F

12. Artificial intelligence systems have been used successfully in all of the following areas *except*
    a. examining equipment failures.
    b. diagnosing medical illness.
    c. evaluating loan applicants.
    d. resolving interpersonal conflicts.
    Ans.: d   LG: 1   Page: 352   QT: A

13. The main challenge for scientists in the field of artificial intelligence systems is to develop machines that can
    a. analyze huge amounts of data.
    b. make decisions based on facts.
    c. duplicate human thinking processes.
    d. keep track of vast amounts of information.
    Ans.: c   LG: 1   Page: 352   QT: C

14. Which of the following is the best definition for *thinking*?
    a. mental manipulation of information
    b. subconscious reactions to stimuli
    c. conditioned response to information
    d. reflexive reactions to stimuli
    Ans.: a   LG: 1   Page: 353   QT: F

15. Which of the following activities does *not* involve thinking?
    a. problem solving
    b. stomach contraction
    c. decision making
    d. concept formation
    Ans.: b   LG: 1   Page: 353   QT: C

16. Which of the following does *not* involve the mental manipulation of information?
    a. deciding between two activities
    b. learning a new skill
    c. making a decision
    d. constricting one's pupils
    Ans.: d   LG: 1   Page: 353   QT: C

Learning Goal 2: Explain concept formation.

17. Mental representations of categories of objects or events are called
    a. concepts.
    b. feelings.
    c. responses.
    d. sensations.
    Ans.: a   LG: 2   Page: 353   QT: F

18. Which of the following would be considered a concept?
    a. objects
    b. skills
    c. events
    d. all of the above
    Ans.: d   LG: 2   Page: 353   QT: A

19. Which of the following is not a function of concepts?
    a. generalization
    b. association
    c. enabling memory
    d. sensing
    Ans.: d   LG: 2   Page: 353   QT: F

20. Which of the following best describes the basic process of forming a concept?
    a. memorizing the differences of each object or idea in detail
    b. grouping objects or ideas on the basis of their common features
    c. rehearsing how one object or idea differs from the others
    d. reciting the unique features of each object or idea
    Ans.: b   LG: 2   Page: 353   QT: C

21. The ability to form concepts helps us with all of the following cognitive activities *except*
    a. generalizing experiences.
    b. relating experience and objects.
    c. feeling tired after a workout.
    d. remembering associations.
    Ans.: c   LG: 2   Page: 353   QT: A

22. Which is the main cognitive benefit of our ability to form concepts?
    a. style
    b. preference
    c. efficiency
    d. capacity
    Ans.: c   LG: 2   Page: 353   QT: C

23. Ignoring differences and looking for similarities is important when forming
    a. language.
    b. knowledge-lean problems.
    c. ill-defined problems.
    d. concepts.
    Ans.: d   LG: 2   Page: 353   QT: C

24. A category for organizing objects and events in the environment is called a
    a. concept.
    b. theory.
    c. hypothesis.
    d. principle.
    Ans.: a   LG: 2   Page: 353 QT: F

25. Which of the following is not a model of how people structure concepts?
    a. the response model
    b. the prototype model
    c. the exemplar model
    d. the classical model
    Ans.: a   LG: 2   Page: 355   QT: F

26. In the classical model of concept structuring,
    a. prototypes are utilized for comparisons.
    b. all instances of a concept share defining properties.
    c. membership in a concept is on a graded scale.
    d. all of the above
    Ans.: b   LG: 2   Page: 355   QT: F

27. Which of the following statements would indicate a problem with the classical model of structuring concepts?
    a. All instances of a concept share defining properties.
    b. Prototypes are not easy to find.
    c. All prototypes share defining properties.
    d. Characteristics of a concept are not always easy to define.
    Ans.: d   LG: 2   Page: 355   QT: C

28. Which of the following would *not* be a defining property of an automobile?
    a. used for transportation
    b. has four tires
    c. is blue
    d. has an engine
    Ans.: c   LG: 2   Page: 355   QT: A

29. Which of the following best describes the difference between the classical model of concepts and the prototype model?
    a. The classical model uses defining properties and the prototype model uses characteristics.
    b. The prototype model uses defining properties and the classical model uses characteristics.
    c. The prototype model is more rigid than the classical model.
    d. The prototype model is all or none regarding concept structure.
    Ans.: a   LG: 2   Page: 355   QT: C

Learning Goal 3: Describe the requirements for solving problems.

30. An attempt to find an appropriate way of attaining a goal when the goal is not readily available is called
    a. a concept
    b. problem solving
    c. use of a prototype
    d. applied intelligence
    Ans.: b   LG: 3   Page: 356   QT: F

31. Which of the following would be the correct sequence for the problem-solving process?
    a. develop good problem-solving strategies, find a problem, evaluate solutions
    b. find and frame problems, develop good problem-solving strategies, evaluate solutions, rethink and redefine problems and solutions over time
    c. develop good problem-solving strategies, evaluate solutions, redefine problems and solutions over time, find and frame problems
    d. rethink and redefine problems and solutions over time, find and frame problems, develop good problem-solving strategies, evaluate solutions
    Ans.: b   LG: 3   Page: 356   QT: C

32. The process of finding and framing a problem involves all of the following *except*
    a. identifying the problem.
    b. asking creative questions.
    c. rejecting unconventional options.
    d. defining the specifics of the problem.
    Ans.: c   LG: 3   Page: 357   QT: C

33. In everyday situations, finding and framing problems can be difficult because most real-life problems
    a. are vague and ill-defined.
    b. suggest obvious operations.
    c. provide clear definitions.
    d. involve well-defined solutions.
    Ans.: a   LG: 3   Page: 357   QT: C

34. Your text describes the experiences of Fred Smith of Federal Express who asked, "Why can't there be reliable overnight mail service?" His question represents which problem-solving step?
    a. rethinking and redefining the problem
    b. finding and framing the problem
    c. evaluating the solutions
    d. employing good problem-solving strategies
    Ans.: b   LG: 3   Page: 357   QT: A

35. Jason would like to build a kayak, but he has no idea how to begin the process. Jason is dealing with what type of problem?
    a. well-defined problem
    b. analytical problem
    c. protocol problem
    d. ill-defined problem
    Ans.: d   LG: 3   Page: 357   QT: A

36. Ill-defined problems can be improved by
    a. clearly specifying the starting point and the final goal.
    b. calling on the help of novices.
    c. using deductive reasoning skills.
    d. examining the problem in general terms.
    Ans.: a   LG: 3   Page: 357   QT: F

37. Sam manages a fast-food restaurant. He is frustrated because employees often call in sick at the last minute before they are supposed to start their shift. Given that Sam recognizes this problem, what should he do next?
    a. select a strategy to solve the problem
    b. ignore the problem
    c. evaluate his solution
    d. define the problem in detail
    Ans.: d   LG: 3   Page: 357   QT: A

38. Which of the following is an often-overlooked dimension of problem solving?
    a. evaluating solutions
    b. developing good problem-solving strategies
    c. finding and framing problems
    d. rethinking and redefining problems and solutions over time
    Ans.: c   LG: 3   Page: 357   QT: F

39. Putting together a mountain bike by following the manufacturer's instructions is *best* described as
    a. protocol analysis.
    b. an expert system.
    c. a knowledge-rich problem.
    d. a well-defined problem.
    Ans.: d   LG: 3   Page: 357   QT: A

40. Which of the following is the *least* effective problem-solving strategy?
    a. subgoaling
    b. trial-and-error
    c. algorithms
    d. heuristics
    Ans.: b   LG: 3   Page: 357   QT: C

41. A good strategy for subgoaling is to
    a. work randomly in establishing subgoals.
    b. work without a specific plan.
    c. work backward in establishing subgoals.
    d. set no more than three subgoals.
    Ans.: c   LG: 3   Page: 357   QT: C

42. You have a major project due at the end of the semester. Which problem-solving strategy would serve you best?
   a. set subgoals
   b. automate the problem-solving process
   c. search for contradictions
   d. redefine the problem
   Ans.: a   LG: 3   Page: 357   QT: A

43. You have to study four chapters of information for your next test. If you decide to use the problem solving strategy of subgoaling, you would do which of the following?
   a. cram the night before the test
   b. do not read the chapters until right before the test
   c. break the topics to be studied into smaller areas and focus on each in an organized sequence
   d. both a and b
   Ans.: c   LG: 3   Page: 357   QT: A

44. An effective way to strategize your organization of subgoals is to
   a. work forward in your planning, first creating a subgoal closest to the start and finally creating a subgoal close to the final goal.
   b. not create more than two subgoals.
   c. not create less than ten subgoals.
   d. work backward in your planning, first creating a subgoal that is closest to the final goal, and then work backward to the subgoal that is closest to the beginning of the problem-solving effort.
   Ans.: d   LG: 3   Page: 357   QT: C

45. A strategy that guarantees a solution to a problem is called a(n)
   a. heuristic.
   b. algorithm.
   c. subgoal.
   d. fixeration.
   Ans.: b   LG: 3   Page: 357   QT: F

46. What is the *main* difference between an algorithm and a heuristic?
   a. A heuristic is a problem-solving strategy.
   b. Algorithms take less time.
   c. An algorithm always leads to a correct solution.
   d. Heuristics should only be applied to a small problem.
   Ans.: c   LG: 3   Page: 357   QT: C

47. Which of the following *best* describes algorithms?
   a. problem-solving strategies that suggest a solution to a problem
   b. problem-solving strategies that are very efficient
   c. problem-solving strategies that guarantee a solution to a problem
   d. problem-solving strategies that can be applied to a large problem
   Ans.: c   LG: 3   Page: 357   QT: F

48. In order to complete your algebra homework, you would use which problem-solving strategy?
    a. algorithms
    b. trial-and-error
    c. heurisitics
    d. subgoaling
    Ans.: a   LG: 3   Page: 357   QT: A

49. What is the *main* disadvantage of using algorithms?
    a. They only work for large problems.
    b. They are very similar to trial-and-error.
    c. Correct solutions are not guaranteed.
    d. Solutions may take a long time.
    Ans.: d   LG: 3   Page: 358   QT: C

50. Which of the following does *not* apply to heuristics?
    a. They always solve the problem correctly.
    b. They are faster.
    c. We use them frequently.
    d. They are short cuts.
    Ans.: a   LG: 3   Page: 358   QT: F

51. Joe has discovered that a particular year penny has a great deal of value. For years, he has been throwing his pennies into a drawer. He is almost certain he has one of the specific pennies of value in the drawer. An algorithmic approach to finding the penny would involve
    a. taking a handful of pennies, seeing if it is there, and if not, throwing them back and grabbing another handful.
    b. removing every penny from the drawer, one by one, and checking each one to see if it is the desired penny.
    c. shuffling the pennies and looking at them to find the valuable penny.
    d. shuffling the pennies, but also turning them over to get better looks.
    Ans.: b   LG: 3   Page: 358   QT: A

52. When solving real-life problems, people tend to prefer using
    a. algorithms.
    b. heuristics.
    c. repression.
    d. the most elaborate approach.
    Ans.: b   LG: 3   Page: 358   QT: F

53. When comparing algorithms and heuristics, what is the advantage of using heuristics for solving real-life problems?
    a. convenience
    b. mental set
    c. accuracy
    d. precision
    Ans.: a   LG: 3   Page: 358   QT: C

54. What is the *main* benefit of rethinking and redefining a problem?
    a. improving on past performance
    b. verifying the problem
    c. recognizing the problem
    d. remembering the problem
    Ans.: a   LG: 3   Page: 358   QT: C

55. Which of the following pairs represents similar concepts?
    a. automobiles and snakes
    b. mental set and functional fixedness
    c. insight and operant conditioning
    d. cognitive and behavioral
    Ans.: b   LG: 3   Page: 358   QT: C

56. Fixation is
    a. the use of the correct problem-solving strategy to fix a problem.
    b. using a fresh new perspective on a problem.
    c. using a prior strategy and failing to consider different perspectives.
    d. fixing a problem with a new solution.
    Ans.: c   LG: 3   Page: 358   QT: F

57. Your car is stuck in the middle of nowhere. You need a screwdriver to tighten a clamp on a radiator hose, but you have no tools with you. All you have is 50 cents in your pocket. What behavior would indicate a lack of functional fixedness?
    a. using the edge of a coin as a screwdriver
    b. walking to the nearest gas station
    c. waiting for roadside help
    d. finding a telephone to make a call
    Ans.: a   LG: 3   Page: 358   QT: A

58. Cathy is working at her desk on her psychology paper. She is enjoying the feeling of a cool breeze coming through the window. Unfortunately, she also notices that her papers are being blown across the desk. If Cathy is limited by functional fixedness, she will
    a. put her stapler on the papers to hold them in place.
    b. put a book on the papers to hold them in place.
    c. drive to a store to purchase a paperweight.
    d. put the papers in a drawer.
    Ans.: c   LG: 3   Page: 358   QT: A

59. Sometimes when people find a good strategy to solve a problem, they use that strategy over and over for other problems, even when better strategies are available. The continued reliance on one particular strategy is called
    a. a mental set.
    b. concept formation.
    c. functional fixedness.
    d. insight learning.
    Ans.: a   LG: 3   Page: 359   QT: A

60. Which of the following would businesses need to avoid to stay successful over a period of many years?
    a. concepts
    b. insight learning
    c. functional fixedness
    d. a mental set
    Ans.: d   LG: 3   Page: 359   QT: A

61. A mathematics instructor is correcting the work of one of her students. The work is neatly done and appears to be correct, but the answer is very wrong. The teacher wants to find the mistake and, hopefully, award partial credit. For ten minutes, she looks for a simple mathematics error, a moved decimal point, or a number that has been copied incorrectly. Frustrated, she gets up and takes a brief break. When she returns, the mistake literally jumps off of the paper—the student had made an error in multiplying positives and negatives. What prevented the teacher from finding this the first time?
    a. algorithms
    b. functional fixedness
    c. subgoaling
    d. mental set
    Ans.: d   LG: 3   Page: 359   QT: A

62. Which picture would be the best visual representation of a mental set?
    a. two people playing chess
    b. a person working on an assembly line
    c. an artist sculpting a famous person
    d. a scientist in a laboratory
    Ans.: b   LG: 3   Page: 359   QT: A

63. Which of the following would enable an individual to fully make use of their problem solving skills?
    a. motivation
    b. emotional control
    c. not being afraid to make mistakes
    d. all of the above
    Ans.: d   LG: 3   Page: 359   QT: C

64. Experts solve problems differently than novices. Which of the following is *not* listed in your text as something that gives an expert an advantage in problem solving?
    a. creative approaches
    b. knowledge base
    c. domain memory
    d. use of strategies
    Ans.: a   LG: 3   Page: 360   QT: F

Learning Goal 4: Discuss the main factors in thinking critically, reasoning, and making decisions.

65. When people grasp a deeper meaning of ideas, keep an open mind, and make their own decisions about what to believe or do, they are using
    a. confirmation bias.
    b. belief perseverance.
    c. hindsight bias.
    d. critical thinking.
    Ans.: d   LG: 4   Page: 362   QT: F

66. Education experts and psychologists stress the importance of teaching critical thinking skills in our schools in order to encourage students to do all of the following *except* to
    a. list information.
    b. gain a deeper understanding of concepts.
    c. rethink prior ideas.
    d. become deeply engaged in meaningful thinking.
    Ans.: a   LG: 4   Page: 362   QT: C

67. According to Ellen Langer, a mindful person is characterized by all of the following *except* that he/she
    a. continues to create new ideas.
    b. engages in automatic behavior.
    c. is open to new information.
    d. is aware of more than one perspective.
    Ans.: b   LG: 4   Page: 363   QT: C

68. From Ellen Langer's perspective, a mindless person
    a. is entrapped in old ideas.
    b. engages in automatic behavior.
    c. operates from a single perspective.
    d. all of the above
    Ans.: d   LG: 4   Page: 363   QT: C

69. Asking good questions would be an important ingredient of
    a. mindless thinking.
    b. mindful thinking.
    c. critical thinking.
    d. both b and c
    Ans.: d   LG: 4   Page: 363   QT: F

70. According to experts who would like to see more emphasis on critical thinking, our schools focus too much on all of the following *except*
    a. evaluation.
    b. recitation.
    c. description.
    d. definition.
    Ans.: a   LG: 4   Page: 362   QT: C

71. Without critical-thinking skills, people are less likely to
    a. stay on the surface of problems.
    b. stretch their minds.
    c. be entrapped in old ideas.
    d. operate from a single perspective.
    Ans.: b   LG: 4   Page: 362   QT: C

72. One important aspect of mindful thinking is
    a. focusing on one perspective.
    b. asking good questions.
    c. sticking with familiar ideas.
    d. engaging in automatic behavior.
    Ans.: b   LG: 4   Page: 363   QT: F

73. Mr. Lawrence encourages his 10th-grade history students to question, connect, and evaluate the material they cover in class. Mr. Lawrence's goal is most likely to
    a. give students an opportunity to talk.
    b. provide a relaxed atmosphere.
    c. teach critical thinking skills.
    d. allow students to waste time.
    Ans.: c   LG: 4   Page: 362   QT: A

74. You are a college English teacher. In order to teach your students critical thinking skills, you would have them do all of the following in your class *except*
    a. recite poems.
    b. analyze the themes of short stories.
    c. critically evaluate newspaper articles.
    d. rethink their own ideas in light of what they read.
    Ans.: a   LG: 4   Page: 362   QT: A

75. Inductive reasoning
    a. always yields the correct answer.
    b. involves reasoning from specific to general.
    c. involves reasoning from general to specific.
    d. is a form of a mental set.
    Ans.: b   LG: 4   Page: 363   QT: F

76. Human beings will often reason from the specific to the general. That is, people will often form general rules and concepts based on specific experiences and examples. This type of reasoning is termed
    a. deductive reasoning.
    b. subgoaling.
    c. inductive reasoning.
    d. problem spacing.
    Ans.: c   LG: 4   Page: 363   QT: C

77. Researchers will often study a sample in order to generalize to a population. This would be referred to as a form of
   a. descriptive study.
   b. inductive reasoning.
   c. deductive reasoning.
   d. analogous application.
   Ans.: b   LG: 4   Page: 363   QT: C

78. Joe believes that all of the people from another part of his town are snobs. He believes that the students from this area are rich and drive expensive sports cars to school. He is scheduled to perform with some of these students in an all-county musical presentation. If he assumes that these students will also be rich and snobby, he is using
   a. inductive reasoning.
   b. deductive reasoning.
   c. critical thinking.
   d. descriptive reasoning.
   Ans.: b   LG: 4   Page: 364   QT: A

79. Bertha met two students from another school at a convention. She enjoyed their company a great deal and was very impressed with how nice they were. Bertha now believes that all of the students from that school must also be nice and is considering transferring there. Bertha is using
   a. inductive reasoning.
   b. deductive reasoning.
   c. critical thinking.
   d. descriptive reasoning.
   Ans.: a   LG: 4   Page: 363   QT: A

80. A conclusion derived from abstract information involves
   a. representative heuristics.
   b. simulation heuristics.
   c. deductive reasoning.
   d. inductive reasoning.
   Ans.: c   LG: 4   Page: 364   QT: F

81. Premises are most likely to be used in
   a. deductive reasoning.
   b. critical thinking.
   c. inference.
   d. hypothesis testing.
   Ans.: a   LG: 4   Page: 364   QT: F

82. Analogies draw on which type of reasoning?
   a. critical
   b. inductive
   c. deductive
   d. hypothetical
   Ans.: b   LG: 4   Page: 363   QT: F

83. Decision making differs from reasoning in that decision making involves
   a. thinking.
   b. cognitive processes.
   c. information.
   d. no established rules.
   Ans.: d   LG: 4   Page: 365   QT: C

84. Cathy just got transferred to a new department, but she has long believed that her new supervisor is a cranky, disagreeable, critical person. According to the confirmation bias, what will Cathy most likely do on her first day in the new supervisor's department?
   a. She will forget about the things she has thought about her new supervisor.
   b. She will look for positive behaviors on the part of her supervisor.
   c. She will tell the new supervisor what she has thought.
   d. She will look for negative behaviors on the part of the supervisor.
   Ans.: d   LG: 4   Page: 365   QT: A

85. Maria is extremely active in politics. She has strong conservative beliefs about what is correct and what is not. Each day when she reads the newspaper, she pays close attention to the editorial section in particular. According to the confirmation bias, what will she do when she reads them?
   a. She will read both the editorials that she agrees with and those that she doesn't to get a balanced view of issues.
   b. She will read the editorials that she agrees with, but not the ones that she disagrees with.
   c. She will read the editorials that she disagrees with to get an idea of what the other perspectives on issues may be.
   d. She will not read any of the editorials.
   Ans.: b   LG: 4   Page: 365   QT: A

86. Tyler comes home to tell his parents about the new teacher that he has. The teacher's name is Mr. Wilson and he is incredibly funny in the way that he teaches the business math class. Tyler's parents realize that Mr. Wilson is actually Skeets Wilson, an unfocused kid who grew up in their old neighborhood. From what they could remember, Skeets was more interested in how to get out of school than working in a school. They did not know what had become of him but had assumed it was not much. According to the notion of belief perseverance, Tyler's parents would have the most difficulty believing which of the following?
   a. Skeets left a very successful business career to work in the teaching field.
   b. Skeets is subbing because of a desperate teacher shortage.
   c. There has to be more than one Skeets Wilson.
   d. Skeets must be related to someone on the school board.
   Ans.: a   LG: 4   Page: 366   QT: A

87. Hindsight bias is to past events as overconfidence bias is to
   a. prior events.
   b. hypothetical events.
   c. future events.
   d. confirmed events.
   Ans.: c   LG: 4   Page: 366   QT: C

244

88. Every week during football season, Fred and his friends have fun following the local high school teams. Before the games, Fred never really talks too much about how the games will turn out. On Monday, however, it is a different scenario altogether. Fred is more than happy to share with his friends that the games came out exactly as he thought they would and why. Fred is demonstrating
   a. overconfidence bias.
   b. hindsight bias.
   c. inductive reasoning.
   d. deductive reasoning.
   Ans.: b   LG: 4   Page: 366   QT: A

89. The fact that we hear about airplane crashes on the news more often than we hear about automobile crashes may lead us to believe that we are more likely to die in a plane than a car. This is an example of a(n)
   a. subgoal strategy.
   b. simulation heuristic.
   c. availability heuristic.
   d. representativeness heuristic.
   Ans.: c   LG: 4   Page: 367   QT: A

90. When decisions are made based on how similar a sample is to the population from which it is drawn, which heuristic is being used?
   a. representativeness
   b. availability
   c. randomness
   d. analogous
   Ans.: a   LG: 4   Page: 367   QT: C

91. Before visiting a showroom, you made a list of the top-ten qualities you want in a new car. If the car that the salesperson shows you matches 8 of the 10 qualities, the probability you will like the car is high. Which heuristic have you used?
   a. subgoal
   b. availability
   c. simulation
   d. representativeness
   Ans.: d   LG: 4   Page: 367   QT: A

Learning Goal 5: Identify the possible connections between language and thought.

92. A system of symbols that can be spoken, written, or signed is considered a
   a. transfer set.
   b. method.
   c. signal.
   d. language.
   Ans.: d   LG: 5   Page: 368   QT: F

93. Which of the following is not true about the system of symbols that comprises a human language?
    a. It has no rules.
    b. It can written.
    c. It can be spoken.
    d. It can be signed.
    Ans.: a   LG: 5   Page: 368   QT: F

94. It is said that if you were to create a unique, original sentence that contained at least ten words, chances are that you would never again see or hear that sequence of words again. You could read newspapers, books, or listen for someone to say it to you, and most likely, it would not happen. The property of language that this demonstrates is called
    a. syntax.
    b. semantics.
    c. morphology.
    d. infinite generativity.
    Ans.: d   LG: 5   Page: 368   QT: C

95. The *main* purpose of language is to
    a. think.
    b. communicate.
    c. be creative.
    d. remember.
    Ans.: b   LG: 5   Page: 368   QT: F

96. The ability to create an infinite number of utterances from a finite set of elements and rules refers to the
    a. infinite generativity of language.
    b. language code.
    c. peripheral property of language.
    d. semantic content.
    Ans.: a   LG: 5   Page: 368   QT: F

97. Which term *best* describes the idea that language allows for creativity?
    a. displacement
    b. phonology
    c. productive constraint
    d. infinite generativity
    Ans.: d   LG: 5   Page: 368   QT: F

98. Which of the following is true of phonemes?
    a. They are the grammatical rules of language.
    b. They are the smallest units of meaning in a language.
    c. They are genetic predispositions for sounds in different languages.
    d. They are the basic units of sound in a language.
    Ans.: d   LG: 5   Page: 368   QT: F

99. The sound of the letter "A" is a
    a. morpheme.
    b. connotation.
    c. phoneme.
    d. holophrase.
    Ans.: c   LG: 5   Page: 368   QT: F

100. Speech involves putting together sound patterns to make words. The sound patterns from which words are made are called
    a. phonemes.
    b. holophrases.
    c. algorithms.
    d. constituents.
    Ans.: a   LG: 5   Page: 368   QT: F

101. Which of the following is true of morphemes?
    a. They are the grammatical rules of language.
    b. They are the basic units of sound in a language.
    c. They are the smallest units of meaning in a language.
    d. They are genetic predispositions for sounds in different languages.
    Ans.: c   LG: 5   Page: 368   QT: F

102. How many morphemes are found in the word "returning"?
    a. 1
    b. 2
    c. 3
    d. 4
    Ans.: c   LG: 5   Page: 368   QT: F

103. Syntax is to structure as semantics is to
    a. meaning.
    b. grammar.
    c. arrangement.
    d. form.
    Ans.: a   LG: 5   Page: 368   QT: C

104. Consider the sentence, "The rock walked up the mountain." This sentence illustrates incorrect
    a. syntax.
    b. phonology.
    c. structure.
    d. semantics.
    Ans.: d   LG: 5   Page: 369   QT: A

105. Consider the sentence, "Maria to the store walked." This sentence illustrates incorrect
    a. semantics.
    b. syntax.
    c. phonology.
    d. morphology.
    Ans.: b   LG: 5   Page: 368   QT: A

106. If one were to translate "white house" to Spanish from English, it would be "casa blanca," or "house white." This demonstrates a difference in _____ between the two languages.
a. phonology
b. morphology
c. syntax
d. sound systems
Ans.: c   LG: 5   Page: 368   QT: A

107. Which of the following language rules is most closely related to the grammar of a language?
a. pragmatics
b. semantics
c. morphology
d. syntax
Ans.: d   LG: 5   Page: 368   QT: C

108. Jason says, "I misplaced my wallet." His wife exclaims, "Oh my goodness, you lost your wallet?" Jason responds, "No, I didn't *lose* my wallet, I misplaced it." This exchange best demonstrates which aspect of language?
a. syntax
b. semantics
c. pragmatics
d. grammar
Ans.: b   LG: 5   Page: 368   QT: A

109. Linguist Benjamin Whorf maintains that
a. thought occurs without language.
b. thought is dependent upon language.
c. language is independent of thought.
d. the function of language is problem solving.
Ans.: b   LG: 5   Page: 369   QT: C

110. According to current research, what is the relationship between language and thought?
a. Language determines thought.
b. Language influences thought.
c. Language occurs before thought.
d. Language is unrelated to thought.
Ans.: b   LG: 5   Page: 370   QT: F

111. According to Benjamin Whorf, if you did not have words to discriminate different flavors, you would
a. not think about the concept of the different flavors.
b. starve to death.
c. think only about how food tastes.
d. not be able to distinguish different foods.
Ans.: a   LG: 5   Page: 369   QT: A

112. A linguist who is known for his work in cognition and language is
    a. Whorf.
    b. Chomsky.
    c. Rosch.
    d. Washoe.
    Ans.: a   LG: 5   Page: 369   QT: F

113. Critics of the work of Benjamin Whorf disagree most strongly with which statement?
    a. Language causes the way people think.
    b. Language influences the way people think.
    c. People of different cultures view the world differently.
    d. Speakers of different languages view the world differently.
    Ans.: a   LG: 5   Page: 369   QT: C

114. Critics of the work of Benjamin Whorf maintain that
    a. linguistic predispositions are universal.
    b. all cultures essentially share the same linguistic experiences.
    c. language determines how we think about our world.
    d. people's perceptions are independent of the words they know.
    Ans.: d   LG: 5   Page: 370   QT: C

115. There was once a dolphin named Ake who could respond to her trainer's hand signals. How would a behaviorist such as Skinner **most likely** explain the dolphin's behavior?
    a. The dolphin has merely been conditioned to respond to particular stimuli in specific ways.
    b. The dolphin has developed the cognitions associated with language in the human sense.
    c. Dolphins use the same signals for communicating among themselves.
    d. The dolphin understands complex language.
    Ans.: a   LG: 5   Page: 374   QT: A

116. Which of the following statements about the research evidence concerning animals' ability to communicate is incorrect?
    a. Animals can learn some aspects of language-like communication.
    b. Animals use abstract symbols and syntax in the wild.
    c. Animals communicate different emotional states with different sounds.
    d. Animals can learn to respond to hand signals.
    Ans.: b   LG: 5   Page: 372   QT: C

117. Which statement best describes the status of the debate over whether or not animals have language in the human sense?
    a. Experts disagree on whether or not animal communication can be considered language.
    b. Experts agree that animal communication is as complex as human language.
    c. Experts agree that animals cannot learn language in the human sense.
    d. Experts disagree on whether or not animals can communicate.
    Ans.: a   LG: 5   Page: 372   QT: C

118. The research of Sue Savage-Rumbaugh and her colleagues indicates that chimps can
    a. not use sign language.
    b. not grasp syntax.
    c. only use about 15 different signs.
    d. understand symbols.
    Ans.: d   LG: 5   Page: 371   QT: F

119. Gardner and Gardner conducted one of the classic studies on chimps' ability to learn language. They taught their chimp, Washoe, to learn which language?
    a. computer language
    b. American Sign Language
    c. synthesized language
    d. symbolic picture language
    Ans.: b   LG: 5   Page: 371   QT: F

120. Which are the two main issues in the debate over whether or not animals can learn language in the human sense?
    a. the ability to learn phonological and morphological rules
    b. the ability to recognize symbols and semantics
    c. understanding the meaning of symbols and the ability to learn syntax
    d. the ability to learn syntax and understand grammar
    Ans.: c   LG: 5   Page: 371   QT: F

121. Your friend Gabriel tells you that he watched a television special that showed that chimps can learn language. When you express your doubts, he tells you excitedly that the television program showed how chimps manipulated symbols and constructed complex sentences. What argument would you raise to point out to Gabriel that these responses by the chimps don't represent language in the human sense?
    a. The chimps' responses were probably faked with film tricks.
    b. The chimps' responses are random, at best, and have no similarity with human language.
    c. The chimps' responses do not show the generativity and the complexity of adult human language.
    d. The chimps' responses do not indicate an understanding of symbols.
    Ans.: c   LG: 5   Page: 372   QT: A

122. Studies on chimps' ability to communicate have, so far, not shown which of the following?
    a. generativity equal to that found in human language
    b. understanding of symbolic systems of communication
    c. ability to produce fairly complex statements
    d. understanding and manipulation of syntax rules
    Ans.: a   LG: 5   Page: 372   QT: C

Learning Goal 6. Summarize how language is acquired and develops.

123. How did Noam Chomsky explain human language?
    a. He believed that language acquisition was the result of reinforcement.
    b. He believed that language acquisition was the result of imitation.
    c. He believed that good parenting brought about language in humans.
    d. He believed that humans are biologically prewired to learn language at a certain time and in a certain way.
    Ans.: d   LG: 6   Page: 373   QT: C

124. Which of the following theorists believed that language acquisition was the result of reinforcement?
    a. Noam Chomsky
    b. B. F. Skinner
    c. Sigmund Freud
    d. Carl Rogers
    Ans.: b   LG: 6   Page: 374   QT: F

125. It is generally accepted that language acquisition is
    a. the result of biological influences
    b. the result of environmental influences
    c. a combination of biological and environmental influences
    d. none of the above
    Ans.: c   LG: 6   Page: 375   QT: F

126. How can language development be enabled by parents talking to their babies
    a. Parents should be an active conversation partner.
    b. Parents should talk as if the infant understands what they are saying.
    c. Parents can use a language style which communicates emotion.
    d. all of the above
    Ans.: d   LG: 6   Page: 375   QT: F

127. What is a critical period of development?
    a. It is a time period of development when something virtually has to happen.
    b. It is a bad time for something to take place in development
    c. It is a dangerous time for something to take place in development
    d. All developmental periods are critical; there is no one period that is more important than others.
    Ans.: a   LG: 6   Page: 376   QT: F

128. What happens when a critical period of development has been passed by?
    a. Learning becomes more difficult, if not impossible.
    b. Problem solving improves.
    c. New ways of thinking develop.
    d. Language development begins.
    Ans.: a   LG: 6   Page: 376   QT: C

129. In Lenneberg's biological theory of language acquisition,
    a. language development was continuous and there were no critical periods.
    b. adults could learn a first language regardless of their backgrounds.
    c. the critical period for language acquisition was 18 months to puberty.
    d. it was established that a second language could be easily learned after puberty.
    Ans.: c   LG: 6   Page: 376   QT: F

130. Which of the following is false regarding Genie, the subject of the deprivation study?
    a. Genie was never allowed to speak until social workers discovered her locked in a room at age 13.
    b. Genie learned to use some words.
    c. Genie developed the ability to create questions.
    d. Genie's case was often compared to that of the Wild Boy of Averyron
    Ans.: c   LG: 6   Page: 376   QT: F

131. Which of the following is true regarding Genie, the girl who had been kept in isolation to age 13 and could not speak when she was found?
    a. She never could be taught language.
    b. She learned to use normal language after age 18 years.
    c. She learned to use correct syntax but not semantics.
    d. She eventually learned to speak in short, mangled sentences.
    Ans.: d   LG: 6   Page: 376   QT: F

132. Between age 3 to 6 months, infants begin to entertain themselves and others with endless repetitions of vowel-consonant combinations. This type of vocalization is known as
    a. babbling.
    b. cooing.
    c. gurgling.
    d. constituent sounding.
    Ans.: a   LG: 6   Page: 376   QT: F

133. Even deaf babies babble. This fact supports which interpretation of the purpose of babbling?
    a. Babbling indicates a biological readiness for language.
    b. Babbling is a form of speech.
    c. Babbling is merely an imitation of the speech environment.
    d. Babbling has meaning.
    Ans.: a   LG: 6   Page: 376   QT: C

134. Telegraphic statements are characterized by all of the following *except*
    a. excluding unnecessary words.
    b. precise, essential words.
    c. two- or three-word combinations.
    d. including all parts of speech.
    Ans.: d   LG: 6   Page: 378   QT: F

135. How do children convey meaning in their telegraphic speech?
    a. with the words only
    b. with rapid expression
    c. with eye contact and volume
    d. with gestures, tone, and context
    Ans.: d   LG: 6   Page: 378   QT: F

136. Which of the following is the *best* example of a telegraphic statement?
    a. ba-ba-ba
    b. Doggie eat.
    c. dada
    d. I want milk.
    Ans.: b   LG: 6   Page: 378   QT: A

137. Which of the following is true about the progression of language development in infants and children?
    a. The sequence of language development is universal, regardless of the particular language.
    b. In many cultures, children use telegraphic speech before they babble.
    c. Most children use telegraphic speech at about one year of age.
    d. Babbling is unique to American babies.
    Ans.: a   LG: 6   Page: 378   QT: C

138. A child's first words *usually* name which of the following?
    a. personal thoughts
    b. uncommon objects
    c. familiar people and objects
    d. abstract concepts
    Ans.: c   LG: 6   Page: 378   QT: F

139. Why is it important to give toddlers sufficient time to express themselves?
    a. to give the adult enough time to think of an answer
    b. to keep the child busy
    c. to improve their creativity
    d. to give them the opportunity to acquire vocabulary and language rules
    Ans.: d   LG: 6   Page: 376   QT: C

140. When you pick up your 3-year-old from day care, she tells you excitedly, "I swimmed today!" How should you respond?
    a. Ignore the child because her statement is grammatically incorrect.
    b. Tell the child that "swimmed" is an incorrect form of the verb "swim."
    c. Ask the child to correct her mistake.
    d. Say, "Wow, you swam today! Tell me all about it."
    Ans.: d   LG: 6   Page: 375   QT: C

141. Which of the following pairs is incorrect regarding language milestones?
    a. 0–6 Months: cooing
    b. 12–18 Months: understands 50 words on average
    c. 3–4 years: word definitions include synonyms.
    d. 15–20 years: understands adult literary works
    Ans.: c   LG: 6   Page: 377   QT: F

142. Which of the following is considered a good strategy to keep in mind when parents are talking to their babies?
    a. Be an active conversational partner
    b. Talk as if the infant understands what you are saying.
    c. Use a language style with which you feel comfortable.
    d. All of the above.
    Ans.: d   LG: 5   Page: 375   QT: F

143. Which of the following statements is not true regarding babbling?
    a. Babbling generally begins at age 3-6 months.
    b. Babbling is endlessly repeating syllables such as bababa.
    c. Babbling is determined by biological readiness.
    d. Deaf babies do not babble.
    Ans.: d   LG: 6   Pages: 376–377 QT: F

144. Which of the following is not true regarding bilingual education in the United States?
    a. A very small number of (as few as ten thousand) children in the United States come from homes in which English is not the primary language.
    b. Some states have passed laws declaring English to be their primary language.
    c. Bilingual education supporters argue that it increases cognitive skills.
    d. Critics of bilingual education argue that it hinders academic performances
    Ans.: a   LG: 6   Page: 379   QT: F

145. Proponents of bilingual education recommend which strategy for immigrant children whose native language is not English?
    a. Teach these children only in English because they have a lot of catching up to do.
    b. Teach these children only in their native language because that is what their parents speak.
    c. Teach these children in their native language for two years before adding English.
    d. Teach these children in their native language while slowly introducing English at the same time.
    Ans.: d   LG: 6   Page: 379   QT: C

146. Research with bilingual children has shown all of the following *except*
    a. bilingual children are usually less proficient in their first than their second language.
    b. bilingual children perform better than monolingual children on intelligence tests.
    c. bilingualism does not interfere with performance in either language.
    d. bilingual children score as well or better than monolingual children on achievement tests.
    Ans.: a   LG: 6   Page: 379   QT: C

147. You believe that all children should begin learning a second language in elementary school. In order to persuade local school officials of your point of view, you would present all of the following arguments except which one?
    a. Childhood is the best age to acquire second-language competence.
    b. Very few people can attain proficiency in two languages.
    c. Bilingualism is associated with higher levels of academic performance.
    d. Bilingualism increases people's appreciation of diversity.
    Ans.: b   LG: 6   Page: 379   QT: C

148. Mr. Aaron's first-graders practice the pronunciation of sounds. Mr. Aaron reinforces this activity with huge, colorful flashcards of the sounds as students say them. In time, Mr. Aaron will teach his students more complex sound combinations, short words, and longer words. Which approach is Mr. Aaron using for his reading instruction?
    a. the visual-kinesthetic approach
    b. the whole language approach
    c. the modern language approach
    d. the basic-skills-and-phonetics approach
    Ans.: d   LG: 6   Page: 380   QT: A

149. A second-grade reading teacher who employs the whole language approach would be least likely to ask students to complete which of the following tasks?
    a. sounding out words
    b. listening to a story
    c. writing a poem
    d. creating a song
    Ans.: a   LG: 6   Page: 380   QT: A

150. Which statement best describes reading experts' consensus on the most effective method of reading instruction?
    a. The whole language approach works best for most children.
    b. Reading instruction should focus exclusively on the basic-skills-and-phonetics approach.
    c. The basic-skills-and-phonetics approach works better with younger readers.
    d. The best approach is to combine the whole language and the basic-skills-and-phonetics approach.
    Ans.: d   LG: 6   Page: 381   QT: C

True/False Items

____ 151.   Modern computers can generalize concepts to novel situations as effectively as the human brain can.
____ 152.   The mental process behind a physical skill is not a concept.
____ 153.   Our ability to form concepts enables us to generalize our experiences to new situations.
____ 154.   In order to reduce violence in schools, educators must first find and frame the problem.
____ 155.   A heuristic is a problem-solving strategy that always guarantees a solution.
____ 156.   Reasoning from the general concept to the specific instances involves deductive reasoning.
____ 157.   When people hold on to a belief despite evidence to the contrary, they are exhibiting belief perseverance.
____ 158.   A language is a system of communication that employs symbols.
____ 159.   All human languages have organizational rules.
____ 160.   The semantics of a language governs how words are sequenced in that language.
____ 161.   Research indicates that chimps can learn the meaning of symbols.
____ 162.   Benjamin Whorf proposes a link between language and thought.
____ 163.   The notion of a critical period of language development is still controversial.
____ 164.   Behaviorists would say that we learn languages because of a neurological language acquisition device.
____ 165.   Children between the ages of 3 and 7 cannot usually achieve competence in a second language.

Answer Key for True/False Items

151.	Ans.: F	LG: 1	Page: 352	159.	Ans.: T	LG: 5	Page: 368
152.	Ans.: F	LG: 2	Page: 355	160.	Ans.: F	LG: 5	Page: 368
153.	Ans.: T	LG: 2	Page: 353	161.	Ans.: T	LG: 5	Page: 371
154.	Ans.: T	LG: 3	Page: 356	162.	Ans.: T	LG: 5	Page: 369
155.	Ans.: F	LG: 3	Page: 358	163.	Ans.: T	LG: 6	Page: 376
156.	Ans.: T	LG: 4	Page: 364	164.	Ans.: F	LG: 6	Page: 373
157.	Ans.: T	LG: 4	Page: 366	165.	Ans.: F	LG: 6	Page: 380
158.	Ans.: T	LG: 5	Page: 368				

Fill-in-the-Blank Items

166. Whereas the human brain can generalize, computers can only process the _____ they have received from a human.
167. Forming concepts, solving problems, reasoning, and decision making are activities that involve _____.
168. _____ allow us to relate experiences and objects and make memory more efficient.
169. _____ involves breaking down a problem and setting intermediate goals that help obtain the final solution.
170. Using a chair as a stepladder indicates a lack of _____.
171. Analyzing information, evaluating evidence, and rethinking one's ideas involve _____ thinking.
172. When you draw a conclusion on a sample based upon knowledge about a population, you are using _____ reasoning.
173. _____ is the tendency to seek information that supports one's opinion or ideas.
174. _____ are the smallest components of a language sound system.
175. _____ determines in what order words will appear when they are used to communicate.
176. Children like Genie, the modern "wild child" discussed in your text, provide evidence for the notion of a _____ period of language development.
177. The typical 2-year-old communicates by using two-word constructions, or _____ speech.
178. Experts recommend that reading instruction should combine the _____ approach and the basic-skills-and-phonetics approach.
179. According to _____ , language determines our thoughts and ideas.
180. The best way to nourish young children's language development is by _____ to them and listening to them.

Answer Key for Fill-in-the-Blank Items

166.	Ans.: information	LG: 1	Page: 352
167.	Ans.: thinking	LG: 1	Page: 353
168.	Ans.: Concepts	LG: 2	Page: 353
169.	Ans.: Subgoaling	LG: 3	Page: 357
170.	Ans.: functional fixedness	LG: 3	Page: 358
171.	Ans.: critical	LG: 4	Page: 362
172.	Ans.: deductive	LG: 4	Page: 364
173.	Ans.: Confirmation bias	LG: 4	Page: 365
174.	Ans.: Phonemes	LG: 5	Page: 368
175.	Ans.: Syntax	LG: 5	Page: 368
176.	Ans.: critical	LG: 6	Page: 376
177.	Ans.: telegraphic	LG: 6	Page: 378
178.	Ans.: whole-language	LG: 6	Page: 380
179.	Ans.: Whorf	LG: 5	Page: 369
180.	Ans.: speaking	LG: 6	Page: 375

Matching Items

<table>
<tr><td>____</td><td>181. thinking</td><td>A.</td><td>the time from 18 months to puberty</td></tr>
<tr><td>____</td><td>182. concept</td><td>B.</td><td>defining properties</td></tr>
<tr><td>____</td><td>183. classical model of concepts</td><td>C.</td><td>thought and language</td></tr>
<tr><td>____</td><td>184. algorithm</td><td>D.</td><td>mentally manipulating information</td></tr>
<tr><td>____</td><td>185. infinite generativity</td><td>E.</td><td>a type of fixation</td></tr>
<tr><td>____</td><td>186. mental set</td><td>F.</td><td>slow but accurate</td></tr>
<tr><td>____</td><td>187. mindful</td><td>G.</td><td>limitless combinations</td></tr>
<tr><td>____</td><td>188. Whorf</td><td>H.</td><td>mental category used to group</td></tr>
<tr><td>____</td><td>189. Chomsky</td><td>I.</td><td>uses critical thinking</td></tr>
<tr><td>____</td><td>190. critical period for language</td><td>K.</td><td>language acquisition</td></tr>
</table>

Answer Key for Matching Items

181.	Ans.: D	LG: 1	Page: 353		186.	Ans.: E	LG: 3	Page: 359
182.	Ans.: H	LG: 2	Page: 353		187.	Ans.: I	LG: 4	Page: 363
183.	Ans.: B	LG: 2	Page: 355		188.	Ans.: C	LG: 5	Page: 369
184.	Ans.: F	LG: 2	Page: 357		189.	Ans.: K	LG: 6	Page: 373
185.	Ans.: G	LG: 5	Page: 368		190.	Ans.: A	LG: 6	Page: 376

Essay Questions

191. Using a problem of your choice, discuss how you would apply the four steps of effective problem solving discussed in your text. (LG: 1)

> Answer Guidelines: Possible options include mentioning the four steps of effective problem solving: (1) finding and framing the problem, (2) developing good problem-solving strategies, (3) evaluating solutions, and (4) rethinking and redefining the problem.

192. Compare and contrast the classical model of concepts and the prototype model of concepts. Give an example of the use of each. (LG: 2)

> Answer Guidelines: The classical model of concepts uses defining properties to decide if an object falls into the category of a particular concept. With the prototype model, people decide on whether an item reflects a concept by comparing it with the most typical item (prototype) of that concept.

193. Identify the critical-thinking skills discussed in your text. Why are these skills necessary in everyday life? (LG: 3)

> Answer Guidelines: Possible options include mentioning that critical thinking involves analyzing, inferring, connecting, synthesizing, criticizing, creating, evaluating, thinking, and rethinking. These thinking skills are important in everyday life because they allow us to engage in meaningful thinking, explore new ideas, adopt new perspectives, and adjust our behavior.

194. Inductive reasoning and deductive reasoning are category labels for different types of logic and problem-solving approaches. Distinguish between inductive and deductive reasoning and give a specific example of each. (LG: 4)

Answer Guidelines: Possible options include mentioning that inductive reasoning works from the specifics and the details to form abstractions (such as theories and hypotheses). Deductive reasoning starts with the abstractions and then works toward finding the details and specifics to support the theories and hypotheses.

195. Discuss three biases or flaws that tend to lead to faulty decision making. Provide your own example for each bias or flaw included in your discussion. (LG: 4)

Answer Guidelines: Possible options include mentioning confirmation bias (tendency to search for and use information that supports our ideas rather than refutes them), belief perseverance (tendency to hold on to a belief in the face of contradictory evidence), overconfidence bias (tendency to have more confidence in our judgments than we should based on the relative frequency of the correct answer), hindsight bias (tendency to report after the fact that one accurately predicted an event), availability heuristic (making a judgment about the probability of an event by recalling the frequency of the event's past occurrences), and representative heuristic (making decisions based on how well something matches a prototype—that is, the most common representative or example).

196. Is there a time period in a child's life when language acquisition is facilitated compared to other time periods? If so, when and why? (LG: 6)

Answer Guidelines: Possible options include mentioning that the idea of a critical period suggests that there is a time frame when language learning is optimally facilitated; after this period, language learning is more difficult. This period seems to be between 18 months of age and the onset of puberty.

197. Discuss the controversy regarding bilingual education. (LG: 6)

Answer Guidelines: Possible options include mentioning that bilingual education attempts to teach academic subjects to immigrant children in their native language while slowly and simultaneously adding English instruction. Those who criticize bilingual education say that bilingual education is a disadvantage to the immigrant children because it fails to instruct them in English, which will leave them behind in the workplace. Those in favor of bilingual education have a great deal of research evidence on their side. There is no evidence to support the notion that maintaining the native language will interfere with learning a second language. In fact, bilingual children tend to score higher on intelligence tests and achievement tests. In addition, bilingual education indicates respect for the value of immigrant children's family and community culture.

198. Explain and contrast the perspectives of Noam Chomsky and B. F. Skinner regarding language acquisition. (LG: 6)

Answer Guidelines: Answers should refer to Chomsky's perspective that human beings are uniquely neurologically "prewired" for language. Chomsky referred to this mechanism as a "language acquisition device." Skinner believed that we acquire language because we are reinforced for doing so. Without this reinforcement, we would not demonstrate this behavior.

199. How would the concept of a "critical period" for language acquisition have an impact upon school curriculum? (LG: 6)

Answer Guidelines: Lenneberg proposed that there is a critical period for language acquisition for humans. The time period that he hypothesized was from approximately 18 months until puberty. If it is known that it is more difficult to learn a language after the onset of puberty than before, then languages should be introduced at an early grade level.

200. Define language and explain four rule systems that shape its structure. (LG: 5)

Answer Guidelines: Language is a form of communication, whether spoken, written, or signed, that is based on a system of symbols. Four rule systems that shape its structure are phonology (sounds), morphology (word formation), syntax (word order) and semantics (meaning).

Chapter 10: Intelligence

Learning Goals

1. Describe what intelligence is.
2. Explain how intelligence is measured and what the limitations of intelligence tests are.
3. Identify four neuroscience approaches to intelligence.
4. Evaluate theories of multiple intelligences.
5. Discuss characteristics of mental retardation, giftedness, and creativity.
6. Analyze the contributions of heredity and environment to intelligence.

Multiple-Choice Items

Learning Goal 1: Describe what intelligence is.

1. Intelligence is defined in your textbook as
   a. problem solving skills.
   b. the ability to adapt to life.
   c. the ability to learn from life's everyday experiences.
   d. all of the above
   Ans.: d   LG: 1   Page: 389   QT: F

2. Which of the following is not a problem associated with the study of intelligence?
   a. Intelligence is defined a number of different ways.
   b. Intelligence cannot be directly seen.
   c. The study of intelligence has no practical application.
   d. Intelligence is difficult to measure.
   Ans.: c   LG: 1   Page: 388   QT: F

3. One of the fundamental difficulties involved with the measurement of intelligence is that
   a. there are no recognized intelligence tests.
   b. not all researchers have come to an agreement on what intelligence is.
   c. different people have different levels of intelligence
   d. intelligence cannot be directly measured.
   Ans.: d   LG: 1   Page: 389 QT: F

4. The stable, consistent ways in which people are different from each other are referred to as
   a. lifestyles.
   b. individual differences.
   c. cognitions.
   d. assessments.
   Ans.: b   LG: 1   Page: 389   QT: F

5. William and Daryl have been friends for years but differ from each other in their talents. William is a better problem solver but Daryl never seems to forget information once he has learned it. How could this be best explained?
   a. individual differences
   b. environmental effects
   c. genetic manifestations
   d. invalidity of assessment devices
   Ans.: a   LG: 1   Page: 389   QT: A

Learning Goal 2: Explain how intelligence is measured and what the limitations of intelligence tests are.

6. Early psychologists studying intelligence were interested in assessing all but which of the following?
   a. higher mental processes
   b. sensory systems
   c. perceptual systems
   d. motor systems
   Ans.: a   LG: 2   Page: 389   QT: F

7. The individual who is considered to be the father of mental tests is
   a. Robert Sternberg.
   b. John Santrock.
   c. Sir Frances Galton.
   d. Stanford Binet.
   Ans.: c   LG: 2   Page: 390   QT: F

8. Which of the following was least influenced by Galton's early work in intelligence?
   a. how intelligence should be measured
   b. group differences in intelligence
   c. components of intelligence
   d. heritability of intelligence
   Ans.: b   LG: 2   Page: 390   QT: F

9. The early tests of Binet were an attempt to
   a. identify low-ability schoolchildren who would not benefit by regular instruction.
   b. evaluate cognitive abilities of adults for vocational training.
   c. identify high-ability schoolchildren who would benefit by advanced classes.
   d. evaluate cognitive abilities of schoolchildren for inclusion classes.
   Ans.: a   LG: 2   Page: 390   QT: F

10. The motivation behind the French Ministry of Education's use of Binet's tests was to
    a. identify low-ability schoolchildren and get them alternative instruction.
    b. evaluate cognitive abilities of adults for vocational training.
    c. identify high-ability schoolchildren who would benefit by advanced classes.
    d. reduce overcrowding.
    Ans.: d   LG: 2   Page: 390   QT: F

11. Which of the following was *not* a significant component of Binet's work?
    a. emphasis on complex cognitive processes
    b. emphasis on developmental differences
    c. emphasis on gifted children
    d. emphasis on individual differences
    Ans.: c   LG: 2   Page: 390   QT: F

12. When psychologists refer to mental age, they mean
    a. Piaget's level of cognitive development.
    b. Galton's individual differences.
    c. Sternberg's elementary school assessment device.
    d. Binet's individual differences in mental development compared to others.
    Ans.: d   LG: 2   Page: 390   QT: F

13. The researcher who was responsible for developing the Intelligence Quotient was
    a. Alfred Binet.
    b. William Stern.
    c. Lewis Terman.
    d. Stanford-Binet.
    Ans.: b   LG: 2   Page: 390   QT: F

14. The intelligence quotient was calculated by which of the following means?
    a. mental age multiplied by chronological age
    b. mental age divided by chronological age and then multiplied by 100
    c. chronological age divided by mental age and then multiplied by 100
    d. mental age over chronological age
    Ans.: b   LG: 2   Page: 390   QT: F

15. According to the intelligence quotient, Katie, who has a mental age of 8 and a chronological age of 8 is
    a. average in intelligence.
    b. below average in intelligence.
    c. above average in intelligence.
    d. gifted in intelligence.
    Ans.: a   LG: 2   Page: 390   QT: C

16. Using the intelligence quotient, an average person's IQ score would be
    a. 75.
    b. 100.
    c. 50.
    d. 150.
    Ans.: b   LG: 2   Page: 390   QT: C

17. Jamal is eight years old, but recently took an IQ test in which he scored the same as the average twelve-year-old. If we were using the intelligence quotient to calculate Jamal's IQ, it would be
    a. 96.
    b. 66.
    c. 200.
    d. 150.
    Ans.: d   LG: 2   Page: 390   QT: C

18. The Stanford-Binet intelligence test analyzes individual responses in all but which of the following areas?
    a. verbal and quantitative reasoning
    b. abstract/visual reasoning
    c. short-term memory
    d. sensory memory
    Ans.: d   LG: 2   Page: 390   QT: F

19. Characteristics of the normal distribution include that
    a. it is symmetrical.
    b. it is bell shaped.
    c. a majority of the scores fall in the middle of the distribution.
    d. all of the above
    Ans.: d   LG: 2   Page: 391   QT: F

20. If we are looking at the normal distribution, and the average score on the Stanford-Binet intelligence test is 100, what percentage of scores will be below this score?
    a. 100 %
    b. 50 %
    c. 34 %
    d. 2 %
    Ans.: b   LG: 2   Page: 391   QT: C

21. Billy takes a Stanford Binet IQ test and finds that he got an average score. Which of the following scores would you say was Billy's?
    a. 50
    b. 75
    c. 100
    d. 125
    Ans.: c   LG: 2   Page: 391   QT: C

22. When using the normal curve and the Stanford-Binet IQ scores shown in the text (mean = 100, standard deviation = 16), what percentage of the population would score above a 132 on the test?
    a. 2 %
    b. 16 %
    c. 50 %
    d. 98%
    Ans.: a   LG: 2   Page: 391   QT: C

23. When using the normal curve and the Stanford-Binet IQ scores shown in the text (mean = 100, standard deviation = 16), what percentage of the population would score below a 68 on the test?
    a. 98 %
    b. 50 %
    c. 16 %
    d. 2 %
    Ans.: d   LG: 2   Page: 391   QT: C

24. The two most widely used intelligence tests are the _____ and the _____.
    a. Stanford-Binet; Sternberg Elementary Test
    b. Raven Matrices Test; Stanford-Binet
    c. Stanford-Binet; Wechsler
    d. Sternberg Elementary Test; Raven Matrices Test
    Ans.: c   LG: 2   Page: 391   QT: F

25. Wechsler's IQ test was an advancement over earlier tests primarily because it
    a. corrected for cultural bias.
    b. used random sampling.
    c. distinguished verbal from non-verbal IQ.
    d. defined intelligence.
    Ans.: c   LG: 2   Page: 391   QT: F

26. Which of the following is not a version of the Wechsler test?
    a. Wechsler Adult Intelligence Scale III (WAIS-III)
    b. Wechsler Intelligence Scale for Children (WISC-III)
    c. Wechsler Preschool and Primary Scale of Intelligence (WPPSI)
    d. Wechsler Prenatal Scale of Intelligence (WPSI)
    Ans.: d   LG: 2   Page: 391   QT: F

27. Which of the following is not an advantage of an individual intelligence test over a group intelligence test?
    a. Individual tests better measure frustration and persistence.
    b. Individual tests are generally more convenient and economical.
    c. Individual tests sample behaviors.
    d. Individual tests sample energy and enthusiasm.
    Ans.: b   LG: 2   Page: 391   QT: C

28. Which of the following is an example of a group test?
    a. Wechsler Adult Intelligence Scale III
    b. Stanford-Binet
    c. Wechsler Preschool and Primary Scale of Intelligence
    d. Scholastic Assessment Test
    Ans.: d   LG: 2   Page: 392   QT: F

29. When placement decisions about an individual student are to be made as a result of a group test, which of the following must also be considered?
    a. An individual test should also be administered.
    b. Information about the child's abilities outside of the testing situation must be considered.
    c. Both a and b are correct.
    d. None of the above. Group test results are sufficient for school placement.
    Ans.: c   LG: 2   Page: 392   QT: C

30. A test that predicts an individual's ability to learn a skill or what can be accomplished with training is a(n)
    a. achievement test.
    b. ability test.
    c. aptitude test.
    d. competency test.
    Ans.: c   LG: 2   Page: 393   QT: F

31. A(n) _____ measures what a person has learned or the skills that a person has mastered.
    a. competency test
    b. ability test
    c. aptitude test
    d. achievement test
    Ans.: d   LG: 2   Page: 393   QT: F

32. Aptitude is to _____ as achievement is to _____.
    a. future performance; current performance
    b. current performance; ability
    c. ability; potential
    d. knowledge; future performance
    Ans.: a   LG: 2   Page: 393   QT: C

33. The recent change of the SAT from the Scholastic Aptitude Test to the Scholastic Assessment Test is a result of
    a. political correctness.
    b. the SAT being both an achievement and an aptitude test.
    c. The SAT no longer is seen as a valid test of aptitude.
    d. The inability of the SAT to predict college success.
    Ans.: b   LG: 2   Page: 393   QT: C

34. Research has found that the SAT prep courses will raise a student's score _____ points on average for the 200-800 point scales.
    a. 100
    b. 200
    c. 0
    d. 15
    Ans.: d   LG: 2   Page: 393   QT: F

35. Juanita has decided to take a test to determine what she might have a talent for. She is most likely taking a(n)
    a. competency test.
    b. ability test.
    c. aptitude test.
    d. achievement test.
    Ans.: c   LG: 2   Page: 393   QT: A

36. At the end of the semester, Lateefa gives her psychology students a test to see what they have learned. Lateefa is most likely giving them a(n)
    a. competency test.
    b. ability test.
    c. aptitude test.
    d. achievement test.
    Ans.: d   LG: 2   Page: 393   QT: A

37. William has joined the Army and wants to drive tanks. William has never learned to drive a car. It is a pretty good assumption that before the Army invests money in training William to drive one of its most expensive and sophisticated vehicles, they will give him an_____.
    a. achievement test
    b. aptitude test
    c. orientation test
    d. altitude test
    Ans.: b   LG: 2   Page: 393   QT: A

38. An individual who specialized in psychological testing would be know as a
    a. psychologist.
    b. tester.
    c. psychometrist.
    d. psychoassesser.
    Ans.: c   LG: 2   Page: 393   QT: F

39. Which of the following would be a responsibility of a psychometrist?
    a. creating tests
    b. interpreting tests
    c. administering tests
    d. all of the above
    Ans.: d   LG: 2   Page: 393   QT: F

40. Psychometrists would work in which of the following fields?
    a. education
    b. business
    c. clinical fields
    d. all of the above
    Ans.: d   LG: 2   Page: 393   QT: F

41. Which of the following is not part of the criteria for a good test?
    a. validity
    b. high scores
    c. reliability
    d. standardization.
    Ans.: b   LG: 2   Page: 394   QT: F

42. The extent to which a test measures what it is intended to measure is called
    a. standardization.
    b. reliability.
    c. validity.
    d. measurability.
    Ans.: c   LG: 2   Page: 394   QT: F

43. The Mad Hatter decides to find out how long that Alice can hold her breath. Each time she holds her breath, he takes a tape measure and measures the distance from her head to her toes. To his surprise, regardless of when she exhales, each time it is the same. What can be said about the Mad Hatter's device for measuring how long she can hold her breath?
    a. It is valid, but not reliable.
    b. It is reliable, but not valid.
    c. It is both valid and reliable.
    d. It is neither valid nor reliable.
    Ans.: b   LG: 2   Page: 394   QT: A

44. After taking a psychology class, Ralph and Ed decide that they can get rich making a better intelligence test that will cost less money than the existing ones. They immediately drop their plans to develop a cheaper cafeteria hot dog and refocus on making their test a valid one. Which of the following would be the best way to measure their test's validity?
    a. They administer their test multiple times to ensure consistency in outcomes.
    b. They compare their test results to how the same subjects did on an established test of intelligence such as the Wechsler or Stanford-Binet.
    c. They make certain that the outcomes of their scores fit the bell curve.
    d. They give the test to a group.
    Ans.: b   LG: 2   Page: 394   QT: A

45. After taking a psychology class, Ralph and Ed decide that they can get rich making a better intelligence test that will cost less money than the existing ones. They immediately drop their plans to train sea snails to clean school showers and refocus on making their intelligence test a reliable one. Which of the following would not be a way to measure their test's reliability?
    a. They administer their test to the same individual multiple times and then measure consistency in test outcomes.
    b. They give alternate forms of the same test to the same individual and then measure consistency in test outcomes.
    c. They give the same test to the same individual twice and then compare his scores to see if they are comparable.
    d. They compare their test results to how the same subjects did on an established test of intelligence such as the Wechsler or Stanford-Binet.
    Ans.: d   LG: 2   Page: 394   QT: A

46. A tester is following a set script in reading instructions to a number of individuals taking a teacher certification test. He reads the instructions word for word, the subjects have assigned seats, and the parts of the test follow a precise time schedule. Which of the following is this an example of?
    a. validity
    b. reliability
    c. criterion validity
    d. standardization
    Ans.: d   LG: 2   Page: 394   QT: A

47. Standardization contributes to all but which of the following *except*
    a. establishing norms for a test.
    b. establishing performance standards for the test.
    c. allowing scores to be compared.
    d. fairness across different cultures.
    Ans.: d   LG: 2   Page: 395   QT: F

48. Tests that are intended to give consistent outcomes that are not influenced by where an individual has acquired their life experiences would be called
    a. unbiased tests.
    b. culturally-biased tests.
    c. fair tests.
    d. cultural-fair tests.
    Ans.: d   LG: 2   Page: 395   QT: F

49. Tests, intentionally or unintentionally, are generally going to show a bias toward
    a. the group that the test maker is a member of.
    b. the group that the test maker is testing.
    c. the majority culture.
    d. the minority culture.
    Ans.: a   LG: 2   Page: 396   QT: C

50. Culture-fair tests are
    a. intended to measure intelligence.
    b. intended to be culturally unbiased.
    c. culturally biased.
    d. universal.
    Ans.: b   LG: 2   Page: 395   QT: F

51. Which of the following is seen as the closest to a culture-fair test?
    a. Scholastic Assessment Test
    b. Raven Progressive Matrices Test
    c. Stanford-Binet
    d. Wechsler Preschool and Primary Scale of Intelligence
    Ans.: b   LG: 2   Page: 395   QT: A

52. Diane moves to Great Britain because she knows that language will not be a problem. She takes a test for employment and is asked the simple question, "If rugby team A scores two tries and one conversion and rugby team B scores three tries and three conversions, how much does team B win by? She has no idea where to begin. This test is
    a. culture-fair.
    b. culturally biased.
    c. too dependent on math skills.
    d. all of the above
    Ans.: b   LG: 2   Page: 395   QT: A

53. Many Native American children are visual learners. They are stronger with manipulating visual representations than they are with verbal representations. Which of the following tests would you recommend for them?
    a. Scholastic Assessment Test
    b. Wechsler Preschool and Primary Scale of Intelligence
    c. Stanford Binet
    d. Raven Progressive Matrices Test
    Ans.: d   LG: 2   Page: 395   QT: C

54. What do the Raven Progressive Matrices Test and the SOMPA have in common?
    a. Both have strict time limits.
    b. Both are entirely non-verbal.
    c. Both are designed for children from low income families.
    d. Both represent efforts to develop culture-fair intelligence tests.
    Ans.: d   LG: 2   Page: 395/396 QT: C

55. Why is the Raven Progressive Matrices Test considered to be a culture-fair test?
    a. It is not a long test.
    b. It is easy for all cultures.
    c. It contains no verbal questions.
    d. It enhances self-esteem.
    Ans.: c   LG: 2   Page: 395   QT: F

56. When utilizing intelligence test scores as an insight into a child's abilities, it is best to
    a. rely on the results as a stand-alone indicator.
    b. use the results as one of many sources of information.
    c. ignore the results.
    d. place the child according to the results.
    Ans.: b   LG: 2   Page: 396   QT: F

57. Intelligence tests can be
    a. an insightful, diagnostic tool.
    b. a stereotyping, damaging tool.
    c. used to identify gifted or special-needs children.
    d. all of the above
    Ans.: d   LG: 2   Page: 396   QT: F

58. According to the text, which of the following is *incorrect* regarding use of intelligence tests?
    a. Intelligence test scores can often establish stereotypes.
    b. Often intelligence tests are given too much weight in placement.
    c. Ability tests only measure current performance.
    d. There are many better alternatives to using intelligence tests.
    Ans.: d   LG: 2   Page: 396/397 QT: F

Learning Goal 3: Identify four neuroscience approaches to intelligence.

59. Which of the following has had the greatest effect on the neuroscience approach to intelligence?
    a. Advances in technology have enabled new looks at brain activity.
    b. Psychologists have finally taken an interest in the brain.
    c. Ethical standards have made human experimentation in intelligence easier.
    d. all of the above
    Ans.: a   LG: 3   Page: 397   QT: F

60. Which of the following is not discussed in your text as an area of interest for neuroscientists studying intelligence at this time?
   a. information processing speed
   b. brain electrical activity
   c. brain cell location
   d. brain energy consumption
   Ans.: c   LG: 3   Page: 398   QT: F

61. Herman has a very large head, and after reading research on brain size, decides that he must also be very intelligent as a result. Which of the following is true regarding brain size and intelligence?
   a. Individuals who have a larger head are more intelligent as a result of it.
   b. There is a small correlation between brain size and intelligence.
   c. Acting intelligently causes a larger brain to take shape.
   d. Both a and c are correct
   Ans.: b   LG: 3   Page: 398   QT: A

62. When neuroscientists are measuring human reaction time while investigating intelligence, they are doing research in
   a. nerve conduction velocity.
   b. information processing speed.
   c. evoked neurological potential.
   d. brain energy consumption.
   Ans.: b   LG: 3   Page: 398   QT: F

63. Which of the following statements is *not* true regarding brain neural activity and intelligence?
   a. There appears to be no consistent connection between nerve conductivity velocity and intelligence.
   b. Evoked potential refers to electrical activity in the sensory areas of the brain that is caused by some external stimulus.
   c. Faster brain activities in the evoked potential areas causes higher intelligence.
   d. Both b and c are correct.
   Ans.: a   LG: 3   Page: 398   QT: F

64. Which of the following statements is *true* regarding energy consumption in the brain?
   a. There is no difference in energy consumption between more and less intelligent individuals.
   b. The brains of lower intelligence individuals use more energy when at rest than the brains of higher intelligence individuals.
   c. The brains of higher intelligence individuals use less energy while completing complex cognitive tasks than the brains of lower intelligence individuals.
   d. Energy consumption in the brain is monitored by an MRI.
   Ans.: c   LG: 3   Page: 399   QT: F

65. The consensus on biological measures of intelligence is that
   a. researchers have learned all they need to know about the brain's activities.
   b. though brain biology is interesting, it is not related to intelligence.
   c. our approach to the study of intelligence should emphasize human behavior.
   d. our understanding of biological measures of intelligence will increase as technology advances.
   Ans.: d   LG: 3   Page: 399   QT: C

Learning Goal 4: Evaluate theories of multiple intelligences.

66. Spearman's perspective that individuals have both a general intelligence and a number of specific abilities is called
    a. Spearman's g.
    b. Spearman's s.
    c. Spearman's multiple intelligences.
    d. Spearman's two-factor theory.
    Ans.: d   LG: 4   Page: 400   QT: F

67. Which of the following was one of the factors in Spearman's two-factor theory?
    a. linguistic intelligence
    b. specific intelligence
    c. general intelligence
    d. both b and c
    Ans.: d   LG: 4   Page: 400   QT: F

68. Spearman's g refers to
    a. global intelligence.
    b. general intelligence.
    c. genetic intelligence.
    d. generic intelligence.
    Ans.: b   LG: 4   Page: 400   QT: F

69. Spearman's s refers to
    a. special intelligence.
    b. seriated intelligence.
    c. spatial intelligence.
    d. specific abilities.
    Ans.: d   LG: 4   Page: 400   QT: F

70. A statistical procedure that correlates test scores to identifying clusters that measure a specific ability is called
    a. regression.
    b. item analysis.
    c. multiple regression.
    d. factor analysis.
    Ans.: d   LG: 4   Page: 400   QT: F

71. Thurstone utilized _____ to develop his _____ theory of intelligence.
    a. regression; two-factor
    b. factor analysis; multiple-factor
    c. regression; multiple-factor
    d. regression; factor analysis
    Ans.: b   LG: 4   Page: 400   QT: F

72. Which of the following best describes Thurstone's Multiple-Factor Theory of Intelligence?
    a. Intelligence is made up of two factors, specific and general.
    b. Intelligence is made up of seven primary mental abilities, not a general intelligence.
    c. Five multiple factors of intelligence are included in a general intelligence that encompasses them all.
    d. Intelligence is made up of eight types of intelligence.
    Ans.: b   LG: 4   Page: 400   QT: C

73. Which of the following sequences regarding the chronological succession of the study of intelligence is correct? (earliest to most recent)
    a. Binet, Wechsler, Spearman, Thurstone
    b. Binet, Spearman, Thurstone, Galton
    c. Spearman, Galton, Binet, Thurstone
    d. Thurstone, Spearman, Galton, Binet
    Ans.: a   LG: 4   Pages: 399–400 QT: F

74. Which of the following is *not true* regarding Gardner's Theory of Eight Intelligences?
    a. Gardner has identified types of intelligence that are important to particular occupations.
    b. Each of Gardner's intelligences involve unique cognitive skills.
    c. Gardner's theory has been applied successfully to education.
    d. Attempts to apply Gardner's theory to education have been unsuccessful.
    Ans.: d   LG: 4   Pages: 400–401 QT: C

75. Caroline is a former dancer who is now an instructor. Despite the fact that she is no longer as physically as fit as she once was, she has an exceptional ability to demonstrate her former skills. She can still perform moves that her physically more capable students cannot master. Which of the following theories of intelligence would explain this?
    a. Spearman's g
    b. Thurstone's Multiple-factor Theory
    c. Gardner's Multiple Intelligences
    d. all of the above
    Ans.: c   LG: 4   Page: 400   QT: A

76. Which of Gardner's intelligences would be *least* important for a car salesperson?
    a. bodily-kinesthetic
    b. verbal
    c. interpersonal skills
    d. mathematical skills
    Ans.: a   LG: 4   Page: 400   QT: A

77. Which of Gardner's intelligences would be *least* important for an actress?
    a. verbal skills
    b. interpersonal
    c. intrapersonal
    d. spatial
    Ans.: d   LG: 4   Page: 400   QT: A

78. Juan wants to work as a park ranger. Which of Gardner's intelligences would be *least* important for him in this career choice?
    a. musical
    b. naturalist
    c. interpersonal
    d. verbal
    Ans.: a   LG: 4   Page: 400   QT: A

79. Lakesha loves the game of golf, and wants to pursue a professional career. Which of Gardner's intelligences would be *least* important to her?
    a. bodily-kinesthetic
    b. musical
    c. intrapersonal
    d. mathematical
    Ans.: b   LG: 4   Page: 400   QT: A

80. Jessica wants to become a biology teacher. Which of Gardner's intelligences would be *least* important for her?
    a. bodily-kinesthetic
    b. naturalist
    c. verbal
    d. interpersonal
    Ans.: a   LG: 4   Page: 400   QT: A

81. Emily has a very good understanding of herself. Gardner would call this _____ intelligence.
    a. interpersonal
    b. intrapersonal
    c. verbal
    d. naturalistic
    Ans.: b   LG: 4   Page: 400   QT: A

82. Which of the following is the most recent addition to Gardner's multiple intelligences?
    a. bodily-kinesthetic
    b. intrapersonal
    c. musical
    d. naturalist
    Ans.: d   LG: 4   Page: 400   QT: F

83. Which of the following is *not true* regarding Gardner's theory of multiple intelligences?
    a. Each of the intelligences involves unique cognitive skills.
    b. Each of the intelligences can be destroyed by brain damage.
    c. One individual cannot have more than one type of intelligence.
    d. Each can show up in an exaggerated fashion in gifted individuals.
    Ans.: c   LG: 4   Page: 400   QT: F

273

84. Advantages of applying Gardner's multiple intelligence theory to the classroom include all of the following *except*
    a. helping children develop their strengths.
    b. providing children with a variety of forms of learning.
    c. grouping children according to IQ scores.
    d. stimulating the range of intelligences in children.
    Ans.: c   LG: 4   Page: 401   QT: C

85. Children in a classroom that utilizes Gardner's multiple intelligences would be *least* likely to be doing which of the following?
    a. copying words from the chalkboard
    b. building things
    c. acting out their own stories
    d. examining leafs and insects
    Ans.: a   LG: 4   Page: 401   QT: C

86. Which of the following theorists recognized creativity as a component of intelligence?
    a. Thurstone
    b. Spearman
    c. Gardner
    d. Sternberg
    Ans.: d   LG: 4   Page: 402   QT: F

87. Which of the following is *not* one of Sternberg's types of intelligence?
    a. application
    b. analytical
    c. creative
    d. practical
    Ans.: a   LG: 4   Page: 402   QT: F

88. Which of Sternberg's types of intelligence is *closest* to what has been traditionally called intelligence?
    a. application
    b. analytical
    c. creative
    d. practical
    Ans.: b   LG: 4   Page: 402   QT: F

89. Byron is very good at acquiring and storing new information, planning, and making decisions. Which of Sternberg's intelligences does Byron demonstrate well?
    a. application
    b. analytical
    c. creative
    d. practical
    Ans.: b   LG: 4   Page: 402   QT: A

90. Dhiraj has an insightful mind and excels at solving new types of problems with unique solutions. Which of Sternberg's intelligences would best explain this?
    a. application
    b. analytical
    c. creative
    d. practical
    Ans.: c   LG: 4   Page: 402   QT: A

91. Jane does not have high IQ scores but functions very well in life. She can fix most common problems around her house, gets along well with others, and has a knack for reading situations and making good decisions. Which of Sternberg's intelligences would best explain this?
    a. application
    b. analytical
    c. creative
    d. practical
    Ans.: d   LG: 4   Page: 402   QT: A

92. Which of Sternberg's intelligences would be a synonym for "street smart?"
    a. application
    b. analytical
    c. creative
    d. practical
    Ans.: d   LG: 4   Page: 402   QT: A

93. According to Sternberg, a child with which of the following types of intelligence would be favored in a conventional school?
    a. application
    b. analytical
    c. creative
    d. practical
    Ans.: b   LG: 4   Page: 402   QT: C

94. From Sternberg's perspective, a student with which of the following types of intelligence would not thrive in a conventional school but would do very well outside of school.
    a. application
    b. analytical
    c. creative
    d. practical
    Ans.: d   LG: 4   Page: 402   QT: C

95. Which of the following is *true* regarding theories of intelligence?
    a. Sternberg developed a theory which included three components of intelligence.
    b. Gardener's theory focuses on multiple intelligences which originate in different areas of the brain.
    c. Sternberg and Gardner proposed a "General Intelligence."
    d. Both a and b are correct
    Ans.: d   LG: 4   Page: 402   QT: C

96. Which of the following is *not true* regarding Gardner's theory of multiple intelligences and Sternberg's triarchic theory of intelligence?
    a. They suggest unconventional approaches of intelligence.
    b. They have had some effect on how teachers instruct students.
    c. They have challenged traditional views of intelligence.
    d. They have produced a research base that refutes traditional views of intelligence.
    Ans.: d   LG: 4   Page: 402   QT: C

97. The idea of emotional intelligence is described by which of the following statements?
    a. Emotional intelligence is similar to Sternberg's practical intelligence.
    b. Emotional intelligence may be more important than intellectual intelligence.
    c. Emotional intelligence is similar to Gardner's interpersonal intelligence.
    d. all of the above
    Ans.: d   LG: 4   Page: 404   QT: C

98. Which of the following is *not* an area of Goleman's emotional intelligence as shown in the text?
    a. emotional awareness
    b. reading emotions
    c. eliminating emotions
    d. handling relationships
    Ans.: c   LG: 4   Page: 404   QT: F

99. Which of the following components of intelligence is the perspective of emotional intelligence most consistent with?
    a. Gardner's interpersonal intelligence
    b. Sternberg's practical intelligence
    c. Gardner's intrapersonal intelligence
    d. all of the above
    Ans.: d   LG: 4   Page: 404   QT: C

100. Criticisms of multiple-intelligence theories include all of the following *except* that
    a. the information that these theories provide has no useful application.
    b. musical intelligence is not a valid form of intelligence.
    c. there is not a strong research base to support the multiple intelligence theories.
    d. creativity is not a form of intelligence,
    Ans.: a   LG: 4   Page: 404-405 QT: C

Learning Goal 5: Discuss characteristics of mental retardation, giftedness, and creativity.

101. Which of the following is a characteristic of mental retardation?
    a. an IQ score below a set criteria
    b. difficulty adapting to everyday life
    c. onset of these characteristics in a developmental period
    d. all of the above
    Ans.: d   LG: 5   Page: 406   QT: F

102. Why are IQ scores alone not used to indicate mental retardation?
    a. Clinicians could not agree if the determining score should be 68 or 70.
    b. There was not a large enough sample of subjects to establish norms.
    c. The mentally retarded do not do well on intelligence tests.
    d. Often subjects with the same low IQ scores can have much different levels of adaptive behaviors.
    Ans.: d   LG: 5   Page: 406   QT: F

103. Which of the following is not a part of the definition of mental retardation?
    a. IQ below 70
    b. brain injury
    c. difficulty adapting to daily life
    d. onset by age 18.
    Ans.: b   LG: 5   Page: 406   QT: F

104. Which of the following would not be a case of mental retardation?
    a. an adult who, after thirty years of normal intellectual functioning, is involved in an automobile accident and has suffered brain damage that has severely limited mental functioning
    b. an adult who was born with Down syndrome and lives in a group home because of cognitive deficits
    c. a seven-year-old child with an IQ of 40 who was born with brain damage and needs constant attention from caregivers
    d. a twelve-year-old child with an IQ score of 55 who has grown up in a severely deprived environment and who struggles in school
    Ans.: a   LG: 5   Page: 406   QT: A

105. Which of the following individuals would be likely to be diagnosed as mentally retarded?
    a. Greg: 16 years old; IQ of 110, no apparent cognitive deficits
    b. Billy: 14 years old; IQ of 100, reading disability
    c. Tom: 13 years old; IQ of 80, difficulty paying attention
    d. John: 12 years old; IQ of 63, difficulty adapting to changes in everyday situations
    Ans.: d   LG: 5   Page: 406   QT: A

106. An individual whose mental retardation was caused by a family genetic disorder would have
    a. organic retardation.
    b. psychosocial retardation.
    c. cultural retardation.
    d. familial retardation.
    Ans.: a   LG: 5   Page: 406   QT: F

107. Which of the following children would not be an example of organic retardation?
    a. William, who has Down syndrome
    b. Scott, who grew up in a deprived environment
    c. Darius, who has fragile X syndrome
    d. Diane, whose brain damage is a direct result of her mother's alcohol abuse during pregnancy
    Ans.: b   LG: 5   Page: 406   QT: C

108. Down's syndrome is a form of
    a. organic retardation.
    b. psychosocial retardation.
    c. cultural retardation.
    d. familial retardation.
    Ans.: a   LG: 5   Page: 406   QT: F

109. Individuals who suffer from organic retardation usually have IQ scores that range from
    a. 70 to 100.
    b. 55 to 70.
    c. 40 to 54.
    d. 0 to 50.
    Ans.: d   LG: 5   Page: 406   QT: F

110. Individuals who suffer from cultural-familial retardation usually have IQ scores that range from
    a. 70 to 100.
    b. 55 to 70.
    c. 40 to 54.
    d. 0 to 50.
    Ans.: b   LG: 5   Page: 406   QT: F

111. Tom has been labeled as mentally retarded, yet he works consistently as a hot dog vender at the beach. He has no trouble counting money. Which type of mental retardation would you suggest that Tom has been labeled with?
    a. organic retardation
    b. behavioral retardation
    c. cultural-familial retardation
    d. id-induced retardation
    Ans.: c   LG: 5   Page: 406   QT: C

112. When environmental effects seem to be the only contributing factors to a child's intellectual deficits, it is referred to as
    a. organic retardation.
    b. behavioral retardation.
    c. cultural-familial retardation.
    d. id-induced retardation.
    Ans.: c   LG: 5   Page: 406   QT: C

113. Which of the following are characteristics of a child who has cultural-familial retardation?
    a. They often prefer tangible rewards to praise.
    b. They will have an IQ score between 55 and 70.
    c. A supportive environment can often raise intelligence levels.
    d. all of the above
    Ans.: d   LG: 5   Page: 406   QT: C

114. Which of the following is not true regarding classification of mental retardation?
    a. Mild: IQ range of 55 to 70, nearly 90 percent of the mentally retarded fall into this category.
    b. Moderate: IQ range of 40 to 54, nearly 90 percent of the mentally retarded fall into this category.
    c. Severe: IQ range of 25 to 39, nearly 5 percent of the mentally retarded fall into this category.
    d. Profound: IQ below 25, nearly 1 percent of the mentally retarded fall into this category.
    Ans.: b   LG: 5   Page: 406   QT: F

115. Individuals who have an IQ score over 120 may be
    a. organically retarded.
    b. culturally retarded.
    c. gifted.
    d. familially retarded.
    Ans.: c   LG: 5   Page: 406   QT: F

116. Which of the following individuals could be considered gifted?
    a. Nika, who has an IQ score of 132
    b. Devon, who is the best cello player that his teacher has ever worked with
    c. Diane, who did not play hockey until she was 15, yet three years later earned a college scholarship
    d. all of the above
    Ans.: d   LG: 5   Page: 406   QT: C

117. Recent research has found that gifted individuals are more likely to demonstrate which of the following?
    a. are more mature
    b. have more emotional problems
    c. be more maladjusted
    d. mental disorders
    Ans.: a   LG: 5   Page: 407   QT: F

118. Which of the following is *not* an adjective that could describe gifted children?
    a. precocious
    b. maladjusted
    c. independent
    d. self-motivated
    Ans.: b   LG: 5   Page: 407   QT: F

119. Which of the following would be the best example of precocity as applied to giftedness?
    a. a child mastering an area earlier than her peers
    b. a child who is not hesitant to speak out
    c. a child who is shy and reserved
    d. a child who is bright but shy
    Ans.: a   LG: 5   Page: 407   QT: F

120. Which of the following would be the *best* way to teach a gifted child?
    a. extensive use of scaffolding
    b. provide plenty of support
    c. rigid rules and instruction
    d. allow them to discover on their own
    Ans.: d   LG: 5   Page: 408   QT: C

121. Which of the following is not given for a reason that gifted children do not always become revolutionary adult creators?
    a. little parental encouragement
    b. difficulty making the transition from child prodigy to adult creator
    c. overzealous parents
    d. loss of intrinsic motivation
    Ans.: a   LG: 5   Page: 408   QT: C

122. Research has found that gifted children grow into _____ adults.
    a. productive
    b. unhappy
    c. maladjusted
    d. both b and c
    Ans.: a   LG: 5   Page: 408   QT: F

123. The ability to think of things in novel and unusual ways is called
    a. giftedness.
    b. creativity.
    c. convergent thinking.
    d. precocity.
    Ans.: b   LG: 5   Page: 408   QT: F

124. Which of the following is true regarding the relationship between creativity and intelligence?
    a. All intelligent people are creative.
    b. All creative people are intelligent.
    c. Intelligence and creativity are the same thing.
    d. Creativity was a component of Sternberg's triarchic theory of intelligence.
    Ans.: d   LG: 5   Page: 408   QT: C

125. _____ thinking involves producing many answers to a question, whereas _____ thinking involves producing one correct answer.
    a. Convergent; creative
    b. Convergent; divergent
    c. Divergent; convergent
    d. Divergent; creative
    Ans.: c   LG: 5   Page: 408   QT: F

126. Creativity is primarily associated with which type of thinking?
    a. divergent
    b. convergent
    c. logical
    d. conventional
    Ans.: a   LG: 5   Page: 408   QT: F

127. Convergent thinking, commonly required on IQ tests, produces
    a. one answer.
    b. two answers.
    c. three answers.
    d. unlimited answers.
    Ans.: a   LG: 5   Page: 408   QT: F

128. Which of the following is not related to divergent thinking?
    a. creativity
    b. intelligence test questions
    c. developing multiple solutions
    d. novel and unusual solutions
    Ans.: b   LG: 5   Page: 408   QT: F

129. Which of the following is related to convergent thinking?
    a. creativity
    b. producing one correct answer
    c. questions on intelligence tests
    d. both b and c
    Ans.: d   LG: 5   Page: 408   QT: F

130. Levon has been hired as a troubleshooter to help a company solve a business problem. He has established a reputation for himself as a creative thinker who can come up with novel solutions that others do not think of. Levon would be considered a(n)
    a. convergent thinker.
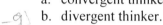
    b. divergent thinker.
    c. linear thinker.
    d. unusual thinker.
    Ans.: b   LG: 5   Page: 408   QT: A

131. The school drama club has recruited Melanie, who will also be the valedictorian, to help with organizing the spring play. As a group, they have wonderful ideas but they cannot seem to decide which ones to put into action. Melanie has a reputation for choosing the best strategy from among many and getting things done. Melanie is most likely a(n)
    a. convergent thinker.
    b. divergent thinker.
    c. creative thinker.
    d. unusual thinker.
    Ans.: a   LG: 5   Page: 408   QT: A

132. Which of the following is a helpful framework for the steps of the creative process?
    a. insight, preparation, incubation, evaluation, elaboration
    b. preparation, incubation, insight, evaluation, elaboration
    c. incubation, preparation, elaboration, evaluation, insight
    d. insight, preparation, elaboration, insight, evaluation
    Ans.: b   LG: 5   Page: 408-409 QT: F

133. Which of the following is *least* characteristic of a creative thinker?
    a. flexibility and playful thinking
    b. inner motivation and a willingness to risk
    c. a sensitivity to the evaluation of others
    d. objective evaluation of work
    Ans.: c   LG: 5   Page: 409   QT: C

134. Rose has decided to work at living a more creative life. Which of the following would you recommend to her to cultivate her creativity?
    a. Try to be surprised by something every day.
    b. Try to surprise someone every day.
    c. When something sparks your interest, follow it.
    d. all of the above
    Ans.: d   LG: 5   Page: 410-411 QT: C

Learning Goal 6: Analyze the contributions of heredity and environment to intelligence.

135. Based on his research, Jensen argued that intelligence is
    a. primarily hereditary.
    b. primarily environmental.
    c. about equally hereditary and environmental.
    d. neither hereditary nor environmental.
    Ans.: a   LG: 6   Page: 412   QT: F

136. What kind of research did Jensen use to examine whether intelligence is due to heredity or to environment?
    a. ethnic research
    b. twin studies
    c. focus groups
    d. none of the above
    Ans.: b   LG: 6   Page: 412   QT: F

137. When researchers use twin studies to investigate heritability, they are interested in
    a. identical twins.
    b. fraternal twins.
    c. biological and adoptive parents.
    d. all of the above
    Ans.: d   LG: 6   Page: 412/413 QT: F

138. In the Jensen study, which of the following pairs showed the highest correlation in IQ scores?
    a. identical twins reared together
    b. identical twins reared apart
    c. fraternal twins reared together
    d. fraternal twins reared apart
    Ans.: a   LG: 6   Page: 412   QT: F

139. Jensen's claims about heredity's influence on intelligence is most similar to whose point of view?
    a. Sternberg
    b. Herrnstein and Murray
    c. Gardner
    d. Skinner
    Ans.: b   LG: 6   Page: 416/417 QT: C

140. Criticisms regarding both Jensen's work and *The Bell Curve* include all of the following *except*
    a. perpetuation of racism, classism, and stereotypes.
    b. cultural bias of IQ tests.
    c. methodological flaws in hereditary studies.
    d. legal limitations of intelligence tests.
    Ans.: d   LG: 6   Page: 416   QT: C

141. The fraction of the variance in IQ in a population that is caused by genetic effects would be called
    a. genetics.
    b. heritability.
    c. environmental effects.
    d. genetic marker.
    Ans.: b   LG: 6   Page: 413   QT: F

142. Which of the following is *not* true regarding the heritability index?
    a. It demonstrates how much genetics cause changes in IQ scores.
    b. It is a numerical value with a high score of 1.00.
    c. It is a correlation coefficient.
    d. It quantifies the relationship between genetics and IQ scores.
    Ans.: a   LG: 6   Page: 413   QT: C

143. Which of the following is not a criticism of conclusions drawn from the heritability index?
    a. The heritability index is a correlation coefficient.
    b. Virtually all of the data that is used to calculate the heritability index comes from traditional IQ tests, which may not be the best measures of intelligence.
    c. The heritability index assumes that we can treat genetic and environmental influences as quanitatively different factors.
    d. Heredity and the environments may so interconnected that their influence is almost impossible to determine.
    Ans.: a   LG: 6   Page: 413   QT: C

144. Which of the following best demonstrates the interactions of genetics and the environment?
    a. Identical twins have the highest correlation of IQ scores.
    b. Environmental interventions have been demonstrated to improve IQ scores significantly.
    c. Identical twins from different environments have similar IQ scores.
    d. By choosing a career path, individuals express genetic tendencies by selecting the environment that they find most compatible.
    Ans.: d   LG: 6   Page: 413   QT: C

145. Jorge's parents talked and communicated with him a great deal from the time he was born. Based on the research in the text, what would you predict for Jorge when his IQ is measured at age 3?
    a. The more that Jorge's parents talked with him, the higher his score will be.
    b. The more that Jorge's parents talked to him, the lower his score will be.
    c. There will be no relationship between how much Jorge's parents talked with him and his IQ score.
    d. If Jorge's parents are from the middle class, they will be less likely to talk to him because of their work schedules.
    Ans.: a   LG: 6   Page: 414   QT: C

146. Based on the Ramey study, which involved exposing children from low-income, poorly educated homes to a more enriched environment and then comparing their IQ scores to a group that had not received such a treatment, which of the following outcomes is *not* true?
    a. The children who were assigned to the enriched environment were less likely than the control group to be held back a year in school.
    b. The children who were assigned to the enriched environment had an average of a 17-point higher IQ score at the end of the treatment.
    c. The children who were assigned to the enriched environment did better on standardized tests of reading and math than the control group.
    d. Over a decade later, the initial advantage in IQ scores that was shown by the children in the enriched environment had increased to 20 points.
    Ans.: d   LG: 6   Page: 414   QT: F

147. Some researchers believe that intelligence can be increased through the appropriate environmental modifications. Which research evidence least supports this belief?
    a. Environmental enrichment can increase a child's IQ score.
    b. Increased communication with young children is associated with higher IQ scores.
    c. High-quality intervention programs enhance children's intellectual development.
    d. Some children from wealthy families perform very poorly in school and on standardized tests.
    Ans.: d   LG: 6   Page: 414   QT: C

148. How do different cultures define intelligence?
    a. They all define it in different ways.
    b. They all use it as a measure of technical skills only.
    c. They all focus on participation in family and social life.
    d. Intelligence is defined similarly in all cultures.
    Ans.: a   LG: 6   Page: 415   QT: F

149. As African Americans have gained social, economic, and educational opportunities, the gap between African Americans and Whites on standardized tests has
    a. stayed the same.
    b. increased.
    c. decreased.
    d. not been studied.
    Ans.: c   LG: 6   Page: 417   QT: F

150. Which of the following statements would best explain gender comparisons of IQ scores?
    a. Average scores of males and females are not different.
    b. Males are more likely than females to have extremely high or low scores.
    c. Females are more likely than males to have extremely high or low scores.
    d. Both a and b are correct.
    Ans.: d   LG: 6   Page: 417   QT: F

True/False Items

___ 151. Intelligence can be defined as the ability to solve problems and adapt and learn from experience.

___ 152. Sir Frances Galton is considered the father of mental tests.

___ 153. Stern's intelligence quotient consists of the chronological age divided by the mental age and multiplied by 100.

___ 154. The normal distribution is a symmetrical bell shaped curve with most scores falling in the middle and few scores appearing at the ends.

___ 155. Aptitude tests measure what a person has learned.

___ 156. Test reliability is the extent to which a test measures what it is supposed to measure.

___ 157. Culture-fair tests provide an advantage for individuals from a particular culture.

___ 158. The results of using biological measures to assess intelligence have not been very robust.

___ 159. Gardner currently has eight different intelligences.

___ 160. Sternberg emphasized the importance of creativity as a form of intelligence.

___ 161. Giftedness is indicated by an IQ score higher than 100.

___ 162. A convergent thinker is generally considered creative.

___ 163. Jensen proposed that the environment largely influenced IQ scores.

___ 164. Different cultures define intelligence in different ways.

___ 165. There is no significant difference between mean IQ scores between males and females.

Answer Key for True/False Items

151.	Ans.: T	LG: 1	Page: 389	159.	Ans.: T	LG: 4	Page: 400
152.	Ans.: T	LG: 2	Page: 390	160.	Ans.: T	LG: 4	Page: 402
153.	Ans.: F	LG: 2	Page: 390	161.	Ans.: F	LG: 5	Page: 406
154:	Ans.: T	LG: 2	Page: 391	162.	Ans.: F	LG: 5	Page: 408
155.	Ans.: F	LG: 2	Page: 393	163.	Ans.: F	LG: 6	Page: 412
156.	Ans.: F	LG: 2	Page: 394	164.	Ans.: T	LG: 6	Page: 415
157.	Ans.: F	LG: 2	Page: 395	165.	Ans.: T	LG: 6	Page: 417
158.	Ans.: T	LG: 3	Page: 399				

Fill-in-the-Blank Items

166. A key aspect of the study of intelligence is the consideration of _____ differences.

167. _____ intelligence tests are convenient and economical.

168. _____ tests predict an individual's ability to learn a skill.

169. The extent to which a test measures what it is supposed to measure is called _____.

170. _____ tests are intended to not favor one group over another.

171. Individuals with a _____ intelligence use less energy to complete challenging tasks.

172. Spearman and Thurstone both used _____ analysis in developing their theories of intelligence.

173. Gardener believes that there are _____ different types of intelligence.

174. Sternberg's triarchic theory states that there are three different types of intelligence: creative, analytical, and _____.

175. _____ is a condition of limited mental ability characterized by an IQ score below 70, difficulty adapting to everyday life, and with onset by age 18.

176. _____ retardation is generally the outcome of a biological problem.
177. Jensen found that _____ twins had the highest correlation of IQ scores.
178. There is a correlation between how much parents _____ with their children in the first three years of life and the children's IQ scores.
179. Intelligence test scores have _____ in recent decades; this is called the Flynn effect.
180. Enrichment programs have shown a(n) _____ in IQ scores for the children who participate in them.

Answer Key for Fill-in-the-Blank Items

166.	Ans.: individual	LG: 1	Page: 389
167.	Ans.: Group	LG: 2	Page: 391
168.	Ans.: Aptitude	LG: 2	Page: 393
169.	Ans.: validity	LG: 2	Page: 394
170.	Ans.: Culture-fair	LG: 2	Page: 395
171.	Ans.: high	LG: 3	Page: 399
172.	Ans.: factor	LG: 4	Page: 400
173.	Ans.: eight	LG: 4	Page: 400
174.	Ans.: practical	LG: 4	Page: 402
175.	Ans.: Mental retardation	LG: 5	Page: 406
176.	Ans.: Organic	LG: 5	Page: 406
177.	Ans.: identical	LG: 6	Page: 412
178.	Ans.: talk	LG: 6	Page: 414
179.	Ans.: increased	LG: 6	Page: 415
180.	Ans.: increase	LG: 6	Page: 414

Matching Questions

___	181. standardization	A.	correlation
___	182. psychometrist	B.	neuroscience
___	183. culture-fair	C.	test specialist
___	184. brain size	D.	55 to 70 IQ
___	185. Spearman's g	E.	general
___	186. creative intelligence	F.	no bias
___	187. emotional Intelligence	G.	over 120 IQ and/or special talent
___	188. cultural-familial retardation	H.	may be as important as IQ
___	189. giftedness	I.	uniform procedures
___	190. heritability index	J.	Sternberg

Answer Key for Matching Items

181.	Ans.: I	LG: 2	Page: 394		186.	Ans.: J	LG: 4	Page: 402
182.	Ans.: C	LG: 2	Page: 393		187.	Ans.: H	LG: 4	Page: 404
183.	Ans.: F	LG: 2	Page: 395		188.	Ans.: D	LG: 5	Page: 406
184.	Ans.: B	LG: 3	Page: 398		189.	Ans.: G	LG: 5	Page: 406
185.	Ans.: E	LG: 4	Page: 400		190.	Ans.: A	LG: 6	Page: 413

Essay Questions

191. What is intelligence and why is it so difficult to assess? (LG: 1)

Answer Guidelines: Intelligence is defined by our text as the ability to solve problems and to adapt and learn from everyday experiences. By this definition alone, it would be extremely difficult to develop an assessment device that would be comprehensive. Compounding this is the fact that not all intelligence theorists view intelligence the same way.

192. Explain how validity, reliability, and standardization are important to a good test. (LG: 2)

Answer Guidelines: A good test of intelligence meets three criteria: validity, reliability, and standardization. Validity is the extent to which a test measures what it is intended to measure. Reliability means how consistently an individual performs on a test. Standardization focuses on uniform procedures for administering and scoring a test.

193. What is the difference between aptitude and achievement? Why is the SAT now called the Scholastic Assessment Test? (LG: 2)

Answer Guidelines: Aptitude tests predict an individual's ability to learn a skill or future performance. Achievement tests assess what a person already knows. The SAT was called the Scholastic Aptitude Test, but because it is arguably also an achievement test, the name was changed.

194. What is cultural bias in testing? How does it take place and what can be done to avoid it? (LG: 2)

Answer Guidelines: Generally, whoever writes a test creates questions that are familiar to both themselves and the culture that they live in. Early intelligence tests favored white, middle socioeconomic status, urban individuals. Often individuals who did not fit into these categories took these tests and did poorly because the questions were not as applicable to their own lives. This cultural bias produced lower test scores. Culture-fair tests attempt to assess intelligence with questions that are applicable to all who take the test. Examples of such tests are the Raven Progressive Matrices Tests and the SOMPA.

195. Identify and explain two neuroscience approaches to the study of intelligence. (LG: 3)

Answer Guidelines: Answers could include research on brain size, information-processing speed, nerve-conduction velocity, and brain energy use during problem solving.

196. Explain the difference between Spearman's g and Gardner's multiple intelligences. (LG: 4)

Answer Guidelines: Spearman's g is a general intelligence. Gardner believes instead that there are eight specific intelligences, all of which would give individuals the ability to do better or worse in a number of diverse career fields.

197. Describe Sternberg's theory of intelligence. (LG: 4)

Answer Guidelines: Sternberg proposed that there are three main types of intelligence: analytical, creative, and practical. Analytical thinking is closest to what has traditionally been called intelligence and what is commonly assessed on intelligence tests. Sternberg was the first to recognize creativity as a form of intelligence. Practical intelligence is applied intelligence, or "street smarts."

198. What is mental retardation? Identify and explain two types of mental retardation. (LG: 5)

Answer Guidelines: Mental retardation is a condition of limited mental ability in which the individual has a low IQ, usually below 70; has difficulty adapting to everyday life; and has the onset of these characteristics during the so-called developmental period. Organic retardation generally has a biological cause and cultural-familial retardation can be social in origin.

199. What is giftedness? (LG: 5)

Answer Guidelines: People who are gifted have high intelligence (IQ of 120 or higher) and/or a superior talent for a particular domain. Characteristics of gifted individuals include precocity, marching to one's own drummer, and a passion to master.

200. Explain the controversy over genetic and environmental influences on intelligence. In your answer, include Jensen's research and give an example of environmental affects on intelligence. (LG: 6)

Answer Guidelines: Researchers argue whether it is our genetics that determine intelligence or if it is the forces of the environment that shape our intellect. Often it is difficult to separate the influence of one from the other. Answers should describe the findings of Jensen's twin studies as support for a genetic link to intelligence. In addition, Ramey's research on the positive effects of educational child care on intelligence would provide support for the environmental affects.

Chapter 11: Motivation and Emotion

Learning Goals

1. Describe psychological approaches to motivation.
2. Explain the physiological basis of hunger and the nature of eating behavior.
3. Discuss the motivation for sex.
4. Characterize the social cognitive motives and how they influence behavior.
5. Summarize views of emotion.

Multiple-Choice Items

Learning Goal 1: Describe psychological approaches to motivation.

1. Joan goes to the kitchen looking for something to eat whenever she sees a television commercial concerning food. If you wanted to study Joan's behavior, you would be doing research on
   a. emotion.
   b. motivation.
   c. cognition.
   d. perception.
   Ans.: b   LG: 1   Page: 425   QT: C

2. Cathy cannot seem to get herself to focus on her schoolwork. She is very involved in school activities, such as student government and drama club, but class work does not interest her. An educational psychologist would be most interested in her
   a. motivation.
   b. performance.
   c. unconscious.
   d. emotion.
   Ans.: a   LG: 1   Page: 425   QT: C

3. Psychologists who focus on why people and organisms do what they do are studying
   a. association.
   b. cognition.
   c. emotion.
   d. motivation.
   Ans.: d   LG: 1   Page: 425   QT: F

4. Which of the following would be the *most appropriate* topic for a motivation researcher to study?
   a. how need for achievement drives people to success
   b. how the polygraph actually detects lies
   c. how animals behave in their natural habitat
   d. how to get the most intense emotional response
   Ans.: a   LG: 1   Page: 428   QT: C

5. Within psychology, the area of motivation involves the study of
   a. effect and facial displays.
   b. weight gain and weight loss.
   c. why people do the things they do.
   d. animal communication systems.
   Ans.: c   LG: 1   Page: 425   QT: F

6. Which of the following terms describes an instinct?
   a. innate
   b. unlearned
   c. biological
   d. all of the above
   Ans.: d   LG: 1   Page: 425   QT: F

7. Which of the following is the *best* example of an instinct?
   a. Nadia's desire to get good grades
   b. a 4-year-old's curiosity
   c. Pierre's daily evening run
   d. the infant's sucking reflex
   Ans.: d   LG: 1   Page: 425   QT: C

8. Which of the following is true regarding instincts?
   a. Humans and animals both rely equally on instincts.
   b. With technology, we have discovered more human instincts than we were aware of in the past.
   c. Instinct theorists name behaviors rather than explain them.
   d. Instinct theory can explain most human behavior.
   Ans.: c   LG: 1   Page: 425   QT: F

9. What is the relationship between needs and drives?
   a. A need activates a drive.
   b. Needs are independent of drives.
   c. A drive activates a need.
   d. Needs are dependent on drives.
   Ans.: a   LG: 1   Page: 426   QT: C

10. A need is to a physiological state as a drive is to a(n)
    a. innate state.
    b. psychological state.
    c. physical state.
    d. biological state.
    Ans.: b   LG: 1   Page: 426   QT: C

11. Which of the following is the *best* example of a drive?
    a. blinking
    b. dreaming
    c. hunger
    d. anger
    Ans.: c   LG: 1   Page: 426   QT: C

12. The theory of motivation that proposes that the purpose of behavior is to reduce arousal is called the
    a. drive reduction theory.
    b. optimum level of arousal theory.
    c. expectancy theory.
    d. opponent process theory.
    Ans.: a   LG: 1   Page: 426   QT: F

13. According to the drive reduction theory, your need for water will lead to a(n)
    a. tendency to obtain water.
    b. instinct to obtain water.
    c. drive to obtain water.
    d. ambition to obtain water.
    Ans.: c   LG: 1   Page: 426   QT: C

14. An aroused state is to drive as a deprived state is to
    a. instinct.
    b. need.
    c. reflex.
    d. habit.
    Ans.: b   LG: 1   Page: 426   QT: C

15. The ultimate goal of drive reduction is to
    a. relieve any pain felt by the individual.
    b. explain human behavior.
    c. explain primary motives.
    d. restore homeostatic balance.
    Ans.: d   LG: 1   Page: 426   QT: C

16. The human body has a natural, built-in tendency to maintain an overall steady state of functioning. It is called
    a. homeostasis.
    b. the set point.
    c. self-actualization.
    d. emotional balance.
    Ans.: a   LG: 1   Page: 426   QT: F

17. Which of the following is an example of homeostasis?
    a. An organism in pain cries out loudly.
    b. A cold organism shivers to reduce heat loss.
    c. A fearful organism huddles in the corner and cries.
    d. Two friends who have been separated for months greet each other with hugs.
    Ans.: b   LG: 1   Page: 426   QT: C

18. Which of the following is the best psychological term for a state of alertness or activation?
    a. motivation
    b. arousal
    c. need
    d. instinct
    Ans.: b   LG: 1   Page: 426   QT: F

19. The Yerkes-Dodson Law states that
    a. high levels of arousal predict optimal performance.
    b. low levels of arousal predict optimal performance.
    c. moderate levels of arousal predict optimal performance.
    d. moderate levels of arousal predict mediocre performance.
    Ans.: c   LG: 1   Page: 426   QT: C

20. Optimal arousal levels are related to task difficulty in that
    a. simple tasks can be optimized with a low level of arousal.
    b. complex tasks can be optimized with a high level of arousal.
    c. complex tasks can be optimized with a low level of arousal.
    d. There is no link between difficulty of task and level of arousal.
    Ans.: c   LG: 1   Page: 426   QT: C

21. According to the Yerkes-Dodson law, performance is generally
    a. best under conditions of high arousal.
    b. best under conditions of low arousal.
    c. best under conditions of moderate arousal.
    d. unrelated to arousal.
    Ans.: c   LG: 1   Page: 426   QT: F

22. Why would you want to be in a moderate state of arousal when you are about to take an important final exam?
    a. to be as relaxed as possible
    b. to be able to concentrate better
    c. to finish as quickly as possible
    d. to stay awake throughout the test
    Ans.: b   LG: 1   Page: 426   QT: C

23. Two teams have just begun to play in the NCAA Final. Both teams are moving up and down the court in a rather frantic manner for the first couple of minutes, missing all of their shots. How would you explain this situation?
    a. These teams don't know how to play basketball; they should never have been in the final.
    b. Both teams are too lethargic to get the job done.
    c. Both teams are too highly aroused by the excitement of the event.
    d. The coaches did not prepare these teams well enough for this important event.
    Ans.: c   LG: 1   Page: 426   QT: C

24. Which of the following would seem to have the best match for task and arousal level?
    a. Dianne is calculating a complex statistical problem for her test and has a high level of arousal.
    b. Fred has to click "sell" on his computer as soon as his stock hits a certain number and has a low level of arousal.
    c. Catherine is trying out for the U.S. Olympic soccer team and has a moderate level of arousal.
    d. George has to speak in front of a group of his peers and has a high level of arousal.
    Ans.: c   LG: 1   Page: 426   QT: A

25. Which of the following is not a term associated with sensation seeking?
    a. risky behavior
    b. thrill
    c. intense
    d. routine
    Ans.: d   LG: 1   Page: 427   QT: C

26. Which of the following events would be most likely to be performed by someone who is high in sensation seeking?
    a. a mile run
    b. the pole vault
    c. the shot put
    d. a 100 meter dash
    Ans.: b   LG: 1   Page: 427   QT: A

27. Someone who is low in sensation seeking would prefer which of the following occupations?
    a. firefighter
    b. air traffic controller
    c. desk job
    d. paramedic
    Ans.: c   LG: 1   Page: 427   QT: A

28. A cognitive psychologist would agree *most* with which of the following statements about motivation?
    a. People are conscious of their motivation.
    b. Motivation was passed from one generation to the next through heredity.
    c. Behavior is motivated by positive or negative consequences.
    d. All motives are biological.
    Ans.: a   LG: 1   Page: 427   QT: C

29. A child who cleans his room every day so he can receive his two-dollar allowance on Saturday is
    a. self-actualizing.
    b. extrinsically motivated.
    c. intrinsically motivated.
    d. probably a Type B personality.
    Ans.: b   LG: 1   Page: 428   QT: C

30. Intrinsic motivation is to _____ as extrinsic motivation is to _____.
    a. reward; reinforcement
    b. challenge; incentive
    c. punishment; incentive
    d. curiosity; self determination
    Ans.: b   LG: 1   Page: 428   QT: C

31. If your major motive for learning the information in a course is a good grade at the end of the semester, you are motivated
    a. intrinsically.
    b. vicariously.
    c. lethargically.
    d. extrinsically.
    Ans.: d   LG: 1   Page: 428   QT: C

32. While he was alive, Van Gogh sold only two of his paintings, and those to his brother! Despite his lack of commercial success, Van Gogh painted for hours each day. He was *most likely* motivated by
    a. opponent-process.
    b. extrinsic factors.
    c. intrinsic factors.
    d. a Type A, workaholic personality.
    Ans.: c   LG: 1   Page: 428   QT: C

33. Diane spends a great deal of her time with animals. She loves riding horses and plans on a career in veterinary medicine even though she knows it is a challenging occupation. Diane is _____ motivated.
    a. extrinsically
    b. intrinsically
    c. vicariously
    d. rationally
    Ans.: b   LG: 1   Page: 428   QT: A

34. Adding external rewards to a situation in which the person is already intrinsically motivated to perform usually results in
    a. enhanced intrinsic motivation.
    b. enhanced extrinsic motivation.
    c. reduced intrinsic motivation.
    d. reduced extrinsic motivation.
    Ans.: c   LG: 1   Page: 428   QT: C

35. Ray played basketball all of his life because he loved the sport. He became so good that he was given the opportunity to play professionally and eventually he signed a very lucrative contract. After that contract ran out, the team offered him slightly more money, but he decided that it was not enough. He chose to sit out a season rather than meet their salary demands. Which of the following best explains this from a motivational perspective?
    a. Ray is being selfish.
    b. The team is not showing Ray the respect that he has earned.
    c. The extrinsic motivation has replaced Ray's intrinsic motivation to play.
    d. The intrinsic motivation has replaced Ray's extrinsic motivation to play.
    Ans.: c   LG: 1   Page: 428   QT: A

36. Which of the following is most related to extrinsic motivation?
    a. persistence
    b. mastery
    c. self-esteem
    d. reward
    Ans.: d   LG: 1   Page: 428   QT: C

37. An internal desire to do well just for the sake of doing well is evidence of
    a. competence motivation.
    b. proficiency motivation.
    c. extrinsic motivation.
    d. intrinsic motivation.
    Ans.: d   LG: 1   Page: 428   QT: F

38. From Maslow's perspective, motivation is primarily the result of
    a. reinforcement of behaviors.
    b. instinctive responses to environmental stimuli.
    c. specific responses to ethological, innate drives.
    d. humans focusing on satisfying basic needs before moving to higher needs.
    Ans.: d   LG: 1   Page: 429   QT: C

39. In Maslow's hierarchy, motives toward the top of the pyramid do not begin to operate until
    a. primary drives are aroused.
    b. curiosity needs are experienced.
    c. the person reaches adulthood.
    d. lower-level needs are satisfied.
    Ans.: d   LG: 1   Page: 429   QT: F

40. If you had to write a research paper on Maslow's hierarchy of motives, which of the following titles would you choose to capture the essence of Maslow's theory?
    a. Keep those reinforcements coming.
    b. The power of the unconscious.
    c. Easy come, easy go.
    d. Be all that you can be.
    Ans.: d   LG: 1   Page: 429   QT: A

41. Which of the following is the correct ascending order for Maslow's hierarchy?
    a. safety, physiological, belongingness, esteem, self actualization
    b. physiological, safety, belongingness, esteem, self actualization
    c. safety, belongingness, physiological, esteem, self actualization
    d. physiological, belongingness, esteem, safety, self actualization
    Ans.: b   LG: 1   Page: 429   QT: F

42. According to Maslow's hierarchy, which of the following human needs has to be satisfied *first*?
    a. the need to belong
    b. the need for self-esteem
    c. the need for physical safety
    d. physiological needs
    Ans.: d   LG: 1   Page: 429   QT: F

43. According to Maslow's hierarchy, which is the highest, and often most elusive, human need?
    a. self-esteem
    b. self-actualization
    c. belongingness
    d. safety
    Ans.: b   LG: 1   Page: 429   QT: F

44. Joanne teaches elementary school in a very poor school district. She noticed that the children in her class had a very difficult time paying attention in the morning. She discovered that if she began the day by covering mathematics, bringing in crackers for the students to count and then eat, her mornings became much more productive. Which of Maslow's needs would this address?
    a. belonging
    b. physiological
    c. safety
    d. esteem
    Ans.: b   LG: 1   Page: 429   QT: A

45. William has volunteered to work in a war-torn country to try to improve the lives of the residents there. Assuming that the citizens have enough to eat and drink, what would they be in need of next? Use the perspective of Abraham Maslow in answering.
    a. safety
    b. esteem
    c. belongingness
    d. esteem
    Ans.: a   LG: 1   Page: 429   QT: A

46. A famous piano-playing musician decides to take time off from his music production to try to improve his skills with his left hand. Unbeknownst to most people, he has long felt that his left hand is not as good as his right. He decides to take a break from the commercial part of his career to see how good he can get at playing the piano. From Maslow's perspective, he is working on
    a. belonging
    b. esteem
    c. self-actualization
    d. physiological needs
    Ans.: c   LG: 1   Page: 429   QT: A

Learning Goal 2: Explain the physiological basis of hunger and the nature of eating behavior.

47. Which of the following chemical substances is not an important factor in eating?
    a. glucose
    b. peptin
    c. insulin
    d. leptin
    Ans.: b   LG: 2   Page: 431   QT: F

48. What research evidence *most strongly* challenged the belief that gastric activity is *the* basis for hunger?
    a. People whose stomachs have been surgically removed still experience hunger pangs.
    b. Some people never experience stomach cues.
    c. The stomach cannot send signals that stop hunger.
    d. A balloon inserted in the stomach can speed up or slow down stomach contractions.
    Ans.: a   LG: 2   Page: 431   QT: C

49. What happens when your blood sugar level gets too low?
    a. You feel energized.
    b. You feel hungry.
    c. You feel self-actualized.
    d. You feel vitalized.
    Ans.: b   LG: 2   Page: 431   QT: C

50. Which of the following is *most closely* related to blood sugar control?
    a. stomach
    b. small intestine
    c. insulin
    d. fat cells
    Ans.: c   LG: 2   Page: 431   QT: C

51. Which of the following monitor blood sugar level?
    a. sugar receptors in the small intestine
    b. sugar receptors in the hypothalamus
    c. sugar receptors in the stomach and liver
    d. sugar receptors in the brain and the liver
    Ans.: d   LG: 2   Page: 431   QT: F

52. You are a high school football coach and your team has an important game tonight. As the coach, you are in charge of the pregame meal menu. Which of the following would you choose and why?
    a. Complex carbohydrates—players need to maintain their energy level.
    b. Simple sugars—players will obtain their maximum energy level quickly.
    c. Fruits, doughnuts, and carbonated drinks—players need to store sugars.
    d. Fruits and juices—players must not be slowed down by heavy foods.
    Ans.: a   LG: 2   Page: 431   QT: A

53. If there is a hunger center in the human brain, which of the following is the *best* candidate?
    a. hypothalamus
    b. hippocampus
    c. amygdala
    d. thalamus
    Ans.: a   LG: 2   Page: 432   QT: C

54. Which intervention would cause a rat to become obese?
    a. destroy the ventromedial hypothalamus
    b. stimulate the ventromedial hypothalamus
    c. enhance the ventromedial hypothalamus
    d. stimulate the mid-sagittal hippocampus
    Ans.: a   LG: 2   Page: 432   QT: C

55. The minimum amount of energy an individual uses in a resting state is referred to as
    a. homeostasis.
    b. the physiological base line.
    c. the physiological base point.
    d. basal metabolism rate.
    Ans.: d   LG: 2   Page: 433   QT: F

56. The basal metabolism rate
    a. declines during adolescence and then increases in adulthood.
    b. surges during adolescence and then increases in adulthood.
    c. declines during adolescence and then continues to decline during adulthood.
    d. increases during adolescence and then declines during adulthood.
    Ans.: c   LG: 2   Page: 433   QT: C

57. Diane is having an animated discussion with her friend Bill over the physiological differences between the sexes. Diane argues that women have a lower BMR than men do. Bill disagrees, saying men have a lower BMR. Who is correct?
    a. Diane is correct, but Bill is not.
    b. Bill is correct and Diane is not.
    c. Neither is correct; there is no difference between the sexes regarding BMR.
    d. BMR cannot be quantified, so the argument is baseless.
    Ans.: a   LG: 2   Page: 433   QT: C

58. The weight that is maintained when no effort is made to gain or lose weight is called the
    a. optimal weight.
    b. set point.
    c. basal metabolism rate.
    d. homeostatic weight.
    Ans.: b   LG: 2   Page: 433   QT: F

59. Which of the following is not true regarding the set point?
    a. A high fat diet may raise a person's set point.
    b. Exercise may lower a person's set point.
    c. There will be individual differences in set points.
    d. Set points are genetically established and are not changed by environmental influences.
    Ans.: d   LG: 2   Page: 433   QT: C

60. Which is true of obesity?
    a. The rate of obesity has been on the decline since the 1960's.
    b. The portions and quantities that Americans are eating are increasing.
    c. Obesity is probably not inherited.
    d. Obese people have a high basal metabolism.
    Ans.: b   LG: 2   Page: 434   QT: F

61. Which of the following plays an important role in the increase in American obesity?
    a. an abundance of food in a culture that encourages food consumption
    b. an increase in the amount of food eaten
    c. a decrease in exercise
    d. all of the above
    Ans.: d   LG: 2   Page: 434   QT: C

62. According to current views, which of the following is *not* an important factor in obesity?
    a. social influences
    b. neurotransmitter balance
    c. cognitive processing
    d. biological predisposition
    Ans.: b   LG: 2   Page: 434   QT: F

63. Which of the following supports the use of diets?
    a. societal norms that promote a lean, aesthetic body
    b. the diet business that makes approximately $30 billion a year in sales
    c. magazine covers that exemplify the perfect man and woman
    d. all of the above
    Ans.: d   LG: 2   Page: 435   QT: C

64. The most effective means of losing weight is through
    a. exercise programs.
    b. hypnosis.
    c. weight-loss cream.
    d. use of compression raps.
    Ans.: a   LG: 2   Page: 435   QT: F

65. Which of the following is *untrue* regarding weight loss programs?
    a. Most diets are successful in keeping weight off long-term.
    b. Frequent changes in weight can lead to chronic disease.
    c. Weight cycling is called yo-yo dieting.
    d. Liquid diets are related to damage of internal organs.
    Ans.: a   LG: 2   Page: 436   QT: C

66. Anorexia nervosa and bulimia have all of the following in common *except* which one?
    a. They occur most often in females.
    b. They are eating disorders.
    c. They can produce major secondary health problems.
    d. They eventually lead to death.
    Ans.: d   LG: 2   Page: 436/437 QT: C

67. Anorexia nervosa is *most* common in
    a. white adolescent or young adult females from well-educated, well-to-do families.
    b. white adolescent males and females from well-educated, well-to-do families.
    c. females of color who struggle with their racial identity.
    d. traditional-age college women.
    Ans.: a   LG: 2   Page: 436   QT: F

68. What is the *main* difference between anorexia nervosa and bulimia?
    a. at-risk population
    b. potential danger
    c. pursuit of thinness
    d. causes
    Ans.: b   LG: 2   Page: 436/437 QT: C

69. According to statistics, which of the following is at *highest* risk for anorexia nervosa?
    a. 21-year-old white college student who works 30 hours a week to pay for school
    b. 18-year-old African American female whose parents are both teachers
    c. 16-year-old Hispanic female who works at a fast food place after school
    d. 15-year-old white female whose parents are both lawyers
    Ans.: d   LG: 2   Page: 436   QT: C

70. Experts consider which of the following as one of the *main* causes of anorexia?
    a. parents who employ an authoritative parenting style
    b. the prevalence of obesity among American males and females
    c. our culture's overemphasis on the importance of thinness in females
    d. the prevalence of depression in the adolescent population
    Ans.: c   LG: 2   Page: 437   QT: C

71. Which of the following *best* describes anorexia nervosa?
    a. bulimia
    b. self-starvation
    c. bingeing-and-purging
    d. depression
    Ans.: b   LG: 2   Page: 436   QT: F

Learning Goal 3: Discuss the motivation for sex.

72. Motivation for sex is centered in the
   a. cerebral cortex.
   b. hypothalamus.
   c. cerebellum.
   d. cerebrum.
   Ans.: b   LG: 3   Page: 438   QT: F

73. Sex hormones are controlled by the
   a. pituitary gland.
   b. adrenal glands.
   c. sex organs.
   d. forebrain.
   Ans.: a   LG: 3   Page: 438   QT: F

74. Sexual motivation involves all of the following *except* the
   a. hypothalamus.
   b. pituitary.
   c. occipital lobe.
   d. limbic system.
   Ans.: c   LG: 3   Page: 438   QT: F

75. Females are to estrogen as males are to
   a. testes.
   b. adrenaline.
   c. estradiol.
   d. androgen.
   Ans.: d   LG: 3   Page: 438   QT: C

76. Estrogens are to ovaries as androgens are to
   a. pituitary gland.
   b. testes.
   c. hypothalamus.
   d. limbic system.
   Ans.: b   LG: 3   Page: 438   QT: C

77. Higher androgen levels are associated with sexual motivation in
   a. males more than in females.
   b. females more than in males.
   c. neither males nor females.
   d. both males and females equally.
   Ans.: a   LG: 3   Page: 438   QT: F

78. What is the correct order of the human sexual response pattern?
    a. engorgement, plateau, pleasure, termination
    b. engorgement, orgasm, plateau, resolution
    c. excitement, refractory period, orgasm, termination
    d. excitement, plateau, orgasm, resolution
    Ans.: d   LG: 3   Page: 438   QT: F

79. Which of the following is *true* regarding orgasm?
    a. It is the second phase of the human sexual response pattern.
    b. Males show four different orgasmic patterns.
    c. It lasts from 3 to 15 seconds.
    d. It occurs during the refractory period.
    Ans.: c   LG: 3   Page: 439   QT: F

80. During the human sexual response cycle, blood vessels return to their normal state during the
    a. orgasmic phase.
    b. plateau phase.
    c. termination phase.
    d. resolution phase.
    Ans.: d   LG: 3   Page: 439   QT: F

81. During the human sexual response cycle, engorgement of blood vessels in genital areas, increased blood flow in genital areas, and muscle tension is characteristic of the
    a. refractory period.
    b. engorgement phase.
    c. excitement phase.
    d. orgasmic phase.
    Ans.: c   LG: 3   Page: 439   QT: F

82. Which of the following is *true* for a male who is in the refractory period?
    a. He is about to have an orgasm.
    b. Blood vessels become engorged
    c. He is experiencing a discharge of neuromuscular tension.
    d. He cannot have an orgasm.
    Ans.: d   LG: 3   Page: 439   QT: F

83. As males get older, they can expect which of the following?
    a. a longer refractory period
    b. more intense orgasms
    c. a shorter plateau phase
    d. no orgasms
    Ans.: a   LG: 3   Page: 439   QT: C

84. Stereotyped patterns of expectancies for how people should sexually behave are called
    a. sexual fantasies.
    b. sexual innuendos.
    c. sexual scripts.
    d. sexual routines.
    Ans.: c   LG: 3   Page: 439   QT: F

85. Which of the following is least correct?
    a. In the traditional religious script, sex is accepted only within marriage.
    b. In the romantic script, sex is equated with love.
    c. Males link love with intercourse.
    d. Women link love with intercourse.
    Ans.: c   LG: 3   Page: 440   QT: C

86. Which of the following *best* explains some of the gender differences found with regard to sexual scripts?
    a. gender-specific socialization and gender stereotypes
    b. biological differences between men and women
    c. neurological differences between men and women
    d. inappropriate attribution and deviant motivation
    Ans.: a   LG: 3   Page: 440   QT: C

87. _____ is the sensory experience that is most likely to arouse sexual motivation in a woman and _____ is most likely to arouse sexual motivation in a man.
    a. Vision; smell
    b. Touch; vision
    c. Smell; touch
    d. Hearing; smell
    Ans.: b   LG: 3   Page: 440   QT: C

88. A person who engages in sexual fantasies becomes aroused to the point of reaching orgasm. In this case, sexual behavior is *primarily* influenced by
    a. perceptual factors.
    b. cognitive factors.
    c. sensory factors.
    d. social factors.
    Ans.: b   LG: 3   Page: 439   QT: C

89. People's ability to control their sexual behavior relates *most strongly* to
    a. sensory factors.
    b. perceptual factors.
    c. social factors.
    d. cognitive factors.
    Ans.: d   LG: 3   Page: 439   QT: C

90. Animals communicate both socially and sexually through
    a. aphrodisiacs.
    b. pheromones.
    c. androgens.
    d. estrogens.
    Ans.: b   LG: 3   Page: 440   QT: F

91. Tom has never had any luck attracting members of the opposite sex. Both contributing to the problem, and as a result of the problem, he has spent much of his youth in the laboratory researching chemistry. His research has yielded a liquid that he believes will attract women. His plan is to use it himself to test it, and then market it. Which of the following is Tom most likely working with?
    a. aphrodisiacs
    b. estrogens
    c. pheromones
    d. androgens
    Ans.: c   LG: 3   Page: 440   QT: A

92. Which statement about aphrodisiacs is *true*?
    a. Certain odors tend to enhance sexual performance in men, but not in women.
    b. No empirical evidence supports the claim that certain foods influence sexual behavior.
    c. Aphrodisiacs tend to increase sexual desire in both men and women.
    d. Visual stimuli influence sexual arousal in women but not in men.
    Ans.: b   LG: 3   Page: 440   QT: C

93. An individual has lost the desire to engage in sexual relations. The individual would be described as having
    a. a psychosexual dysfunction.
    b. reached the resolution phase.
    c. developed premature ejaculation.
    d. a pattern of inhibited orgasm.
    Ans.: a   LG: 3   Page: 442   QT: F

94. An inability to go beyond the excitement phase of the human sexual response pattern would be classified as a
    a. premature ejaculation.
    b. loss of desire for gratification.
    c. refractory period.
    d. psychosexual dysfunction.
    Ans.: d   LG: 3   Page: 442   QT: F

95. Your friend confides in you that she has no desire whatsoever to engage in sexual relations with her husband. What would you advise your friend to do?
    a. Ignore the problem for now; the desire will return if she doesn't obsess about it.
    b. Seek psychoanalysis; obviously this problem has an unconscious cause.
    c. Seek therapy; modern techniques have yielded good success rates.
    d. Leave her husband; desire will return once she meets someone new.
    Ans.: c   LG: 3   Page: 442   QT: A

96. A friend tells you that he intends to start taking Viagra. You would advise your friend of all of the following *except* which one?
    a. Discuss this plan with a physician.
    b. Be aware that Viagra doesn't work for everyone.
    c. A natural aphrodisiac would be more effective.
    d. Viagra can have unpleasant and serious side effects.
    Ans.: c   LG: 3   Page: 442   QT: A

97. Viagra has received a great deal of attention in the media lately. Although this drug seems to be an effective treatment for sexual dysfunction in some people, consumers should keep in mind which of the following?
    a. The long-term effects of this drug have not yet been determined.
    b. Natural aphrodisiacs are much cheaper than this drug.
    c. Viagra has only been proven effective in men.
    d. The media have misrepresented the effectiveness of this drug.
    Ans.: a   LG: 3   Page: 442   QT: C

98. To summarize the findings of the 1994 Michael survey, it can be said that
    a. American's sexual lives are more conservative than was previously believed.
    b. American's sexual lives are more liberal than was previously believed.
    c. American men and women now see sex from the same perspective.
    d. marriage is on the decline.
    Ans.: a   LG: 3   Page: 443   QT: F

99. Which of the following statements is *not* true according to the Michael survey of 1994?
    a. Adultery is the exception, rather than the rule.
    b. Three-quarters of married men admit to having an extramarital affair.
    c. Men think about sex more than women do.
    d. Two-thirds of American couples report having sex less than once a week.
    Ans.: b   LG: 3   Page: 443   QT: F

100. If a contemporary psychologist could go back in time and have a conversation with a psychologist of the 1950s, the two psychologists would *most likely* disagree on which question?
    a. Can children learn aggression by observing aggressive models?
    b. Are most Americans latent homosexuals?
    c. What is the human sexual response cycle?
    d. Is homosexuality a mental disorder?
    Ans.: d   LG: 3   Page: 445   QT: C

101. A study that compared the brains of heterosexual and homosexual males found a difference in a specific area of the
    a. pituitary gland.
    b. amygdala.
    c. hypothalamus.
    d. limbic system.
    Ans.: c   LG: 3   Page: 445   QT: F

102. Which of the following statements about research on homosexuality is *incorrect*?
    a. Research has not yielded definite answers about the causes of homosexuality.
    b. Research results have consistently supported the critical-period hypothesis.
    c. Researchers know less about what does than what does not cause homosexuality.
    d. Results of hormone studies have been inconsistent.
    Ans.: b   LG: 3   Page: 445   QT: F

103. Which of the following *best* describes psychologists' current perspective on the causes of homosexuality?
    a. Homosexuality is caused by multiple factors.
    b. Homosexuality is caused by genetic factors.
    c. Homosexuality is caused by environmental factors.
    d. Homosexuality is caused by hormonal factors.
    Ans.: a   LG: 3   Page: 445   QT: F

104. With respect to the causes of homosexuality, what would be the *main* benefit of empirical verification of the critical-period hypothesis?
    a. It would explain why more males than females are homosexual.
    b. It would explain the different factors that cause homosexuality.
    c. It would explain why homosexuality is a mental disorder.
    d. It would explain sexual orientation's resistance to modification.
    Ans.: d   LG: 3   Page: 445   QT: C

Learning Goal 4: Characterize the social cognitive motives and how they influence behavior.

105. The need for achievement refers to desires for
    a. power over and control of other people.
    b. high status and acclaim.
    c. arousing activities.
    d. reaching a standard of excellence.
    Ans.: d   LG: 4   Page: 447   QT: F

106. Which of the following would *not* be indicative of someone with a high need to achieve?
    a. They are moderate risk takers.
    b. They are high risk takers.
    c. They persist when things get difficult.
    d. They have a stronger hope for success than fear of failure.
    Ans.: b   LG: 4   Page: 447   QT: C

107. Research on achievement motivation indicates achievement motivation
    a. is a genetic trait and cannot be changed by the environment.
    b. may be influenced by the environment.
    c. is a construct which cannot be measured.
    d. is the highest level of Maslow's hierarchy.
    Ans.: b   LG: 4   Page: 447   QT: C

108. Danielle works very hard and gets very upset if she gets anything less than an A on a test. Danielle can be *best* described as having a high need to
    a. control.
    b. achieve.
    c. affiliate.
    d. get attention.
    Ans.: b   LG: 4   Page: 447   QT: C

109. Jamie, a good math student, is taking an advanced math class. Sometimes the teacher covers the material in class so fast that Jamie can barely keep up with his notes. Jamie works on his math problems for at least two hours every evening. Sometimes, he spends more than three hours because he will not stop until he has fully understood each problem that was covered in class and assigned for homework. Jamie can be *best* described as having high
    a. achievement motivation.
    b. risk-taking behavior.
    c. self-esteem.
    d. extrinsic motivation.
    Ans.: a   LG: 4   Page: 447   QT: C

110. Which of the following is *not* associated with high achievement motivation?
    a. moderate risk taking
    b. persistence
    c. high fear of failure
    d. effort
    Ans.: c   LG: 4   Page: 447   QT: F

111. Attribution theory
    a. is a biological theory which looks at the neurology of emotion.
    b. is a humanist perspective which addresses physiological responses.
    c. is a behavioral theory which places emphasis upon reward.
    d. is a cognitive theory which looks for the underlying causes of behavior.
    Ans.: d   LG: 4   Page: 447   QT: F

112. Caroline took a psychology test and did not do well. She is not too upset, however, because she feels that the teacher did a poor job of covering the material. Which of the following perspectives of attribution theory would explain this?
    a. The teacher's methods of instruction are external to Caroline.
    b. The teacher's methods of instruction are internal to Caroline.
    c. There is no difference in internal or external attributions when considering Caroline's response.
    d. Caroline did not study.
    Ans.: a   LG: 4   Page: 448   QT: A

113. Which of the following is not a critical aspect of achievement?
    a. external monitoring
    b. self-monitoring
    c. planning
    d. goal setting
    Ans.: a   LG: 4   Page: 448   QT: F

114. Research has found that an individual's achievement improves when they set goals for themselves that are all but which of the following?
    a. specific
    b. short term
    c. challenging
    d. general
    Ans.: d   LG: 4   Page: 448   QT: C

115. A psychologist who approaches motivation from the sociocultural perspective would agree *most* with which of the following statements about motivation?
    a. The environment dictates the majority of human motives.
    b. The contexts in which we live contributes to our motivation.
    c. Higher human motives cannot be activated until lower motives have been reduced.
    d. Most human motives are universal.
    Ans.: b   LG: 4   Page: 449   QT: C

116. Compared to their counterparts in nonindustrialized countries, parents in industrialized countries place
    a. higher value on achievement and independence.
    b. lower value on achievement and independence.
    c. equal value on achievement and independence.
    d. no value on achievement and independence.
    Ans.: a   LG: 4   Page: 449   QT: F

117. Picture an American first grader (in an American school) and a Chinese first grader (in a Chinese school). Which of the two is spending more time on math-related activities?
    a. The American first grader is spending more time on math in school but not at home.
    b. The Chinese first grader is spending more time on math in school and at home.
    c. The American first grader is spending more time on math at home but not in school.
    d. They both are spending about the same amount of time on math in school and at home.
    Ans.: b   LG: 4   Page: 449   QT: F

118. Sport psychology is an important medium for the application of motivational theory. Which of the following statements would a sport psychologist *not* agree with?
    a. Emphasize the outcome rather than the process.
    b. Use positive self-talk.
    c. When facing adversity, cope and move on.
    d. Use visualization.
    Ans.: a   LG: 4   Page: 452   QT: C

119. Which of the following statements would a sport psychologist most likely agree with?
    a. Winning isn't everything, it is the only thing.
    b. It is not whether you win or lose, it is how you play the game.
    c. Do not dwell on the negative.
    d. both b and c
    Ans.: d   LG: 4   Page: 452   QT:C

120. One of Murray's social motives addressing the need to be with other people is
    a. aggression.
    b. achievement.
    c. affiliation.
    d. alignment.
    Ans.: c   LG: 4   Page: 452   QT: F

121. Frieda is a very social person. She is always concerned with personal relationships and is not the same when she is not involved in one. Frieda is high in a need for
   a. aggression.
   b. achievement.
   c. affiliation.
   d. alignment.
   Ans.: c   LG: 4   Page: 453   QT: A

122. In which of the following countries is affiliation emphasized the most?
   a. Japan
   b. The United States
   c. Canada
   d. Italy
   Ans.: a   LG: 4   Page: 453   QT: F

123. When Ryan and Deci (2000) refer to the factors necessary for well-being, they mean all but which of the following?
   a. financial wealth
   b. competence
   c. autonomy
   d. affiliation
   Ans.: a   LG: 4   Page: 453   QT: F

124. Which of the following factors for well-being is related to the need to be with other people?
   a. affiliation
   b. competence
   c. autonomy
   d. all of the above
   Ans.: a   LG: 4   Page: 453   QT: C

125. Devon is intrinsically motivated, self-initiated and very self-determined. All of these refer to her
   a. affiliation.
   b. emotions.
   c. autonomy.
   d. competence.
   Ans.: c   LG: 4   Page: 453   QT: F

Learning Goal 5: Summarize views of emotion.

126. What is another word for emotion?
   a. thought
   b. behavior
   c. consciousness
   d. feeling
   Ans.: d   LG: 5   Page: 455   QT: F

127. According to your text, emotions can involve all of the following *except*
    a. physiological arousal.
    b. conscious experience.
    c. unconscious experience.
    d. behavioral expression.
    Ans.: c   LG: 5   Page: 455   QT: F

128. Which of the following physiological responses is not monitored by the polygraph?
    a. heart rate
    b. breathing
    c. electrodermal response
    d. pupil dilation
    Ans.: d   LG: 5   Page: 456   QT: F

129. What do polygraphs detect?
    a. lies
    b. psychological responses associated with lies
    c. physiological responses associated with lies
    d. unconscious information
    Ans.: c   LG: 5   Page: 456   QT: F

130. What is the *main* problem with using polygraph results as an indication of whether or not a person is lying?
    a. Different emotions can cause the same physiological changes.
    b. Most people can camouflage their response patterns.
    c. Examiners are usually biased against the person being tested.
    d. The accuracy rate of polygraphs is very low.
    Ans.: a   LG: 5   Page: 456   QT: C

131. Which of the following statements about polygraphs is *untrue*?
    a. The polygraph measures physiological arousal.
    b. Most courts consider polygraph results inadmissible evidence.
    c. Strategies to deceive the polygraph are usually unsuccessful.
    d. The accuracy rate of the polygraph is almost equal to chance.
    Ans.: c   LG: 5   Page: 456   QT: F

132. The statement, "You are happy because you are jumping up and down" *best* describes which theory of emotion?
    a. James-Lange theory
    b. Cannon-Bard theory
    c. Yerkes-Dodson theory
    d. Schachter-Singer theory
    Ans.: a   LG: 5   Page: 457   QT: C

133. Which of the following best summarizes the James-Lange theory of emotion.
    a. Emotion occurs after physiological reactions.
    b. Emotion occurs before physiological reactions.
    c. Emotion occurs at the same time as physiological reactions.
    d. Emotion is a result of a cognitive assessment.
    Ans.: a   LG: 5   Page: 456   QT: C

134. The Cannon-Bard theory predicts that after witnessing a shocking event, a person will
    a. first experience shock and then be motivated to turn away.
    b. be motivated to turn away and then will experience shock.
    c. experience cathartic shock as a release of anxiety.
    d. experience physical and emotional reactions simultaneously.
    Ans.: d   LG: 5   Page: 457   QT: C

135. What is the *main* difference between the James-Lange theory of emotion and the Cannon-Bard theory of emotion?
    a. They propose that perception of a fear stimulus occurs after the emotion of fear.
    b. They propose different relationships between physiological arousal and emotion.
    c. They disagree on the number of factors involved in emotion.
    d. They disagree on which comes first—physiological arousal or cognitive labeling.
    Ans.: b   LG: 5   Page: 457   QT: C

136. According to Schachter and Singer, the specific emotion we experience depends on the
    a. rate of neuron activity in the area leading from the hypothalamus to the neocortex.
    b. actual nature of the cause of the arousal.
    c. specific pattern of heart rate, blood pressure, and skin resistance.
    d. environmental circumstances to which we attribute our arousal.
    Ans.: d   LG: 5   Page: 459   QT: C

137. Schachter and Singer tested their theory of emotion in a situation involving injection of epinephrine and the use of a confederate. The results indicated
    a. that the confederate influenced the uninformed subjects' cognitive interpretations of their arousal.
    b. that the confederate had no influence on the subjects' cognitive interpretations of their arousal.
    c. considerable support for the James-Lange theory of emotion.
    d. that cognitive interpretation was not affected by the adrenaline.
    Ans.: a   LG: 5   Page: 460   QT: F

138. Which of the following theories of emotion stresses the importance of cognition in the response?
    a. James-Lange theory
    b. Cannon-Bard theory
    c. Yerkes-Dodson theory
    d. Schachter-Singer theory
    Ans.: d   LG: 5   Page: 460   QT: C

139. The facial feedback hypothesis relates *primarily* to which theory of emotion?
    a. two-factor theory
    b. Cannon-Bard theory
    c. Schachter-Singer theory
    d. James-Lange theory
    Ans.: d   LG: 5 Page: 462   QT: C

140. According to the facial feedback hypothesis, what will happen if you smile?
    a. You will feel sad.
    b. You will feel angry.
    c. You will feel happy.
    d. You will feel no different than before.
    Ans.: c   LG: 5   Page: 462   QT: C

141. A therapist is trying to get her depressed client to smile as much as possible during their therapy sessions. What is the therapist *most likely* hoping for?
    a. The client will get upset
    b. The client will get angry
    c. The client's mood will change
    d. The client will return for more sessions
    Ans.: c   LG: 5   Page: 462   QT: C

142. Bill was raised to believe that males should not cry in public except at an immediate relative's funeral. Bill adheres to these
    a. flow responses.
    b. display rules.
    c. stereotypes.
    d. set points.
    Ans.: b   LG: 5   Page: 464   QT: C

143. Display rules determine
    a. where, when, and how we express emotions.
    b. the intensity of the emotion we experience.
    c. the specific type of emotion we feel.
    d. how often we experience a particular emotion.
    Ans.: a   LG: 5   Page: 464   QT: F

144. Plutchik's wheel model of emotions contains all of the following dimensions *except* which one?
    a. Emotions are primary or mixed.
    b. Emotions are polar opposites.
    c. Emotions have equal intensity.
    d. Emotions are positive or negative.
    Ans.: c   LG: 5   Page: 465   QT: F

145. Which of the following is not true regarding the role that positive emotions play in well being.
    a. Positive emotions can improve coping.
    b. Positive emotions can undo lingering negative emotions.
    c. Anger overrides positive emotions..
    d. Positive emotions help in adaptation.
    Ans.: c   LG: 5   Page: 466   QT: C

146. The release of anger or aggressive energy by directly or vicariously engaging in anger or aggression is called
    a. catharsis.
    b. arousal.
    c. repressed anger.
    d. negativity affect.
    Ans.: a   LG: 5   Page: 467   QT: F

147. When Harriet left work, she was still very angry with a coworker. According to the catharsis hypothesis, Harriet would reduce her anger *most* effectively through which action?
    a. going to the mall and buying herself something nice
    b. watching a tragic love story on television
    c. working out on a punching bag in a gym
    d. having a few drinks at a bar
    Ans.: c   LG: 5   Page: 467   QT: A

148. When you feel yourself getting angry, appropriate anger control would involve which of the following?
    a. postponing a response until arousal has decreased
    b. venting the anger publicly
    c. venting the anger privately
    d. confronting the source of your anger directly
    Ans.: a   LG: 5   Page: 467   QT: A

149. Carol Tavris suggests all of the following for managing one's anger *except*
    a. gaining perspective on one's own anger by helping others.
    b. continuing to think about one's reasons for being angry.
    c. forming a self-help group.
    d. avoiding chronic anger.
    Ans.: b   LG: 5   Page: 467   QT: F

150. Why is it quite difficult to conduct research on happiness?
    a. People do not usually like to talk about happiness.
    b. Happiness is a subjective experience.
    c. People often don't know that they are happy.
    d. Researchers don't agree on the definition of happiness.
    Ans.: b   LG: 5   Page: 468   QT: C

True/False Items

____ 151. Motivated behavior is energized, directed, and sustained.
____ 152. The Yerkes Dodson Theory relates to optimum arousal.
____ 153. High arousal always facilitates performance.
____ 154. Extrinsic reinforcers can have a negative effect on intrinsic motivation.
____ 155. Maslow's hierarchy of motives reflects his belief that people are aware of what motivates them.
____ 156. Stomach signals are the only factors that affect hunger.

___ 157. Approximately one-half of the American population is overweight enough to be at increased risk for health problems.
___ 158. Anorexia is associated with self-starvation and can eventually lead to death.
___ 159. Sexual motivation in humans is strictly cognitive.
___ 160. Human males and females tend to have different sexual scripts.
___ 161. American's sex lives are more conservative than what was once thought.
___ 162. People with a high need for achievement are usually high risk takers.
___ 163. The need for affiliation is consistent across cultures.
___ 164. "Put on a happy face" would be most related to the Cannon-Bard theory of emotion.
___ 165. Schacter and Singer emphasized the importance of instincts in emotion.

Answer Key for True/False Items

151.	Ans.: T	LG: 1	Page: 425	159.	Ans.: F	LG: 3	Page: 438
152.	Ans.: T	LG: 1	Page: 426	160.	Ans.: T	LG: 3	Page: 439
153.	Ans.: F	LG: 1	Page: 426	161.	Ans.: T	LG: 3	Page: 443
154.	Ans.: T	LG: 1	Page: 428	162.	Ans.: F	LG: 4	Page: 447
155.	Ans.: T	LG: 1	Page: 429	163.	Ans.: F	LG: 4	Page: 453
156.	Ans.: F	LG: 2	Page: 431	164.	Ans.: F	LG: 5	Page: 457
157.	Ans.: F	LG: 2	Page: 433	165.	Ans.: F	LG: 5	Page: 459
158.	Ans.: T	LG: 2	Page: 436				

Fill-in-the-Blank Items

166. An innate pattern of behavior that is assumed to be universal throughout a species is known as an _____.

167. In order to perform your best on a task, you should try to maintain a _____ state of arousal.

168. Julie hates her job but needs the money. Julie is _____ motivated.

169. _____-motivated students tend to work for mastery goals rather than for performance goals.

170. From Maslow's perspective, our most fundamental need is _____.

171. Your body's tendency to maintain a steady temperature is an example of _____.

172. When sugar levels in your body get too low, you will feel _____.

173. The weight level that one maintains without making an effort to gain or lose weight is referred to as the _____ .

174. The rate of obesity in the United States is _____ than past generations.

175. _____ and bulimia are the two most common psychologically-based eating disorders.
176. Culturally-imposed, stereotyped expectations about people's sexual behavior are known as sexual _____ .
177. A man who cannot maintain an erection during the excitement phase of the human sexual response cycle would be diagnosed with a _____ .
178. Individuals who have high _____ motivation tend to persist with effort even when tasks become difficult.
179. You are happy about your promotion, but _____ rules prevent you from expressing your joy too ecstatically while your boss is around.
180. The problem with the _____ in lie detection is that it cannot distinguish between such feelings as anxiety and guilt.

Answer Key for Fill-in-the-Blank Items

166.	Ans.: instinct	LG: 1	Page: 425
167.	Ans.: moderate	LG: 1	Page: 426
168.	Ans.: extrinsically	LG: 1	Page: 428
169.	Ans.: Intrinsically	LG: 1	Page: 428
170.	Ans.: physiological	LG: 1	Page: 429
171.	Ans.: homeostasis	LG: 2	Page: 426
172.	Ans.: hungry	LG: 2	Page: 431
173.	Ans.: set point	LG: 2	Page: 433
174.	Ans.: higher	LG: 2	Page: 433
175.	Ans.: Anorexia	LG: 2	Page: 436
176.	Ans.: scripts	LG: 3	Page: 439
177.	Ans.: psychosexual dysfunction	LG: 3	Page: 442
178.	Ans.: achievement	LG: 4	Page: 447
179.	Ans.: display	LG: 5	Page: 464
180.	Ans.: polygraph	LG: 5	Page: 456

Matching Items

181. drive
182. Yerkes Dodson Law
183. internal and external
184. internal hunger cue
185. estrogens
186. bisexual
187. Viagra
188. The need to be with others
189. Wheel Model
190. catharsis

A. low blood sugar level
B. Plutchik's classification system of emotions
C. intrinsic and extrinsic
D. sexually attracted to individuals of both sexes
E. release of an emotion by engaging in that emotion
F. a drug used to treat sexual dysfunctions
G. female sex hormone
H. affiliation
I. arousal based on a physiological need
J. moderate arousal facilitates performance

Answer Key for Matching Items

181.	Ans.: I	LG: 1	Page: 425
182.	Ans.: J	LG: 1	Page: 426
183.	Ans.: C	LG: 1	Page: 428
184.	Ans.: A	LG: 2	Page: 431
185.	Ans.: G	LG: 3	Page: 438

186.	Ans.: D	LG: 3	Page: 444
187.	Ans.: F	LG: 3	Page: 442
188.	Ans.: H	LG: 4	Page: 452
189.	Ans.: B	LG: 5	Page: 465
190.	Ans.: E	LG: 5	Page: 467

Essay Questions

191. Explain the concept of optimal arousal and the Yerkes-Dodson law. Give examples of how high levels of arousal, moderate levels of arousal, and low levels of arousal would be associated with performance in different tasks. (LG: 1)

Answer Guidelines: Answers should address that arousal is a state or alertness or activation and that according to Yerkes-Dodson, too much arousal or too little arousal is associated with decreased performance. For simple tasks, arousal can be quite high but for difficult tasks, arousal level should be less.

192. Explain the difference between intrinsic and extrinsic motivation and discuss how these motivation patterns relate to the need for achievement. (LG: 1)

Answer Guidelines: Possible options include mentioning that intrinsic motivation is due to internal factors such as the desire to master a task; extrinsic motivation depends on external rewards or incentives, such as a good grade. In general, mastery and competency are related to strong intrinsic motivation. The need to achieve is affected by both intrinsic and extrinsic motivation. Successful individuals tend to have strong intrinsic motivation that allows them to initiate and sustain behavior even in the absence of external rewards. However, even the most intrinsically motivated person eventually enjoys seeing some external validation of his/her accomplishments, such as a compliment, a raise, etc.

193. Describe each of the levels of Maslow's hierarchy of motives, giving an example of each. Finally, briefly discuss which level(s) of the hierarchy you are currently working on and how. (LG: 1)

Answer Guidelines: Possible options include mentioning the levels, including physiological, safety, love and belongingness, esteem, and self-actualization. Physiological would be how hungry you might be. Safety would be related to whether or not you feel threatened. (Sept. 11) Belongingness would be related to groups that you associate with, such as clubs, friends, or family. Esteem would be your affective assessment of where you stand in your world. Self-actualization would be your efforts to be as good as you can be in a particular domain.

194. What are some factors that may be contributing to the increase of obesity in the United States in recent years? In your answer, include the terms basal metabolism and set point. (LG: 2)

Answer Guidelines: Obesity is influenced by heredity, basal metabolism (BMR), and set point. BMR is the minimum amount of energy an individual uses in a resting state. Set point is the weight that is maintained without attempting to gain or lose weight. Answers should reflect an understanding of how Americans eat too much of the wrong things and do not exercise enough. A high-fat diet can actually raise an individual's set point. Obesity, or excessive body weight, appears to have a genetic component and is more common with age, especially in females. Often it is due to an interaction of biological, cognitive, and social factors that produce a pattern of overeating behaviors that focus primarily on external food cues. Obesity is associated with hypertension, diabetes, and cardiovascular disease.

195. What are the causes, the symptoms, and incidence of bulimia nervosa and anorexia nervosa. (LG: 2)

Answer Guidelines: Possible options include mentioning that anorexia nervosa is most common in white adolescent or young-adult females from well-educated, middle- and upper-class families. Its causes are strictly psychological. Psychologists believe that it is the result of social pressure about being thin and high achievement demands by parents. Anorexics starve themselves and develop a very distorted body image. Unless anorexia nervosa is discovered and treated in time, it can lead to death. Bulimia nervosa is an eating disorder in which the individual consistently follows a binge-and-purge pattern. It is difficult to detect because it usually occurs within a normal weight range. one to two percent of females are estimated to develop bulimia nervosa. 70 percent eventually recover from it.

196. Define the term sexual script and describe the different types of sexual scripts. (LG: 3)

Answer Guidelines: Possible options include mentioning that sexual script are stereotyped patterns of expectancies of how people should behave sexually. Two types of sexual scripts are the traditional religious script, which prescribes that sex is accepted only within marriage, and the romantic script, which represents the belief that sex is synonymous with love. Sex differences in sexual scripts indicate that females tend to link sex with love whereas males tend to link sex with conquest.

197. In terms of the psychological research that has been conducted, how are the attitudes of homosexual and heterosexual individuals different? What are the proposed causes for each sexual orientation? (LG: 3)

Answer Guidelines: Possible options include mentioning that homosexuals and heterosexuals differ little in their attitudes. Current research suggests genetic, hormonal, anatomical, and environmental influences in exploring sexuality issues.

198. Explain the cognitive perspective of attribution theory and motivation. In your answer, include need for achievement and internal and external attributions. (LG: 4)

Answer Guidelines: Attribution theory looks for the underlying causes of behavior in an effort to make sense of that behavior. An important part of this is to determine if the causes for success or failure are internal or external. Individuals with a high need to achieve attribute success to internal causes and failure to external causes. Individuals with a low need to achieve attribute their success to external sources and failure to internal causes. High achievers set specific, proximal, and challenging, but attainable goals.

199. On a hiking trip, you have an encounter with a bear in the woods and you feel afraid. Your textbook described three major theories of emotion: James-Lange, Cannon-Bard, and Schachter and Singer's theories of emotion. How would each of these three theories explain your fear of the bear? (LG: 5)

Answer Guidelines: Possible options include mentioning James-Lange (emotion occurs after physiological reactions), Cannon-Bard (emotion and physiological reactions happen simultaneously), and Schachter-Singer (intense arousal leads to cognitive explanations of that arousal).

200. What are some perspectives mentioned in the text that can be used to control anger. (LG: 5)

Answer Guidelines: Possible answers can include the positives and negatives associated with catharsis, which is the release of anger by directly or vicariously engaging in anger or aggression. Tavris recommends that we can lower anger arousal by letting time pass before we act, getting involved with a self-help group of others who struggle with anger, taking action to help others, and seeking ways to break out of our perspectives.

Chapter 12: Personality

Learning Goals

1. Define personality and identify the major issues in the study of personality.
2. Summarize the psychodynamic perspectives.
3. Explain the behavioral and social cognitive perspectives.
4. Describe the humanistic perspectives.
5. Discuss the trait perspectives.
6. Characterize the main methods of personality assessment.

Multiple-Choice Items

Learning Goal 1: Define personality and identify the major issues in the study of personality.

1. The enduring and distinctive thoughts, emotions, and behaviors that are characteristic of an individual comprise
    a. the conscious.
    b. the superego.
    c. personality.
    d. consciousness.
    Ans.: c   LG: 1   Page: 477   QT: F

2. Which of the following is *not* an aspect of personality?
    a. distinctive thoughts
    b. characteristic behaviors
    c. particular emotions
    d. personal unconscious
    Ans.: d   LG: 1   Page: 477   QT: F

3. As we get to know people, we recognize their style of thinking, feeling, and reacting to things. This individual style is referred to as
    a. personality.
    b. the superego.
    c. the hierarchy of traits.
    d. the hierarchy of states.
    Ans.: a   LG: 1   Page: 477   QT: C

4. Which of the following examples does *not* provide information about an individual's personality?
    a. Beth always expects the worst out of other people.
    b. Tommy often feels low and depressed.
    c. Carmen is usually kind to other people.
    d. Michael has brown hair and weighs 200 pounds.
    Ans.: d   LG: 1   Page: 477   QT: C

5. Psychologists who study personality investigate which of the following?
   a. the enduring traits and qualities we demonstrate over time
   b. relatively permanent changes in behavior due to experience
   c. the organization of sensation into a meaningful interpretation
   d. the pleasantness or sociability of an individual
   Ans.: a   LG: 1   Page: 477   QT: C

6. Which of the following is the *least* important issue in the study of personality?
   a. Is personality innate or learned?
   b. Which part of the brain is the id located in?
   c. Is personality conscious or unconscious?
   d. Is personality influenced by internal or external factors?
   Ans.: b   LG: 1   Page: 477   QT: F

7. The strongest proponents of the human unconscious mind's role in personality are
   a. humanists.
   b. psychodynamic theorists.
   c. behaviorists.
   d. trait theorists.
   Ans.: b   LG: 1   Page: 477   QT: C

8. Which of the following perspectives places the *least* emphasis on the influence of the environment in shaping personality?
   a. psychodynamic theorists
   b. humanists
   c. behaviorists
   d. social cognitive theorists
   Ans.: a   LG: 1   Page: 478   QT: C

9. Which of the following perspectives *least* emphasizes the internal dimensions of personality?
   a. trait theorists
   b. psychodynamic theorists
   c. humanistic theorists
   d. behaviorists
   Ans.: d   LG: 1   Page: 477   QT: C

10. Which personality theory pays little attention to the conscious-unconscious issue?
    a. humanistic
    b. psychoanalytic
    c. social learning theory
    d. trait theory
    Ans.: d   LG: 1   Page: 477   QT: F

Learning Goal 2: Summarize the psychodynamic perspectives.

11. Psychodynamic theorists would *not* agree with which of the following statements?
    a. Personality is primarily unconscious.
    b. Personality develops in stages.
    c. Personality is merely a surface characteristic.
    d. We must explore the inner workings of the mind.
    Ans.: c   LG: 2   Page: 478   QT: C

12. The psychodynamic perspective views personality in terms of all of the following *except* for
    a. early childhood experiences.
    b. the unconscious.
    c. positive potential.
    d. stages.
    Ans.: c   LG: 2   Page: 478   QT: F

13. Which of the following statements is true regarding the theories of Sigmund Freud?
    a. Freud's theories were largely influenced by his life experiences.
    b. Freud was first trained as a psychologist.
    c. Freud had a strained relationship with his mother.
    d. Freud's work has been relatively uncontroversial.
    Ans.: a   LG: 2   Page: 478   QT: C

14. A prosecutor in a rape trial argues that the defendant has never learned to control his sexual instincts and failed to develop a conscience because of ineffective parental controls. This description is most compatible with
    a. psychodynamic theory.
    b. social learning theory.
    c. humanistic theory.
    d. existential theory.
    Ans.: a   LG: 2   Page: 481   QT: C

15. In order to examine a painting from the Freudian perspective, you would be *least* likely to ask which of the following questions?
    a. What unconscious thoughts and wishes are expressed in this painting?
    b. What type of relationship did the artist have with his mother?
    c. What symbolic meanings are contained in the painting?
    d. What is the artist charging for this painting?
    Ans.: d   LG: 2   Page: 479   QT: A

16. Tom is interested in Tiffany for one reason—her family is very wealthy. One day when Tom is speaking to her he says, "Money, would you like to go to the horse races today?" He realizes his mistake immediately and explains to her that he meant to say "Honey." From the psychodynamic perspective, Tom's error would be called a
    a. behavioral response.
    b. Freudian slip.
    c. cognitive misrepresentation.
    d. negative trait.
    Ans.: b   LG: 2   Page: 479   QT: A

17. According to Freud, whatever you are thinking about at this moment is in your
    a. unconscious mind.
    b. preconscious mind.
    c. conscious mind.
    d. subconscious mind.
    Ans.: c   LG: 2   Page: 479   QT: F

18. Freud compared human consciousness to a(n)
    a. iceberg.
    b. computer.
    c. funnel.
    d. forest.
    Ans.: a   LG: 2   Page: 479   QT: F

19. According to Freud's theory, conflict and tension in our everyday lives can be revealed by our
    a. conditioned responses.
    b. sensations.
    c. defense mechanisms.
    d. dreams.
    Ans.: d   LG: 2   Page: 479   QT: F

20. According to Freud, the major responsibility of the ego is to
    a. find socially acceptable ways for the id to be gratified.
    b. prevent the death instinct from destroying the ego ideal.
    c. fulfill all the desires of the id.
    d. make sure that the process of identification is not hampered.
    Ans.: a   LG: 2   Page: 479   QT: F

21. The spoiled child within you is to the id as the referee within you is to the
    a. pleasure principle.
    b. superego.
    c. libido.
    d. ego.
    Ans.: b   LG: 2   Page: 479   QT: C

22. Carolyn was reared in a home where high moral principles dominated. She has attended Sunday school and church since early childhood. In high school, her boyfriend talked her into "sleeping" with him. Which Freudian personality structure ruled Carolyn's behavior in this scenario?
    a. superego
    b. reality principle
    c. id
    d. ego
    Ans.: c   LG: 2   Page: 479   QT: C

23. An angry young boy who decides to tear up his father's collection of baseball cards is ruled by the
    a. id
    b. ego
    c. superego
    d. oral stage
    Ans.: a   LG: 2   Page: 479   QT: C

24. Cartoons sometimes depict personal conflict by showing an individual with an angel speaking into one ear and a devil speaking into the other ear. The angel corresponds to Freud's idea of the
    a. id.
    b. ego.
    c. superego.
    d. phallic symbol.
    Ans.: c   LG: 2   Page: 480   QT: C

25. In Freudian theory, the part of the self that functions as the censoring conscience is called the
    a. ego.
    b. id.
    c. libido.
    d. superego.
    Ans.: d   LG: 2   Page: 480   QT: F

26. Jane has to make a decision. She wants to go to a party and have fun tonight; however, she has a test tomorrow and knows she will fail the test if she doesn't study. Her ego would say,
    a. "You'd better stay home and study. Failing the test will be difficult to overcome later."
    b. "Go to the party! You deserve a good time! You'll feel better."
    c. "You're a bad girl if you go to that party, and you'll feel terrible if you fail that test."
    d. "Don't do anything. It's too complicated."
    Ans.: a   LG: 2   Page: 479   QT: C

27. Michelle was reared in a home where high moral principles dominated. She has attended Sunday school and church since early childhood. In high school, her boyfriend tried to talk her into "sleeping" with him, but something from inside her told her not to. She felt very proud of herself afterward for holding her ground. Which Freudian personality structure made Michelle feel proud of her response?
    a. superego
    b. reality principle
    c. id
    d. ego
    Ans.: a   LG: 2   Page: 480   QT: C

28. From Freud's perspective, which personality structure dominates earliest in childhood?
    a. pseudoego
    b. ego
    c. id
    d. superego
    Ans.: c   LG: 2   Page: 479   QT: C

29. Which personality structure is completely unconscious and consists of instincts?
    a. ego
    b. id
    c. superego
    d. pseudoego
    Ans.: b   LG: 2   Page: 479   QT: F

30. According to psychodynamic theory, defense mechanisms are necessary because of conflict
    a. between the ego and the libido.
    b. between the id and the superego.
    c. within the ego.
    d. between the id and the archetype.
    Ans.: b   LG: 2   Page: 480   QT: F

31. According to Freud, memories and emotions that are so threatening to the conscious mind that they have been repressed are stored in the
    a. subconscious.
    b. unconscious.
    c. personal conscious.
    d. primal conscious.
    Ans.: b   LG: 2   Page: 480   QT: F

32. Phillip is very much influenced by Freudian psychology. He is trying to convince his friend Bill, who takes a behavioral perspective, that Bill went through the phallic stage, including the Oedipus conflict. Bill says that he does not remember anything of the kind and that Phillip and Freud were both wrong. Which of the following would be Phillip's response?
    a. Bill has been conditioned to make responses like that.
    b. Bill is incorrect but is trying to self-actualize.
    c. Bill is demonstrating a classic Freudian defense mechanism—repression—which proves that both Phillip and Freud are correct.
    d. Bill has a bad memory.
    Ans.: c   LG: 2   Page: 480   QT: A

33. Redirecting our instinctual urges of sex and aggression into socially acceptable behavior is termed
    a. sublimation.
    b. projection.
    c. denial.
    d. reaction formation.
    Ans.: a   LG: 2   Page: 480   QT: F

34. When we attribute our own shortcomings, faults, and problems to others, we are using which defense mechanism?
    a. sublimation
    b. projection
    c. reaction formation
    d. regression
    Ans.: b   LG: 2   Page: 480   QT: F

35. Jeff experiences a lot of aggressive feelings toward his overprotective stepfather. Because he is powerless to aggress openly against his stepfather, Jeff becomes a very aggressive forward on his basketball team. According to Freud, this is an example of
    a. castration anxiety.
    b. sublimation.
    c. repression.
    d. displacement.
    Ans.: b   LG: 2   Page: 480   QT: C

36. Tina had a big argument with her best friend. She feels that the argument was her friend's fault. For several days after the argument, Tina "punishes" her friend by not returning her phone calls. This type of behavior is an example of which ego defense mechanism?
    a. regression
    b. repression
    c. sublimation
    d. rationalization
    Ans.: a   LG: 2   Page: 480   QT: C

37. Your friend had a car crash in which his brother was killed. Even though he knows the crash occurred, your friend cannot remember any of the details of the accident. Your friend is engaging in which ego defense mechanism?
    a. displacement
    b. rationalization
    c. reaction formation
    d. repression
    Ans.: d   LG: 2   Page: 480   QT: C

38. If you had to write a research paper on ego defense mechanisms, which of the following would be the *most* appropriate title?
    a. Defense mechanisms are people's conscious attempts to escape their problems.
    b. The most effective way to deal with a problem is to use ego defense mechanisms.
    c. In some situations, the use of defense mechanisms can be beneficial to psychological health.
    d. The use of defense mechanisms always indicates an impending psychological breakdown.
    Ans.: c   LG: 2   Page: 481   QT: A

39. Jane was not accepted into her top college choice. She told her friends that she did not want to go there anyway because the college faculty was too snobbish. She is using the defense mechanism of
    a. sublimation.
    b. reaction formation.
    c. displacement.
    d. rationalization.
    Ans.: d   LG: 2   Page: 480   QT: C

40. Seven-year-old Erica gets mad at her schoolteacher but cannot show her anger. After school, she takes out her frustration on her four-year-old brother Adam. According to Freud, Erica is using which ego defense mechanism?
    a. projection
    b. sublimation
    c. displacement
    d. regression
    Ans.: c   LG: 2   Page: 480   QT: C

41. According to Freud, an erogenous zone is a(n)
    a. area of the body undergoing rapid growth during childhood.
    b. area of the body that provides strong pleasure.
    c. period of time in which unconscious conflict can be dangerous.
    d. period of time during which we are most sensitive to social errors and embarrassment.
    Ans.: b   LG: 2   Page: 481   QT: F

42. Which of the following represents the correct order of Freud's stages of personality development?
    a. anal, oral, phallic, latency, genital
    b. oral, anal, phallic, genital, latency
    c. oral, anal, phallic, latency, genital
    d. anal, oral, latency, phallic, genital
    Ans.: c   LG: 2   Page: 481   QT: F

43. Which of the following persons is *best* described as fixated at the oral stage?
    a. a person who compulsively rearranges his desk and drawers
    b. a person who constantly smokes, chews, or puts things into the mouth
    c. a person who marries someone old enough to be his mother
    d. a person who cannot figure out why anyone would be interested in sex
    Ans.: b   LG: 2   Page: 482   QT: F

44. According to Freud's stages of psychosexual development, you would expect a nine-year-old to show the *most* interest in which of the following activities?
    a. going to the mall with her father
    b. helping his mother with the dishes
    c. going to the movies with his girlfriend
    d. talking to and playing with her friends
    Ans.: d   LG: 2   Page: 481   QT: C

45. Sean is five and has a strong attachment to his mother. According to Freud, Sean has a(n)
    a. anal complex.
    b. genital complex.
    c. Oedipus complex.
    d. Electra complex.
    Ans.: c   LG: 2   Page: 481   QT: C

46. The Oedipus complex develops and is resolved during which stage of Freud's theory of psychosexual development?
    a. genital
    b. phallic
    c. anal
    d. oral
    Ans.: b   LG: 2   Page: 481   QT: F

47. A critic of Freudian theory would agree *most* with which of the following statements?
    a. Human behavior is governed primarily by the unconscious.
    b. Early childhood experiences are the critical influence on personality development.
    c. Sociocultural factors play an important role in personality development.
    d. The id dominates personality throughout life.
    Ans.: c   LG: 2   Page: 482   QT: C

48. Criticisms of Freudian theory include all of the following *except* that
    a. Freud overestimated the importance of sexuality in personality development.
    b. Freud placed too much emphasis on the instinctual impulses of the id.
    c. Freud underestimated the importance of later experiences in personality development.
    d. Freud placed too much emphasis on conscious control of behavior.
    Ans.: d   LG: 2   Page: 482   QT: F

49. Critics have accused Freud of gender bias based on his concept of the
    a. Oedipus complex.
    b. id.
    c. unconscious.
    d. oral stage.
    Ans.: a   LG: 2   Page: 482   QT: F

50. Freud's view that gender differences in personality development are due to anatomical differences between males and females was criticized primarily for
    a. ignoring cultural and environmental influences on personality development.
    b. underestimating cognitive differences between males and females.
    c. dismissing the importance of parenting style on personality development.
    d. overestimating intelligence differences between males and females.
    Ans.: a   LG: 2   Page: 482   QT: C

51. Which of the following is the central idea in Karen Horney's personality theory?
    a. The need for security is the prime motive in human existence.
    b. Self-actualization is the most basic human motive.
    c. Conflict is the inevitable result of the inborn motives of the id.
    d. We each possess both a personal unconscious and a collective unconscious.
    Ans.: a   LG: 2   Page: 483   QT: F

52. Which of the following *best* summarizes Horney's perspective of personality development?
    a. Anatomy is destiny.
    b. Hypotheses need not be supported with observable data.
    c. Personality is a matter of biology.
    d. Social experiences and culture shape personality.
    Ans.: d   LG: 2   Page: 483   QT: C

53. Which of the following is *not* a coping mechanism proposed by Karen Horney?
    a. moving toward people
    b. moving away from people
    c. moving against people
    d. moving within the unconscious
    Ans.: d   LG: 2   Page: 483   QT: F

54. In reaction to Freud, Horney said women really did *not* want to have a man's physiological features; what they really wanted was
    a. stronger personalities.
    b. power and opportunities.
    c. adequate superegos and stronger moral convictions.
    d. ego defense mechanisms, particularly intellectualization.
    Ans.: b   LG: 2   Page: 483   QT: C

55. According to Jung, emotionally laden ideas and images are called
    a. the personal unconscious.
    b. archetypes.
    c. the mandala.
    d. dreams.
    Ans.: b   LG: 2   Page: 483   QT: F

56. Even if they are not told this directly, most people intuitively understand that incest is wrong. Jung would explain that the incest taboo is part of the
    a. innate id.
    b. collective unconscious.
    c. feelings of inferiority.
    d. unconscious superego.
    Ans.: b   LG: 2   Page: 483   QT: C

57. Which theorist placed the greatest emphasis on the unconscious?
    a. Freud
    b. Adler
    c. Jung
    d. All of them placed an equal emphasis on the unconscious.
    Ans.: c   LG: 2   Page: 483   QT: C

58. According to Adler, which of the following plays an important role in our adaptation and striving for goals?
    a. uncovering the unconscious mind
    b. playing out aggressive instincts
    c. understanding the collective unconscious
    d. dealing with feelings of inferiority
    Ans.: d   LG: 2   Page: 484   QT: C

59. According to Adler, from the time that we are infants, larger, more powerful people make us feel
    a. inferior.
    b. superior.
    c. adequate.
    d. comparable.
    Ans.: a   LG: 2   Page: 484   QT: F

60. Aaron has never felt very good about his accomplishments and typically will focus on any error he has made as a way of demonstrating that he is not adequate. From Adler's perspective, Aaron
    a. had difficulty resolving the trust vs. mistrust stage.
    b. is suffering from basic anxiety.
    c. has developed an inferiority complex.
    d. has not yet developed a personal unconscious.
    Ans.: c   LG: 2   Page: 484   QT: A

61. Which of the following psychoanalytic principles has had the *most* lasting impact on the field of personality psychology?
    a. Sexuality rules human personality development.
    b. Personality should be studied observationally.
    c. Personality should be studied developmentally.
    d. The unconscious dominates human personality.
    Ans.: c   LG: 2   Page: 484   QT: C

62. Which of the following represents a major criticism of psychoanalytic theories?
   a. Early psychoanalytic theorists overestimated positive human potential.
   b. Human behavior is not subject to the influence of unconscious motives.
   c. Psychoanalytic theory underestimates the importance of early childhood experiences.
   d. Most psychoanalytic concepts have not been verified empirically.
   Ans.: d   LG: 2   Page: 485   QT: C

63. Which of the following is *not* a criticism of the psychoanalytic approach?
   a. The psychodynamic approach placed too much emphasis on sexuality.
   b. The psychodynamic approach placed too much emphasis on the unconscious.
   c. The psychodynamic approach overestimated the human capacity for change.
   d. The psychodynamic approach lacks empirical verification.
   Ans.: c   LG: 2   Page: 485   QT: C

Learning Goal 3: Explain the behavioral and social cognitive perspectives.

64. Roberta is described as caring, friendly, and helpful. According to Skinner's view of personality, Roberta's personality would be defined by her
   a. traits.
   b. body type.
   c. cognitions.
   d. behavior.
   Ans.: d   LG: 3   Page: 486   QT: C

65. Environment as a determinant of personality was strongly advocated by
   a. Freud.
   b. Eysenck.
   c. Allport.
   d. Skinner.
   Ans.: d   LG: 3   Page: 486   QT: F

66. In a discussion regarding the significance of the unconscious in personality, _____ would say that the unconscious is significant, and _____ would state that only observable behaviors matter.
   a. Skinner, Freud
   b. Watson, Skinner
   c. Skinner, Horney
   d. Freud, Skinner
   Ans.: d   LG: 3   Page: 486   QT: C

67. According to Skinner, an individual's personality is the result of
   a. learning.
   b. age.
   c. thinking.
   d. heredity.
   Ans.: a   LG: 3   Page: 486   QT: F

68. "Once a person has reached adolescence, little can be done to alter her personality." Which of the following would *most* strongly disagree with this statement?
    a. Horney
    b. Jung
    c. Freud
    d. Skinner
    Ans.: d   LG: 3   Page: 486   QT: C

69. Bandura and Skinner would *most* strongly disagree about the answer to which of these questions?
    a. Is personality learned or primarily due to biological factors?
    b. Are person variables and cognitive factors important in understanding personality?
    c. Is personality development influenced by environmental factors?
    d. Can personality change over time?
    Ans.: b   LG: 3   Page: 487   QT: C

70. The theory that stresses the importance of reinforcement and punishment in personality development is
    a. the psychoanalytic theory.
    b. the humanistic theory.
    c. behaviorism.
    d. the cognitive theory.
    Ans.: c   LG: 3   Page: 486   QT: F

71. Who would be *most* likely to say that a person is dishonest because of environmental factors?
    a. Skinner
    b. Freud
    c. Rogers
    d. Jung
    Ans.: a   LG: 3   Page: 486   QT: C

72. Which of the following is *not* a component of Bandura's model of reciprocal determinism?
    a. behavior
    b. environment
    c. person/cognitive factors
    d. biological instincts
    Ans.: d   LG: 3   Page: 487   QT: F

73. Bandura's idea of reciprocal determinism implies that
    a. the environment dictates behaviors.
    b. cognition controls the environment.
    c. cognition, the environment, and behavior are bidirectional in their influence upon each other.
    d. cognition is not significant in the stimulus-response of learning.
    Ans.: c   LG: 3   Page: 487   QT: F

74. Which of the following places the *most* emphasis on cognition in personality?
    a. operant conditioning
    b. reciprocal determinism
    c. collective unconscious
    d. inferiority complex
    Ans.: b   LG: 3   Page: 487   QT: C

75. Which of the following is the *best* example of how social learning can influence personality?
    a. Billy stops himself from cheating by looking at a classmate's test because he feels guilty.
    b. Billy stops himself from cheating by looking at a classmate's test because the teacher has told everyone that they will be punished if caught.
    c. Billy stops himself from cheating by looking at a classmate's test because he saw another student get caught cheating and have their test torn up.
    d. None of these is an example.
    Ans.: c   LG: 3   Page: 487   QT: A

76. A book designed to help people develop the personality features they desire suggests that readers pattern their lives on the model provided by someone they admire a great deal. The approach employed by this book is *most* compatible with
    a. psychoanalytic theory.
    b. social cognitive theory.
    c. humanistic theory.
    d. existential theory.
    Ans.: b   LG: 3   Page: 487   QT: C

77. According to Bandura, self-efficacy represents a person's belief that
    a. the environment regulates human behavior.
    b. the unconscious id dominates personality.
    c. she can master a situation and produce positive outcomes.
    d. he cannot overcome negative childhood experiences.
    Ans.: c   LG: 3   Page: 488   QT: F

78. Diane believes that she can succeed at almost anything she sets her mind to. As a result, she tends to do her best at everything that she attempts. Bandura would say that Diane has a high level of
    a. drive.
    b. self-esteem.
    c. self-efficacy.
    d. self-determination.
    Ans.: c   LG: 3   Page: 488   QT: F

79. Which of the following is *not* a strategy for increasing self-efficacy?
    a. Select achievable goals.
    b. Distinguish between past performances and the present.
    c. Pay close attention to your failures.
    d. As self-efficacy increases, challenge yourself with more daunting tasks.
    Ans.: c   LG: 3   Page: 488   QT: C

80. The student who does poorly on a test and complains that he normally does well but the questions were tricky and the professor did not teach the unit well is demonstrating
    a. low self-efficacy and an internal locus of control.
    b. low self-efficacy and an external locus of control.
    c. high self-efficacy and an internal locus of control.
    d. high self-efficacy and an external locus of control.
    Ans.: d   LG: 3   Page: 488   QT: A

81. Which of the following is *not* a criticism of behavioral and social cognitive approaches to personality?
    a. Both approaches place too much emphasis on biology.
    b. Both approaches are too concerned with change and situational influences on personality and do not pay enough attention to enduring qualities.
    c. Both try to explain the complex concept of personality in one or two factors.
    d. Both approaches miss the creative, spontaneous, human dimensions of personality.
    Ans.: a   LG: 3   Page: 490   QT: C

Learning Goal 4: Describe the humanistic perspectives.

82. Which of the following would *not* be consistent with the humanistic perspective of personality?
    a. Each of us has the ability to cope with stressors.
    b. We have the ability to control our own lives.
    c. Our subconscious gives us either a sense of control or a lack of control.
    d. We have the ability to understand our world and ourselves.
    Ans.: c   LG: 4   Page: 491   QT: C

83. An optimist is *most* likely to prefer which personality theory?
    a. social cognitive
    b. psychodynamic
    c. humanistic
    d. trait
    Ans.: c   LG: 4   Page: 491   QT: C

84. Humanistic psychologists tend to see people as
    a. highly resilient and possessing positive qualities.
    b. failing to break loose from instinctive control.
    c. possessing inherited aggressive tendencies.
    d. products of their environmental experiences.
    Ans.: a   LG: 4   Page: 491   QT: F

85. Your five-year-old nephew is spending a few days with you. One morning before breakfast, he attempts to give your cat a bath in the toilet. You are not happy about the mess; neither is the cat. Which response would you choose to show your nephew unconditional positive regard despite your displeasure at his behavior?
    a. "Don't worry about the mess; it doesn't matter."
    b. "I am not happy about the mess you made, but I love you as a person."
    c. "I guess you are just too little to reach the shower controls."
    d. "Look at this mess! How can you be so stupid and careless?"
    Ans.: b   LG: 4   Page: 492   QT: A

86. The central term to Rogers' theory that refers to an individual's overall perceptions of their abilities, behavior, and personality is called
    a. self-esteem.
    b. self-efficacy.
    c. self-concept.
    d. self-evaluation.
    Ans.: c   LG: 4   Page: 491   QT: F

87. Which of the following statements is *not* true regarding the real self and the ideal self?
   a. The real self is the self that results from our experiences.
   b. The ideal self is what we would like to be.
   c. The greater the discrepancy between the real self and the ideal self, the more problems we will have adjusting.
   d. Our perception of our real self and our ideal self is set and cannot be changed.
   Ans.: d   LG: 4   Page: 491   QT: C

88. According to Rogers, in order to develop a positive self-concept, a person needs to receive from others all of the following *except*
   a. unconditional positive regard.
   b. empathy.
   c. genuineness.
   d. negative feedback.
   Ans.: d   LG: 4   Page: 492   QT: F

89. What do Carl Rogers' and Abraham Maslow's theories have in common?
   a. They emphasize the need for empathy.
   b. They propose a hierarchy of human needs.
   c. They focus on positive human potential.
   d. They deal with the difference between the real and ideal self.
   Ans.: c   LG: 4   Page: 492   QT: C

90. Self-actualization is a term used by Maslow to refer to a state in which people
   a. are highly motivated by physiological or safety needs.
   b. have an inner-directed need to reach their full potential.
   c. have overcome a period of mental illness.
   d. have achieved their self-concept.
   Ans.: b   LG: 4   Page: 493   QT: F

91. Carl Rogers sees maladjustment as the result of
   a. a discrepancy between the ideal self and the real self.
   b. rejection and fear of certain archetypes.
   c. faulty reinforcement patterns.
   d. poor childhood experiences.
   Ans.: a   LG: 4   Page: 491   QT: F

92. Another term for self-esteem is
   a. self-concept.
   b. self-efficacy.
   c. self-worth.
   d. self-confidence.
   Ans.: c   LG: 4   Page: 493   QT: F

93. Which of the following is *not* a recommended strategy for improving a person's self-esteem?
   a. identifying the causes of low self-esteem
   b. participating in competitive situations
   c. experiencing emotional support and approval
   d. achieving and coping
   Ans.: b   LG: 4   Page: 495   QT: F

94. Emotional support and approval tend to facilitate self-esteem. This finding corresponds *most* closely with which of Carl Rogers' principles?
    a. unconditional positive regard
    b. ideal self
    c. genuineness
    d. the hierarchy of human needs
    Ans.: a   LG: 4   Page: 495   QT: C

95. Which of the following is *not* considered a weakness of the humanistic perspective?
    a. Humanistic psychologists are overly optimistic about human nature.
    b. Humanists may encourage excessive self-love and narscissism.
    c. Humanists are overly scientific in the experimentation that supports their theories.
    d. There was no real need for another theory in addition to the behaviorists and psychodynamic theorists.
    Ans.: c   LG: 4   Page: 495   QT: C

Learning Goal 5: Discuss the trait perspectives.

96. An enduring personality characteristic that tends to lead to certain behaviors is a(n)
    a. goal.
    b. trait.
    c. attribute.
    d. delusion.
    Ans.: b   LG: 5   Page: 496   QT: F

97. Which of the following terms *best* describes the trait theory of personality?
    a. personality characteristics
    b. explanations
    c. development
    d. motives
    Ans.: a   LG: 5   Page: 496   QT: F

98. Which of the following is *not* one of Allport's main categories of human traits?
    a. secondary traits
    b. central traits
    c. periodic traits
    d. cardinal traits
    Ans.: c   LG: 5   Page: 497   QT: F

99. From Allport's perspective, which of the following traits are the *most* powerful and dominating in a person's personality?
    a. cardinal traits
    b. central traits
    c. primary traits
    d. secondary traits
    Ans.: a   LG: 5   Page: 497   QT: F

100. According to Allport, people who possess cardinal traits are
    a. difficult to classify.
    b. rare.
    c. eccentric.
    d. maladjusted.
    Ans.: b   LG: 5   Page: 497   QT: F

101. According to Allport, most people's personalities can be described with a limited number of
    a. cardinal traits.
    b. secondary traits.
    c. primary traits.
    d. central traits.
    Ans.: d   LG: 5   Page: 497   QT: F

102. How would Gordon Allport *most* likely describe the characteristics associated with Eysenck's introversion-extraversion dimension?
    a. as secondary traits
    b. as central traits
    c. as cardinal traits
    d. as primary traits
    Ans.: b   LG: 5   Page: 497   QT: C

103. What do Allport's and Eysenck's theories of personality have in common?
    a. They consist of sets of opposites with positive and negative poles.
    b. They feel that people with psychological disorders require additional explanatory dimensions.
    c. They group personality traits into four main categories.
    d. They assume that personality can be described in terms of traits.
    Ans.: d   LG: 5   Page: 497   QT: C

104. What is the main difference between Allport's and Eysenck's theories of personality?
    a. Eysenck's theory is more detailed than Allport's.
    b. Allport proposes more basic human traits than Eysenck.
    c. Allport explains personality traits in terms of polar opposites.
    d. Eysenck describes general categories rather than specific traits.
    Ans.: a   LG: 5   Page: 497   QT: C

105. Hans Eysenck said that three main dimensions were needed to explain personality. Which of the following is *not* one of the three that he mentioned?
    a. static-dynamic
    b. introversion-extroversion
    c. stable-unstable
    d. psychoticism
    Ans.: a   LG: 5   Page: 497   QT: F

106. Which of the following is included in the big five factors of personality?
    a. truthfulness
    b. intelligence
    c. cynicism
    d. extraversion
    Ans.: d   LG: 5   Page: 498   QT: F

107. An acronym that can be used to remember the big five factors of personality is
    a. HOMES.
    b. OCEAN.
    c. LAKES.
    d. FREUD.
    Ans.: b   LG: 5   Page: 498   QT: F

108. Sociable, fun loving, and affectionate are attributes associated with which of the big five factors of personality?
    a. conscientiousness
    b. agreeableness
    c. extraversion
    d. openness
    Ans.: c   LG: 5   Page: 499   QT: F

109. Softhearted, trusting, and helpful are characteristics used to describe Alex. In terms of the big five factors of personality, Alex would be described as strong on
    a. emotional stability.
    b. openness.
    c. conscientiousness.
    d. agreeableness.
    Ans.: d   LG: 5   Page: 499   QT: C

110. Based on the big five factors of personality, someone who is calm, secure, and self-satisfied would be described as strong on which factor?
    a. openness
    b. emotional stability
    c. conscientiousness
    d. extraversion
    Ans.: b   LG: 5   Page: 499   QT: C

111. Dennis is imaginative rather than practical and prefers variety to routine. Dennis would probably rank high on which of the big five factors of personality?
    a. agreeableness
    b. openness
    c. emotional stability
    d. introversion
    Ans.: b   LG: 5   Page: 499   QT: C

112. Carla doesn't like to interact with too many people. Most of the time, her mood is gloomy. In interpersonal interactions, she tends to be reserved. Carla would probably rank low on which of the big five factors of personality?
    a. extraversion
    b. conscientiousness
    c. emotional stability
    d. agreeableness
    Ans.: a   LG: 5   Page: 499   QT: C

113. Based on cross-cultural research on the big five personality factors, which conclusion can be drawn?
    a. The big five personality factors have only been supported in industrialized countries.
    b. Support of the big five is limited because research has been conducted only in Western countries.
    c. There is currently little evidence that the big five exist anywhere other than the United States.
    d. Research results support the existence of the big five personality factors around the world.
    Ans.: d   LG: 5   Page: 499   QT: C

114. How stable are the big five personality factors across the life span?
    a. very unstable over the life span
    b. unstable until age 30, then very stable
    c. quite stable over the life span
    d. stable until age 50, then rapid decline
    Ans.: c   LG: 5   Page: 499   QT: F

115. The theory of the big five personality factors has recently been challenged by which research findings?
    a. The big five factors of personality are defined too narrowly.
    b. More than five basic factors may be needed to fully describe personality.
    c. The polar opposites within each of the big five factors are too vague.
    d. The big five factors of personality are not distinct enough.
    Ans.: b   LG: 5   Page: 499   QT: C

116. Felicia came home and found that her friends had arranged a surprise party to celebrate her promotion at work. Felicia was so overwhelmed that she began crying with happiness. Which view of personality would explain Felicia's reaction as due to a combination of her personality characteristics and the circumstances of her promotion, the party, and her friends' caring?
    a. somatotype theory
    b. collectivism
    c. trait-situation interaction
    d. the big five theory
    Ans.: c   LG: 5   Page: 500   QT: C

117. A psychologist who believes in the trait-situation interaction would say that consistency in personality depends on
    a. the person.
    b. the situation.
    c. the behavior sampled.
    d. all of the above.
    Ans.: d   LG: 5   Page: 499   QT: F

118. A cross-cultural psychologist would agree with which of the following statements pertaining to trait-situation interactions?
    a. Both the immediate setting and the broader cultural context must be considered.
    b. Only the broader cultural context must be considered.
    c. Individual differences are always the result of cultural influence.
    d. Traits are not influenced by culture.
    Ans.: a   LG: 5   Page: 500   QT: C

119. A personality psychologist who believes in trait-situation interaction would primarily criticize which aspect of trait theories?
    a. the view that traits are consistent across time and circumstances
    b. the notion that there is an identifiable number of traits
    c. the idea that there are primary and secondary traits
    d. the notion that traits can be defined in terms of polar opposites
    Ans.: a   LG: 5   Page: 500   QT: C

Learning Goal 6: Characterize the main methods of personality assessment.

120. Which of the following is *not* true regarding personality assessment?
    a. The kind of test chosen by psychologists often depends on the psychologist's theoretical perspective.
    b. Personality tests are susceptible to situational influence.
    c. Personality tests assess stable characteristics.
    d. Psychologists today use scientifically developed methods to measure personality.
    Ans.: b   LG: 6   Page: 501   QT: C

121. Which of the following is *not* true regarding projective tests?
    a. Projective tests present subjects with ambiguous stimuli and then ask them to describe it or tell a story about it.
    b. Projective tests are most closely aligned with the trait perspective of personality.
    c. Projective tests are designed to prove an assessment that goes deeper than the surface of personality.
    d. Projective tests go beyond how you overtly present yourself.
    Ans.: b   LG: 6   Page: 502   QT: C

122. Which of the following perspectives would be most closely aligned with projective tests?
    a. Psychodynamic.
    b. Behavioral.
    c. Humanistic.
    d. Social Cognitive.
    Ans.: a   LG: 6   Page: 500   QT: C

123. The subject looks at the image and says, "I see my psychology professor chasing me because my research paper is late…" This would most likely be which type of personality test?
    a. the GRE
    b. the MMPI
    c. a projective test
    d. a self-report measure
    Ans.: c   LG: 6   Page: 502   QT: C

124. A clinician told Mark that a sample of his handwriting was required in order to assess his personality. This type of measure is considered a
    a. self-report.
    b. projective technique.
    c. Thematic Apperception Test.
    d. regression test.
    Ans.: b   LG: 6   Page: 503   QT: C

125. The Rorschach test could also be called the
    a. photograph test
    b. drawing test
    c. multiple-choice test
    d. inkblot test
    Ans.: d   LG: 6   Page: 502   QT: F

126. The Rorschach inkblot test is based on the assumption that
    a. people have insight into their personalities.
    b. people will project repressed feelings onto ambiguous stimuli.
    c. people use defense mechanisms without any awareness.
    d. the unconscious is expressed in dreams.
    Ans.: b   LG: 6   Page: 502   QT: F

127. Which of the following is *most* similar to the Rorschach inkblot test?
    a. the Myers-Briggs Type indicator
    b. the Thematic Apperception Test
    c. the Minnesota Multiphasic Personality Inventory
    d. the Stanford-Binet
    Ans.: b   LG: 6   Page: 503   QT: C

128. The Rorschach test is to _____ as the Thematic Apperception Test is to _____.
    a. geometric shapes, realistic pictures
    b. cartoon drawings, inkblots
    c. inkblots, objective questions
    d. inkblots, realistic pictures
    Ans.: d   LG: 6   Page: 503   QT: C

129. Fred looks at a realistic picture and then tells the examiner that he thinks the subject in the picture looks frustrated because he cannot do as well as he would like in school. Fred is *most* likely taking a(n)
    a. Rorschach test.
    b. Thematic Apperception Test.
    c. Minnesota Multiphasic Personality Inventory.
    d. self-report test.
    Ans.: b   LG: 6   Page: 503   QT: F

130. What is graphology?
    a. analysis of geometric shapes
    b. the statistical analysis of projective data
    c. handwriting analysis
    d. art therapy
    Ans.: c   LG: 6   Page: 503   QT: F

131. Your company is trying to decide whether or not to hire a graphologist in order to obtain more information about potential employees. If you were on a committee that will make a recommendation on this question to your company's president, which recommendation would you endorse?
    a. Hiring a graphologist will be a waste of money.
    b. Hiring a graphologist will provide useful information.
    c. Hiring a graphologist will make the company more competitive.
    d. Hiring a graphologist will intimidate potential employees.
    Ans.: a   LG: 6   Page: 503   QT: A

132. What is the *main* criticism of projective personality tests?
    a. They contain bias.
    b. They are not very useful to clinicians.
    c. They confuse subjects.
    d. They have low reliability and validity.
    Ans.: d   LG: 6   Page: 503   QT: C

133. The goal of self-report tests is to
    a. reveal unconscious personality characteristics.
    b. use the handwriting sample to measure personality.
    c. uncover the true id, ego, and superego relationships.
    d. assess personality traits by asking about them.
    Ans.: d   LG: 6   Page: 504   QT: F

134. Projective personality tests and self-report tests differ with respect to all of the following aspects *except* for
    a. what they intend to measure.
    b. underlying theoretical assumptions.
    c. the type of responses asked for.
    d. the type of stimuli presented.
    Ans.: a   LG: 6   Page: 504   QT: C

135. Projective tests are to subjective as self-report tests are to
    a. ambiguous.
    b. objective.
    c. deceptive.
    d. biased.
    Ans.: b   LG: 6   Page: 504   QT: C

136. Which of the following is *not* a self-report personality test?
    a. Minnesota Multiphasic Personality Inventory
    b. NEO-PI-R
    c. Thematic Apperception Test
    d. Hogan Personality Inventory
    Ans.: c   LG: 6   Page: 507   QT: F

137. A testing instrument that assesses the Big Five Factors of personality is the
    a. Neuroticism Extraversion Openness Personality Inventory.
    b. Rorschach Test.
    c. Thematic Apperception Test.
    d. none of the above.
    Ans.: a   LG: 6   Page: 506   QT: F

138. Which of the following tests would have the highest test reliability and validity?
    a. Rorschach test, black and white images
    b. Thematic Apperception Test
    c. Minnesota Multiphasic Personality Inventory
    d. Rorschach test, color images
    Ans.: c   LG: 6   Page: 507   QT: C

139. The goal of an empirically keyed test is to
    a. provide therapeutic instruction.
    b. have answer keys made available.
    c. avoid research interpretations.
    d. predict some criterion.
    Ans.: d   LG: 6   Page: 506   QT: F

140. Which of the following would *not* be true regarding an empirically keyed test?
    a. An empirically keyed test relies on items to predict some criterion.
    b. An empirically keyed test is especially susceptible to social desirability.
    c. Empirically keyed tests make no assumptions about the nature of test items.
    d. Empirically keyed tests often contain questions that do not seem relevant, but are very important.
    Ans.: b   LG: 6   Page: 506   QT: C

141. Juan recently took a test for a job. The test itself had a variety of questions that did not really seem applicable to the work he was seeking. Nonetheless, he did his best and a week later got the job offer. Juan was *most* likely taking a(n)
    a. Thematic Apperception Test.
    b. empirically keyed test.
    c. Rorschach test.
    d. dexterity test.
    Ans.: b   LG: 6   Page: 506   QT: C

142. The main problem with self-report personality tests is
    a. poor validity.
    b. social desirability.
    c. low clinical utility.
    d. reliance on empirical criteria.
    Ans.: b   LG: 6   Page: 506   QT: C

143. What would be a psychologist's main reason for using the MMPI instead of a projective personality test?
    a. reliance on face validity
    b. less problems with reliability and validity
    c. focus on unconscious determinants of personality
    d. desire to keep the test session as short as possible
    Ans.: b   LG: 6   Page: 506   QT: C

144. Critics of self-report personality tests have addressed all of the following issues *except* that they do not
    a. focus on the unconscious determinants of personality.
    b. reflect situational variation in personality.
    c. capture the individual's personality traits.
    d. examine the environmental influence on personality.
    Ans.: c   LG: 6   Page: 506   QT: F

145. Which of the following would *most* favor the use of self-report personality tests?
    a. B.F. Skinner
    b. Sigmund Freud
    c. Hans Eysenck
    d. Carl Rogers
    Ans.: c   LG: 6   Page: 506   QT: C

146. What is the main disadvantage of direct behavioral assessment?
    a. It is often impractical.
    b. It is often invalid.
    c. It is often biased.
    d. It is often skewed.
    Ans.: a   LG: 6   Page: 508   QT: C

147. Dr. Chandler is observing young children's reactions to separation from their mothers. The scenario goes like this: The mother brings the child (age 3 or 4) to a playroom with an assortment of toys and stays there with the child for a few minutes. Then, an adult comes into the room and asks the mother to step out for a moment to complete some paperwork. Dr. Chandler observes the child's reactions to being left alone in the playroom through a two-way mirror. She notes that some children continue playing calmly whereas others get quite distressed by the mother's departure and start crying. Which assessment technique is Dr. Chandler using?
    a. behavioral assessment
    b. projective assessment
    c. self-report assessment
    d. standardized assessment
    Ans.: a   LG: 6   Page: 508   QT: C

148. How does behavioral assessment differ from projective personality tests and self-report personality tests?
    a. It tends to be more subjective.
    b. It focuses on situational influences.
    c. It usually takes place in a controlled setting.
    d. It occurs without the subject's knowledge.
    Ans.: b   LG: 6   Page: 508   QT: C

149. When direct observation is not possible, a therapist might attempt to assess behavior by
    a. interpreting the client's dreams.
    b. asking the client to keep a journal.
    c. examining the client's irrational thoughts.
    d. asking the client to complete a behavior checklist.
    Ans.: d   LG: 6   Page: 508   QT: C

150. When tests are given by industrial psychologists to predict job performance, they include assessment of
    a. personality tests, such as the MMPI.
    b. vocational inventories, such as the Strong Interest Inventory.
    c. aptitude tests, such as IQ tests.
    d. all of the above.
    Ans.: d   LG: 6   Page: 510   QT: C

True/False Items

___ 151. Personality involves thoughts, emotions, and behaviors.
___ 152. The psychodynamic perspective of personality development emphasizes the importance of early childhood experiences.
___ 153. According to Freud, the ego becomes more developed as infants get older.
___ 154. Freud would say that an individual who is compulsively neat is fixated in the oral stage.
___ 155. Freud's personality theory was criticized for its overemphasis on sexuality and the unconscious.
___ 156. Karen Horney developed the concept of the collective unconscious.
___ 157. A behaviorist defines personality in terms of observable behavior.
___ 158. According to Bandura, an individual's personality is the result of a reciprocal interaction among behavior, environment, and person/cognitive factors.
___ 159. Humanistic psychologists stress people's positive potential and their ability to control their lives.
___ 160. Self-concept is an overall evaluation of self-worth.
___ 161. All trait theorists agree on the basic characteristics that comprise personality.
___ 162. Cross-cultural studies show little consistency of the big five personality factors across the world.
___ 163. Projective tests are an objective measure of personality.
___ 164. Self-report tests are objective tests.
___ 165. Empirically keyed tests are often used to minimize the influence of socially desirable answers.

Answer Key for True/False Items

				158.	Ans.: T	LG: 3	Page: 487
151.	Ans.: T	LG: 1	Page: 477	159.	Ans.: T	LG: 4	Page: 491
152.	Ans.: T	LG: 2	Page: 478	160.	Ans.: F	LG: 4	Page: 493
153.	Ans.: T	LG: 2	Page: 479	161.	Ans.: F	LG: 5	Page: 497
154.	Ans.: F	LG: 2	Page: 482	162.	Ans.: F	LG: 5	Page: 499
155.	Ans.: T	LG: 2	Page: 482	163.	Ans.: F	LG: 6	Page: 501
156.	Ans.: F	LG: 2	Page: 483	164.	Ans.: T	LG: 6	Page: 504
157.	Ans.: T	LG: 3	Page: 486	165.	Ans.: T	LG: 6	Page: 506

Fill-in-the-Blank Items

166. _____ is the enduring, distinctive thoughts, emotions, and behaviors that characterize the way an individual adapts to the world.
167. According to Freud's psychodynamic perspective, our mind is more _____ than conscious.
168. According to Freud, the _____ abides by the pleasure principle.
169. The _____ stage is the last stage of psychosexual development.
170. In order to resolve the Oedipus complex, the male child identifies with the _____.
171. Carl Jung proposed the idea that all humans share a collective _____.
172. One main criticism that _____, who also took a psychodynamic perspective, had of Freud's theories concerns their male bias.
173. Skinner would say that personality is a person's observable behavior that has been learned through interaction with the _____.
174. Bandura views _____ learning as having a powerful influence on personality development.
175. According to Carl Rogers, people need _____ positive regard, empathy, and genuineness.
176. Abraham Maslow believed that _____ was not only an important part of motivation, but also of personality.
177. _____ theorists study personality in terms of characteristic responses or enduring dispositions.
178. According to Gordon Allport, personality traits can be classified as _____, central, or secondary.
179. The _____ is also referred to as the inkblot test.
180. Self-report personality tests are more _____ than projective personality tests.

Answer Key for Fill-in-the-Blank Items

166.	Ans.: personality	LG: 1	Page: 477
167.	Ans.: unconscious	LG: 2	Page: 479
168.	Ans.: id	LG: 2	Page: 479
169.	Ans.: genital	LG: 2	Page: 481
170.	Ans.: father	LG: 2	Page: 481
171.	Ans.: unconscious	LG: 2	Page: 483
172.	Ans.: Horney	LG: 2	Page: 482
173.	Ans.: environment	LG: 3	Page: 486
174.	Ans.: social	LG: 3	Page: 487
175.	Ans.: unconditional	LG: 4	Page: 492
176.	Ans.: self-actualization	LG: 4	Page: 493
177.	Ans.: Trait	LG: 5	Page: 496
178.	Ans.: cardinal	LG: 5	Page: 497
179.	Ans.: Rorschach test	LG: 6	Page: 502
180.	Ans.: objective	LG: 6	Page: 504

Matching Items

____ 181. projection
____ 182. graphology
____ 183. real self
____ 184. objective test
____ 185. projective test

A. Freudian stage
B. collective unconscious
C. handwriting analysis
D. inferiority complex
E. cognitive factor that affects personality

344

	186.	self-efficacy		F.	Thematic Apperception Test
___	186.	self-efficacy		F.	Thematic Apperception Test
___	187.	cardinal trait		G.	self-concept
___	188.	anal		H.	defense mechanism
___	189.	Adler		I.	Minnesota Multiphasic Personality Inventory
___	190.	archetype		J.	trait theory

Answer Key for Matching Items

181.	Ans.: H	LG: 2	Page: 480		186.	Ans.: E	LG: 3	Page: 488
182.	Ans.: C	LG: 6	Page: 503		187.	Ans.: J	LG: 5	Page: 497
183.	Ans.: G	LG: 4	Page: 491		188.	Ans.: A	LG: 2	Page: 481
184.	Ans.: I	LG: 6	Page: 506		189.	Ans.: D	LG: 2	Page: 484
185.	Ans.: F	LG: 6	Page: 503		190.	Ans.: B	LG: 2	Page: 483

Essay Questions

191. The id, ego, and superego are Freudian structures of personality. Describe each of these structures, and discuss how they are related to and influenced by each other. (LG: 2)

Answer Guidelines: Possible options include mentioning the id (pleasure principle; instincts as source of energy), ego (reality principle; mediates between id and superego), and superego (conscience; moral principle).

192. Briefly discuss the stages of Freud's theory of psychosexual development. (LG: 2)

Answer Guidelines: Possible options include mentioning the oral stage (birth to 18 months; pleasure centered on oral activities), the anal stage (1½ to 3 years; pleasure associated with the anus and eliminative functions), the phallic stage (3 to 6 years; pleasure associated with genitals; Oedipus and Electra complex), the latency stage (6 years to puberty; pleasure associated with the development of social and intellectual skills), and the genital stage (puberty and beyond; pleasure associated with sexual activity).

193. Discuss the influence of Sigmund Freud on the work of Karen Horney and Alfred Adler. Include similarities and differences in theories. (LG: 2)

Answer Guidelines: Answers should reflect the commonalities of the theories including the role of the unconscious and the significance of development. Answers should also acknowledge Freud's psychosexual perspective and libido as compared to Horney's anxiety and Adler's inferiority. The gender differences that existed between Freud and Horney's perspectives should also be mentioned.

194. Explain the concept of Jung's collective unconscious. In your answer, include archetypes. (LG: 2)

Answer Guidelines: The collective unconscious was Jung's term for the impersonal, deepest layer of the unconscious mind, shared by all human beings because of their ancestral past. Archetypes were emotionally laden ideas and images in the collective unconscious that have rich and symbolic meaning.

195. Discuss how the fundamental assumptions of the behavioral and social cognitive theories of personality differ from Freud's psychoanalytic approach? (LG: 3)

Answer Guidelines: Possible options include mentioning that Freud's theory is based primarily on the unconscious determinants of personality. Neither behaviorism (personality is observed behavior, learned through experiences with the environment) nor social cognitive theory (person/cognitive factors, in addition to behavior and environment, affect personality) attributes any significance to the unconscious.

196. Define Bandura's concepts of reciprocal determinism, self-efficacy, and observational learning. (LG: 3)

Answer Guidelines: Possible options include mentioning that reciprocal determinism refers to the interaction between the environment and person/cognitive factors; as much as the person can influence the environment, the environment can influence a person's behavior. Self-efficacy is one person/cognitive factor that can influence how a person acts upon his/her environment. Self-efficacy refers to the belief that one can master a situation and produce positive outcomes. Observational learning occurs through the observation of models.

197. What is the humanistic approach to personality? Discuss the key ideas of Rogers' and Maslow's theories. (LG: 4)

Answer Guidelines: Possible options include mentioning that the humanistic approach assumes positive human potential and people's ability to exercise conscious control over their behavior. The highest human need is to fulfill one's potential, which Maslow called self-actualization. This need constitutes the top of Maslow's hierarchy of human needs. Rogers proposed that people need unconditional positive regard, empathy, and genuineness to develop a healthy self and be able to fulfill their potential.

198. Describe the perspective of trait theories. List and describe each of the big five personality factors. Are these factors consistent across cultures and over time? (LG: 5)

Answer Guidelines: Traits are broad dispositions that tend to lead to characteristic responses. Personality factors include mentioning emotional stability, extraversion, openness, agreeableness, and conscientiousness. Research has supported the notion that these five personality factors are fairly consistent around the world and over time.

199. Distinguish between projective and objective personality tests. Give at least one example of each category. From the test administrator's perspective, what are the important differences between the two approaches? (LG: 6)

Answer Guidelines: Possible options include mentioning that an objective test is based on trait theory, whereas projective tests are based on psychoanalytic theory. Projective tests present ambiguous stimuli, and the subject is asked to create a story or explanation of the stimuli, the assumption being that subjects will project their unconscious thoughts onto the ambiguous stimuli. The problem with projective tests, such as the Rorschach inkblot test, is that they have low reliability and validity. Nevertheless, clinicians insist that these tests are very useful for the diagnosis of psychological disorders. The problem with objective, or self-report tests, is that the subjects may not answer honestly. Therefore, some of these tests, like the Minnesota Multiphasic Personality Inventory, are empirically keyed to overcome this problem.

200. Describe ways that personality assessment can be used. (LG: 6)

Answer Guidelines: Clinical and school psychologists assess personality to better understand individuals. Industrial and vocational psychologists use personality testing in assisting individuals to find careers. Research psychologists assess personality to investigate theories.

Chapter 13: Psychological Disorders

Learning Goals

1. Discuss the characteristics and classifications of abnormal behavior.
2. Distinguish among the various anxiety disorders.
3. Describe the dissociative disorders.
4. Compare the mood disorders and specify risk factors for depression and suicide.
5. Characterize schizophrenia.
6. Identify the behavior patterns typical of personality disorders.

Multiple-Choice Items

Learning Goal 1: Discuss the characteristics and classifications of abnormal behavior.

1. Which of the following is a characteristic of abnormal behavior?
   a. deviant
   b. maladaptive
   c. personally distressful
   d. All of the above can be characteristic of abnormal behavior.
   Ans.: d   LG: 1   Page: 520   QT: F

2. Which of the following is *not* true regarding psychological disorders?
   a. People with psychological disorders often cannot be distinguished form normal people.
   b. People with psychological disorders are for the most part, dangerous.
   c. Most people can be successfully treated for psychological disorders.
   d. Abnormal behavior consists of a poor fit between the behavior and the situation in which it is enacted.
   Ans.: b   LG: 1   Page: 519   QT: C

3. Of the following, whose behavior would be considered abnormal?
   a. an eccentric genius with an IQ of 200
   b. a bodybuilder who bulks up with special diet and exercise
   c. a security guard who believes everyone is out to harm him
   d. a sexually promiscuous teen whose culture encourages sexual encounters
   Ans.: c   LG: 1   Page: 519   QT: C

4. Behavior is considered abnormal if the behavior is
   a. atypical.
   b. statistically skewed.
   c. excessive and medically diagnosed.
   d. maladaptive and harmful.
   Ans.: d   LG: 1   Page: 520   QT: F

5. For John to be described as exhibiting abnormal behavior, his behavior must be
   a. excessive.
   b. atypical.
   c. maladaptive.
   d. genetically based.
   Ans.: c   LG: 1   Page: 520   QT: F

6. When it is said that abnormal behavior is maladaptive, it infers that
   a. abnormal behavior is unusual.
   b. abnormal behavior interferes with a person's ability to function effectively in the world.
   c. individuals with psychological disorders cannot learn.
   d. abnormal behavior deviates from what is considered appropriate in a culture.
   Ans.: b   LG: 1   Page: 520   QT: F

7. Emma recently moved to the big city from a rural area. She is having trouble adjusting, is so afraid that she has not gone to the grocery store for three weeks, and is eating poorly. Emma's behavior is best described as
   a. maladaptive.
   b. a dissociative disorder.
   c. anorexia nervosa.
   d. normal adjustment anxiety.
   Ans.: a   LG: 1   Page: 520   QT: C

8. Which of the following statements about atypical behavior is true?
   a. Atypical behavior is usually a clear sign of impending psychological illness.
   b. Atypical behavior may be unusual, but it is not necessarily abnormal.
   c. Atypical behavior is judged according to objective social criteria.
   d. Atypical behavior is usually classified as abnormal.
   Ans.: b   LG: 1   Page: 520   QT: F

9. Which of the following is *not* one of the myths about abnormal behavior?
   a. Abnormal behavior is always bizarre.
   b. People with psychological disorders cannot be treated.
   c. Most people can be successfully treated for a psychological disorder.
   d. Normal behavior and abnormal behavior are different in kind.
   Ans.: c   LG: 1   Page: 519   QT: F

10. The term insanity
    a. is a psychological term.
    b. is a legal term.
    c. has no usefulness.
    d. is used only in clinical psychology.
    Ans.: b   LG: 1   Page: 520   QT: F

11. The medical model is to drug therapy as the psychological approach is to
    a. psychotherapy.
    b. the interactionist approach.
    c. diathesis-stress.
    d. the social cognitive approach.
    Ans.: a   LG: 1   Page: 521   QT: C

12. A major problem with the medical model of abnormal behavior is that it
    a. overemphasizes cultural factors.
    b. ignores gender differences.
    c. describes mental illness in terms of problems of living.
    d. focuses primarily on biological rather than psychological causes.
    Ans.: d   LG: 1   Page: 520   QT: C

13. Which of the following perspectives would describe psychological disorders as mental illnesses?
    a. medical model
    b. psychodynamic perspective
    c. behavioral perspective
    d. humanistic perspective
    Ans.: a   LG: 1   Page: 520   QT: C

14. Which of the following is not a category of the biological view of psychological disorders?
    a. psychological view
    b. structural view
    c. biochemical view
    d. genetic view
    Ans.: a   LG: 1   Page: 520   QT: C

15. The concept that abnormalities in the brain's structure cause mental disorders is consistent with the
    a. genetic view
    b. biochemical view
    c. structural view
    d. psychological view
    Ans.: c   LG: 1   Page: 520   QT: C

16. The idea that imbalances in neurotransmitters or hormones cause mental illness comes from which of the following perspectives?
    a. learning view
    b. genetic view
    c. structural view
    d. biochemical view
    Ans.: d   LG: 1   Page: 520   QT: C

17. The psychological approach to psychological disorders includes all but which of the following?
    a. Psychodynamic perspectives
    b. Behavioral perspectives
    c. Mental illness perspective
    d. Humanistic perspective
    Ans.: c   LG: 1   Page: 521   QT: C

18. The belief that abnormal behavior results primarily from inappropriate learning represents which approach?
    a. biological
    b. interactionist
    c. psychological
    d. medical
    Ans.: c   LG: 1   Page: 521   QT: C

19. The viewpoint that sees psychological disorders as stemming from inherited or acquired brain disorders that involve imbalances in neurotransmitters *best* represents which approach to abnormal behavior?
   a. cognitive
   b. behavioral
   c. psychoanalytical
   d. biological
   Ans.: d   LG: 1   Page: 520   QT: C

20. Robert is very compulsive in all of the things he does. He has difficulty working with others because he insists that everything always be done perfectly. He gets very upset if anyone leaves anything out of place. How would a psychodynamic theorist explain this behavior?
   a. Rewards and punishments have shaped his behavior.
   b. It is his effort toward self-actualization that manifests these outcomes.
   c. It is a neurological imbalance that is creating these problems.
   d. Unconscious conflicts that result from ineffective early relationships with parents have influenced his behaviors.
   Ans.: d   LG: 1   Page: 521   QT: C

21. Tami will do anything that she can to promote herself. She takes advantage of others constantly and feels no remorse when she hurts others. She seems to have no conscience. How would a behavioral theorist explain this?
   a. Unconscious conflicts that result from ineffective early relationships with parents have influenced her behaviors.
   b. Rewards and punishments have shaped her behavior.
   c. It is her effort toward self-actualization that manifests these outcomes.
   d. It is a neurological imbalance that is creating these problems.
   Ans.: b   LG: 1   Page: 521   QT: A

22. Jerry is a social recluse who has few interactions with others. He believes that others who have been critical of him are responsible for his lack of self-esteem and his inability to be successful at anything that he tries. How would a humanist explain this?
   a. Rewards and punishments have shaped his behavior.
   b. Jerry has a low self-concept because of the excessive criticism that he has experienced.
   c. Jerry has a chemical imbalance.
   d. Unconscious conflicts that result from ineffective early relationships with his mother have influenced his behaviors.
   Ans.: b   LG: 1   Page: 521   QT: A

23. Which of the following would a sociocultural theorist be *least* interested in investigating when researching psychological abnormalities?
   a. self-concept
   b. socioeconomic status
   c. ethnicity
   d. gender
   Ans.: a   LG: 1   Page: 521   QT: F

24. The sociocultural factor *most* strongly related to rates of mental disorder is
    a. gender.
    b. race.
    c. socioeconomic status.
    d. ethnicity.
    Ans.: c   LG: 1   Page: 521   QT: F

25. The biopsychosocial perspective is also known as the
    a. learning perspective
    b. interactionist perspective
    c. operational perspective
    d. genetic perspective
    Ans.: b   LG: 1   Page: 522   QT: F

26. According to the interactionist perspective, abnormal behaior can be influenced by
    a. biological factors
    b. psychological factors
    c. sociocultural factors
    d. all of the above
    Ans.: d   LG: 1   Page: 522   QT: F

27. Which of the following factors is related to the highest rates of mental disorders?
    a. low income
    b. ethnicity
    c. high income
    d. gender
    Ans.: a   LG: 1   Page: 521   QT: C

28. When investigating gender differences in psychological disorders, it has been found that women are most associated with _____ disorders and men are most associated with _____ disorders.
    a. internalizing, medical
    b. externalizing, internal
    c. externalizing, medical
    d. internalizing, externalizing
    Ans.: d   LG: 1   Page: 521   QT: C

29. A woman is more likely than a man to be diagnosed with
    a. depression.
    b. antisocial personality disorder.
    c. substance abuse.
    d. alcoholism.
    Ans.: a   LG: 1   Page: 521   QT: F

30. Which of the following would be *most* associated with an internalizing disorder?
    a. aggression
    b. anxiety
    c. substance abuse
    d. antisocial behavior
    Ans.: b   LG: 1   Page: 521   QT: F

31. Which of the following would be *most* associated with an externalizing disorder?
    a. aggression
    b. depression
    c. anxiety
    d. all of the above
    Ans.: a   LG: 1   Page: 521   QT: F

32. In a recent study that looked at 20,000 randomly selected subjects, it was discovered that nearly _____ of the respondents indicated that they had experienced one or more psychological disorders in their lifetime.
    a. two-thirds
    b. one-third
    c. 10%
    d. 90%
    Ans.: b   LG: 1   Page: 518   QT: F

33. A psychologist may refer to the DSM-IV for all of the following reasons *except*
    a. communicating with other psychologists.
    b. keeping informed about the changes in the classification of mental disorders.
    c. determining the best course of treatment for a mental disorder.
    d. finding neurosurgeons whose certification is current.
    Ans.: d   LG: 1   Page: 522   QT: F

34. You happen to hear two psychologists discussing a client. They refer to the DSM-IV. What area of behavior were the psychologists *most* likely talking about?
    a. learning and memory
    b. abnormal behavior
    c. sensation and perception
    d. motivation and emotion
    Ans.: b   LG: 1   Page: 522   QT: C

35. In an attempt to classify psychological disorders in the United States, the American Psychological Association developed
    a. the *Mental Measurement Yearbook*.
    b. the *Psychiatric Dictionary*.
    c. the *Diagnostic and Statistical Manual of Mental Disorders*.
    d. *Roget's Psychological Thesaurus*.
    Ans.: c   LG: 1   Page: 522   QT: F

36. The current classification of mental disorders is called the
    a. OCD-10.
    b. ICD-9.
    c. DSM-3-R.
    d. DSM-IV.
    Ans.: d   LG: 1   Page: 522   QT: F

37. The *Diagnostic and Statistical Manual of Mental Disorders*, 4th edition, has
    a. two axes.
    b. three axes.
    c. four axes.
    d. five axes.
    Ans.: d   LG: 1   Page: 523   QT: F

38. The main controversy surrounding the DSM-IV involves its
    a. behavioral orientation.
    b. strong reliance on psychoanalytic concepts.
    c. humanistic orientation.
    d. strong reliance on the medical model.
    Ans.: d   LG: 1   Page: 523   QT: C

39. What is the main benefit of listing learning disorders in the DSM-IV?
    a. Clients' insurance companies will cover the treatment costs.
    b. Teachers will become aware of the seriousness of these disorders.
    c. Parents will begin to understand what is wrong with their children.
    d. Psychologists will realize how these disorders need to be treated.
    Ans.: a   LG: 1   Page: 525   QT: C

40. Which of the following is a criticism of the DSM-IV?
    a. Five axes are not sufficient for the classification of all mental disorders.
    b. The classification is not comprehensive enough.
    c. The classification is not current enough.
    d. Labels can become self-fulfilling prophecies.
    Ans.: d   LG: 1   Page: 525   QT: F

41. Criticisms of the DSM-IV include all of the following *except* its
    a. reliance on the medical model.
    b. focus on pathology and deviance.
    c. narrow selection of disorders.
    d. promotion of the use of labels.
    Ans.: c   LG: 1   Page: 525   QT: F

42. Which of the following is not an everyday problem that is listed as a psychological disorder in DSM-IV?
    a. reading disorders
    b. paronoid schizophrenia
    c. caffeine overuse
    d. mathematical disorders
    Ans.: b   LG: 1   Page: 525   QT: C

Learning Goal 2: Distinguish among the various anxiety disorders.

43. When one refers to the etiology of a psychological disorder, they mean the
    a. medical definition.
    b. causes or significant antecedents.
    c. long-term effects.
    d. unconscious conflicts.
    Ans.: b   LG: 2   Page: 527   QT: F

44. Anxiety disorders do *not* include
    a. motor tension.
    b. hyperactivity.
    c. apprehension.
    d. a lowering of mood tone.
    Ans.: d   LG: 2   Page: 527   QT: F

45. Intense feelings of fear without focus, pounding heart, and breathlessness are all characteristics of
    a. a somatoform disorder.
    b. an anxiety disorder.
    c. schizophrenic reactions.
    d. obsessive-compulsions.
    Ans.: b   LG: 2   Page: 527   QT: F

46. Your friend Daniel refuses to leave his house and reports that if he is not in his own home he begins to have "tremendous fears." Daniel *most* likely suffers from a(n)
    a. affective disorder.
    b. somatoform disorder.
    c. dissociative disorder.
    d. anxiety disorder.
    Ans.: d   LG: 2   Page: 527   QT: C

47. Generalized anxiety disorder differs from panic disorder in that it
    a. can lead to agoraphobia.
    b. is a milder kind of anxiety disorder.
    c. usually occurs for only a short time.
    d. can lead to heart failure.
    Ans.: b   LG: 2   Page: 527   QT: C

48. Brad seems to be in a continuous state of anxiety though he is unable to identify the source of his feelings. The *most* likely diagnosis for Brad is
    a. a generalized anxiety disorder.
    b. a phobia.
    c. a panic disorder.
    d. dysthymia.
    Ans.: a   LG: 2   Page: 527   QT: C

49. The anxiety disorder characterized by a persistent, pervasive feeling of anxiety for which no specific reason can be identified is a(n)
   a. panic anxiety disorder.
   b. agoraphobia.
   c. generalized anxiety disorder.
   d. somatoform disorder.
   Ans.: c   LG: 2   Page: 527   QT: F

50. Agoraphobia is maladaptive because it involves
   a. an intense fear of professionals.
   b. a loss of touch with reality.
   c. isolating oneself.
   d. unwanted thoughts.
   Ans.: c   LG: 2   Page: 528   QT: C

51. Lynn does not like to ride on public buses. She has an unreasonable fear that once on the bus, if she suddenly needed to get off, she would be unable to and would be trapped. Which of the following anxiety disorders would *best* explain this?
   a. agoraphobia
   b. post-traumatic stress disorder
   c. generalized anxiety disorder
   d. phobic disorder
   Ans.: a   LG: 2   Page: 528   QT: A

52. An anxiety disorder that is marked by the recurrent sudden onset of intense apprehension or terror is called a(n)
   a. generalized anxiety disorder.
   b. panic disorder.
   c. obsessive-compulsive disorder.
   d. post-traumatic stress disorder
   Ans.: b   LG: 2   Page: 528   QT: F

53. Jack was sitting reading a book when all of a sudden he felt he was "losing his mind." His heart beat faster, and he began to sweat and tremble. He was *most* likely experiencing a(n)
   a. generalized anxiety disorder.
   b. specific anxiety disorder.
   c. obsessive-compulsive disorder.
   d. panic disorder.
   Ans.: d   LG: 2   Page: 528   QT: C

54. Which of the following is not true regarding the etiology of panic disorder?
   a. In terms of biological factors, individuals who experience panic disorder may have an autonomic nervous system that is predisposed to be overly active.
   b. In terms of psychological factors, agoraphobia may involve a "fear of fear."
   c. In terms of psychosocial factors panic attacks involve two potential neurotransmitters: norepinephrine and GABA.
   d. In terms of psychosocial factors, U.S. women are twice as likely as men to have panic attacks.
   Ans.: c   LG: 2   Page: 529   QT: C

55. Larry's mother did not enjoy going to the mall. Whenever she went, she invariably would ask Larry to take her home within 10 minutes. One day, Larry wanted to stay and insisted that she wait for him. After about 10 more minutes, his mother reported feeling a smothering and choking sensation, like she was trapped and could not get enough air. Her symptoms were *most* likely the result of a(n)
    a. obsessive disorder.
    b. phobic disorder.
    c. conversion disorder.
    d. compulsive disorder.
    Ans.: b   LG: 2   Page: 529   QT: C

56. Edward is afraid of riding in elevators, and he quit his job because he was being moved to the 27th floor of his office building. He would *most* likely be classified as exhibiting a(n)
    a. phobic disorder.
    b. generalized anxiety disorder.
    c. somatoform reaction.
    d. hysterical reaction.
    Ans.: a   LG: 2   Page: 529   QT: C

57. An intense fear of being humiliated or embarrassed in social situations is called
    a. social phobia
    b. mysophobia
    c. arachnophobia
    d. acrophobia
    Ans.: a   LG: 2   Page: 530   QT: C

58. Which of the following is a diagnostic criterion for obsessive-compulsive disorder?
    a. memory loss for at least one week
    b. anxiety-provoking thoughts that will not go away
    c. physical symptoms with no organic cause
    d. major sudden mood swings
    Ans.: b   LG: 2   Page: 531   QT: F

59. Mr. Dodge engages in very rigid and structured behavior. He is preoccupied with cleanliness. He washes his hands more than 20 times per day and brings two changes of underwear to work with him. He would probably be diagnosed as suffering from a(n)
    a. conversion disorder.
    b. phobia.
    c. generalized anxiety disorder.
    d. obsessive-compulsive disorder.
    Ans.: d   LG: 2   Page: 531   QT: C

60. Each of the following is a compulsion *except*
    a. repeatedly washing one's hands.
    b. checking and rechecking the locks on doors.
    c. touching a spot on one's shoulder over and over.
    d. uncontrollable thoughts about someone.
    Ans.: d   LG: 2   Page: 531   QT: C

61. Stanley was fearful of developing cancer, which was the cause of death of both of his parents. Wherever he was, he constantly had thoughts of himself wasting away with cancer. Stanley's thoughts were
    a. a generalized anxiety disorder.
    b. compulsions.
    c. obsessions.
    d. a conversion disorder.
    Ans.: c   LG: 2   Page: 531   QT: C

62. If someone feels an irresistible need to touch every parking meter on the street as he walks along, he is exhibiting
    a. agoraphobia.
    b. a dissociative state.
    c. a compulsion.
    d. obsessive rumination.
    Ans.: c   LG: 2   Page: 531   QT: C

63. An anxiety disorder that develops through exposure to a traumatic event is called
    a. agoraphobia.
    b. obsessive-compulsive disorder.
    c. phobic disorder.
    d. post-traumatic stress disorder.
    Ans.: d   LG: 2   Page: 532   QT: F

64. Which of the following is not a symptom of PTSD?
    a. flashbacks
    b. obsessions
    c. constricted ability to feel emotions
    d. feelings of apprehension
    Ans.: b   LG: 2   Page: 532   QT: C

65. Since he left the service 10 years ago, Walter has been reliving his experiences in Vietnam. He has recurrent nightmares, and he is frequently tense and easily aroused. The *most* likely diagnosis is
    a. undifferentiated schizophrenia.
    b. obsessive-compulsive disorder.
    c. post-traumatic stress disorder.
    d. antisocial personality disorder.
    Ans.: c   LG: 2   Page: 532   QT: C

66. Sandy experienced a horrific childhood. She was physically and verbally abused by her mother and sexually abused by a stepfather. Years later, she began experiencing anxiety symptoms. Which of the following anxiety disorders would *best* apply to her situation?
    a. generalized anxiety disorder
    b. post-traumatic stress disorder
    c. phobic disorder
    d. panic disorder
    Ans.: b   LG: 2   Page: 532   QT: A

Learning Goal 3: Describe the dissociative disorders.

67. Psychological disorders that involve a sudden loss of memory or a change in identity are called
    a. mood disorders.
    b. dissociative disorders.
    c. anxiety disorders.
    d. phobic disorders.
    Ans.: b   LG: 3   Page: 535   QT: F

68. Which of the following is *not* a type of dissociative disorder?
    a. dissociative amnesia
    b. dissociative depression
    c. dissociative fugue
    d. dissociative identity
    Ans.: b   LG: 3   Page: 535   QT: F

69. What was formerly known as multiple personality disorder is now known as
    a. dissociative amnesia disorder.
    b. dissociative depression disorder.
    c. dissociative fugue disorder.
    d. dissociative identity disorder.
    Ans.: d   LG: 3   Page: 535   QT: F

70. A woman wandered away from her hometown and was discovered, under a different name and identity, five years later in a distant city. She is *most* likely suffering from
    a. multiple personality disorder.
    b. depersonalization.
    c. dissociation amnesia.
    d. a fugue state.
    Ans.: d   LG: 3   Page: 535   QT: C

71. If an individual shifts abruptly from one personality to another whenever he is confronted with a stressful situation, this person probably has
    a. dissociative identity disorder.
    b. schizophrenia.
    c. low self-esteem.
    d. amnesia.
    Ans.: a   LG: 3   Page: 535   QT: C

72. Amnesia caused by extensive psychological stress is termed
    a. physiogenic amnesia.
    b. dissociative amnesia.
    c. retrograde amnesia.
    d. anterograde amnesia.
    Ans.: b   LG: 3   Page: 535   QT: F

73. Which of the following is not true regarding dissociative identity disorder?
    a. The disorder is characterized by an inordinately high rate of sexual abuse during childhood.
    b. The disorder is characterized by an inordinately high rate of physical abuse during childhood.
    c. The vast number of individuals with dissociative disorder are adult males.
    d. Dissociative identity disorder is very rare.
    Ans.: c   LG: 3   Page: 536   QT: C

Learning Goal 4: Compare the mood disorders and specify risk factors for depression and suicide.

74. Psychological disorders in which there is a primary disturbance in the emotional state of the individual are called
    a. mood disorders.
    b. somatoform disorders.
    c. phobic disorders.
    d. dissociative disorders.
    Ans.: a   LG: 4   Page: 537   QT: F

75. Mood disorders can include symptoms of all but which of the following?
    a. cognitive symptoms
    b. subconscious symptoms
    c. behavioral symptoms
    d. somatic symptoms
    Ans.: b   LG: 4   Page: 537   QT: C

76. Which of the following would be the best synonym for the term "somatic"
    a. physical
    b. psychological
    c. subconscious
    d. environmental
    Ans.: a   LG: 4   Page: 537   QT: F

77. Which of the following individuals experienced depression?
    a. Virginia Woolf
    b. Ernest Hemingway
    c. Abraham Lincoln
    d. all of the above
    Ans.: d   LG: 4   Page: 538   QT: C

78. If you had to write a research paper on depression, which of the following would be the *most* appropriate title for your paper?
    a. The most commonly misdiagnosed mental disorder is depression.
    b. If you think you are immune to depression, think again.
    c. Unless there is a history of depression in your family, you have nothing to worry about.
    d. Most types of depression do not require treatment; they will disappear on their own.
    Ans.: b   LG: 4   Page: 538   QT: A

79. Which of the following statements is not true regarding depression?
   a. Depression is so widespread that it is referred to as the "common cold" of mental disorders.
   b. Depression is caused by genetics, and the environment does not play a significant role in its onset.
   c. Abraham Lincoln and Winston Churchill experienced depression.
   d. More than 250,000 individuals are hospitalized every year for depression.
   Ans.: b   LG: 4   Page: 538   QT: C

80. Which of the following is not true regarding dysthymic disorder?
   a. Dysthymic disorder is generally less chronic than major depressive disorder.
   b. Dysthymic disorder has fewer symptoms than major depressive disorder.
   c. Possible symptoms include poor appetite or overeating, sleep problems, and low energy.
   d. Possible symptoms include low self-esteem, inability to concentrate, and feelings of hopelessness.
   Ans.: a   LG: 4   Page: 538   QT: C

81. Your aunt goes through periods of deep depression followed by periods in which she is euphoric and unrealistically optimistic. She is probably suffering from
   a. bipolar disorder.
   b. schizophrenia.
   c. major depression.
   d. dissociation reaction.
   Ans.: a   LG: 4   Page: 539   QT: C

82. Trouble sleeping, fatigue, significant weight loss, and feelings of worthlessness are symptoms of
   a. major depressive disorder.
   b. schizophrenia.
   c. bipolar disorder.
   d. dissociative identity disorder.
   Ans.: a   LG: 4   Page: 538   QT: F

83. Unlike major depressive disorder, bipolar disorder involves
   a. loss of interest in life.
   b. pessimism.
   c. schizophrenia.
   d. mania.
   Ans.: d   LG: 4   Page: 539   QT: C

84. After a very stressful period, Mr. Stepanek quit his job, stayed home, and shut out his family and friends. He appeared to get better, but one day, he walked out on his family. Two months later he came home depressed and wouldn't talk with anybody. Mr. Stepanek is *most* likely suffering from
   a. paranoid schizophrenia.
   b. major depressive disorder.
   c. dysthymic disorder.
   d. a dissociative reaction.
   Ans.: b   LG: 4   Page: 538   QT: C

85. What is the *greatest* risk associated with major depressive disorder?
   a. suicide
   b. weight loss
   c. amnesia
   d. insomnia
   Ans.: a   LG: 4   Page: 538   QT: C

86. How does dysthymic disorder differ from major depressive disorder?
   a. It has more symptoms than major depressive disorder.
   b. It is more chronic than major depressive disorder.
   c. It is easier to cure.
   d. It includes mania.
   Ans.: b   LG: 4   Page: 538   QT: C

87. Which of the following is not true regarding heredity and mood disorders?
   a. One of the greatest risks for having a mood disorder is having a parent with a mood disorder.
   b. For bipolar disorder, there is a higher concordance rate among identical twins than fraternal twins.
   c. Researchers are closing in on the exact genetic location of bipolar.
   d. If you have and identical twin with bipolar, you will have bipolar.
   Ans.: d   LG: 4   Page: 540   QT: C

88. The neurotransmitters that appear to play a role in mood disorders are
   a. dopamine, tyrosine, and endorphin.
   b. acetylcholine, endorphin, and epinephrine.
   c. GABA, endorphin, and norepinephrine.
   d. serotonin, norepinephrine, and dopamine.
   Ans.: d   LG: 4   Page: 541   QT: F

89. A physiological aspect of depression seems to be an incorrect sequence of interactions between the
   a. amygdala and limbic system.
   b. brain stem and limbic system.
   c. amygdala and prefrontal cortex.
   d. prefrontal cortex and brain stem.
   Ans.: c   LG: 4   Page: 541   QT: C

90. What is the consensus on hormonal links to depression?
   a. The research supports a strong influence for women.
   b. The research supports a strong influence for men.
   c. The research is inconclusive at this time.
   d. Both a and b are correct.
   Ans.: c   LG: 4   Page: 542   QT: C

91. Which of the following individuals is at *highest* risk for developing a mood disorder?
   a. Angela, whose aunt is often moody and withdrawn
   b. Fred, whose father is a diagnosed manic depressive
   c. Roslyn, who is often in a bad mood
   d. Andrew, whose brother has a personality disorder
   Ans.: b   LG: 4   Page: 540   QT: C

92. Which of the following *best* represents a negative schema?
    a. "I had a bad day at work today."
    b. "Whenever things start to look pretty good, something bad happens to me."
    c. "I'm glad tomorrow is Saturday."
    d. "I haven't heard from my best friend Alice in over a month. I hope she is OK."
    Ans.: b   LG: 4   Page: 543   QT: C

93. What is the relationship between negative schema and depression?
    a. Depressed individuals process information more inefficiently.
    b. Depression limits negative schema.
    c. Negative schemas interfere with depression.
    d. Depressed individuals engage in habitual negative thought patterns.
    Ans.: d   LG: 4   Page: 543   QT: C

94. Your friend Ashley complains that no matter what she does or how she studies, she always gets the same low grade on exams. Ashley's attitude *best* reflects which of the following?
    a. bipolar aphasia
    b. dissociative helplessness
    c. psychogenic fear
    d. learned helplessness
    Ans.: d   LG: 4   Page: 542   QT: C

95. Joshua has received low grades in math throughout his school years. In the lower grades, he would try to study hard, but the results were always the same. Eventually, he stopped trying to do better in math because nothing he tried seemed to work. Joshua has developed
    a. learned helplessness.
    b. major depressive disorder.
    c. bipolar disorder.
    d. post-traumatic stress disorder.
    Ans.: a   LG: 4   Page: 542   QT: C

96. Fred is struggling with depression. His therapist has pointed out that Fred's lifestyle and work schedule is so stressful that it seems he never gets any good news. There seem to be no positive reinforcers in his life and this has led to his depression. What psychological perspective would you say that his therapist is basing his analysis on?
    a. psychoanalytic
    b. behavioral
    c. cognitive
    d. humanist
    Ans.: b   LG: 4   Page: 542   QT: A

97. The incidence of depressive disorders is lower in less industrialized, less modernized countries than in more industrialized, modernized countries. This appears to be related to the _____ lifestyles and _____ families and communities in more industrialized countries.
    a. slower, stronger
    b. faster, stronger
    c. faster, weaker
    d. slower, weaker
    Ans.: c   LG: 4   Page: 545   QT: C

98. What is the relationship between learned helplessness and depression?
    a. The depressed individual has no time to worry about learned helplessness.
    b. Learned helplessness causes hopelessness, a major symptom of depression.
    c. Depression interferes with learned helplessness.
    d. Depression reduces learned helplessness.
    Ans.: b   LG: 4   Page: 542   QT: C

99. Which of the following behaviors would indicate learned helplessness?
    a. anger
    b. aggression
    c. apathy
    d. delusions
    Ans.: c   LG: 4   Page: 542   QT: F

100. A depressed individual who realistically sees her situation as negative and accurately realizes she does not have control over her circumstances would be an example of
    a. delusional
    b. bipolar
    c. depressive realism
    d. psychodynamic deregulation
    Ans.: c   LG: 4   Page: 554   QT: C

101. Gender differences in suicide are described *best* in which of the following statements?
    a. Women attempt suicide more often, but males succeed more often.
    b. Each year, more women than men die from suicide.
    c. Women are more likely than men to choose violent methods of suicide.
    d. Men are more likely than women to attempt suicide.
    Ans.: a   LG: 4   Page: 546   QT: F

102. According to your text, which of the following statements about suicide is *most* correct?
    a. Suicide accounts for 50% of the mortality rate in adolescents.
    b. Two of every three college students have thought about suicide on at least one occasion.
    c. The rate of suicide in the United States has doubled since the 1950s.
    d. For every successful suicide in the general population, 10 to 15 suicide attempts occur.
    Ans.: b   LG: 4   Page: 546   QT: F

103. Which cultural factor is strongly related to suicide?
    a. extraversion
    b. family instability
    c. achievement orientation
    d. anxiety
    Ans.: b   LG: 4   Page: 547   QT: C

104. Which question would you ask to determine whether or not someone is seriously considering suicide?
    a. Are you seeing a counselor?
    b. Is there a history of suicide in your family?
    c. Are you crazy?
    d. What method would you use?
    Ans.: d   LG: 4   Page: 547   QT: A

105. Which of the following is *not* a predictor of suicide?
    a. depression
    b. instability in personal relationships
    c. birth of a child
    d. alcoholism
    Ans.: c   LG: 4   Page: 546   QT: F

106. Someone you know is very depressed and talking about committing suicide. You should do all of the following *except*
    a. listen calmly.
    b. encourage the person to get professional help.
    c. ask straightforward questions.
    d. reassure the person that everything will be all right.
    Ans.: d   LG: 4   Page: 547   QT: A

Learning Goal 5: Characterize schizophrenia.

107. A severe psychological disorder that is characterized by highly disordered thought processes is called
    a. depression.
    b. personality disorder.
    c. hypochondriasis.
    d. schizophrenia.
    Ans.: d   LG: 5   Page: 548   QT: F

108. Which psychological disorder is characterized by a disintegration of perception, emotion, and thought?
    a. depression
    b. bipolar disorder
    c. dissociative personality disorder
    d. schizophrenia
    Ans.: d   LG: 5   Page: 548   QT: C

109. Schizophrenia is a disorder that affects *about* what percent of the American population?
    a. 1%
    b. 4%
    c. 9%
    d. 15%
    Ans.: a   LG: 5   Page: 548   QT: F

110. A belief that is held despite obvious evidence to the contrary is called a(n)
    a. delusion.
    b. hallucination.
    c. catatonia.
    d. conditioned response.
    Ans.: a   LG: 5   Page: 548   QT: F

111. Max had been in the hospital for 12 years. Everyone knew him, but they didn't call him Max. He insisted that they call him J.C. and that he had died once for their sins. Max suffered from delusions of
    a. persecution.
    b. reference.
    c. grandeur.
    d. paranoia.
    Ans.: c   LG: 5   Page: 550   QT: C

112. Patients sometimes hear, see, smell, or taste things that are not there. These false perceptions are known as
    a. defense mechanisms.
    b. hallucinations.
    c. paraphilias.
    d. thought disorders.
    Ans.: b   LG: 5   Page: 548   QT: F

113. In a recent movie about the life of a genius who was schizophrenic, the main character consistently interacted with other characters who were only figments of his imagination. As real as they seemed, these imaginary characters were only
    a. defense mechanisms.
    b. hallucinations.
    c. paraphilias.
    d. thought disorders.
    Ans.: b   LG: 5   Page: 548   QT: C

114. A delusions of reference involves the belief that
    a. you have been singled out for attention.
    b. there is a conspiracy against you.
    c. others are jealous of you.
    d. your food may be poisoned.
    Ans.: a   LG: 5   Page: 550   QT: F

115. Even though *schizo* is Latin for "split," what is the main difference between schizophrenia and dissociative personality disorder?
    a. The schizophrenic has one personality that has split from reality.
    b. The schizophrenic has split their personality into more than two components.
    c. The schizophrenic never has more than one alternate personality.
    d. The schizophrenic always has more than two alternate personalities.
    Ans.: a   LG: 5   Page: 548   QT: C

116. Paranoid schizophrenia differs from disorganized schizophrenia primarily in which way?
    a. the inappropriateness of affect
    b. the complexity and systematic nature of hallucinations and delusions
    c. the disorganization of thought
    d. the extreme bizarreness of motor behavior, ranging from stupor to agitation
    Ans.: b   LG: 5   Page: 550   QT: F

117. Which of the following correctly states the "one-fourth rule" for schizophrenia?
    a. One-fourth of schizophrenics are children, one-fourth are adolescents, and one-fourth are adults.
    b. One-fourth of schizophrenics get better, one-fourth are able to live independently, and one-fourth are institutionalized.
    c. One-fourth of schizophrenics are hospitalized, and one-fourth get outpatient treatment.
    d. One-fourth of schizophrenics are males, and one-fourth are females.
    Ans.: b   LG: 5   Page: 548   QT: F

118. Delusions of grandeur, persecution, and reference are characteristic of
    a. paranoid schizophrenia.
    b. disorganized schizophrenia.
    c. catatonic schizophrenia.
    d. undifferentiated schizophrenia.
    Ans.: a   LG: 5   Page: 550   QT: F

119. William lives in fear that foreign spies will abduct him. He knows that he possesses military secrets that they need, even though he cannot remember what they could be. He has attempted to tell the police of the danger that is everywhere, but they do not take him seriously. He believes that they are in on the plot. His therapist attempts to tell him that he may be mistaken. He knows and trusts his therapist, but he believes that she is simply naïve and is unaware of the dangers. Which of the following types of schizophrenia *most* likely affects William?
    a. catatonic schizophrenia
    b. paranoid schizophrenia
    c. undifferentiated schizophrenia
    d. disorganized schizophrenia
    Ans.: b   LG: 5   Page: 550   QT: A

120. If you developed a drug that eliminated motor dysfunctions in schizophrenia, it would be *most* useful in treating
    a. paranoid schizophrenia.
    b. catatonic schizophrenia.
    c. disorganized schizophrenia.
    d. psychotic schizophrenia.
    Ans.: b   LG: 5   Page: 549   QT: C

121. Inappropriate affective behavior, especially giggling and silliness, is characteristic of which type of schizophrenia?
    a. catatonic
    b. delusional
    c. disorganized
    d. affective
    Ans.: c   LG: 5   Page: 549   QT: F

122. Judith has been experiencing delusions and hallucinations. She has been gradually withdrawing from human contact and often acts silly, with childlike behaviors. She would *most* likely be diagnosed with which form of schizophrenia?
    a. dissociative
    b. catatonic
    c. disorganized
    d. paranoid
    Ans.: c   LG: 5   Page: 549   QT: C

123. A schizophrenic disorder for which the symptoms do not fall neatly into one of the main types of schizophrenia is known as
    a. disorganized schizophrenia.
    b. catatonic schizophrenia.
    c. paranoid schizophrenia.
    d. undifferentiated schizophrenia.
    Ans.: d   LG: 5   Page: 550   QT: F

124. I realize that everyone is talking about me, mostly behind my back. Yesterday, I read the paper and found that several reporters were writing specifically for me. I found coded messages in a number of articles which, of course, only I could decipher. This afternoon, my doctor here at the hospital told me that I have been diagnosed as suffering from
    a. paranoid schizophrenia.
    b. catatonic schizophrenia.
    c. dissociative schizophrenia.
    d. somatoform disorder.
    Ans.: a   LG: 5   Page: 550   QT: C

125. Martha has been sitting in a hunched-over position on her hospital bed for several hours. When you speak to her, her position remains unchanged, and she doesn't answer. When you lift her arm, she remains sitting motionless, with her arm in a raised position. Martha is *most* likely suffering from which type of schizophrenia?
    a. paranoid
    b. catatonic
    c. disorganized
    d. undifferentiated
    Ans.: b   LG: 5   Page: 549   QT: C

126. Abnormal levels of which neurotransmitter are suspected to be involved in schizophrenia?
    a. norepinephrine
    b. dopamine
    c. serotonin
    d. epinephrine
    Ans.: b   LG: 5   Page: 552   QT: F

127. How would someone who is looking at a brain scan have an indication that the subject is schizophrenic?
    a. incorrect neurological pathways
    b. enlarged ventricles
    c. larger brain size
    d. enlarged brain stem
    Ans.: b   LG: 5   Page: 552   QT: C

128. A person whose identical twin has schizophrenia has about a 46% chance of also developing the disorder. This finding *most* strongly supports which causal factor for schizophrenia?
    a. genetic
    b. environmental
    c. diathesis-stress
    d. sociocultural
    Ans.: a   LG: 5   Page: 550   QT: C

129. Which of the following is a plausible neurobiological factor in causing schizophrenia?
    a. genetic similarity
    b. diathesis-stress
    c. cultural isolation
    d. excessive dopamine
    Ans.: d   LG: 5   Page: 552   QT: C

130. According to the psychological view of schizophrenia, which of the following is the *most* significant factor in the development of the disorder?
    a. dopamine
    b. stress
    c. genetic makeup
    d. culture
    Ans.: b   LG: 5   Page: 552   QT: F

131. A program interested in addressing the psychological factors involved in the development of schizophrenia would attempt to provide which of the following?
    a. education about and assistance in stress reduction
    b. education about the risks of genetic predisposition
    c. medication for control of neurotransmitter levels
    d. assistance with child care and elderly care
    Ans.: a   LG: 5   Page: 552   QT: A

132. Which view suggests that schizophrenia results from an interaction between biogenetic disposition and stress?
    a. sociocultural
    b. neurobiological
    c. undifferentiated
    d. diathesis-stress
    Ans.: d   LG: 5   Page: 552   QT: C

133. The diathesis-stress view of schizophrenia argues that the cause of the disorder is
    a. stress alone.
    b. biogenetic disposition alone.
    c. both stress and biogenetic disposition.
    d. neither stress nor biogenetic disposition.
    Ans.: c   LG: 5   Page: 552   QT: F

134. If Eileen has a predisposition for developing schizophrenia, the diathesis-stress model of schizophrenia states that Eileen
    a. will have symptoms of the disease by age 20.
    b. is most likely to develop the disease during periods of stress.
    c. has excess serotonin in her frontal lobes.
    d. has schizophrenic siblings.
    Ans.: b   LG: 5   Page: 552   QT: C

Learning Goal 6: Identify the behavior patterns typical of personality disorders.

135. Chronic, maladaptive cognitive-behavioral patterns that are thoroughly integrated into the individual's personality are known as
    a. adjustment disorders.
    b. neurotic disorders.
    c. psychotic disorders.
    d. personality disorders.
    Ans.: d   LG: 6   Page: 553   QT: F

136. Personality disorders differ from other types of mental disorders in all of the following ways *except* in the
    a. intensity of the symptoms.
    b. occurrence in males only.
    c. degree of personal distress.
    d. bizarreness of the symptoms.
    Ans.: b   LG: 6   Page: 553   QT: C

137. Why might personality disorders be confused with other mental disorders?
    a. They have very similar treatment.
    b. They have very similar symptoms.
    c. They have very similar names.
    d. They have very similar intensity.
    Ans.: c   LG: 6   Page: 554   QT: F

138. How many clusters of personality disorders are discussed in your text?
    a. two
    b. three
    c. four
    d. five
    Ans.: b   LG: 6   Page: 553   QT: F

139. Which of the following is *not* one of the clusters of personality disorders mentioned in your text?
    a. odd/eccentric
    b. dramatic/emotionally problematic
    c. chronic-fearfulness/avoidant
    d. hyperactive/debilitated
    Ans.: d   LG: 6   Page: 553   QT: F

140. Which of the following is a personality disorder from the odd/eccentric cluster?
    a. obsessive-compulsive personality disorder
    b. borderline personality disorder
    c. antisocial personality disorder
    d. schizotypal personality disorder
    Ans.: d   LG: 6   Page: 553   QT: F

141. Pat has trouble keeping friends because she exhibits several strange and eccentric behaviors in public that are embarrassing to them. Pat has tried to change but cannot; she has become increasingly lonely. Her loneliness seems to intensify her odd behavior. Pat's symptoms resemble those found in
    a. bipolar disorder.
    b. undifferentiated schizophrenia.
    c. organic mental disorders.
    d. personality disorders.
    Ans.: d   LG: 6   Page: 554   QT: C

142. Obsessive-compulsive personality disorder falls within the cluster of
    a. odd/eccentric personality disorders.
    b. chronic-fearfulness/avoidant personality disorders.
    c. dramatic/emotionally problematic personality disorders.
    d. neurotic/psychotic personality disorders.
    Ans.: b   LG: 6   Page: 555   QT: F

143. When can personality disorders usually be recognized?
    a. by adolescence or earlier
    b. between age 20–25
    c. after age 30
    d. by middle adulthood
    Ans.: a   LG: 6   Page: 553   QT: F

144. Andrea has an excessive need to be the center of attention whenever she is with other people. At work, she is highly competitive and gets very angry if anyone criticizes her. She constantly manipulates others, especially younger coworkers. These behaviors are associated with
    a. paranoid disorder.
    b. borderline disorder.
    c. schizoid disorder.
    d. narcissistic disorder.
    Ans.: d   LG: 6   Page: 554   QT: C

145. The obsessive-compulsive personality disorder differs from the obsessive-compulsive anxiety disorder in all of the following ways *except* for
a. a lack of distress over one's lifestyle.
b. an absence of a dominant compulsion.
c. a lack of major obsession.
d. its occurrence mostly in females.
Ans.: d   LG: 6   Page: 555   QT: C

146. Jennifer's personality disorder involves very dramatic and sometimes questionable behavior. She is often irritable, anxious, and bored. She also divides the world into good and evil. Her disorder would *best* be characterized as
a. schizotypal.
b. avoidant.
c. obsessive-compulsive.
d. borderline.
Ans.: d   LG: 6   Page: 554   QT: C

147. Which psychosocial factor appears to play a role in the development of antisocial personality disorder?
a. neurotransmitter deficiency
b. inadequate socialization
c. genetic predisposition
d. hormonal imbalance
Ans.: b   LG: 6   Page: 554   QT: C

148. Gerald has been diagnosed as having antisocial personality disorder. Gerald's parents were probably *not*
a. neglectful.
b. punitive.
c. nurturing.
d. inconsistent.
Ans.: c   LG: 6   Page: 554   QT: C

149. Which statement about the biological causes of antisocial personality disorder is *most* correct?
a. There is some indication of a genetic link in antisocial personality disorder.
b. A specific gene that carries antisocial personality disorder has been identified.
c. Antisocial personality disorder appears to be caused by a neurotransmitter imbalance.
d. Antisocial personality disorder is due to a chromosomal abnormality.
Ans.: a   LG: 6   Page: 554   QT: C

150. James, age 18, was caught again trying to pawn some of his parents' antique jewelry. He has skipped so much school that he will have to repeat his courses. He is also unconcerned that he has gotten two different girls pregnant in the past year. He would probably be diagnosed as having a(n)
a. adventurous adolescent period.
b. antisocial personality disorder.
c. schizoid personality disorder.
d. borderline personality disorder.
Ans.: b   LG: 6   Page: 554   QT: C

True/False Items

___ 151. Psychologists employ absolutely objective criteria when they define abnormal behavior.
___ 152. Insanity is a legal term, not a psychological term.
___ 153. The newest *Diagnostic and Statistical Manual of Mental Disorders* (DSM-IV) has abandoned the medical approach to mental disorders.
___ 154. Nearly one-third of individuals surveyed reported that they had experienced a psychological disorder at one time in their lifetimes.
___ 155. Post-traumatic stress disorder is classified as an anxiety disorder.
___ 156. Obsessive-compulsive disorder is classified as a somatoform disorder.
___ 157. Dissociative identity disorder is quite common in the general U.S. population.
___ 158. An individual who is diagnosed as having major depressive disorder has experienced a manic episode.
___ 159. No biological causes have been identified for mood disorders.
___ 160. Schizophrenia is a mental disorder that involves a severe disintegration of an individual's personality.
___ 161. The type of schizophrenia that is accompanied by bizarre motor behavior, which sometimes takes the form of a completely immobile stupor, is known as catatonic schizophrenia.
___ 162. Heredity has been implicated as an important factor in schizophrenia.
___ 163. Personality disorders are grouped into three diagnostic clusters.
___ 164. People who have antisocial personality disorder regularly violate the rights of others without experiencing guilt or remorse.
___ 165. Personality disorders have been explained in terms of biological and psychosocial causal factors.

Answer Key for True/False Items

151.	Ans.: F	LG: 1	Page: 520		159.	Ans.: F	LG: 4	Page: 540
152.	Ans.: T	LG: 1	Page: 520		160.	Ans.: T	LG: 5	Page: 548
153.	Ans.: F	LG: 1	Page: 523		161.	Ans.: T	LG: 5	Page: 549
154.	Ans.: T	LG: 1	Page: 518		162.	Ans.: T	LG: 5	Page: 550
155.	Ans.: T	LG: 2	Page: 532		163.	Ans.: T	LG: 6	Page: 553
156.	Ans.: F	LG: 2	Page: 531		164.	Ans.: T	LG: 6	Page: 554
157.	Ans.: F	LG: 3	Page: 535		165.	Ans.: T	LG: 6	Page: 554
158.	Ans.: F	LG: 4	Page: 539					

Fill-in-the-Blank Items

166. _____ behavior is behavior that is deviant, maladaptive, or personally distressful.
167. From the medical model approach to psychological disorders, abnormalities are called_____.
168. The modern _____ defense standard requires that the defendant was unable to appreciate the nature and quality or wrongfulness of his/her acts.
169. The _____ model describes mental disorders as biologically caused diseases.
170. The DSM-IV's use of labels has been criticized because labels can become _____ prophecies.
171. The anxiety disorder marked by recurrent sudden onset of intense apprehension or terror is known as _____ disorder.

373

172. An individual who has a fear of germs that keeps them from leaving their home probably suffers from a _____.
173. Dissociative identity disorder was formerly known as _____.
174. Dissociative amnesia accompanied by physical flight is known as dissociative _____.
175. Sleep problems, reduced interest in everyday activities, concentration problems, and weight loss are symptoms associated with _____.
176. _____ disorder was once known as manic depression.
177. A type of schizophrenia that is accompanied by complex systematic delusions and hallucinations is known as _____ schizophrenia.
178. The _____ model of schizophrenia views the disorder as caused by a combination of biogenetic predisposition and stress.
179. _____ disorders involve chronic patterns of behavior that are troublesome to others or whose pleasure sources are either harmful or illegal.
180. _____ personality disorder is primarily characterized by a lack of trust in and suspicion of others.

Answer Key for Fill-in-the-Blank Items

166.	Ans.: Abnormal	LG: 1	Page: 520
167.	Ans. mental illness	LG: 1	Page: 520
168.	Ans.: insanity	LG: 1	Page: 520
169.	Ans.: medical	LG: 1	Page: 520
170.	Ans.: self-fulfilling	LG: 1	Page: 525
171.	Ans.: panic	LG: 2	Page: 528
172.	Ans.: phobia	LG: 2	Page: 529
173.	Ans.: multiple personality disorder	LG: 3	Page: 535
174.	Ans.: fugue	LG: 3	Page: 535
175.	Ans.: major depressive disorder	LG: 4	Page: 538
176.	Ans.: Bipolar	LG: 4	Page: 539
177.	Ans.: paranoid	LG: 5	Page: 550
178.	Ans.: diathesis-stress	LG: 5	Page: 552
179.	Ans.: Personality	LG: 6	Page: 553
180.	Ans.: Paranoid	LG: 6	Page: 553

Matching Items

____ 181. deviant, maladaptive
____ 182. phobia
____ 183. medical model
____ 184. DSM-IV
____ 185. somatic
____ 186. multiple personality disorder
____ 187. mania
____ 188. diathesis-stress model
____ 189. delusion of grandeur
____ 190. personality disorder

A. someone who believes that he is Napoleon
B. mental illness
C. irrational fear of a particular object or situation
D. three main clusters
E. former term for dissociative identity disorder
F. criteria for defining abnormal behavior
G. overexcited state associated with bipolar disorder
H. physical
I. classification system
J. biogenetic disposition and stress

Answer Key for Matching Items

181.	Ans.: F	LG: 1	Page: 520	186.	Ans.: E	LG: 3	Page: 535
182.	Ans.: C	LG: 2	Page: 529	187.	Ans.: G	LG: 4	Page: 539
183.	Ans.: B	LG: 1	Page: 520	188.	Ans.: J	LG: 5	Page: 552
184.	Ans.: I	LG: 1	Page: 522	189.	Ans.: A	LG: 5	Page: 550
185.	Ans.: H	LG: 4	Page: 537	190.	Ans.: D	LG: 6	Page: 553

Essay Questions

191. Discuss the criteria for defining abnormal behavior. What are the problems associated with each of these criteria? Which criterion determines whether or not a person can be committed to a mental institution against his or her will? (LG: 1)

    Answer Guidelines: Possible options include mentioning deviance (somewhat subjective in terms of what is considered to deviate from acceptable cultural norms), maladaptive behavior (inability to function in everyday world), and personal distress (subjective). Involuntary commitment requires the assessment that the individual is a danger either to self or to others.

192. What is the *Diagnostic and Statistical Manual of Mental Disorders*? Why was it necessary, and how is it used? (LG: 1)

    Answer Guidelines: The DSM is used to classify mental disorders. It assisted in more consistent diagnoses and allowed professionals to communicate with each other in common terms. DSM contains diagnostic criteria for psychological disorders. The DSM-IV contains 17 major classifications and more than 200 specific disorders.

193. How do the biological approach, the psychological approach and the sociocultural approaches to psychological disorders differ? What is the biopsychosocial approach?

    Answer Guidelines: The biological approach attributes psychological disorders to organic, internal causes. The psychological approach includes the psychodynamic, behavioral, social cognitive, and humanistic perspectives. The psychological approach focuses on the individual. The sociocultural approach places emphasis on the larger social contexts in which a person lives. The biopsychosocial approach combines biological, psychological, and sociocultural components into what is called an interactionist perspective.

194. Describe three myths related to psychological disorders, and explain the facts related to them. (LG: 1)

    Answer Guidelines: Some of the myths regarding psychological disorders are that abnormal behavior is always bizarre, people with mental disorders are dangerous, and once people have a mental disorder, they will never be able to get rid of it. Students should also present the facts related to these myths in their answers.

195. Imagine you are in charge of an anxiety disorder clinic. A variety of subjects come to see you with all sorts of anxiety problems. For each of the following specific problems, give an example of the type of behavior that would commonly be seen: generalized anxiety disorder, panic disorder, phobic disorder, obsessive-compulsive disorder, and post-traumatic disorder. (LG: 2)

Answer Guidelines: Possible options include mentioning generalized anxiety disorder (persistent anxiety), panic disorder (recurrent sudden onset of terror), phobic disorder (irrational fear of object or situation), obsessive-compulsive disorder (anxiety-provoking thoughts that do not go away and/or urges to perform repetitive, ritualistic behaviors), and post-traumatic stress disorder (anxiety symptoms following trauma).

196. What are dissociative disorders? Name two dissociative disorders and describe the characteristics of each. (LG: 3)

Answer Guidelines: Dissociate disorders are psychological disorders that involve a sudden loss of memory or change in identity. Dissociative amnesia involves extreme memory loss caused by extensive psychological stress. Dissociative fugue involves the individual not only developing amnesia, but unexpectedly traveling from home and establishing a new identity. Dissociative identity disorder is formerly called multiple personality disorder. It is the least common dissociative disorder. Individuals suffering from this disorder have two or more distinct personalities.

197. Compare and contrast the similarities and differences between major depressive disorder and bipolar disorder. (LG: 4)

Answer Guidelines: Possible options include mentioning that each shares a depression component. Whereas major depressive disorder is characterized by severe depression, bipolar disorder involves extreme mood swings alternating between depression and mania.

198. Explain how negative schemas and learned helplessness are related to depression. (LG: 4)

Answer Guidelines: Possible options include mentioning that negative schemas are cognitive structures that cause the individual to perceive the negative aspect of situations, think pessimistic thoughts, and catastrophize. According to Beck, the accumulation of such negative thoughts can lead to depression. Learned helplessness, according to Seligman, is a behavior pattern that is characterized by the individual's perception of lack of control. This may be due to chronic stress or pain. Ultimately, the individual gives up and becomes depressed.

199. A much-studied area of psychological disorders is schizophrenia. Describe the general characteristics of a schizophrenic, and list and describe two specific forms of schizophrenia. Finally, discuss two explanations for the causes of schizophrenia. (LG: 5)

Answer Guidelines: Possible options include mentioning schizophrenic characteristics such as delusions, hallucinations, and word salad. Types of schizophrenia include disorganized, catatonic, paranoid, and undifferentiated schizophrenia. Causes of schizophrenia have been linked to heredity, neurotransmitter imbalance (dopamine), and stress (diathesis-stress model).

200. Explain how personality disorders differ from other major mental health disorders. (LG: 6)

Answer Guidelines: Possible options include mentioning that chronic, maladaptive cognitive-behavioral patterns are thoroughly integrated into the person's personality. They are not characterized by loss of touch with reality, hallucinations, or delusions. Personality disorders involve behavior patterns, or lack of behavior, that are troublesome to others and whose pleasure source is either harmful or illegal.

Chapter 14: Therapies

Learning Goals

1. Describe the biological therapies.
2. Define psychotherapy and characterize four types of psychotherapies.
3. Explain the sociocultural approaches and issues in treatment.
4. Evaluate the effectiveness of psychotherapy.

Multiple-Choice Items

Learning Goal 1: Describe the biological therapies.

1. A therapeutic approach to reducing or eliminating symptoms of psychological disorders by altering the way an individual's body functions is called
   a. biological therapy.
   b. psychotherapy.
   c. behavioral therapy.
   d. sociocultural therapy.
   Ans.: a   LG: 1   Page: 562   QT: F

2. William is taking lithium to help control his psychological disorder. What type of therapy is he receiving?
   a. psychotherapy
   b. cognitive therapy
   c. biological therapy
   d. sociocultural therapy
   Ans.: c   LG: 1   Page: 562   QT: F

3. Another term for biological therapies would be
   a. biomedical therapy.
   b. bicultural therapies.
   c. psychophysiological therapies.
   d. none of the above.
   Ans.: a   LG: 1   Page: 562   QT: F

4. Which of the following is the *most* common form of biological therapy?
   a. psychosurgery
   b. drug therapy
   c. electroconvulsive therapy
   d. brain fade
   Ans.: b   LG: 1   Page: 562   QT: F

5. The process by which mental health professionals help individuals recognize, define, and overcome their psychological and interpersonal difficulties is called
   a. biological therapy.
   b. biomedical therapy.
   c. drug therapy.
   d. psychotherapy.
   Ans.: d   LG: 1   Page: 562   QT: F

6. Which of the following statements is *most* correct?
   a. Psychiatrists, who are medical doctors, can prescribe drugs as a part of therapy.
   b. Psychologists and other mental health professionals may provide psychotherapy.
   c. In many cases, a combination of psychotherapy and medication is effective.
   d. All of the above are correct.
   Ans.: d   LG: 1   Page: 562   QT: C

7. Psychotherapeutic drugs are used mainly to alleviate symptoms of all but which of the following diagnostic categories?
   a. personality disorders
   b. anxiety disorders
   c. mood disorders
   d. schizophrenia
   Ans.: a   LG: 1   Page: 563   QT: F

8. What is the primary reason for using drug therapy as a treatment for psychological disorders?
   a. to sedate mental patients
   b. to correct neurochemical imbalances
   c. to be able to release patients from mental hospitals
   d. to enable patients to sleep through the night
   Ans.: b   LG: 1   Page: 563   QT: C

9. Antianxiety drugs are commonly known as
   a. amphetamines.
   b. stimulants.
   c. depressants.
   d. tranquilizers.
   Ans.: d   LG: 1   Page: 563   QT: F

10. Which of the following people is *most* likely to be treated with Xanax or Valium?
    a. a person with hallucinations
    b. a violent, delusional patient
    c. a patient with bipolar disorder
    d. a patient with an anxiety disorder
    Ans.: d   LG: 1   Page: 563   QT: C

11. Which of the following would *not* be considered a side effect of antianxiety medications?
    a. addiction
    b. hyperactivity
    c. loss of coordination
    d. fatigue
    Ans.: b   LG: 1   Page: 563   QT: C

12. Juan has been taking a benzodiazepine to reduce his anxiety, but he has also been drinking alcohol, because he thinks it makes him feel better. Juan is putting himself at risk for
    a. additional anxiety due to an interaction effect.
    b. no reduction in anxiety due to an interaction effect.
    c. depression.
    d. schizophrenia.
    Ans.: c   LG: 1   Page: 563   QT: C

13. If a patient were taking a drug to regulate mood, they would most likely be taking a(n)
    a. antianxiety drug.
    b. antidepressant drug.
    c. antipsychotic drug.
    d. benzodiazepine.
    Ans.: b   LG: 1   Page: 563   QT: F

14. Which of the following is *not* a class of antidepressant?
    a. monocyclic
    b. tricyclic
    c. MAO inhibitors
    d. SSRI drugs
    Ans.: a   LG: 1   Page: 563   QT: F

15. Three days ago, a doctor prescribed a tricyclic for your friend's depression. Your friend is complaining that she feels no better today than she did three days ago. In order to reassure her, what would you tell your friend?
    a. Tricyclics really don't work for most people.
    b. Ask your doctor to prescribe Valium.
    c. You should feel better in about two to four weeks.
    d. See another doctor and demand lithium.
    Ans.: c   LG: 1   Page: 563   QT: A

16. Which of the following is *not* a common side effect associated with tricyclics?
    a. restlessness
    b. faintness
    c. trembling
    d. delusions
    Ans.: d   LG: 1   Page: 563   QT: F

17. Zoloft, Prozac, and Paxil are all
    a. neuroleptics.
    b. tricyclics.
    c. MAO inhibitors.
    d. SSRI drugs.
    Ans.: d   LG: 1   Page: 564   QT: F

18. Which of the following is *not* true regarding SSRI drugs?
    a. They are widely prescribed.
    b. They interfere with serotonin reuptake in the brain.
    c. They have no side effects.
    d. They include Zoloft and Prozac.
    Ans.: c   LG: 1   Page: 564   QT: F

19. Which of the following drugs is widely used as a treatment for bipolar disorder?
    a. lithium
    b. Xanax
    c. Prozac
    d. neuroleptics
    Ans.: a   LG: 1   Page: 564   QT: F

20. After a period of several weeks during which Ted experienced heightened excitability, acceleration of thought and speech, and feelings of grandiosity, he became deeply depressed. The drug that would probably be *most* effective in treating Ted's mood disorder is
    a. Thorazine.
    b. lithium.
    c. Valium.
    d. Tofranil.
    Ans.: b   LG: 1   Page: 564   QT: A

21. Which of the following is *not* true regarding the controversy over whether depression should be treated with drugs?
    a. Research has found a large placebo effect.
    b. We understand depression well enough to know how the drugs are affecting subjects.
    c. Dietary changes can lower depression.
    d. Exercise is correlated with levels of depression.
    Ans.: b   LG: 1   Page: 565   QT: F

22. Powerful drugs that diminish agitated behavior, reduce tension, decrease hallucinations, improve social behavior, and produce better sleep patterns are called
    a. antipsychotic drugs.
    b. antianxiety drugs.
    c. antidepressant drugs.
    d. MAO inhibitors.
    Ans.: a   LG: 1   Page: 565   QT: F

23. The *most* widely prescribed class of antipsychotic drugs are
    a. MAO inhibitors.
    b. SSRI drugs.
    c. neuroleptics.
    d. benzodiazepines.
    Ans.: c   LG: 1   Page: 565   QT: F

24. Which is the *most* severe side effect associated with neuroleptics?
    a. tardive dyskinesia
    b. insomnia
    c. hallucinations
    d. restlessness
    Ans.: a   LG: 1   Page: 566   QT: C

25. Larry has been treated with neuroleptics for several years. Recently, he has started to display strange, involuntary contortions of the face and mouth. In addition, he cannot control the frequent twitching of his legs, arms, and neck. How can you *best* explain Larry's condition?
    a. The medication is no longer working, and his schizophrenic symptoms have returned.
    b. He probably drank alcohol, which causes a bizarre interaction with neuroleptics.
    c. He has developed tardive dyskinesia, a common side effect of neuroleptics.
    d. The symptoms indicate that he took an overdose of neuroleptics.
    Ans.: c   LG: 1   Page: 566   QT: C

26. Which individual is *most* likely to be treated with neuroleptics?
    a. a person with anxiety disorder
    b. a person with schizophrenia
    c. a person with bipolar disorder
    d. a person with dissociative identity disorder
    Ans.: b   LG: 1   Page: 566   QT: C

27. The *most* promising treatment strategy for schizophrenia to date is
    a. a one-time administration of a large dosage of antipsychotic drugs.
    b. several administrations of large dosages of antipsychotic drugs.
    c. psychotherapy in the form of strict and consistent behavior modification.
    d. a combination of psychotherapy and low-dosage, long-term drug therapy.
    Ans.: d   LG: 1   Page: 566   QT: C

28. Research has indicated that electroconvulsive therapy, or ECT, is somewhat effective in treating severe
    a. mania.
    b. depression.
    c. sociopathy.
    d. conversion disorders.
    Ans.: b   LG: 1   Page: 566   QT: F

29. Carlos is very depressed, and the danger of suicide is imminent. He is not responding to the drugs normally employed with depression. Which of the following treatments is *most* likely to prove helpful in reducing Carlos' depression and suicidal behavior?
    a. psychoanalysis
    b. electroconvulsive therapy
    c. encounter groups
    d. minor tranquilizers
    Ans.: b   LG: 1   Page: 567   QT: A

30. The physical purpose of electroconvulsive therapy is to
    a. produce restoration of neurotransmitter imbalance.
    b. decrease involuntary movements of the facial muscles.
    c. induce seizures that stimulate neural activity.
    d. reduce amnesia.
    Ans.: c   LG: 1   Page: 567   QT: C

31. One side effect of electroconvulsive therapy, or ECT, is that the client may
    a. experience severe depression.
    b. develop tardive dyskinesia.
    c. become extremely aggressive.
    d. experience severe memory loss.
    Ans.: d   LG: 1   Page: 567   QT: F

32. In a study by Seligman, it was shown that electroconvulsive therapy is
    a. the most effective treatment for major depressive disorder.
    b. comparable in effectiveness to cognitive therapy and drug therapy.
    c. is more effective than cognitive therapy, but not as effective as drug therapy.
    d. less effective than both cognitive therapy and drug therapy.
    Ans.: b   LG: 1   Page: 567   QT: F

33. Which of the following would describe psychosurgery?
    a. Psychosurgery is a biological therapy.
    b. Psychotherapy involves removal of tissue.
    c. Psychotherapy involves destruction of tissue.
    d. All of the above are correct.
    Ans.: a   LG: 1   Page: 568   QT: F

34. The precursor of modern psychosurgery was the
    a. biopsy.
    b. corpus callosum procedure.
    c. prefrontal lobotomy.
    d. split brain procedure.
    Ans.: c   LG: 1   Page: 568   QT: F

35. Which of the following is *not* true regarding prefrontal lobotomies?
    a. They are still a common surgical procedure today.
    b. A surgical instrument was inserted into the brain and rotated, severing neural fibers.
    c. Some subjects improved, but many were left in a vegetative state.
    d. The researcher who developed the procedure was awarded the Nobel Prize.
    Ans.: a   LG: 1   Page: 568   QT: C

36. Psychosurgery can be described *best* as a(n)
    a. economical treatment option.
    b. last-resort treatment option.
    c. debilitating treatment option.
    d. preferred treatment option.
    Ans.: b   LG: 1   Page: 568   QT: C

Learning Goal 2: Define psychotherapy and characterize four types of psychotherapies.

37. An individual wanting to recognize, define, and overcome their psychological and interpersonal difficulties and improve their adjustment would be most interested in
    a. biological therapies.
    b. electroconvulsive therapies.
    c. drug therapies.
    d. psychotherapies.
    Ans.: d   LG: 2   Page: 568   QT: C

38. Which of the following was the first approach to psychotherapy?
    a. psychodynamic
    b. behavioral
    c. humanistic
    d. cognitive
    Ans.: a   LG: 2   Page: 569   QT: F

39. Two approaches to psychotherapy that are associated with insight therapy are _____ therapy and _____ therapy.
    a. behavioral, humanistic
    b. psychodynamic, humanistic
    c. behavioral, psychodynamic
    d. cognitive, behavioral
    Ans.: b   LG: 2   Page: 568   QT: F

40. Which of the following is true regarding insight therapy?
    a. It is used with an MRI as a biological insight.
    b. It is very controversial because of a placebo effect.
    c. It is used with behavioral therapy to give an insight into the unconscious.
    d. It encourages self-awareness.
    Ans.: d   LG: 2   Page: 569   QT: C

41. Which of the following is *not* a focus of psychodynamic therapies?
    a. unconscious mind
    b. early-childhood experiences
    c. extensive interpretation by the therapist
    d. conditioning
    Ans.: d   LG: 2   Page: 569   QT: F

42. The *main* goal of psychoanalysis is to analyze the client's
    a. irrational thinking.
    b. unconscious thoughts.
    c. ideal self.
    d. lack of self-actualization.
    Ans.: b   LG: 2   Page: 569   QT: C

43. The underlying belief of psychoanalysis is that emotional problems result from
    a. the inability to feel guilt.
    b. excessive sexual activity.
    c. repressed conflicts.
    d. conscious indecision over major stressors.
    Ans.: c   LG: 2   Page: 569   QT: F

44. Kathy has begun to see a psychoanalyst. During her therapy sessions, she will spend *most* of the time talking about her
    a. children.
    b. current problems.
    c. future goals.
    d. childhood.
    Ans.: d   LG: 2   Page: 570   QT: C

45. Which type of therapist would be *most* likely to use free association and dream analysis to explain your unconscious motivations?
    a. transactional therapist
    b. psychoanalyst
    c. cognitive process therapist
    d. person-centered therapist
    Ans.: b   LG: 2   Page: 570   QT: F

46. In a psychoanalytic session, Rob remembered a traumatic childhood experience and, as a result, sobbed uncontrollably for about 15 minutes. Freud would have regarded this situation as an example of
    a. transference.
    b. resistance.
    c. rational emotion.
    d. catharsis.
    Ans.: d   LG: 2   Page: 570   QT: C

47. The technique used by Freud to encourage the patient to talk about whatever comes to mind, giving the unconscious mind the opportunity to slip past the censorship of the ego, is known as
    a. dream interpretation.
    b. transference.
    c. free association.
    d. catharsis.
    Ans.: c   LG: 2   Page: 570   QT: F

48. Your friend Angela has been very moody lately and often gets angry with others without any apparent reason. If you wanted to use the psychodynamic approach to finding out what is really on your friend's mind, which of the following would you do?
    a. let Angela talk about whatever she wants and listen carefully
    b. ask Angela very specific questions about the most recent events in her life
    c. remind Angela that others are getting tired of her moodiness
    d. tell Angela that her childish behavior is jeopardizing your friendship
    Ans.: a   LG: 2   Page: 570   QT: A

49. Interpretation in psychoanalysis involves
    a. the search for symbolic meaning.
    b. the provision of unconditional positive regard.
    c. rewarding desirable behavior.
    d. establishing an anxiety hierarchy.
    Ans.: a   LG: 2   Page: 570   QT: F

50. The psychoanalyst explains to the patient that his dream symbolizes an unresolved conflict involving his parents. This typical psychoanalytic strategy is called
    a. interpretation.
    b. free association.
    c. catharsis.
    d. counter-transference.
    Ans.: a   LG: 2   Page: 570   QT: F

51. James dreamed that he went to his neighbor's house at midnight and made himself a sandwich. His psychoanalyst interpreted the dream to mean that James really wanted to go to bed with his neighbor's wife. Making the sandwich was the
    a. symbolic content of the dream.
    b. manifest content of the dream.
    c. latent content of the dream.
    d. resistant content of the dream.
    Ans.: b   LG: 2   Page: 571   QT: C

52. Jack tells his therapist about the dream that he had about he and his female neighbor playing basketball in the back yard. The therapist tells him this represents the fact that his mother did not interact with him when he was young. The therapist's interpretation represents
    a. the manifest content.
    b. the latent content.
    c. the behavioral content.
    d. symbolic interactionism.
    Ans.: b   LG: 2   Page: 571   QT: C

53. A woman is unhappy because her husband does not give her enough attention, but she is quite taken with her male therapist because he gives her his undivided attention. How would a psychoanalyst interpret the woman's growing affection for the therapist?
    a. resistance
    b. latent content
    c. transference
    d. manifest content
    Ans.: c   LG: 2   Page: 571   QT: C

54. Jennifer canceled her next appointment with her psychoanalyst after a particularly disturbing session. The psychoanalyst would probably suggest that Jennifer's behavior is an example of
    a. resistance.
    b. transference.
    c. blocked association.
    d. working through.
    Ans.: a   LG: 2   Page: 572   QT: C

55. How would a psychoanalyst describe a client's tendency to express feelings of affection and approval toward the therapist?
    a. transference
    b. interpretation
    c. free association
    d. catharsis
    Ans.: a   LG: 2   Page: 571   QT: F

56. Harold has been in psychoanalysis for several weeks. The analyst noticed that Harold has spent the majority of the last two sessions just talking about insignificant matters. If you were Harold's analyst, what notation would you make in Harold's file?
    a. Client's free association is mostly unproductive.
    b. Client exaggerates minor events in his life.
    c. Client is experiencing catharsis.
    d. Client is displaying resistance behaviors.
    Ans.: d   LG: 2   Page: 572   QT: A

57. What is the *main* difference between contemporary psychoanalysis and traditional Freudian psychoanalysis?
    a. Contemporary psychoanalysis focuses more on early childhood experiences.
    b. Contemporary psychoanalysis focuses more on unconscious thought.
    c. Contemporary psychoanalysis focuses more on repressed conflicts.
    d. Contemporary psychoanalysis focuses more on current problems and relationships.
    Ans.: d   LG: 2   Page: 572   QT: C

58. Contemporary psychoanalysts have abandoned which traditional Freudian technique?
    a. dream interpretation
    b. free association
    c. having a client lie on a couch
    d. scheduling weekly appointments for clients
    Ans.: c   LG: 2   Page: 572   QT: F

59. Contemporary psychoanalysts *most* differ from Freud in their emphasis on which of the following?
    a. importance of conscious thought
    b. attention to transference
    c. importance of early childhood experiences
    d. utility of free association
    Ans.: a   LG: 2   Page: 572   QT: C

60. Humanistic therapists believe that
    a. interpretation is central to the therapy session.
    b. clients have a basic ability to help themselves.
    c. clients are not rational about their emotions.
    d. free association will help the client to gain insight into his/her problem.
    Ans.: b   LG: 2   Page: 572   QT: F

61. Which of the following is *not* a focus of humanistic therapy?
    a. conscious thoughts
    b. past experiences
    c. personal growth
    d. self-fulfillment
    Ans.: b   LG: 2   Page: 572   QT: F

62. Humanistic therapy focuses primarily on
    a. the person or client.
    b. unconscious thoughts.
    c. interpretation.
    d. the person's past.
    Ans.: a   LG: 2   Page: 573   QT: F

63. Who developed the client-centered therapy approach?
    a. Carl Rogers
    b. Heinz Kohut
    c. Fritz Perls
    d. B.F. Skinner
    Ans.: a   LG: 2   Page: 573   QT: F

64. According to Carl Rogers, client-centered therapy requires all of the following *except*
   a. unconditional positive regard.
   b. genuineness.
   c. interpretation.
   d. active listening.
   Ans.: c   LG: 2   Page: 573   QT: F

65. Which of the following would *not* be a part of client-centered therapy?
   a. active listening
   b. genuineness
   c. unconditional positive regard
   d. conditional positive regard
   Ans.: d   LG: 2   Page: 573   QT: C

66. The therapist's principal role in client-centered therapy is to convey
   a. thoughtful interpretations.
   b. unconditional positive regard.
   c. a critical attitude toward the patient's symptomatic behavior.
   d. step-by-step directions about goal setting.
   Ans.: b   LG: 2   Page: 573   QT: F

67. Which of the following is a client-centered therapy technique?
   a. interpretation
   b. free association
   c. confrontation
   d. genuineness or congruence
   Ans.: d   LG: 2   Page: 573   QT: F

68. What type of therapist would conduct therapy sessions in the *least* directive manner?
   a. behaviorist
   b. Gestalt therapist
   c. client-centered therapist
   d. cognitive therapist
   Ans.: c   LG: 2   Page: 573   QT: C

69. What does it mean when we say that a therapist is "nondirective"?
   a. The therapist only interprets symbolic meanings.
   b. The therapist uses Gestalt techniques.
   c. The therapist engages in decision making.
   d. The therapist tries not to lead the client to any particular revelation.
   Ans.: d   LG: 2   Page: 573   QT: C

70. Gary's therapist seeks to engage in a warm and understanding relationship with him. He offers Gary no advice or direction. He openly shares his own feelings and tries hard to understand what it is like to be in Gary's roles in life and how Gary perceives the world. This therapist would identify his approach as
   a. psychoanalytic.
   b. rational-emotive.
   c. client-centered.
   d. a cognitive therapy.
   Ans.: c   LG: 2   Page: 573   QT: C

71. Gestalt therapy is considered a
    a. psychoanalytic therapy.
    b. humanistic therapy.
    c. behavioral therapy.
    d. biological therapy.
    Ans.: b   LG: 2   Page: 573   QT: F

72. Alicia decides to meet with a therapist that has a humanistic perspective because she has heard that humanists are very warm and engaging in their approach. She visits a therapist who instead is very confrontational and pushes her to face her problems. What explains this?
    a. Alicia has chosen a Gestalt therapist.
    b. Humanists are confrontational by nature.
    c. The therapist is using client-centered techniques.
    d. Both a and c are true.
    Ans.: a   LG: 2   Page: 573   QT: C

73. What distinguishes Gestalt therapy from client-centered therapy?
    a. Gestalt therapy encourages personal growth.
    b. Gestalt therapy uses aversion techniques.
    c. Gestalt therapy is more directive.
    d. Gestalt therapy is not a humanistic therapy.
    Ans.: c   LG: 2   Page: 574   QT: C

74. After several sessions of psychotherapy, Ralph protests to his therapist that she is being confrontational. The therapist responds by saying that her approach is directive and based on the premise that people must become aware of their feelings and face their problems. This therapist can be described *best* as a
    a. biological therapist.
    b. behavior therapist.
    c. client-centered therapist.
    d. Gestalt therapist.
    Ans.: d   LG: 2   Page: 573   QT: C

75. In which type of psychotherapy is heavy emphasis placed on the congruence between verbal and nonverbal behavior, being open about one's feelings, and role-playing activities?
    a. Gestalt therapy
    b. aversive therapy
    c. psychoanalysis
    d. rational-emotive therapy
    Ans.: a   LG: 2   Page: 574   QT: C

76. Vigorously challenging and questioning clients about critical issues and forcing them to face their problems are techniques used in
    a. psychodynamic therapy.
    b. humanistic therapy.
    c. Gestalt therapy.
    d. person-centered therapy.
    Ans.: c   LG: 2   Page: 574   QT: F

77. Behavioral therapy uses _____ to reduce or eliminate maladaptive behavior.
    a. psychoanalysis
    b. principles of learning
    c. drug therapy
    d. unconditional positive regard
    Ans.: b   LG: 2   Page: 574   QT: F

78. Behavioral therapies are based upon all but which of the following?
    a. insight
    b. operant conditioning
    c. classical conditioning
    d. social cognitive theory
    Ans.: a   LG: 2   Page: 574   QT: F

79. In behavior therapy, abnormal behavior is viewed as being
    a. innate.
    b. learned.
    c. instinctive.
    d. caused by regression.
    Ans.: b   LG: 2   Page: 575   QT: F

80. Which type of therapist is *most* likely to maintain that a client is acting depressed because the behavior is being rewarded by the people around him?
    a. psychoanalyst
    b. person-centered therapist
    c. rational-emotive therapist
    d. behavior therapist
    Ans.: d   LG: 2   Page: 575   QT: C

81. Systematic desensitization is a technique used in
    a. psychoanalysis.
    b. humanistic therapies.
    c. behavior therapy.
    d. Gestalt therapy.
    Ans.: c   LG: 2   Page: 575   QT: F

82. Your roommate Rachel has terrifying memories of having been bitten by a pit bull when she was a child. To this day, she gets extremely nervous if a dog is anywhere near her. In order to help Rachel overcome this fear of dogs, you have brought home a puppy and intend to use systematic desensitization. Which of the following *best* describes your procedure?
    a. bringing the puppy closer and closer to Rachel after she has been given time to completely relax
    b. keeping the puppy in a separate room where Rachel does not have to interact with it
    c. forcing Rachel to hold the dog because fear of a puppy is ridiculous
    d. letting young children handle the dog in front of Rachel
    Ans.: a   LG: 2   Page: 576   QT: A

83. Bart, an alcoholic, was given an alcoholic drink containing a substance that made him very nauseous and induced vomiting. What technique was used?
    a. flooding
    b. transference
    c. aversive conditioning
    d. operant conditioning
    Ans.: c   LG: 2   Page: 577   QT: C

84. Systematic desensitization appears to be an effective treatment for
    a. OCD.
    b. mania.
    c. phobias.
    d. dissociative disorders.
    Ans.: c   LG: 2   Page: 576   QT: F

85. A teacher intentionally ignores a student in an attempt to stop the student's incessant questioning. Which behavior modification approach is this teacher using?
    a. punishment
    b. systematic desensitization
    c. assertive confrontation
    d. operant conditioning
    Ans.: d   LG: 2   Page: 577   QT: C

86. The idea that anxiety and relaxation are incompatible is central to
    a. Gestalt theory.
    b. aversive conditioning.
    c. dream interpretation.
    d. systematic desensitization.
    Ans.: d   LG: 2   Page: 575   QT:F

87. Patients in a mental hospital can attend a movie or eat in the hospital restaurant only if they have accumulated enough coupons. Hospital personnel give out the coupons whenever the patient displays healthy responses. The technique being employed at this hospital is
    a. exposure.
    b. encounter therapy.
    c. a token economy.
    d. modeling.
    Ans.: c   LG: 2   Page: 577   QT: C

88. Which of the following is an operant conditioning technique?
    a. systematic desensitization
    b. free association
    c. aversive conditioning
    d. behavior modification
    Ans.: d   LG: 2   Page: 577   QT: F

89. The *main* goal of behavior modification is to
    a. help the individual to develop a stronger self-concept.
    b. replace maladaptive responses with adaptive responses.
    c. substitute rational thoughts for irrational thoughts.
    d. identify repressed conflicts in the unconscious.
    Ans.: b   LG: 2   Page: 577   QT: C

90. What do operant conditioning and classical conditioning have in common?
    a. They both are highly nondirective.
    b. They both focus on insight and self-awareness.
    c. They both are behavior therapies.
    d. They both emphasize the importance of unconscious conflicts.
    Ans.: c   LG: 2   Page: 575–577 QT: C

91. Your friend suffers from an extreme phobia of insects. In order to get the *most* effective help for this
    problem, you would advise your friend to seek help from a
    a. behavior therapist.
    b. humanistic therapist.
    c. rational-emotive therapist.
    d. psychoanalyst.
    Ans.: a   LG: 2   Page: 576   QT: A

92. Which type of therapy would place the highest emphasis on the idea that individuals' conscious
    thoughts are the main source of their psychological problems?
    a. humanistic
    b. psychodynamic
    c. cognitive
    d. rational-emotive
    Ans.: c   LG: 2   Page: 578   QT: F

93. Therapy based on the assumption that abnormal behavior is due to faulty ways of thinking and
    believing is known as
    a. humanistic psychotherapy.
    b. cognitive therapy.
    c. psychoanalysis.
    d. behavior modification.
    Ans.: b   LG: 2   Page: 578   QT: F

94. Modification of thoughts is the goal of
    a. cognitive therapies.
    b. behavior modification.
    c. antidepressant drugs.
    d. token economies.
    Ans.: a   LG: 2   Page: 578   QT: F

95. Changing a pattern of thought that is presumed to be causing maladaptive behavior is called
    a. behavior modification.
    b. operant conditioning.
    c. unconscious modification.
    d. cognitive restructuring.
    Ans.: d   LG: 2   Page: 578   QT: F

96. Which therapist is associated with rational-emotive therapy?
    a. Carl Rogers
    b. Aaron Beck
    c. Albert Ellis
    d. Albert Bandura
    Ans.: c   LG: 2   Page: 579   QT: F

97. Mika flunked a history test and told himself, "I'm a failure." According to rational-emotive therapy, this is an example of
    a. an activating experience.
    b. beliefs.
    c. consequence.
    d. transference.
    Ans.: b   LG: 2   Page: 579   QT: C

98. What is the *main* goal of rational-emotive therapy?
    a. identifying and changing an individual's irrational beliefs
    b. producing adaptive responses by changing environmental consequences
    c. identifying and resolving an individual's repressed conflicts
    d. improving the individual's self-regard
    Ans.: a   LG: 2   Page: 579   QT: C

99. Helping clients make connections between their patterns of thinking and their emotions is the first step in which type of cognitive therapy?
    a. rational-emotive therapy
    b. Beck's cognitive therapy
    c. family systems therapy
    d. self-instructional methods
    Ans.: b   LG: 2   Page: 579   QT: C

100. What is the *main* difference between Ellis' rational-emotive therapy and Beck's cognitive therapy?
    a. Rational-emotive therapy is a briefer type of therapy.
    b. Rational-emotive therapy focuses more on illogical thinking.
    c. Rational-emotive therapy focuses more on conscious thoughts.
    d. Rational-emotive therapy is more confrontational.
    Ans.: d   LG: 2   Page: 581   QT: C

101. Which of the following types of therapy places a high emphasis on self-efficacy?
    a. rational-emotive therapy
    b. cognitive-behavior therapy
    c. humanistic therapy
    d. behavioral therapy
    Ans.: b   LG: 2   Page: 581   QT: F

102. Cognitive-behavior techniques that teach individuals to modify their own behavior are called
    a. self-instructional methods.
    b. cognitive restructuring.
    c. behavior modifications.
    d. token economies.
    Ans.: a   LG: 2   Page: 581   QT: F

103. Damian has a very stressful piano audition in the next hour. He runs the following statements through his mind in preparation.

"I can meet the challenge."

"I'll keep on taking one step at a time."

"I can handle it. I'll just relax, breathe deeply, and use one of my strategies."

Damian is making use of

a. psychodynamic techniques.

b. behavioral techniques.

c. self-instructional methods.

d. operant techniques.

Ans.: c   LG: 2   Page: 581   QT: A

104. Cognitive therapy has been especially helpful in treating all of the following *except*

a. depression.

b. schizophrenia.

c. obsessive-compulsive disorders.

d. dissociative disorders.

Ans.: d   LG: 2   Page: 582   QT: F

Learning Goal 3: Explain the sociocultural approaches and issues in treatment.

105. Which of the following statements is *not* true?

a. Biological therapies change a person's body

b. Behavioral therapies change a person's behavior

c. Cognitive therapies change a person's thinking

d. Sociocultural approaches agree that all of the above are correct and sufficient in dealing with psychological disorders.

Ans.: d   LG: 3   Page: 584   QT: C

106. Seeing individuals in a social context is an advantage of which type of therapy?

a. group

b. client-centered

c. situational

d. behavior modification

Ans.: a   LG: 3   Page: 584   QT: F

107. Which of the following is a *main* advantage of group therapy?

a. lower cost

b. briefer sessions

c. more attention from the therapist

d. less focus on irrational thinking

Ans.: a   LG: 3   Page: 584   QT: C

108. Which of the following therapies can be used in a group format?

a. psychodynamic

b. behavior

c. cognitive and humanistic

d. all of the above

Ans.: d   LG: 3   Page: 584   QT: F

109. Development of social skills is *most* immediately facilitated in which type of therapy approach?
    a. behavior modification
    b. individual
    c. group
    d. client-centered
    Ans.: c   LG: 3   Page: 585   QT: C

110. Which factor is *most* likely to make a therapist decide that group therapy may be more beneficial than individual therapy?
    a. uniqueness
    b. unconditional positive regard
    c. context
    d. cost
    Ans.: c   LG: 3   Page: 584   QT: F

111. Typically, what effect does group therapy have on social skills?
    a. Group members tend to feel self-conscious.
    b. Group feedback has a positive effect.
    c. The therapist provides a positive role model.
    d. Group members are too critical of each other.
    Ans.: b   LG: 3   Page: 585   QT: F

112. Universality in the group therapy situation refers to the belief that group members
    a. all have similar problems.
    b. value other people's cultural value system.
    c. take into consideration how many people there are in the world.
    d. receive information about the world.
    Ans.: a   LG: 3   Page: 584   QT: F

113. Bertha has been hesitant to seek therapy because she thinks she is the only person in the world who feels the way that she does. Which feature of group therapy will be most beneficial for her?
    a. universality
    b. development of social skills
    c. interpersonal learning
    d. corrective recapitulation of the family group
    Ans.: a   LG: 3   Page: 584   QT: C

114. What is facilitated when therapy group members support and learn from each other?
    a. information transfer
    b. conditional positive regard
    c. altruism
    d. irrational thinking
    Ans.: c   LG: 3   Page: 585   QT: F

115. What do family therapy and couple therapy have in common?
    a. They usually employ the humanistic approach.
    b. They are forms of group therapy.
    c. They are intended to be confrontational.
    d. They usually last for years.
    Ans.: b   LG: 3   Page: 585   QT: C

116. Which of the following is *not* true regarding couples therapy?
    a. The major problem is the relationship.
    b. Tthe couples must be married.
    c. The couples do not have to be married.
    d. Psychodynamic, humanistic, and behavioral therapies are used.
    Ans.: b   LG: 3   Page: 585   QT: F

117. The principle of validation in family therapy is similar to the concept of
    a. aversive conditioning.
    b. counterconditioning.
    c. unconditional positive regard.
    d. unconditional stimulation.
    Ans.: c   LG: 3   Page: 585   QT: C

118. A therapeutic strategy used primarily by family therapists is called
    a. desensitization.
    b. social-skills training.
    c. reframing.
    d. self-label identification.
    Ans.: c   LG: 3   Page: 585   QT: F

119. Ozzie feels that he is the only parent in the family responsible for discipline. It is always he that has to dole out the discipline and his wife who acts like the loving parent. A family therapist recommends that they both share more of the responsibility of disciplining the children. The therapist is using
    a. restructuring.
    b. social-skills training.
    c. reframing.
    d. detriangulation.
    Ans.: a   LG: 3   Page: 586   QT: C

120. Ann and the children feel that they are not getting enough of Jerry's attention. Ann complains that Jerry works too much. Their family therapist told them all that Jerry is not the problem and that they should not complain to or about him for two weeks. The therapist is using
    a. restructuring.
    b. detriangulation.
    c. something other than the systems approach.
    d. reframing.
    Ans.: b   LG: 3   Page: 585   QT: C

121. When a family therapist uses validation, the therapist
    a. expresses an understanding of each family member.
    b. tells the family which member is responsible for the problem.
    c. teaches families that their problem is universal.
    d. encourages each family member to be open and honest.
    Ans.: a   LG: 3   Page: 585   QT: C

122. What kind of professional therapist leads a self-help group?
    a. They are led by psychoanalytic therapists.
    b. They are led by cognitively trained therapists.
    c. They are not led by professional therapists.
    d. They use computer-based professional help.
    Ans.: c   LG: 3   Page: 586   QT: C

123. Which of the following is *not* true regarding paraprofessionals?
    a. They have formal mental health training.
    b. They have been taught by a professional.
    c. They provide some mental health services.
    d. They can conduct self-help groups.
    Ans.: a   LG: 3   Page: 586   QT: C

124. Why are self-help groups an important resource for people who need help?
    a. They are relatively inexpensive and use community resources.
    b. They can easily be reached by dialing 911.
    c. Professionals can be contacted over the Internet, and the advice is free.
    d. They use humanistically trained leaders who give unconditional positive regard.
    Ans.: a   LG: 3   Page: 586   QT: C

125. Alcoholics Anonymous (AA) is an example of which type of group situation?
    a. group therapy
    b. self-help group
    c. family therapy
    d. encounter group
    Ans.: b   LG: 3   Page: 586   QT: F

126. Which of the following factors was related to the community mental health movement origin in the 1960s?
    a. mental health care was not reaching the poor
    b. development of new drugs for treating disorders
    c. deinstitutionalization
    d. all of the above
    Ans.: d   LG: 3   Page: 587   QT: C

127. Community mental health is intended to do all of the following *except*
    a. make the treatment of mental disorders more humane.
    b. care for patients released due to deinstitutionalization.
    c. prevent and treat mental disorders.
    d. provide community-based mental health services.
    Ans.: a   LG: 3   Page: 587   QT: F

128. Which of the following courses of community mental health is intended to reduce the number of new cases of psychological disorders?
    a. primary prevention
    b. secondary prevention
    c. tertiary prevention
    d. pre-diagnosis prevention
    Ans.: a   LG: 3   Page: 587   QT: F

129. With ethnic minority clients, success of psychotherapy depends primarily on the
   a. age of the psychotherapist.
   b. gender of the psychotherapist.
   c. ethnic background of the psychotherapist.
   d. professional competence and cultural sensitivity of the psychotherapist.
   Ans.: d   LG: 3   Page: 588   QT: C

130. An ethnic match between the therapist and the client appears to provide which *main* advantage for psychotherapy?
   a. professional similarity
   b. cultural commonality
   c. educational similarity
   d. socioeconomic commonality
   Ans.: b   LG: 3   Page: 588   QT: C

131. A psychotherapist who recommends that clients and therapists be ethnically matched is *most* likely aware of which research findings?
   a. In many cases, ethnic matches produce better treatment outcomes.
   b. In most cases, ethnic matches result in more confrontational therapy sessions.
   c. Ethnically matched therapists have most likely experienced the same problems as their clients.
   d. Ethnically matched clients tend to be more defensive about their behavioral choices.
   Ans.: a   LG: 3   Page: 588   QT: F

132. If you were a psychotherapist who expected to work with a diverse clientele, you could improve your cultural sensitivity through all of the following *except* by
   a. learning as much as possible about the cultural backgrounds of your clients.
   b. studying and attempting to understand the sociopolitical influences affecting different cultural groups.
   c. continuing to study the traditional psychological theories and their therapeutic applications.
   d. interacting as much as possible with people from different cultural backgrounds.
   Ans.: c   LG: 3   Page: 588   QT: A

133. If you were doing a research paper on the challenges involved in providing psychotherapy for women, which would be the *best* title for your paper?
   a. The ultimate purpose of psychotherapy is self-determination of the client.
   b. The new direction of psychotherapy: Relatedness and connection with others.
   c. Psychotherapy for women: The focus on interpersonal dependence.
   d. Psychotherapy should facilitate maximum autonomy of the client.
   Ans.: b   LG: 3   Page: 588   QT: A

Learning Goal 4: Evaluate the effectiveness of psychotherapy.

134. Which research technique is used to combine many different studies to answer one research question?
   a. meta-analysis
   b. factor analysis
   c. correlation
   d. discrimination function analysis
   Ans.: a   LG: 4   Page: 590   QT: F

135. You want to do a meta-analysis to determine which therapy approach is the most effective for individuals who suffer from dissociative identity disorder. Which of the following *best* describes your procedure?
    a. Find many studies on different therapy approaches and compare their results.
    b. Locate one study using each therapy approach and compare their results.
    c. Compare therapies for dissociative identity disorder with therapies for schizophrenia.
    d. Ask individuals who have dissociative identity disorder which therapy they feel works best.
    Ans.: a   LG: 4   Page: 590   QT: A

136. A meta-analysis involves the combination of
    a. many kinds of mental disorders in a single study.
    b. psychoanalytic and behavior modification techniques.
    c. several different drug treatments at the same time.
    d. many studies to draw a single conclusion.
    Ans.: d   LG: 4   Page: 590   QT: F

137. Based on the most current research, psychotherapy is
    a. effective overall.
    b. not very effective.
    c. effective only for those with schizophrenia.
    d. effective only for those with phobias.
    Ans.: a   LG: 4   Page: 590   QT: F

138. Which of the following was *not* a common element of successful psychotherapies?
    a. expectations
    b. mastery
    c. longevity
    d. emotional arousal
    Ans.: c   LG: 4   Page: 591   QT: C

139. What was the effect of psychotherapy on 88% of the outcomes measured by Smith, Glass, and Miller?
    a. no effect
    b. a positive effect
    c. a negative effect
    d. a culture-specific effect
    Ans.: b   LG: 4   Page: 590   QT: F

140. Based on the research results discussed in your text, what overall conclusion can you draw about the effectiveness of psychotherapy?
    a. For most people, psychotherapy is a waste of time; most people would get better on their own.
    b. Different types of therapy are equally effective for different types of psychological disorders.
    c. Most types of psychotherapy provide only temporary relief.
    d. The type of therapy that might be the most effective depends on the specific disorder to be treated.
    Ans.: d   LG: 4   Page: 590   QT: C

141. Dr. Burgess describes herself as an eclectic therapist. What does she mean?
    a. She employs different therapy approaches, depending on the client and the problem.
    b. She has a hard time making up her mind about which therapy approach she likes best.
    c. She has studied many different types of therapy approaches and uses them randomly.
    d. She employs therapy techniques that were developed by the eclectic approach to psychology.
    Ans.: a   LG: 4   Page: 591   QT: C

142. Another term for the integrative approach is the
    a. biological approach.
    b. isolation approach.
    c. eclectic approach.
    d. singular approach.
    Ans.: c   LG: 4   Page: 591   QT: C

143. What is the *main* advantage of an integrative approach to psychotherapy?
    a. It is usually more cost effective.
    b. It is usually less time consuming.
    c. It requires less formal training on the part of the psychotherapist.
    d. It utilizes the strengths of a variety of approaches to meet the specific needs of the client.
    Ans.: d   LG: 4   Page: 592   QT: C

144. If you were to consider seeking professional psychological help, you would do all of the following *except*
    a. research the services offered by potential therapists.
    b. identify the professional credentials of potential therapists.
    c. pick a therapist on-line and make an appointment.
    d. set specific therapy goals and frequently assess whether or not these goals are being met.
    Ans.: c   LG: 4   Page: 592   QT: A

145. A process that uses external reviewers to approve the type and length of psychological treatment is called
    a. psychodynamic consultation.
    b. eclectic care.
    c. tailored management.
    d. managed care.
    Ans.: d   LG: 4   Page: 592   QT: F

146. With respect to the treatment of psychological disorders, managed care systems differ from traditional health care systems in all of the following ways *except* by
    a. focusing on short-term treatment.
    b. limiting traditional services.
    c. offering services at lower costs.
    d. providing diagnostic information.
    Ans.: d   LG: 4   Page: 592   QT: C

147. Managed care systems place a primary emphasis on
    a. long-term therapy.
    b. cost management.
    c. psychodynamic treatment.
    d. finding medical specialists.
    Ans.: b   LG: 4   Page: 592   QT: C

148. Dr. Burrow has diagnosed one of his patients as having a mental illness. Before payment is issued for treatment, Dr. Burrow is required to submit a report to a review committee, detailing the type and length of treatment recommended for this patient. This patient is part of a(n)
    a. managed care system.
    b. collective medical system.
    c. eclectic system.
    d. fourth-party system.
    Ans.: a   LG: 4   Page: 592   QT: C

149. Which of the following is *not* a criticism of managed care systems?
    a. Managed care organizations are reluctant to provide for more than a few therapy sessions for a given patient.
    b. Long-term psychotherapy has been eliminated except for a relatively few wealthy clients who can pay their own way.
    c. Managed care systems have not saved money.
    d. Some managed care organizations are employing less well-trained therapist who work at lower fees.
    Ans.: c   LG: 4   Page: 593   QT: C

150. Which of the following is *not* a good guideline for seeking professional help?
    a. Identify the professional's credentials.
    b. Expect fast results.
    c. Be a thoughtful and careful consumer of mental health services.
    d. Give therapy some time.
    Ans.: b   LG: 4   Page: 594–595 QT: C

True/False Items

___ 151. The most common form of biological therapy is psychosurgery.
___ 152. The excessive and prolonged use of antianxiety drugs can lead to addiction.
___ 153. Electroconvulsive therapy is often used for mildly depressed patients because it works so quickly.
___ 154. Sigmund Freud's therapy method focused on the unconscious and on early childhood experiences.
___ 155. Modern psychoanalysts have abandoned Freud's concept of the unconscious.
___ 156. Humanistic therapists focus on people's strengths and potentials.
___ 157. Gestalt therapy is less directive than person-centered therapy.
___ 158. Behavior therapists focus on providing unconditional positive regard.
___ 159. Systematic desensitization is an effective treatment method for phobias.
___ 160. Rational-emotive therapy and Beck's cognitive therapy both focus on conscious thought.
___ 161. Group therapy is more expensive than individual psychotherapy.
___ 162. When dealing with female clients, traditional psychotherapy overemphasizes relatedness and connection with others.
___ 163. Research has shown that ethnic minority individuals have been generally less likely to seek professional help for their personal problems.
___ 164. Self-help groups require a professional therapist to lead discussions.
___ 165. Society retains control over those who practice psychotherapy through licensing and certification.

Answer Key for True/False Items

151.	Ans.: F	LG: 1	Page: 562		159.	Ans.: T	LG: 2	Page: 576
152.	Ans.: T	LG: 1	Page: 563		160.	Ans.: T	LG: 2	Page: 579
153.	Ans.: F	LG: 1	Page: 566		161.	Ans.: F	LG: 3	Page: 584
154.	Ans.: T	LG: 2	Page: 569		162.	Ans.: F	LG: 3	Page: 588
155.	Ans.: F	LG: 2	Page: 572		163.	Ans.: T	LG: 3	Page: 588
156.	Ans.: T	LG: 2	Page: 572		164.	Ans.: F	LG: 3	Page: 586
157.	Ans.: F	LG: 2	Page: 574		165.	Ans.: T	LG: 4	Page: 594
158.	Ans.: F	LG: 2	Page: 573					

Fill-in-the-Blank Items

166. _____ therapies include drug therapy, electroconvulsive therapy, and psychosurgery.
167. _____ drugs are commonly known as tranquilizers.
168. Modern techniques of _____ are much more refined than the crude lobotomies of the past.
169. According to psychodynamic theorists, psychological disorders are caused by unresolved unconscious _____.
170. Sigmund Freud said that dreams reveal important information about a person's _____ thoughts.
171. According to Rogers, a person-centered therapist must provide active listening, accurate empathy, genuineness, and, most importantly, _____.
172. _____ believe that maladaptive behaviors can be unlearned by reinforcing only acceptable, adaptive behaviors.
173. A therapist who uses the _____ approach intentionally confronts the client about his or her irrational beliefs.
174. In cognitive-behavior therapy, self-efficacy and self-_____ methods are utilized.
175. The main advantage of _____ therapy is the context of interpersonal relationships.
176. _____ groups provide social support, role modeling, and the sharing of concrete problem-solving strategies.
177. A _____ sensitive therapist would offer tea rather than coffee to a Chinese-American client.
178. Evaluating past research through _____ allows researchers to study how effective psychotherapy is.
179. Many contemporary psychotherapists are in favor of an _____ approach to psychotherapy.
180. _____ providers do not encourage long-term psychotherapy.

Answer Key for Fill-in-the-Blank Items

166.	Ans.: Biological	LG: 1	Page: 562
167.	Ans.: Antianxiety	LG: 1	Page: 563
168.	Ans.: psychosurgery	LG: 1	Page: 568
169.	Ans.: conflicts	LG: 2	Page: 569
170.	Ans.: unconscious	LG: 2	Page: 571
171.	Ans.: unconditional positive regard	LG: 2	Page: 573
172.	Ans.: Behaviorists	LG: 2	Page: 574
173.	Ans.: rational-emotive	LG: 2	Page: 579
174.	Ans.: instructional	LG: 2	Page: 581
175.	Ans.: group	LG: 3	Page: 584
176.	Ans.: Self-help	LG: 3	Page: 586

177.	Ans.: culturally	LG: 3	Page: 588
178.	Ans.: meta-analysis	LG: 4	Page: 590
179.	Ans.: eclectic	LG: 4	Page: 591
180.	Ans.: Managed care	LG: 4	Page: 593

Matching Items

___ 181. SSRI
___ 182. deinstitutionalization
___ 183. tranquilizers
___ 184. psychotherapy success
___ 185. client-centered therapy
___ 186. free association
___ 187. token economy
___ 188. eclectic
___ 189. group therapy
___ 190. managed care

A. behavior modification technique
B. integrative
C. humanistic theory
D. psychoanalysis
E. less expensive than individual psychotherapy
F. linked to community mental health growth
G. antidepressant
H. good therapist/client relationship
I. antianxiety
J. focus on reduced costs for mental health care

Answer Key for Matching Items

181.	Ans.: G	LG: 1	Page: 563		186.	Ans.: D	LG: 2	Page: 570
182.	Ans.: F	LG: 3	Page: 587		187.	Ans.: A	LG: 2	Page: 577
183.	Ans.: I	LG: 1	Page: 563		188.	Ans.: B	LG: 4	Page: 591
184.	Ans.: H	LG: 4	Page: 591		189.	Ans.: E	LG: 3	Page: 584
185.	Ans.: C	LG: 2	Page: 572		190.	Ans.: J	LG: 4	Page: 593

Essay Questions

191. A variety of classes of drugs are available for treating mental disorders. Briefly describe the functions of drugs in the following categories: antianxiety, antidepressant, and antipsychotic. (LG: 1)

Answer Guidelines: Possible options include mentioning that antianxiety drugs make individuals less excitable and more tranquil; antidepressant drugs regulate mood (except in the case of bipolar disorder, which is usually treated with lithium); and antipsychotic drugs diminish agitated behavior and reduce tension.

192. Discuss how contemporary psychoanalytic therapies differ from traditional Freudian psychoanalysis. (LG: 2)

Answer Guidelines: Possible options include mentioning that contrary to traditional psychoanalysis contemporary psychodynamic therapies focus more on conscious thought, current relationships, and the development of the self in social contexts. Modern psychodynamic therapies are also briefer than traditional psychoanalysis. Also, clients sit in a comfortable chair while they talk to the therapist.

193. Describe the key characteristics of Carl Rogers' client-centered therapy. According to Rogers, who is responsible for change, and what is the therapist's role? (LG: 2)

Answer Guidelines: Possible options include mentioning that client-centered therapy is based on the humanistic approach, which focuses on people's positive potential, ability to grow, and need for self-fulfillment. According to Rogers, the client is responsible for change. The therapist merely assists the client in this process. In order to do so effectively, the therapist must be genuine, listen actively, provide unconditional positive regard, and display accurate empathy.

194. Describe how behavioral therapies use principles of learning to reduce or eliminate maladaptive behavior. (LG: 2)

Answer Guidelines: Behavioral therapies seek to eliminate the symptoms rather than help individuals gain insight into their problems. Fundamentals of classical conditioning and operant conditioning are used to apply such techniques as systematic desensitization and aversive conditioning.

195. Compare and contrast Ellis' rational-emotive therapy with Beck's cognitive therapy. (LG: 2)

Answer Guidelines: Possible options include mentioning that both of these approaches are cognitive therapies that attempt to change people's behaviors by changing their cognitions, or thoughts. Ellis' rational-emotive therapy is based on the belief that people's irrational, self-defeating beliefs cause psychological problems. In order to change the individual's belief system, this type of therapy openly confronts the individual about the irrational, or illogical, nature of his/her beliefs and thoughts. Beck's cognitive therapy is mostly used with depression. It is also based on the idea that people's psychological problems stem from illogical thinking. However, this approach is less confrontational; it is more of an open-ended dialogue in which the therapist encourages the client to gather information and conduct experiments to reveal the inaccuracies of the client's beliefs.

196. Describe some of the elements of group therapy. Include family therapy, couples therapy, and self-help support groups in your answer. (LG: 3)

Answer Guidelines: Group therapies emphasize that relationships can hold the key to successful therapy. They are generally less expensive than individual therapy for the client. Family therapy is group therapy with family members. Family therapy techniques include validation, reframing, structural change, and detriangulation. Couples therapy is group therapy with married or unmarried couples whose major problem is within their relationships.

197. How are sociocultural considerations related to psychotherapy? (LG: 3)

Answer Guidelines: Psychotherapies have been mainly focused on the individual, but some cultures may have more of a collectivist influence. Many ethnic-minority individuals prefer to discuss problems with parents, friends, and relatives rather than mental health professionals. Some research finds that therapy is more effective when there is an ethnic match between the therapist and the client, although culturally sensitive therapy can be successfully provided by a therapist who is from a different ethnic background.

198. A controversial issue for some time has been the evaluation of the effectiveness of psychotherapy. Trace the history of the answers to this issue, and summarize the empirical evidence on this question. (LG: 4)

Answer Guidelines: Possible options include mentioning Eysenck's study (1952) and the Smith, Glass, and Miller study (1980). More recent studies conclude that psychotherapy is generally effective although specifics about cause and effect are elusive. We do know that certain therapy approaches work better for some disorders than for others; we also know that no single approach is effective across disorders.

199. Many psychotherapists identify themselves as eclectic. What does this mean, and what are the advantages and disadvantages of this approach? (LG: 4)

Answer Guidelines: Possible options include mentioning that eclectic therapists use an integrative approach, drawing on a variety of approaches to psychotherapy to match the approach to the specific needs of each individual client.

200. Describe the major issues you would consider if you were trying to find a professional therapist. (LG: 4)

Answer Guidelines: Possible options include mentioning that what is effective therapy depends on the problem experienced by the client, the client's personality and expectations, and the therapist's approach. What works in one situation may not work in the next situation. Some general guidelines for finding the appropriate therapist include: (1) educate yourself about the various approaches to psychological therapy and decide which approach might best fit your needs; (2) think about whether you would be more comfortable with a male or female therapist; (3) ask about the therapist's professional credentials either before or during the first visit; (4) ask about the therapist's experience with and/or licensure for dealing with your specific problem; (5) ask about the approach the therapist prefers or suggests for your problem; (6) together with your therapist, set specific therapy goals with specific time expectations; and (7) give a new therapy situation between four to six weeks before deciding whether or not you find it useful.

Chapter 15: Stress, Coping, and Health

Learning Goals

1. Describe the scope of health psychology and behavioral medicine.
2. Define stress and identify its sources.
3. Explain how people respond to stress.
4. Discuss links between stress and illness.
5. Outline strategies for coping with stress.
6. Summarize how to promote health.

Multiple-Choice Items

Learning Goal 1: Describe the scope of health psychology and behavioral medicine.

1. What do behavioral medicine and health psychology have in common?
   a. They both study the connection between stress and health.
   b. They both set and monitor certification standards for health professionals.
   c. They both study the causes of mental illness.
   d. They both develop biological treatments for psychological disorders.
   Ans.: a   LG: 1   Page: 603   QT: C

2. Which field is *most* closely related to health psychology?
   a. psychotherapy
   b. behavioral medicine
   c. social psychology
   d. clinical psychology
   Ans.: b   LG: 1   Page: 603   QT: C

3. Dr. Flintstone is interested in studying the relationship between the degree to which people follow doctor's orders and health care outcomes. Of the following, Dr. Flintstone *most* likely works in the field of
   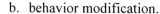
   a. clinical psychology.
   b. behavior modification.
   c. psychoanalysis.
   d. behavioral medicine.
   Ans.: d   LG: 1   Page: 603   QT: C

4. Which of the following is the main difference between health psychology and behavioral medicine?
   a. scope
   b. topics of interest
   c. subjects studied
   d. importance
   Ans.: a   LG: 1   Page: 603   QT: C

5. Which of the following areas of study would a health psychologist be *least* interested in?
   a. immune functioning
   b. psychological factors in losing weight
   c. maximizing performance in an athletic event
   d. using exercise to reduce stress
   Ans.: c   LG: 1   Page: 603   QT: C

6. Which of the following is the major cause of death in the United States?
   a. diabetes
   b. cancer
   c. heart disease
   d. stroke
   Ans.: c   LG: 1   Page: 603   QT: F

7. If you were a health psychologist, you would be *most* likely to examine which of the following research questions?
   a. Does behavior modification cure phobias?
   b. What personality type is achievement oriented?
   c. Does short-term memory decrease with age?
   d. Does physical exercise effectively reduce stress?
   Ans.: d   LG: 1   Page: 603   QT: A

8. In the United States, _____ of the leading causes of death can be attributed to personal habits and lifestyles.
   a. 10%
   b. 25%
   c. 40%
   d. 70%
   Ans.: d   LG: 1   Page: 603   QT: C

9. Willard is trying to climb the corporate ladder. He has no real regard for the people that work under him but is very concerned with both corporate productivity and profits. Which of the following would Willard be *least* likely to do to meet these goals?
   a. Cut back on spending for employee health promotion
   b. Create on-site exercise facilities
   c. Sponsor company athletic events
   d. Give bonuses for quitting smoking and weight loss
   Ans.: a   LG: 1   Page: 603   QT: A

Learning Goal 2: Define stress and identify its sources.

10. According to the American Academy of Family Physicians, _____ office visits to family doctors are for stress-related symptoms.
    a. one-tenth of
    b. one-third of
    c. two-thirds of
    d. all
    Ans.: c   LG: 2   Page: 604   QT: F

407

11. Psychologists view stress as a(n)
    a. sign of the times.
    b. unconscious event.
    c. external event.
    d. innate event.
    Ans.: a   LG: 2   Page: 604   QT: C

12. Which of the following is the *best* example of a stressor?
    a. taking a vacation
    b. talking to a friend
    c. getting an A on an exam
    d. being fired from a job
    Ans.: d   LG: 2   Page: 604   QT: C

13. Which of the following is *not* a personality characteristic that is being studied for its relation to stress coping?
    a. Type A/Type B
    b. hardiness
    c. personal control
    d. unconscious conflicts
    Ans.: d   LG: 2   Page: 604   QT: F

14. Psychologists have identified a hard-driving, achievement-oriented, coronary-prone personality pattern known as
    a. Type A personality.
    b. Type B personality.
    c. dissonant personality.
    d. hardiness personality.
    Ans.: a   LG: 2   Page: 605   QT: F

15. Dick always feels like he is running out of time. He rarely takes a vacation and finds it hard to relax at home. He demands perfection of himself and is competitive in all areas of his life. Dick has a(n)
    a. avoidant personality.
    b. Type A personality.
    c. Type B personality.
    d. bulimic personality.
    Ans.: b   LG: 2   Page: 605   QT: C

16. Jason gets angry very quickly. The slightest mishap causes him to become hostile and explosive toward others. Which of the following is true about Jason?
    a. He is more likely to have a depressed immune system.
    b. He is more likely to develop cancer.
    c. He is less likely to be a Type A personality.
    d. He is more likely to develop heart disease.
    Ans.: d   LG: 2   Page: 605   QT: C

17. Janice is usually a relaxed and easygoing person. She rarely gets upset and takes things in stride. Janice could be described *best* as a(n)
    a. detached personality.
    b. Type A personality.
    c. Type B personality.
    d. passive personality.
    Ans.: c   LG: 2   Page: 605   QT: C

18. Sam is an intense, hard-driven, competitive, and impatient manager. He would probably have the *most* difficulty working with an employee who is a
    a. Type B personality.
    b. Type A personality.
    c. compatible personality.
    d. workaholic.
    Ans.: a   LG: 2   Page: 605   QT: C

19. Which of the behaviors associated with the Type A personality ultimately was shown to be the *best* predictor of coronary problems?
    a. impatience
    b. competitiveness
    c. flexibility
    d. hostility
    Ans.: d   LG: 2   Page: 605   QT: F

20. A sense of commitment, a feeling of control, and a perception of problems as challenges, rather than crises, are all characteristics of
    a. business executives.
    b. a Type A personality.
    c. a Type B personality.
    d. hardiness.
    Ans.: d   LG: 2   Page: 605   QT: F

21. Crystal has a hardy personality. If she were to lose her job, her reactions would probably include all of the following *except* which one?
    a. She would see this event as a challenge rather than a threat.
    b. She would take control and start looking for a new job immediately.
    c. She would fall into deep depression and start overeating.
    d. She would talk to her friends and family about her situation.
    Ans.: c   LG: 2   Page: 605   QT: C

22. In a study that looked at stress in executives' lives, which of the following did *not* play an important role in reducing illness?
    a. hardy personalities
    b. exercise
    c. income level
    d. social support
    Ans.: c   LG: 2   Page: 606   QT: C

23. An individual's perception that they have an influence on their situation would be referred to as
    a. personal advocacy.
    b. personal control.
    c. interpersonal direction.
    d. subconscious control.
    Ans.: b   LG: 2   Page: 606   QT: F

24. Holmes and Rahe developed the Social Readjustment Rating Scale in an attempt to assign
    a. explanations to life events.
    b. numerical values to life events.
    c. interpretations to life events.
    d. justification to life events.
    Ans.: b   LG: 2   Page: 607   QT: F

25. Research has discovered that the Social Readjustment Rating Scale
    a. predicts physical health very well.
    b. does not have any relationship with physical health.
    c. predicts physical health modestly.
    d. rates mental health very well.
    Ans.: c   LG: 2   Page: 608   QT: C

26. Which of the following is accounted for by the Social Readjustment Rating Scale?
    a. physiological makeup
    b. major life events
    c. coping methods
    d. support systems
    Ans.: b   LG: 2   Page: 607   QT: F

27. Researchers who are investigating the influence of daily hassles on health would be interested in all but which of the following?
    a. wasting time
    b. being lonely
    c. graduating from college
    d. worrying about meeting high standards
    Ans.: c   LG: 2   Page: 607   QT: C

28. Two different approaches to stress and health look at _____, which are larger events, and _____ , which are the things that provide stress for us on a daily basis.
    a. hassles, life events
    b. life events, daily hassles
    c. stressful decisions, daily decisions
    d. life events, daily decisions
    Ans.: b   LG: 2   Page: 606   QT: C

29. Diane is planning to get married next week. Unfortunately, it is also the Christmas holiday, she is graduating from college, her fiancé is being released from prison, her mother is going into the hospital for surgery, and she still has to plan the honeymoon vacation. She is very stressed and feels run down and sick. Which of the following theories would *best* explain this?
   a. daily hassles approach
   b. life events approach
   c. lack of coping skills
   d. constitutional weakness
   Ans.: b   LG: 2   Page: 607   QT: A

30. Often, we have difficulty making choices regarding both attractive and unattractive alternatives. In health psychology, when investigating stress, the term that is used for this is
   a. disequilibrium.
   b. consensus.
   c. decision process.
   d. conflict.
   Ans.: d   LG: 2   Page: 608   QT: G

31. An approach/approach conflict is *best* defined as a situation in which an individual must choose between two
   a. positive goals of unequal value.
   b. alternatives that contain both positive and negative properties.
   c. positive goals of approximately equal value.
   d. opposing challenges.
   Ans.: c   LG: 2   Page: 608   QT: C

32. You may not enjoy studying for the exams in this course, but you do like the better grades that result from studying. The mixed feelings that you have when you try to get yourself to study are an example of a(n)
   a. self-efficacy problem.
   b. avoidance strategy.
   c. approach/approach conflict.
   d. approach/avoidance conflict.
   Ans.: d   LG: 2   Page: 608   QT: C

33. Sandra is holding up the cafeteria line because she is trying to decide between the dried out meatloaf and the overcooked hot dogs. Sandra is *most* likely experiencing a(n)
   a. approach/frustration conflict.
   b. approach/approach conflict.
   c. avoidance/avoidance conflict.
   d. approach/avoidance conflict.
   Ans.: c   LG: 2   Page: 608   QT: C

34. Of the possible conflicts discussed in your text, the *least* stressful is the
   a. approach/approach conflict.
   b. avoidance/avoidance conflict.
   c. approach/avoidance conflict.
   d. frustration conflict.
   Ans.: a   LG: 2   Page: 608   QT: C

35. Kenneth can't decide whether or not to ask Debra to marry him. He really loves her, but he knows his parents will object if he marries her before he finishes college. Kenneth's situation exemplifies which type of conflict?
    a. active/coping
    b. approach/avoidance
    c. avoidance/avoidance
    d. approach/approach
    Ans.: b   LG: 2   Page: 608   QT: C

36. Juanita is experiencing stress. Both of her boyfriends have asked her out for the same night. Assuming she is equally attracted to both guys, she is *most* likely experiencing which conflict?
    a. approach/avoidance
    b. approach/approach
    c. assimilation
    d. marginalization
    Ans.: b   LG: 2   Page: 608   QT: C

37. A feeling of hopelessness and helplessness brought on by constant work-related stress is termed
    a. overload.
    b. burnout.
    c. frustration.
    d. fatigue.
    Ans.: b   LG: 2   Page: 609   QT: F

38. What type of stress produces burnout?
    a. work-related
    b. approach/approach stress
    c. avoidance/avoidance stress
    d. self-efficacy stress
    Ans.: a   LG: 2   Page: 609   QT: F

39. Susan is in her tenth year of teaching. Since the beginning of the new school year, Susan hasn't been feeling herself. She is extremely tired all the time and barely has the energy to make it through the day. Given that Susan is basically in good physical health, what might be the *best* explanation for her condition?
    a. She is just beginning to realize that she never really liked teaching.
    b. She has personal problems that are interfering with her effectiveness as a teacher.
    c. She doesn't like the way the new principal is running the school.
    d. She is experiencing some of the classic symptoms of burnout.
    Ans.: d   LG: 2   Page: 609   QT: C

40. The *least* likely situation to produce burnout is
    a. work that involves dealing with others in highly emotional situations.
    b. work that allows for autonomy and flexibility in decision making.
    c. work that affords little control over the outcomes of one's effort.
    d. work that presents a gradual accumulation of stress over time.
    Ans.: b   LG: 2   Page: 609   QT: C

41. Burnout appears to be a widespread phenomenon among college students. In order to avoid this situation, a college student should do all of the following *except*
    a. take well-balanced class loads.
    b. avoid class overloads.
    c. use available campus support resources.
    d. plan to graduate in three years.
    Ans.: d   LG: 2   Page: 609   QT: A

42. For the past couple of years, Quentin has been working long, hard hours as the director of a shelter for the homeless. He receives little encouragement and few funds. Quentin would like to do much more but has no resources. Lately, he often feels that his efforts are just a "drop in the bucket." Quentin is a prime candidate for
    a. learned helplessness.
    b. Type A behavior.
    c. burnout.
    d. acquired immune deficiency syndrome.
    Ans.: c   LG: 2   Page: 609   QT: C

43. Which of the following is the *least* adaptive response to acculturation?
    a. assimilation
    b. marginalization
    c. integration
    d. resolution
    Ans.: b   LG: 2   Page: 611   QT: C

44. Negative consequences that result from contact between two distinctive cultural groups are called
    a. frustration.
    b. integration.
    c. assimilation stress.
    d. acculturative stress.
    Ans.: d   LG: 2   Page: 610   QT: F

45. In an attempt to deal with acculturative stress, Karem has decided to move to a sparsely populated area and to practice the traditions of his culture. This is an example of
    a. separation.
    b. marginalization.
    c. integration.
    d. segregation.
    Ans.: a   LG: 2   Page: 611   QT: C

46. Sagrita feels that she does not fit within any cultural group and that she has lost her identity. Sagrita is experiencing
    a. assimilation.
    b. separation.
    c. marginalization.
    d. integration.
    Ans.: c   LG: 2   Page: 611   QT: C

413

47. Which of the following is the *most* psychologically adaptive response to acculturation?
    a. assimilation
    b. integration
    c. separation
    d. marginalization
    Ans.: b   LG: 2   Page: 611   QT: C

48. The *main* disadvantage of assimilation is
    a. bicultural functioning.
    b. isolation.
    c. learning a new language.
    d. loss of original cultural identity.
    Ans.: d   LG: 2   Page: 610   QT: C

49. Assimilation is associated with which cultural model?
    a. stew
    b. mosaic
    c. melting pot
    d. multiculturalism
    Ans.: c   LG: 2   Page: 611   QT: F

50. The multicultural approach in which people move into the larger culture but maintain many aspects of their distinct cultural identities is called
    a. assimilation.
    b. integration.
    c. separation.
    d. marginalization.
    Ans.: b   LG: 2   Page: 611   QT: F

Learning Goal 3: Explain how people respond to stress.

51. Selye's term for the common effects on the body when demands are placed upon it is the
    a. adjustment syndrome.
    b. general adaptation syndrome.
    c. physiological/psychological response syndrome.
    d. general physiological adjustment.
    Ans.: b   LG: 3   Page: 612   QT: F

52. Which stage of the general adaptation syndrome is associated with the highest risk of physical illness?
    a. alarm
    b. resistance
    c. conversion
    d. countershock
    Ans.: a   LG: 3   Page: 613   QT: F

53. The first stage of the general adaptation syndrome is called the
    a. alarm stage.
    b. flight stage.
    c. exhaustion stage.
    d. resistance stage.
    Ans.: a   LG: 3   Page: 613   QT: F

54. Seyle's three-stage pattern of reaction to stress is known as the
    a. cognitive appraisal scale.
    b. social readjustment scale.
    c. personality adjustment system.
    d. general adaptation syndrome.
    Ans.: d   LG: 3   Page: 612   QT: F

55. According to Seyle, in which stage does the person exert an all-out effort to combat stress?
    a. alarm stage
    b. resistance stage
    c. primary appraisal
    d. secondary appraisal
    Ans.: b   LG: 3   Page: 614   QT: F

56. Two years ago, Walter's business went bankrupt. Two months ago, his wife left him. Two days ago, Walter had a nervous breakdown. Seyle would say that Walter is in which stage of the general adaptation syndrome?
    a. alarm
    b. reaction
    c. resistance
    d. exhaustion
    Ans.: d   LG: 3   Page: 614   QT: C

57. Which of the following accurately describes the sequence of the general adaptation syndrome?
    a. alarm, resistance, and challenge
    b. primary appraisal, alarm, secondary appraisal
    c. challenge, frustration, and exhaustion
    d. alarm, resistance, and exhaustion
    Ans.: d   LG: 3   Page: 613   QT: F

58. .According to Seyle, which of the following symptoms will appear as a result of stress?
    a. loss of appetite
    b. muscular weakness
    c. decreased interest in the world
    d. all of the above
    Ans.: d   LG: 3   Page: 612   QT: F

59. Selye's alarm reaction is consistent with Cannon's _____, which prepares the body by a physiological response that best supports survival.
    a. autonomic response
    b. central nervous system automasticity
    c. fight-or-flight response
    d. coping response
    Ans.: c   LG: 3   Page: 614   QT: C

60. The fight-or-flight response
    a. is an evolutionary leftover of our ancestors.
    b. maximizes our chances of survival under physical threat.
    c. involves rapid blood circulation, muscular tension, and increased respiration.
    d. does all of the above.
    Ans.: d   LG: 3   Page: 614   QT: C

61. Recent research finds that while _____ are more likely to utilize the fight-or-flight response, _____ are more likely to "tend and befriend."
    a. dogs, cats
    b. males, females
    c. females, males
    d. adults, children
    Ans.: b   LG: 3   Page: 614   QT: C

62. Cognitive appraisal is *best* explained as
    a. how much a person remembers about a given event.
    b. the degree to which a person expected a given event.
    c. what a person thinks about and how a person interprets a given event.
    d. the number of times a person has already experienced a given event.
    Ans.: c   LG: 3   Page: 615   QT: F

63. Charles has been assessing whether or not he should attend a football game. The weather is cold and damp, and he thinks he might become ill if he sits outside all afternoon. His assessment is an example of which step of cognitive appraisal?
    a. challenge
    b. coping
    c. primary appraisal
    d. secondary appraisal
    Ans.: c   LG: 3   Page: 615   QT: C

64. The evaluation of the potential harm, threat, or challenge of a situation defines which process?
    a. general adaptation
    b. acculturation
    c. cognitive restructuring
    d. primary appraisal
    Ans.: d   LG: 3   Page: 615   QT: F

65. If you have evaluated a situation as potentially harmful and threatening, you will be better able to cope with the stress if you
    a. perceive the situation as a challenge and your coping resources are high.
    b. avoid the situation and focus on something else altogether.
    c. become alarmed about the situation and recognize when you are exhausted.
    d. withdraw from the situation in order to reduce resistance and conflict.
    Ans.: a   LG: 3   Page: 615   QT: C

66. Ashley decides that an event is stressful. Next, she evaluates how effectively she can cope with this stressful event. She is engaging in
    a. primary appraisal.
    b. counterstress.
    c. secondary appraisal.
    d. cognitive restructuring.
    Ans.: c   LG: 3   Page: 615   QT: C

67. What do primary and secondary appraisal have in common?
    a. They both take about the same amount of time.
    b. They both are cognitive activities.
    c. They both occur at the same time.
    d. They both are basically passive activities.
    Ans.: b   LG: 3   Page: 615   QT: C

Learning Goal 4: Discuss links between stress and illness.

68. Rosemary is interested in studying the relationships between emotion, the nervous system, and the immune system. She would be most interested in the field of
    a. cognitive psychology.
    b. psychopharmacology.
    c. psychoneuroimmunology.
    d. anatomy and physiology.
    Ans.: c   LG: 4   Page: 616   QT: A

69. Which statement is *not* correct concerning the relationship between the immune system and stress?
    a. Acute stressors produce superior immune system functioning.
    b. Acute stressors produce poor immune system functioning.
    c. Chronic stressors are associated with poor immune system response.
    d. Positive social circumstances are associated with an increased ability to fight cancer.
    Ans.: a   LG: 4   Page: 617   QT: C

70. Which of the following would *not* be one of the preliminary hypotheses of the relatively new field of psychoneuroimmunology?
    a. Stressful experiences lower the efficiency of the immune system, making individuals more susceptible to disease.
    b. Stress directly promotes disease-producing processes.
    c. Stress is the cause of all illness.
    d. Stressful experiences may diminish the individual's ability to cope with a disease.
    Ans.: c   LG: 4   Page: 617   QT: C

71. According to the sympathetic nervous system pathway to stress, prolonged stress would *most* likely be associated with an increased risk for which illness?
   a. Alzheimer's
   b. eating disorder
   c. heart disease
   d. pneumonia
   Ans.: c   LG: 4   Page: 618   QT: C

72. Suppose Janet's cold is associated with her increased exposure to stress at work. This demonstrates a(n)
   a. biological pathway for stress and illness.
   b. immunological eustress reaction.
   c. Type C behavior pattern for illness.
   d. example of behavioral noncompliance.
   Ans.: a   LG: 4   Page: 618   QT: C

73. Why is it important for patients with HIV or cancer to avoid stress?
   a. These patients do not appear to use primary appraisal.
   b. Stress does not trigger general adaptation syndrome in these patients.
   c. The Type A behavior pattern is more likely to appear in these patients.
   d. Stress is associated with poor immune functioning in these patients.
   Ans.: d   LG: 4   Page: 619   QT: C

74. Which of the following cancer patients would you predict to have the weakest immune system?
   a. Meagan, who is a college graduate, has a good job, and lives with a loving family
   b. Charles, who is homeless, sleeps and eats at shelters whenever he can, and is generally alone
   c. Anita, who has raised three children and enjoys spending time with her grandchildren
   d. James, who owns a business, has many friends, but lives by himself
   Ans.: b   LG: 4   Page: 619   QT: C

75. If you were a psychoneuroimmunologist, you would *most* likely study which of the following hypotheses?
   a. Acute stress causes the release of cortisol or norepinephrine.
   b. Physiological arousal represents a "flight-or-fight" response.
   c. People who react to a cancer diagnosis with depression are less likely to get well.
   d. Stress creates physiological arousal by activating the sympathetic nervous system.
   Ans.: c   LG: 4   Page: 619   QT: A

76. Research has found not only that _____ emotional factors are related to promoting illness but also that _____ emotional factors are related to reducing illness.
   a. negative, positive
   b. neutral, positive
   c. negative, neutral
   d. positive, negative
   Ans.: a   LG: 4   Page: 619   QT: C

77. Researchers have found an increase in the levels of the antibody immunoglobulin, which is believed to be the first line of defense against the common cold, when subjects
    a. watched a sad video.
    b. were exposed to humor.
    c. were exposed to neutral stimuli.
    d. were in a bad mood.
    Ans.: b   LG: 4   Page: 619   QT: C

78. Which of the following is related to positive emotions?
    a. use of more coping styles
    b. use of more objective appraisal of situations
    c. increase in social support
    d. all of the above
    Ans.: d   LG: 4   Page: 620   QT: C

Learning Goal 5: Outline strategies for coping with stress.

79. Which of the following is *not* a part of coping?
    a. managing taxing circumstances
    b. expending effort to solve life's problems
    c. seeking to master or reduce stress
    d. surrendering to life's problems
    Ans.: d   LG: 5   Page: 621   QT: F

80. Which of the following scenarios would yield the highest stress?
    a. perceiving a situation as harmful and having few or no coping resources available
    b. perceiving a situation as a challenge and having good coping resources available
    c. perceiving a situation as threatening and having adequate coping resources available
    d. perceiving a situation as a challenge and having few coping resources available
    Ans.: a   LG: 5   Page: 621   QT: C

81. Social support, prior experience with stress, exercise, and perceived control over stressors are all factors that
    a. are associated with increased physiological arousal.
    b. reduce reactions to stress.
    c. make it easier to apply defense mechanisms.
    d. inhibit coping mechanisms.
    Ans.: b   LG: 5   Page: 621   QT: F

82. Which individual will cope *most* successfully with stress?
    a. Tara, who has several really close friends, exercises regularly, and sees problems as challenges
    b. Jim, who spends most of his free time alone, catastrophizes, and feels powerless
    c. Sarah, who is overweight, often feels lonely, and perceives most events as problems
    d. Matt, who is sedentary, feels helpless, and never lets anyone see when he is angry
    Ans.: a   LG: 5   Page: 621   QT: C

83. Seamus is having trouble in his algebra class. The worse he does in the class, the more likely he is to be upset. Finally, he decides to make an effort not to get too happy when he does well or too angry when he does not do well. According to Lazarus, Seamus is
    a. using problem-focused coping.
    b. using emotion-focused coping.
    c. using an active cognitive strategy.
    d. a Type C personality.
    Ans.: b   LG: 5   Page: 621   QT: C

84. After being promoted to department head, Alex found the job to be uncomfortable and highly stressful. Ultimately, Alex resigned from the position and returned to his former job, where he reported being much happier. Which method of coping with stress did Alex use?
    a. denial
    b. emotion-focused coping
    c. problem-focused coping
    d. defense mechanisms
    Ans.: c   LG: 5   Page: 621   QT: C

85. Which of the following is generally the *most* effective method of reducing stress?
    a. defense mechanisms
    b. problem-focused coping
    c. withdrawing from the stressful situation
    d. emotion-focused coping
    Ans.: b   LG: 5   Page: 621   QT: F

86. Which of the following *best* describes problem-focused coping?
    a. employing psychological defense mechanisms
    b. rationalizing the stressful situation
    c. avoiding the stress-producing situation
    d. attacking the stressful problem directly
    Ans.: d   LG: 5   Page: 621   QT: F

87. Emotion-focused coping works *best* in combination with
    a. avoidance strategies.
    b. defense mechanisms.
    c. the general adaptation syndrome.
    d. problem-focused coping.
    Ans.: d   LG: 5   Page: 621   QT: C

88. While Chris was trying to study at the library, two people near his study area kept talking to each other. Chris was annoyed by the noise and moved to a quieter area. This is an example of
    a. emotion-focused coping.
    b. passive coping.
    c. avoidance coping.
    d. problem-focused coping.
    Ans.: d   LG: 5   Page: 621   QT: C

89. Emilio's wife of 40 years is terminally ill. Although her physical condition has deteriorated drastically over the past three months, Emilio keeps talking about the trip he is planning for the two of them, once she is feeling better again. In this particular situation, Emilio's denial of his wife's impending death is a(n)
    a. unhealthy coping strategy.
    b. adaptive coping strategy.
    c. problem-focused coping strategy.
    d. maladaptive coping strategy.
    Ans.: b   LG: 5   Page: 621   QT: C

90. When Chloe made mistakes in the past, she told herself that she was a failure. Recently, however, she has learned to tell herself to try again and that she is a competent person. Chloe is using
    a. cognitive restructuring.
    b. problem-focused coping.
    c. assimilation.
    d. behavioral modification.
    Ans.: a   LG: 5   Page: 622   QT: C

91. A technique that is helpful in cognitive restructuring is
    a. learned helplessness.
    b. integration.
    c. self-talk.
    d. biofeedback.
    Ans.: c   LG: 5   Page: 622   QT: F

92. Why is it important to monitor your self-talk?
    a. to limit the time spent on self-statements
    b. to identify and change negative self-statements
    c. to discuss self-statements with a therapist
    d. to share self-statements with others
    Ans.: b   LG: 5   Page: 622   QT: C

93. Rick is one of those people who always sees "the glass as half empty." His thoughts are dominated by negative themes and pessimism. What method could be used to improve Rick's negative thoughts about himself and the world around him?
    a. biofeedback
    b. cognitive restructuring
    c. behavior modification
    d. psychoanalysis
    Ans.: b   LG: 5   Page: 622   QT: A

94. Which of the following appears to be a characteristic of happy people?
    a. a firm grasp of reality
    b. seeing themselves for what they are
    c. an avoidant personality
    d. positive self-illusion
    Ans.: d   LG: 5   Page: 622   QT: F

95. Which degree of self-illusion tends to be the *most* effective?
    a. grandiose positive self-illusion
    b. mildly positive self-illusion
    c. mildly negative self-illusion
    d. extremely negative self-illusion
    Ans.: b   LG: 5   Page: 623   QT: F

96. A student must write a 15-page paper to complete a seminar course. At the beginning of the semester, the student began to worry and imagine what would happen if he wrote a bad paper. Can these negative thoughts help the student?
    a. Negative thoughts will only cause added stress.
    b. No, according to cognitive restructuring, the student will fail.
    c. They will help only if he avoids using self-talk strategies.
    d. They may motivate the student to avoid failure.
    Ans.: d   LG: 5   Page: 624   QT: C

97. According to your text, defensive pessimism may actually be an effective strategy for handling stress because it
    a. prepares the individual for eventual failure.
    b. restructures the individual's cognitions.
    c. creates adaptive self-illusions.
    d. motivates the individual to avoid failure.
    Ans.: d   LG: 5   Page: 624   QT: F

98. Self-efficacy is the belief that you can
    a. teach others to be self-reliant.
    b. show unconditional positive regard for others.
    c. be empathetic to your own problems.
    d. master a situation and produce positive outcomes.
    Ans.: d   LG: 5   Page: 624   QT: F

99. Which of the following has *not* been linked to high self-efficacy?
    a. the ability to solve personal problems
    b. persistence toward a goal
    c. stress-free living
    d. how much stress is experienced.
    Ans.: c   LG: 5   Page: 624   QT: C

100. Belief in one's own capability to produce successful outcomes is called
    a. deindividuation.
    b. self-instruction.
    c. self-efficacy.
    d. ethnocentrism.
    Ans.: c   LG: 5   Page: 624   QT: F

101. Rob has his first piano recital on Sunday. He has a difficult piece to master but is confident he will be ready in time. Rob would probably rate high in
    a. Type A behavior.
    b. acculturative stress.
    c. Type C behavior.
    d. self-efficacy.
    Ans.: d   LG: 5   Page: 624   QT: C

102. Self efficacy is closely linked to the concept of
    a. control.
    b. self-control.
    c. authority.
    d. perceived control.
    Ans.: d   LG: 5   Page: 625   QT: F

103. Self efficacy has been linked with which of the following factors of health psychology?
    a. how much stress people experience
    b. how much effort people expend in coping with stress.
    c. how long people persist in the face of obstacles.
    d. all of the above
    Ans.: d   LG: 5   Page: 625   QT: F

104. Individuals who have high self-efficacy are *least* likely to do which of the following?
    a. persist in the face of obstacles
    b. expend effort in coping with stress
    c. experience less stress in challenging situations
    d. perceive that they have no control over the situation
    Ans.: d   LG: 5   Page: 625   QT: C

105. Feedback from others that one is loved and cared for, esteemed and valued, and included in a network of communication and mutual obligation is
    a. self-efficacy.
    b. social support.
    c. positive self-illusion.
    d. assertive behavior.
    Ans.: b   LG: 5   Page: 624   QT: F

106. Lindsay has attended the funerals of three of her friends in the past month. According to research on stress, she should
    a. seek social support.
    b. use avoidance strategies.
    c. avoid problem-focused coping.
    d. try not to think about the deaths.
    Ans.: a   LG: 5   Page: 624   QT: A

107. You just spent a full hour and a half talking to your best friend about how stressful school has been, how stressful it will be to go through graduation, and how stressful it will be to find a job after four years without one. What effect is this talk *most* likely going to have on you?
    a. It will increase your stress.
    b. It will decrease your stress.
    c. It will have little effect on your stress.
    d. It will trigger marginalization.
    Ans.: b   LG: 5   Page: 624   QT: C

108. Diane is a single mom who is raising her child by herself. There are days when she feels so stressed out she is not certain that she can keep her composure. On one particular day when her son put pennies in their DVD machine, she shared her experience with her friend Shante. She is no sooner finished relaying her horrible plight, when Shante tells her about the time that her daughter attempted to flush the cat down the toilet. Soon, what seemed to be catastrophic is a source of humor as each of them exchanges stories of parenthood. Diane's reduction in stress can be attributed to
    a. social support.
    b. self-efficacy.
    c. problem-focused coping.
    d. hardiness.
    Ans.: a   LG: 5   Page: 624   QT: A

109. Social support includes
    a. tangible assistance.
    b. information.
    c. emotional support.
    d. all of the above.
    Ans.: d   LG: 5   Page: 624   QT: F

110. When Erin and Josh brought their new baby home, several of their friends brought food to their home so Josh and Erin would not have to cook. This is an example of
    a. tangible assistance.
    b. stress management.
    c. biofeedback.
    d. acculturation.
    Ans.: a   LG: 5   Page: 624   QT: C

111. What is the relationship between social support and depression?
    a. Researchers have found no correlation between stress and social support.
    b. Researchers have found a negative correlation between stress and social support.
    c. Researchers have found a positive correlation between stress and social support.
    d. Researchers have found inconsistent correlations between stress and social support.
    Ans.: b   LG: 5   Page: 625   QT: F

112. What is the relationship between social support and life span?
    a. People who have numerous social relationships live longer.
    b. Life span is not affected by the diversity of a person's social networks.
    c. People who interact primarily with family members live longer.
    d. Family and close friends are the crucial social networks affecting life span.
    Ans.: a   LG: 5   Page: 626   QT: F

113. Assertive coping is *most* relevant
    a. when one is making an important personal decision.
    b. when one is selecting the best of several bargains.
    c. when one is trying to resolve an interpersonal conflict.
    d. when one is studying for an important exam.
    Ans.: c   LG: 5   Page: 626   QT: C

114. Which of the following is *not* one of the positive effects of assertive coping?
    a. standing up for one's legitimate rights
    b. acting in one's own best interest
    c. running roughshod over others
    d. expressing one's feelings freely
    Ans.: c   LG: 5   Page: 626   QT: F

115. Assertive coping has beneficial effects on mental health because it
    a. is a method of active and effective coping that reduces stress.
    b. relies on defense mechanisms.
    c. requires the internalization of anger.
    d. makes others feel guilty for not meeting their responsibility.
    Ans.: a   LG: 5   Page: 626   QT: C

116. Which of the following is *not* true when speaking of the relationship between religion and health?
    a. Research has proven that religious involvement causes an improvement in health.
    b. Religion can help people cope better.
    c. Religious thoughts play a role in maintaining hope and stimulating motivation.
    d. Religious involvement stimulates social involvement.
    Ans.: a   LG: 5   Page: 628   QT: C

117. What is the *best* way to cope with stress?
    a. positive self-talk
    b. problem-focused coping
    c. biofeedback
    d. multiple coping strategies
    Ans.: d   LG: 5   Page: 629   QT: C

118. Geraldine is attending a stress management program. At this program, she can expect to learn all but which of the following?
    a. how to appraise stressful events
    b. how to end stress
    c. how to develop skills for coping with stress
    d. how to handle stress
    Ans.: b   LG: 5   Page: 629   QT: A

119. Don is learning a system that incorporates exercises that can help him improve mental self-control and well-being, as well as enlightenment. Don is *most* likely learning
    a. attributions.
    b. self-efficacy.
    c. meditation.
    d. assertive behavior.
    Ans.: c   LG: 5   Page: 629   QT: A

120. Strategies of meditation usually take which of the following forms?
    a. cleansing the mind to have new experiences
    b. forgetting your stressors forever
    c. increased concentration
    d. both a and c
    Ans.: d   LG: 5   Page: 629   QT: C

121. A mantra is a phrase used to focus attention when you engage in an activity called
    a. biofeedback.
    b. behavioral medicine.
    c. positive self-illusion.
    d. transcendental meditation.
    Ans.: d   LG: 5   Page: 629   QT: F

122. In which way is meditation *most* similar to relaxation?
    a. physiological effects
    b. posture
    c. duration of session
    d. cognitive effects
    Ans.: a   LG: 5   Page: 629   QT: C

123. What technique are you using if you are trying to reduce muscle tension by monitoring instruments that are recording your muscle tension?
    a. cognitive restructuring
    b. transcendental meditation
    c. biofeedback
    d. psychoneuroimmunology
    Ans.: c   LG: 5   Page: 630   QT: C

124. With biofeedback, an individual can learn to
    a. develop active coping techniques.
    b. voluntarily control their physiological activities.
    c. restructure cognitions.
    d. use assertive coping techniques.
    Ans.: b   LG: 5   Page: 630   QT: F

125. If you had to write a research paper on biofeedback, which of the following would be the *most* appropriate title for your paper?
    a. The magic word can help you relax.
    b. You have more control over your body than you think.
    c. Don't be afraid to stand up for your legitimate rights.
    d. Monitor your successes rather than your failures.
    Ans.: b   LG: 5   Page: 630   QT: A

Learning Goal 6: Summarize how to promote health.

126. Aerobic exercise is defined as
    a. any form of physical activity.
    b. a lack of exercise.
    c. an inability to exercise.
    d. sustained exercise that stimulates heart and lung activity.
    Ans.: d   LG: 6   Page: 632   QT: F

127. Leslie wishes to improve her health and wants to participate in aerobic exercise. Which of the following activities would you *least* recommend for her?
    a. swimming
    b. biking
    c. jogging
    d. shuffleboard
    Ans.: d   LG: 6   Page: 632   QT: A

128. Aerobic exercises help with weight loss because
    a. most people stay with them once they start.
    b. they raise the body's metabolic rate.
    c. they raise the body's setpoint.
    d. they cause an aversion to food.
    Ans.: b   LG: 6   Page: 632   QT: F

129. Which of the following individuals would be *least* likely to suffer from heart disease?
    a. Fred, who is a longshoreman
    b. Barbara, who climbs poles for a utility company
    c. Ray, who is a college professor
    d. Emily, who is a doctor, but also rockclimbs
    Ans.: a   LG: 6   Page: 632   QT: C

130. Health experts recommend that adults engage in 30 minutes or more of physical activity each day in which they raise their heart rates to at least 60% of maximum heart rate. What percentage of Americans are currently doing this?
    a. 50%
    b. 75%
    c. none
    d. 20%
    Ans.: d   LG: 6   Page: 632   QT: C

131. Theresa finds time to get exercise nearly every day. She maintains a busy schedule, and her workouts vary, but she makes a point of participating in some form of physical activity as much as possible. Which of the following is *least* likely to be true about Theresa?
    a. Theresa has a high self-concept.
    b. Theresa has lower anxiety.
    c. Theresa is less likely to be affected by depression.
    d. Theresa is prone to injury.
    Ans.: d   LG: 6   Page: 632   QT: A

132. Your text discusses a study where nonexercisers were assigned to four exercise conditions. Which group(s) showed psychological as well as aerobic benefits?
    a. both the high-intensity and the moderate-intensity aerobic groups
    b. only the low-intensity nonaerobic group
    c. only the moderate-intensity aerobic group
    d. All but the control group showed psychological benefits.
    Ans.: c   LG: 6   Page: 633   QT: F

133. A friend of yours who is a nonexerciser asks you for advice regarding an exercise plan in order to help them feel better psychologically. Which of the following would you recommend?
    a. join a competitive swim club
    b. in order to reduce competitive stress, do sprints in the back yard each day
    c. start competitive mountain biking
    d. begin with brisk walks and gradually work up to short jogs
    Ans.: d   LG: 6   Page: 633   QT: C

134. Proper nutrition is an important element of all of the following health goals *except* for
    a. more energy.
    b. lower blood pressure.
    c. lower cancer risk.
    d. a crash diet.
    Ans.: d   LG: 6   Page: 635   QT: F

135. The *best* nutritional plan consists of a
    a. diet high in fibers.
    b. low fat and low cholesterol diet.
    c. well-balanced diet that includes all the nutrients we need.
    d. high vitamin and high mineral diet.
    Ans.: c   LG: 6   Page: 635   QT: C

136. Which of the following statements regarding nutrition and health is *not* true?
    a. Some of our confusion about which foods we should eat is because nutritional standards have changed over time.
    b. High fat diets have been linked with some forms of cancer.
    c. There is a higher incidence of breast, colon, and prostate cancer in the United States than in Japan.
    d. Watching television is linked to healthy eating habits.
    Ans.: d   LG: 6   Page: 635   QT: C

137. Smokers are positively reinforced because nicotine
    a. takes away the craving for more nicotine.
    b. blocks the release of acetylcholine.
    c. releases our inhibitions.
    d. increases energy and alertness.
    Ans.: d   LG: 6   Page: 635   QT: F

138. Smokers who want to quit often fail because nicotine provides all of the following *except*
    a. positive reinforcement.
    b. a calming or pain-reducing effect.
    c. negative reinforcement.
    d. punishment.
    Ans.: d   LG: 6   Page: 635   QT: C

139. When smokers ingest cigarette smoke, it provides relief from the craving for nicotine or aversive state. As such, the cigarette provides a
    a. positive reinforcement.
    b. negative reinforcement.
    c. punishment.
    d. neutral stimuli.
    Ans.: b   LG: 6   Page: 635   QT: C

140. Levon has smoked for years and would like to quit. Which of the following methods would you *least* recommend for him?
    a. Use a substitute source of nicotine such as a patch
    b. Learn more about social cues that are associated with smoking and work to avoid them or find a substitute
    c. Take the antidepressant Zyban
    d. Go "cold turkey"
    Ans.: c   LG: 6   Page: 636   QT: A

141. What do national surveys indicate about the U.S. population's knowledge about sexual issues?
    a. Adults are generally pretty well informed.
    b. Teenagers know more about sexual issues than adults.
    c. Both adults and adolescents are often uninformed or misinformed on sexual issues.
    d. Male adolescents are better informed than female adolescents.
    Ans.: c   LG: 6   Page: 636   QT: F

142. Your text points out that the United States has the dubious distinction of having the highest adolescent pregnancy rate in the industrialized world. The main reason for this situation appears to be the adolescents'
    a. lack of knowledge about effective methods of contraception and the importance of their use.
    b. inability to obtain contraceptives.
    c. lack of money to cover the expense associated with contraceptives.
    d. desire to become a parent.
    Ans.: a   LG: 6   Page: 637   QT: C

143. The National Center for Health Statistics (2001) found that sexually transmitted diseases affect _____ adults.
    a. one in every 10
    b. one in every 20
    c. one in every two
    d. one in every six
    Ans.: d   LG: 6   Page: 638   QT: F

144. Which of the following is *not* true about acquired immune deficiency syndrome?
    a. AIDS is considered to be an STD.
    b. AIDS is caused by the human immunodeficiency virus, which destroys the body's immune system.
    c. Because of more effective drug treatments and education, deaths from AIDS are on the decline in the United States.
    d. Because of awareness and education, AIDS is on the decline in sub-Saharan Africa.
    Ans.: d   LG: 6   Page: 638   QT: F

145. AIDS can be transmitted in which of the following ways?
    a. sexual contact
    b. sharing hypodermic needles
    c. direct contact of cuts or mucous membranes with blood and sexual fluids
    d. all of the above
    Ans.: d   LG: 6   Page: 638   QT: F

146. AIDS can be transmitted in all but which of the following ways?
    a. sexual contact
    b. hugging an individual who is infected
    c. sharing hypodermic needles
    d. direct contact of cuts or mucous membranes with blood and sexual fluids
    Ans.: b   LG: 6   Page: 638   QT: F

147. In the study that addressed lying and sexual behavior in college students, all but which of the following was revealed?
    a. Less than 5% of students indicated they had lied about their sexual past in order to have sex with a partner.
    b. Nearly a third of men and one-tenth of women indicated they had lied to a partner in order to have sex with them.
    c. Nearly 50% of men and 60% of women indicated that they had been lied to.
    d. About 20% of men indicated that they would lie about results from an AIDS blood test in order to have sex.
    Ans.: a   LG: 6   Page: 638   QT: F

148. Which of the following STDs are latex condoms *least* effective in helping to prevent?
    a. syphilis
    b. gonorrhea
    c. herpes
    d. AIDS
    Ans.: c   LG: 6   Page: 639   QT: F

149. One of the *best* predictors of getting an STD is
    a. having sex with multiple partners.
    b. obtaining medical examinations.
    c. knowing your partner's risk status.
    d. all of the above.
    Ans.: a   LG: 6   Page: 639   QT: C

150. It is estimated that without some form of contraception, _____ of women would become pregnant in their first year of being (heterosexually) sexually active.
   a. 10%
   b. 25%
   c. 50%
   d. 90%
   Ans.: d   LG: 6   Page: 638   QT: F

True/False Items

___ 151. Health psychology emphasizes lifestyle issues as an influence on wellness.
___ 152. In order to understand stress, we must consider biological, personality, cognitive, environmental, and sociocultural factors.
___ 153. A person with a Type B behavior pattern is more likely than a person with a Type A behavior pattern to have a heart attack.
___ 154. Burnout tends to occur after one traumatic job-related event.
___ 155. An example of a daily hassle would be planning a family vacation.
___ 156. People generally experience the approach/approach conflict as the most stressful.
___ 157. According to the general adaptation syndrome, vulnerability to disease is highest during the exhaustion stage.
___ 158. Males and females respond the same (fight or flight) when stressed.
___ 159. Whether or not two people perceive the same event as equally stressful will depend on their cognitive appraisal.
___ 160. Psychoneuroimmunology examines the connections among psychological factors, the nervous system, and the immune system.
___ 161. Emotion-focused coping is an easier strategy to use successfully than problem-focused coping.
___ 162. Research generally supports the claim that meditation decreases physiological arousal.
___ 163. The majority of adults in the United States exercise more than the recommended minimum for cardiovascular benefits.
___ 164. People who smoke less and have been smoking for a shorter period of time probably have a greater chance of quitting successfully by going "cold turkey."
___ 165. Before starting a sexual relationship, research indicates that both partners can rely on each other's honesty in determining the existence of an STD.

Answer Key for True/False Items

				158.	Ans.: F	LG: 3	Page: 614
151.	Ans.: T	LG: 1	Page: 603	159.	Ans.: T	LG: 3	Page: 615
152.	Ans.: T	LG: 1	Page: 603	160.	Ans.: T	LG: 4	Page: 616
153.	Ans.: F	LG: 2	Page: 605	161.	Ans.: F	LG: 5	Page: 621
154.	Ans.: F	LG: 2	Page: 609	162.	Ans.: T	LG: 5	Page: 630
155.	Ans.: F	LG: 2	Page: 607	163.	Ans.: F	LG: 6	Page: 632
156.	Ans.: F	LG: 2	Page: 608	164.	Ans.: T	LG: 6	Page: 636
157.	Ans.: F	LG: 3	Page: 613	165.	Ans.: F	LG: 6	Page: 638

Fill-in-the-Blank Items

166. A _____ psychologist would say that treatment of physical illness must include an understanding of the contributing psychological and social factors.
167. Circumstances or events that tax our coping ability are called _____.
168. The key component of the Type A behavior pattern that is linked with the risk for coronary disease is _____.
169. When confronted with a problem, a _____ personality maintains a sense of control rather than powerlessness.
170. A person who has to choose between "the lesser of two evils" is facing an _____ conflict.
171. Chronic overload and work-related stress may result in _____.
172. A major criticism of the life events model is that it does not account for _____ in coping.
173. The three stages of the _____ are alarm, resistance, and exhaustion.
174. A physiological response to a stressor that has evolutionary significance is the _____ response.
175. _____ emotional states are thought to be associated with healthy patterns of physiological functioning in both the cardiovascular system and the immune system.
176. Individuals with high _____ believe that they can produce positive outcomes when confronted with challenging circumstances.
177. The benefits of _____ support are tangible assistance, information, and emotional support.
178. Aerobic exercise has been shown to have positive effects on both physical and _____ health.
179. For most habitual smokers, quitting is difficult because of the various reinforcing properties of _____.
180. Recent statistics have shown an increase of AIDS in individuals who have _____ sex partners.

Answer Key for Fill-in-the-Blank Items

166.	Ans.: health	LG: 1	Page: 603
167.	Ans.: stressors	LG: 2	Page: 604
168.	Ans.: hostility	LG: 2	Page: 605
169.	Ans.: hardy	LG: 2	Page: 605
170.	Ans.: avoidance/avoidance	LG: 2	Page: 608
171.	Ans.: burnout	LG: 2	Page: 609
172.	Ans.: individual differences	LG: 2	Page: 607
173.	Ans.: general adaptation syndrome	LG: 3	Page: 612
174.	Ans.: fight-or-flight	LG: 3	Page: 614
175.	Ans.: Positive	LG: 4	Page: 619
176.	Ans.: self-efficacy	LG: 5	Page: 624
177.	Ans.: social	LG: 5	Page: 624
178.	Ans.: mental	LG: 6	Page: 632
179.	Ans.: nicotine	LG: 6	Page: 635
180.	Ans.: multiple	LG: 6	Page: 639

Matching Items

_____ 181. health psychology
_____ 182. self-efficacy
_____ 183. Type B behavior
_____ 184. hardiness
_____ 185. marginalization
_____ 186. resistance
_____ 187. psychoneuroimmunologist
_____ 188. tend or befriend
_____ 189. biofeedback
_____ 190. multiple sex partners

A. personality style that appears to buffer stress
B. voluntary control of physiological processes
C. associated with a lower risk for heart disease
D. female response
E. increases risk for STDs
F. acculturation associated with alienation
G. middle stage of general adaptation syndrome
H. focuses on the link between stress and the immune system
I. perceived control
J. interested in psychological factors and physiological factors

Answer Key for Matching Items

181.	Ans.: J	LG: 1	Page: 603	186.	Ans.: G	LG: 3	Page: 614
182.	Ans.: I	LG: 5	Page: 625	187.	Ans.: H	LG: 4	Page: 616
183.	Ans.: C	LG: 2	Page: 605	188.	Ans.: D	LG: 3	Page: 614
184.	Ans.: A	LG: 2	Page: 605	189.	Ans.: B	LG: 5	Page: 630
185.	Ans.: F	LG: 2	Page: 611	190.	Ans.: E	LG: 6	Page: 639

Essay Questions

191. Describe health psychology and behavioral medicine. (LG: 1)

Answer Guidelines: Health psychology emphasizes psychology's role in promoting and maintaining health and preventing and treating illness. Behavioral medicine is an interdisciplinary field that focuses on developing and integrating behavior and biomedical knowledge to promote health and reduce illness. Both are relatively new fields.

192. Briefly summarize the characteristics of the Type A behavior pattern, and discuss its relationship to coronary disease. (LG: 2)

Answer Guidelines: Possible options include mentioning that the Type A individual is likely to be competitive, hard-driven, impatient, and hostile. Earlier research showed that the Type A behavior pattern was associated with higher risk for coronary disease. More recent research has shown that it is the component of hostility that is related to the risk of coronary disease.

193. Briefly summarize the types of conflict that may lead to stress. Which of these is the least stressful, and which of these is the most stressful? (LG: 2)

Answer Guidelines: Possible options include mentioning approach/approach (choosing between two positive options; least stressful), approach/avoidance (reacting to one stimulus that involves both positive and negative aspects; highly stressful), and avoidance/avoidance conflict (choosing the lesser of two evils).

194. Using an example of your choice, discuss the stages of the general adaptation syndrome as proposed by Seyle. What criticisms have been raised about this model of coping with stress? (LG: 3)

Answer Guidelines: Possible options include mentioning the alarm stage (shock stage; rather short stage; lowered resistance), the resistance stage (all-out effort to combat stress; increased immune system activity), and the exhaustion stage (if stress persists, increased vulnerability to disease and exhaustion). Critics charge that the stress response is not merely physical and not as uniform across individuals as proposed by Seyle.

195. Describe the aim of the field of psychoneuroimmunology. Explain how acute stress can have an effect on immune system functioning as related to quality of life and behavioral factors. (LG: 4)

Answer Guidelines: Answers should connect psychoneuroimmunology with the study of psychological factors, the nervous system, and the immune system. Research has shown that a good quality of life is associated with a healthier immune system. Emotional stress has been linked to cardiovascular disease. People under emotional stress also are more likely to manifest unhealthy behaviors such as smoking, poor diet, and not exercising.

196. Optimism and a positive outlook on life have been shown to be related to successful coping in stressful situations. Briefly describe the benefits of positive self-talk and positive self-illusions in coping with stressful situations. (LG: 5)

Answer Guidelines: Possible options include mentioning that positive self-talk keeps the focus on successes rather than failures; it improves confidence and reinforces the feeling of being in control of the stressful situation. Thus, it is important to monitor one's self-talk for negative thinking. If needed, negative thoughts might need to be restructured, or changed, into positive ones. Research has shown that people who maintain a moderate level of self-illusion are happier people. They also cope with stress more effectively because they have confidence and a positive outlook.

197. Briefly discuss the relationship between self-efficacy and health. Then summarize the specific steps recommended in your text for improving someone's self-efficacy. (LG: 5)

Answer Guidelines: Possible options include mentioning that self-efficacy describes a person's belief that he/she can master a situation and produce positive outcomes. The stronger this belief, the better able the person is to cope with stress and challenging circumstances. Steps for improving self-efficacy: (1) choose something you expect to be able to do; (2) focus on the present project, not past failures; (3) keep good records; (4) focus on your successes; and (5) make a list of situations and rank them by the difficulty you expect to have with them, then start with an easier task and gradually work your way up to the more difficult tasks.

198. List the benefits of social support. Summarize the results of studies that have found a correlation between social support and health. (LG: 5)

Answer Guidelines: Possible options include mentioning that social support can provide tangible assistance, information, and emotional support. Research has shown that social support helps individuals cope with stress and, thus, has positive effects on people's health. Specifically, social support has been linked to depression, prognosis of cancer, mental illness, suicide, life span, and even the common cold.

199. Explain the connection between aerobic exercise and physical and mental wellness. In your answer, include optimal levels of exercise and health benefits. (LG: 6)

Answer Guidelines: Both moderate and intense exercise produce important physiological and psychological gains. Experts claim that 30 minutes of moderate exercise per day will yield significant improvements. One study found that psychological benefits were higher in moderate exercise conditions than in intense exercise conditions.

200. Discuss at least three strategies for protecting oneself against AIDS and other sexually transmitted diseases. (LG: 6)

Answer Guidelines: Possible options include mentioning that individuals who are considering a sexual relationship with someone should (1) know their own and their partner's risk status; (2) obtain medical exams for both partners; (3) have protected, not unprotected sex; and (4) not have sex with multiple partners.

Chapter 16: Social Psychology

Learning Goals

1. Describe how people think about the social world.
2. Identify how people are influenced in social settings.
3. Discuss intergroup relations.
4. Explain how aggression and altruism characterize social interaction.
5. Understand the nature of relationships.

Multiple-Choice Items

Learning Goal 1: Describe how people think about the social world.

1. The study of how people think about, influence, and relate to other people is called
   a. personality.
   b. social psychology.
   c. biopsychology.
   d. motivation theory.
   Ans.: b   LG: 1   Page: 646   QT: F

2. The difference between sociology and social psychology is that
   a. sociology focuses more on the individual than social psychology does.
   b. sociology is not a scientific discipline.
   c. social psychology places more emphasis on the individual than sociology does.
   d. social psychology predicts all human behavior.
   Ans.: c   LG: 1   Page: 646   QT: C

3. Bill is observing a child to see how her play patterns change relevant to the number of playmates she is interacting with. Bill is *most* likely a
   a. psychiatrist.
   b. sociologist.
   c. social psychologist.
   d. behavioral therapist.
   Ans.: c   LG: 1   Page: 646   QT: A

4. Which of the following is true regarding attribution theory?
   a. Attribution theorists have discovered a causational relationship between all attitudes and behaviors.
   b. Attributions are thoughts about why people behave the way they do.
   c. Attributions are most often connected to unconscious desires.
   d. Attribution theory is only relevant to social psychology.
   Ans.: b   LG: 1   Page: 647   QT: C

5. Bethany has been pretty grumpy all day although she is not quite sure why. When her friends ask, she says she probably didn't get enough sleep last night. Bethany's attempt to find an underlying cause for her bad mood is in keeping with
   a. cognitive dissonance theory.
   b. attribution theory.
   c. conformity theory.
   d. diffusion of responsibility.
   Ans.: b   LG: 1   Page: 647   QT: A

6. People will often try to relate the behavior of others to external or internal causes. This process is known as
   a. attribution.
   b. social comparison.
   c. dissonance reduction.
   d. impression management.
   Ans.: a   LG: 1   Page: 647   QT: F

7. If you decide that your roommate broke your psychology CD because she is a nasty person, you are making a(n)
   a. implicit impression.
   b. internal attribution.
   c. external attribution.
   d. social comparison.
   Ans.: b   LG: 1   Page: 647   QT: C

8. Which of the following *most* clearly illustrates an internal attribution?
   a. John believes his sister plays the piano to make a good impression on others.
   b. Larry believes that his father is hostile because of the difficulties at work.
   c. Maria believes Rob gossips about others because of a mean and spiteful streak.
   d. Diane believes her son lies to her to avoid possible punishment.
   Ans.: c   LG: 1   Page: 647   QT: C

9. The three dimensions of causality involved in making attributions include all of the following *except*
   a. internal/external causes.
   b. stable/unstable causes.
   c. conscious/unconscious causes.
   d. controllable/uncontrollable causes.
   Ans.: c   LG: 1   Page: 647   QT: F

10. Robin says, "I got a good grade on my last physics test because I got lucky; most of the questions came from the material I studied." Robin is making a(n)
    a. internal/stable/controllable attribution.
    b. external/unstable/uncontrollable attribution.
    c. internal/unstable/controllable attribution.
    d. external/stable/uncontrollable attribution.
    Ans.: b   LG: 1   Page: 647   QT: C

11. The teacher just returned a math test. Whose self-esteem will be affected *most* positively?
    a. Lateef's—he attributes his low grade to the fact that he barely studied for the test.
    b. Tamara's—she attributes her high grade to the fact that the test was easy.
    c. Chris's—he attributes his high grade to the fact that he studied hard for the test.
    d. Helen's—she attributes her low grade to the fact that she is just no good in math.
    Ans.: c   LG: 1   Page: 648   QT: C

12. The fundamental attribution error involves
    a. blaming others for our problems.
    b. blaming ourselves for our problems.
    c. overestimating the importance of internal traits and underestimating the importance of external situations.
    d. underestimating the importance of internal traits and overestimating the importance of external situations.
    Ans.: c   LG: 1   Page: 648   QT: F

13. We tend to attribute our own behavior to
    a. circumstances.
    b. fate.
    c. external causes.
    d. internal causes.
    Ans.: c   LG: 1   Page: 648   QT: C

14. In general, we tend to attribute the behavior of others to
    a. circumstances.
    b. fate.
    c. external causes.
    d. internal causes.
    Ans.: d   LG: 1   Page: 648   QT: F

15. In the actor/observer relationship, actors tend to attribute their own behavior to _____ and observers attribute an actor's behavior to _____.
    a. internal causes, conditioning
    b. external causes, internal causes
    c. internal causes, external causes
    d. external causes, external causes
    Ans.: b   LG: 1   Page: 648   QT: C

16. You watch as another student stumbles and drops their books in the hall. Given the fundamental attribution error, how would you explain the student's behavior?
    a. She must have tripped over something.
    b. She is a clumsy person.
    c. She couldn't help it; there were too many books to carry.
    d. She was trying to get out of someone else's way.
    Ans.: b   LG: 1   Page: 648   QT: A

17. Your boss criticizes you because you dropped a plastic bottle of mustard. The mustard did not spill, and there was no mess to clean up, but the boss got very upset. Given the fundamental attribution error, how would you explain your boss's behavior?
    a. The boss is in a stressful position.
    b. The boss is a bad person.
    c. The boss must be having a bad day.
    d. The boss must be under a great deal of pressure.
    Ans.: c   LG: 1   Page: 648   QT: A

18. Jordan attributes his successes to internal factors and his failures to external factors. Jordan is exhibiting which bias?
    a. cultural bias
    b. fundamental attribution bias
    c. irrational bias
    d. self-serving bias
    Ans.: d   LG: 1   Page: 649   QT: F

19. Cindy recently played in a softball game in which she misplayed a ground ball for an error. Later in the same game, she made a great catch on a very difficult play. According to the self-serving bias, she would attribute her error to _____ and her good catch to _____.
    a. bad fielding skills, luck
    b. bad fielding skills, good fielding skills
    c. a bad bounce, luck
    d. a bad bounce, good fielding skills
    Ans.: d   LG: 1   Page: 649   QT: A

20. A good phrase to describe the primacy effect would be
    a. "first come, first serve."
    b. "the first impression is the lasting impression."
    c. "he who gets there first, with the most, wins."
    d. "who's on first?"
    Ans.: b   LG: 1   Page: 649   QT: F

21. The enduring quality of initial impressions is termed
    a. social comparison.
    b. a prototype.
    c. the primacy effect.
    d. the recency effect.
    Ans.: c   LG: 1   Page: 649   QT: F

22. Suppose you are interviewing for a job. Based on what you know about the primacy effect, you should
    a. present yourself honestly so that the interviewer does not expect too much from you.
    b. make sure that the interviewer first notices your positive traits.
    c. present your positive and negative qualities at the same time.
    d. use the foot-in-the-door technique.
    Ans.: b   LG: 1   Page: 649   QT: A

23. In developing impressions of others, what do unification and integration have in common?
    a. They are methods of cognitively organizing information about others.
    b. They are methods of explaining other people's behavior.
    c. They are methods of making ourselves look good in front of others.
    d. They are methods of persuading others to comply with our request.
    Ans.: a   LG: 1   Page: 650   QT: C

24. What is the relationship between unification and integration?
    a. Unification follows integration.
    b. Unification is the opposite of integration.
    c. Unification precedes integration.
    d. Unification takes longer than integration.
    Ans.: c   LG: 1   Page: 650   QT: C

25. Our everyday notion of the manner in which personality traits fit together in a person is known as
    a. heuristic personality theory.
    b. implicit personality theory.
    c. algorithmic personality theory.
    d. dissonance personality theory.
    Ans.: b   LG: 1   Page: 650   QT: F

26. Dwayne has developed the idea that all extraverted people are optimistic, based upon a group of friends that he has. This would be an example of
    a. the implicit personality theory.
    b. the fundamental attribution error.
    c. impression management.
    d. cognitive dissonance.
    Ans.: a   LG: 1   Page: 650   QT: A

27. "Am I as popular as Cathy?" This question is an example of gaining self-knowledge through the process of
    a. peer-review.
    b. peripheral attribute.
    c. wishful thinking.
    d. social comparison.
    Ans.: d   LG: 1   Page: 650   QT: C

28. By spending a great amount of time around her peers, an adolescent may be gaining self-knowledge through
    a. social primacy.
    b. social recency.
    c. social comparison.
    d. group schemata.
    Ans.: c   LG: 1   Page: 650   QT: F

29. Michael was surprised to learn that one of his favorite teachers thought he was aggressive. According to social comparison theory, if Michael begins to wonder about this quality within himself, he will compare himself to
    a. introverted students.
    b. people in competitive sports.
    c. members of the opposite gender.
    d. other students taught by this teacher.
    Ans.: d   LG: 1   Page: 650   QT: A

30. Alphonzo usually dresses very casually and uses a lot of colloquialisms in his speech. However, when he went to a job interview, Alphonzo wore a brand new, tailored suit and used his best grammar. Alphonzo's behavior is *best* described as
    a. impression management.
    b. social conformity.
    c. social comparison.
    d. obedience training.
    Ans.: a   LG: 1   Page: 651   QT: C

31. Another name for impression management is
    a. attribution formation.
    b. self-perception.
    c. self-presentation.
    d. social competence.
    Ans.: c   LG: 1   Page: 651   QT: F

32. Nonverbal cues, behavioral matching, conforming to situational norms, and showing appreciation of others are
    a. attribution patterns.
    b. impression management strategies.
    c. compliance techniques.
    d. behavior management strategies.
    Ans.: b   LG: 1   Page: 651   QT: F

33. When Laura was trying to show one of her coworkers how to prepare the quarterly office report, she noticed that her coworker was getting defensive. Laura realized that she might have been sounding too critical of the coworker's report. She began to phrase her comments more in terms of suggestions, rather than criticisms. Laura's behavior can *best* be described as
    a. waffling.
    b. self-monitoring.
    c. indecisiveness.
    d. attribution bias.
    Ans.: b   LG: 1   Page: 652   QT: C

34. Self-monitoring helps *least* with
    a. awareness of one's impression on others.
    b. adjusting one's behavior according to the situation.
    c. presenting oneself in the appropriate manner.
    d. others' attitudes about issues and people.
    Ans.: d   LG: 1   Page: 651   QT: C

35. Beliefs or opinions about people, objects, and ideas describe a person's
    a. attitudes.
    b. motivation.
    c. predispositions.
    d. biases.
    Ans.: a   LG: 1   Page: 653   QT: F

36. Social psychologists are interested in which of the following?
    a. how attitudes can be changed
    b. how attitudes affect behavior
    c. how behavior affects attitude
    d. all of the above
    Ans.: d   LG: 1   Page: 653   QT:

37. Which of the following has the *weakest* influence on attitudes leading to behaviors?
    a. When the person's attitudes are strong
    b. When the person rehearses and practices attitudes and behaviors
    c. When the attitudes are relevant to the behavior
    d. When the person is not aware of their attitudes
    Ans.: d   LG: 1   Page: 653   QT: C

38. People's attitudes do not always predict their behavior. Which of the following statements about the relationship between attitudes and behavior is *not* correct?
    a. Strong attitudes are better predictors of behavior.
    b. We can predict behavior better when the person shows a strong awareness of his/her attitudes.
    c. General attitudes are the best predictors of behavior.
    d. When attitudes are relevant to the behavior, predicting behavior from attitudes is more likely.
    Ans.: c   LG: 1   Page: 653   QT: F

39. Cognitive dissonance occurs when there are inconsistencies between
    a. the way we think and the way we feel.
    b. sensations and perceptions.
    c. our attitudes and our behavior.
    d. our self-concept and our concept of others.
    Ans.: c   LG: 1   Page: 653   QT: C

40. Cognitive dissonance theory states that individuals
    a. change attitudes in order to be more popular.
    b. change behavior in order to be more popular.
    c. do not perceive a discrepancy between attitudes and behavior.
    d. try to make attitudes conform to behavior.
    Ans.: d   LG: 1   Page: 653   QT: C

41. Which of the following is true of individuals experiencing cognitive dissonance?
    a. They show an inability to make up their mind.
    b. They have lost their sense of self and the ability to make decisions.
    c. They are preoccupied with how they are perceived by others.
    d. They are experiencing a conflict between their attitudes and behavior.
    Ans.: d   LG: 1   Page: 653   QT: C

42. "Drinking may be harmful to my health, but I'll die having a good time." This statement illustrates an attempt to reduce
    a. the exposure effect.
    b. cognitive dissonance.
    c. a classical dilemma.
    d. attitude consistency.
    Ans.: b   LG: 1   Page: 654   QT: C

43. According to the theory of cognitive dissonance, if I wanted to change a person's attitude, I should
    a. present a high-fear persuasive speech.
    b. present a medium-fear persuasive speech.
    c. tell him about effort justification.
    d. get him to change his behavior first.
    Ans.: d   LG: 1   Page: 654   QT: A

44. Which of the following is *not* an effective way to avoid dissonance reduction?
    a. Know your dissonance-reducing tendencies.
    b. Develop enough competencies to be able to tolerate your own mistakes without having to rationalize them away.
    c. Realize that behaving in stupid ways probably means that you are a stupid person.
    d. Know your defensive tendencies.
    Ans.: c   LG: 1   Page: 655   QT: C

45. According to self-perception theory, information about our attitudes comes primarily from
    a. authority figures.
    b. our own behaviors.
    c. our belief systems.
    d. our cognitive dissonance.
    Ans.: b   LG: 1   Page: 655   QT: F

46. We infer our attitudes from our behavior in the same way that we infer other people's attitudes from their behavior. This statement *best* describes
    a. cognitive dissonance theory.
    b. self-perception theory.
    c. social learning theory.
    d. attribution theory.
    Ans.: b   LG: 1   Page: 655   QT: F

47. Juanita returned home after being away for several years. When she saw her father, whom she thought she disliked, she hugged him and cried. Based on her crying when she saw him, she determined that she must like him more than she thought. This is *most* consistent with which theory of attitudes?
    a. reactance theory
    b. social learning theory
    c. self-perception theory
    d. balance theory
    Ans.: c   LG: 1   Page: 655   QT: C

48. Which theory of attitude development is reflected in the following statement? "I was very aggressive with those people. They are very undesirable types to have in our neighborhood."
    a. social humanistic theory
    b. self-perception theory
    c. introspection theory
    d. self-assessment theory
    Ans.: b   LG: 1   Page: 655   QT: C

49. Advertisers use negative appeals to play to the audience's _____ and positive appeals to engage the audience's _____.
    a. attention, emotions
    b. emotions, logic
    c. logic, attention
    d. logic, emotions
    Ans.: b   LG: 1   Page: 656   QT: C

50. With the elaboration likelihood model, the _____ route engages someone thoughtfully, while the _____ route involves such nonmessage factors, such as the source's credibility, attractiveness, or emotional appeal.
    a. primary, secondary
    b. peripheral, central
    c. central, secondary
    d. central, peripheral
    Ans.: d   LG: 1   Page: 657   QT: C

51. Which of the following factors would *not* be a part of the peripheral route of the elaboration likelihood model?
    a. the message of the source
    b. the source's credibility
    c. the source's attractiveness
    d. an emotional appeal
    Ans.: a   LG: 1   Page: 657   QT: F

52. When people pay close attention to the facts, the _____ is (are) the most persuasive, but when subjects are not paying full attention, such as during a television commercial, the _____ may work better.
    a. message of the source, attractiveness of the source
    b. emotional factors, attractiveness of the source
    c. source's credibility, emotional factors
    d. emotional factors, credibility of the source
    Ans.: a   LG: 1   Page: 657   QT: C

53. When we speak of the change that television has made in our response to the messages of political leaders, we are referring to television as a
    a. target.
    b. medium.
    c. communicator.
    d. route.
    Ans.: b   LG: 1   Page: 657   QT: C

54. If attitudes are _____, attitude change is more likely. If attitudes are _____, the communicator will have more difficulty changing them.
    a. negative, strong
    b. strong, negative
    c. neutral, strong
    d. weak, strong
    Ans.: d   LG: 1   Page: 657   QT: C

Learning Goal 2: Identify how people are influenced in social settings.

55. A change in a person's behavior to coincide more closely with a group standard is called
    a. conformity.
    b. compliance.
    c. obedience.
    d. attitude adjustment.
    Ans.: a   LG: 2   Page: 658   QT: F

56. Solomon Asch asked college students to make judgments about the lengths of lines. Confederates purposely made errors, and the subjects followed by giving incorrect responses. This experiment analyzed the phenomenon of
    a. conformity.
    b. compliance.
    c. attribution.
    d. obedience.
    Ans.: a   LG: 2   Page: 659   QT: F

57. What is the relationship between self-esteem and conformity?
    a. High self-esteem equals high conformity.
    b. No self-esteem leads to resistance rather than conformity.
    c. Self-esteem is necessary for conformity.
    d. Low self-esteem usually produces higher conformity.
    Ans.: d   LG: 2   Page: 660   QT: C

58. When Charles arrived at school, he discovered that the class president had declared the day to be "sockless day." As he scanned his class, Charles noticed that no one was wearing socks, and, even though he felt stupid, he proceeded to remove his socks. Charles's behavior is an example of
    a. deindividuation.
    b. conformity.
    c. disinhibition.
    d. counter-conditioning.
    Ans.: b   LG: 2   Page: 658   QT: C

59. Conformity is more likely to occur when prior commitment has
    a. been strongly made.
    b. not been made.
    c. been made weakly but privately.
    d. been announced publicly.
    Ans.: b   LG: 2   Page: 660   QT: F

60. Research shows that people tend to conform to group norms
    a. when the group is from an individualistic society.
    b. when the group members are experts.
    c. when the group members are diverse.
    d. when the individual has high self-esteem.
    Ans.: b   LG: 2   Page: 660   QT: F

61. When others have an influence on us that makes us want to conform to seek their approval, it is called
    a. normative social influence.
    b. informational social influence.
    c. cognitive dissonance.
    d. variable social influence.
    Ans.: a   LG: 2   Page: 659   QT: F

62. Joyce has the potential to be an honor student but frustrates her teachers because of her actions. Rather than work to succeed, she tends to "dummy down" to act more like the students that she hangs out with. She has at times answered questions incorrectly in class on purpose to be more like her friends. Which of the following perspectives would explain this?
    a. informational social influence
    b. cognitive social influence
    c. defense mechanisms
    d. normative social influence
    Ans.: d   LG: 2   Page: 659   QT: A

63. When we conform to a group because we want to be correct, it is called
    a. informational social influence.
    b. cognitive social influence.
    c. a defense mechanism.
    d. normative social influence.
    Ans.: a   LG: 2   Page: 659   QT: F

64. Emily has decided to purchase a new computer. She knows a little about computers but decides to ask some of the members of the computer club for suggestions. Contrary to what she has read in computer magazines, they advise her to purchase the new ACME 43 Gazillion Megabyte Turbo Annihilator. She decides to follow their advice. Emily is conforming because of
    a. cognitive social influence.
    b. defense mechanisms.
    c. normative social influence.
    d. informational social influence.
    Ans.: c   LG: 2   Page: 659   QT: A

65. Which of the following factors would *not* cause a subject to conform to a group?
    a. unanimity of the group
    b. subject having a high level of prior commitment
    c. group members' characteristics
    d. cultural values
    Ans.: b   LG: 2   Page: 660   QT: C

66. A behavior by an individual that complies with the explicit demands of an individual in authority is called
   a. conformity.
   b. obedience.
   c. rationalization.
   d. subliminal manifestation.
   Ans.: b   LG: 2   Page: 660   QT: F

67. In Milgram's classic study, how many "teachers" delivered the XXX 450-volt shock to the "learners"?
   a. none of them
   b. one-third of them
   c. two-thirds of them
   d. all of them
   Ans.: c   LG: 2   Page: 661   QT: F

68. In Milgram's classic study, the "teacher" was
   a. a confederate.
   b. shocked by the "learner."
   c. the subject.
   d. afraid of the "learner."
   Ans.: c   LG: 2   Page: 660   QT: F

69. Which of the following was the *most* serious criticism of Milgram's classic study on obedience?
   a. Subjects were paid too little for their participation.
   b. The experimenters used unethical deception of the subjects.
   c. The experimenters used unethical force to get the subjects to comply.
   d. The study was a waste of time because it produced no useful results.
   Ans.: b   LG: 2   Page: 662   QT: C

70. Milgram's study demonstrated that people obey when they are
   a. under great pressure to do so.
   b. unsure of themselves.
   c. directed by an authority figure.
   d. in stressful situations.
   Ans.: c   LG: 2   Page: 661   QT: C

71. All members of your group are required to wear a blazer when traveling. This rule *best* exemplifies
   a. laws.
   b. altruism.
   c. a norm.
   d. roles.
   Ans.: c   LG: 2   Page: 663   QT: C

72. Rules that apply to all members of a group are called
   a. norms.
   b. roles.
   c. stereotypes.
   d. laws.
   Ans.: a   LG: 2   Page: 663   QT: F

73. Todd is expected to make sure that everyone in his company division has turned in his or her time card by Thursday at noon. Todd's responsibility *best* illustrates
    a. the risky shift.
    b. a stereotype.
    c. a role.
    d. contingency leadership.
    Ans.: c   LG: 2   Page: 663   QT: C

74. When an individual's performance improves because of the presence of others, it is a result of
    a. social facilitation.
    b. increased arousal.
    c. social loafing.
    d. both a and b.
    Ans.: d   LG: 2   Page: 663   QT: F

75. Mike is a good piano player whose performance seems to improve as the crowd watching him gets larger. The *best* explanation for this pattern is
    a. the bystander effect.
    b. deindividuation.
    c. social facilitation.
    d. egoism.
    Ans.: c   LG: 2   Page: 663   QT: C

76. The college instructor found that class projects were of poorer quality when students worked in groups compared to when each student did an individual project. This difference can be explained by the phenomenon of
    a. groupthink.
    b. social loafing.
    c. the sleeper effect.
    d. polarization.
    Ans.: b   LG: 2   Page: 663   QT: C

77. Adam has the habit of giving assignments to his entire production crew, but lately he has been unhappy about their work output. Given the effect of social loafing, what might be Adam's *best* strategy for increasing the crew's work output?
    a. giving individual assignments to each worker
    b. doing some of the work himself
    c. reporting the crew to the foreman
    d. docking the crew members' pay for incomplete work
    Ans.: a   LG: 2   Page: 663   QT: A

78. Deindividuation refers to
    a. a schizophrenic personality.
    b. a suppression of selfish needs for the good of society.
    c. feelings of anonymity that result from immersion in a crowd.
    d. disobedience of one's own rules of conduct.
    Ans.: c   LG: 2   Page: 664   QT: F

79. June is a very quiet individual, but she recently discovered a different side of herself. She was at the Mardi Gras and found herself swept up in the festivities, doing the things that the other party revelers were doing. These were not behaviors that she would have ever considered doing on her own. Social psychologists would *most* likely attribute June's behavior to
    a. groupthink.
    b. social loafing.
    c. deindividuation.
    d. the id coming out.
    Ans.: c   LG: 2   Page: 664   QT: A

80. When individuals make decisions on their own, their decisions tend to be more conservative than the decision they will agree to in a group. The tendency for a group's decision to be more daring is called
    a. deindividuation.
    b. emergent boldness.
    c. disinhibition.
    d. the risky shift.
    Ans.: d   LG: 2   Page: 664   QT: F

81. Lynn feels that her company should hire a certain job candidate. At the company meeting, she starts to feel even more strongly about her position. This is *most* likely the result of
    a. groupthink.
    b. the group polarization effect.
    c. a majority influence.
    d. the risky shift.
    Ans.: b   LG: 2   Page: 664   QT: C

82. Katie, who is moderately liberal, attends a very liberal college. After four years at this college, Katie is likely to
    a. become more politically conservative as a result of the boomerang effect.
    b. hold moderately liberal values as a result of social learning.
    c. become more liberal as a result of group polarization.
    d. become indifferent to social causes as a result of diffusion of responsibility.
    Ans.: c   LG: 2   Page: 664   QT: C

83. What process tends to maintain harmony and unanimity during group decision making while suffocating differences of opinions?
    a. deindividuation
    b. pluralism
    c. social facilitation
    d. groupthink
    Ans.: d   LG: 2   Page: 665   QT: F

84. Which of the following is *not* a symptom of groupthink?
    a. overestimation of the power of the group
    b. closed-mindedness
    c. pressures toward uniformity
    d. critical thinking
    Ans.: d   LG: 2   Page: 665   QT: F

85. If you were leading a group discussion for the purpose of making an important decision, how could you *most* effectively avoid groupthink?
    a. encourage dissenting opinions
    b. vote on all decisions
    c. have a charismatic leader
    d. maintain the social harmony of the group
    Ans.: a   LG: 2   Page: 666   QT: A

86. Which theory is reflected in the following statement? "Abraham Lincoln was a great president because he was a natural-born leader who effectively rose to meet stressful and complicated situations."
    a. situational view
    b. contingency model
    c. great-person theory
    d. natural-leader theory
    Ans.: c   LG: 2   Page: 667   QT: C

87. If you believe in the great-person theory, then you believe that leadership develops through the influence of
    a. developmental abilities.
    b. environmental factors.
    c. training and education.
    d. inborn personality traits.
    Ans.: d   LG: 2   Page: 667   QT: C

88. Which of the following *best* describes a leader according to the great-person theory of leadership?
    a. having great strength in disastrous situations
    b. gains power from adoration
    c. was born with leadership abilities
    d. has earned the position of leadership
    Ans.: c   LG: 2   Page: 667   QT: C

89. According to the contingency theory of leadership, a task-oriented leader will be more effective than a relationship-oriented leader if the
    a. leader is in charge of earthquake disaster relief.
    b. production crew is barely above their daily quota.
    c. country is running at a moderately effective level.
    d. company has recovered from a hostile takeover.
    Ans.: a   LG: 2   Page: 667   QT: C

90. No one realized what a good leader Oman was until he formed a group to combat a problem with crime in his neighborhood. Oman's leadership role *best* supports
    a. the theory of social facilitation.
    b. the contingency model of leadership.
    c. superordinate goals.
    d. group polarization.
    Ans.: b   LG: 2   Page: 667   QT: C

91. In a group decision-making situation, a minority would *most* effectively sway the opinion of the majority by using which strategy?
    a. use informational pressure
    b. use normative influence
    c. demand their opinion be followed
    d. sway the group leader through ingratiation
    Ans.: a   LG: 2   Page: 666   QT: A

Learning Goal 3: Discuss intergroup relations.

92. Social identity theory states that
    a. when individuals are assigned to a group, they invariably think of the group as an in-group for them.
    b. individuals form groups based upon what they want their social identity to be.
    c. we join groups in order to get a sense of belonging on the way to self-actualization.
    d. we join groups because they provide evolutionary advantages for us.
    Ans.: a   LG: 3   Page: 669   QT: F

93. Which of the following is *not* true regarding social identity and between group relations?
    a. Our group is the "in-group," and the other groups are therefore "out-groups."
    b. We focus more on differences between groups than similarities.
    c. We most often remain objective about the strengths and weaknesses of both groups.
    d. In order to promote our own social identity, we tend to promote positive things about our group and negative things about other groups.
    Ans.: c   LG: 3   Page: 669   QT: C

94. When assigned to a group, people automatically tend to think more highly of *their* group. Which of the following *best* explains this phenomenon?
    a. They engage in groupthink.
    b. They experience deindividuation.
    c. They want a positive self-image.
    d. They adhere to the contingency model.
    Ans.: c   LG: 3   Page: 669   QT: C

95. Conflicts in the Middle East have existed for centuries. Often, one group feels that its culture is normal and that its members behave naturally while the opposing culture is abnormal and its members behave unnaturally. This type of conflict illustrates
    a. assimilation.
    b. culture shock.
    c. ethnocentrism.
    d. pluralism.
    Ans.: c   LG: 3   Page: 669   QT: C

96. Juan and Diane are in a friendly discussion over which of their favorite teams will do better in the Soccer World Cup. Each is certain that their national style of play is superior to the others. Both are third-generation Americans, but each has maintained a close connection to their ethnic heritage. Juan is rooting for Brazil, and Diane is supporting the Italian effort. Which of the following terms would explain this?
    a. assimilation
    b. cultural blending
    c. multicultural awareness
    d. ethnocentrism
    Ans.: d   LG: 3   Page: 669   QT: A

97. A negative attitude involving inappropriate generalizations about a group of people is called
    a. ethnocentrism.
    b. stereotyping.
    c. deindividuation.
    d. prejudice.
    Ans.: d   LG: 3   Page: 670   QT: F

98. Which of the following is *not* true regarding prejudice?
    a. outside of the United States, prejudice rarely exists.
    b. individuals with an authoritarian personality are more likely to be prejudiced.
    c. feelings of hostility between groups can last for generations.
    d. discrimination is often associated with prejudice.
    Ans.: a   LG: 3   Page: 671   QT: C

99. Which of the following has *not* been found to contribute to prejudice?
    a. competition between groups over scarce resources
    b. high self-esteem
    c. cognitive processes
    d. cultural learning
    Ans.: b   LG: 3   Page: 671   QT: C

100. A social schema that incorporates characteristics supposedly shared by almost all members of a group is called
    a. a stereotype.
    b. racism.
    c. obedience.
    d. a self-fulfilling prophecy.
    Ans.: a   LG: 3   Page: 672   QT: F

101. The fifth-grade teacher was surprised when her Japanese-American student, Hiroko, performed poorly in math. The teacher's reaction was due to
    a. polarization.
    b. stereotyping.
    c. groupthink.
    d. deindividuation.
    Ans.: b   LG: 3   Page: 672   QT: C

102. On the first day of psychology class, Alicia is told to choose a partner for her research assignment. She does not know anyone in the class but has heard that Latrell is a member of the school chess club. She immediately approaches him because she needs a high grade in the course. Alicia is demonstrating
   a. discrimination.
   b. conformity.
   c. compliance.
   d. stereotyping.
   Ans.: d   LG: 3   Page: 672   QT: A

103. In order to improve interactions among students from different ethnic backgrounds, a teacher would be *best* advised to use which of the following?
   a. a reward structure based on race
   b. competition among students
   c. group polarization
   d. the jigsaw classroom
   Ans.: d   LG: 3   Page: 674   QT: A

104. Why does intimate contact tend to facilitate interethnic relations?
   a. It allows people to discover their similarities.
   b. It allows people to confirm their stereotypes.
   c. It encourages people to re-categorize others.
   d. It reinforces ethnic and cultural differences.
   Ans.: a   LG: 3   Page: 675   QT: C

Learning Goal 4: Explain how aggression and altruism characterize social interaction.

105. From an ethological perspective, aggression would be
   a. linked to survival of a species.
   b. conditioned.
   c. learned by observation.
   d. driven by the ego.
   Ans.: a   LG: 4   Page: 676   QT: C

106. Which of the following is *not* true regarding human aggression?
   a. Freud viewed aggression as biologically based.
   b. Aggression is a result of primarily environmental factors.
   c. Alcohol is linked to violence and aggression.
   d. There appears to be a genetic link to aggression.
   Ans.: b   LG: 4   Page: 676   QT: C

107. Which type of research evidence suggests a genetic basis for aggression?
   a. Identical twins tend to have more similar aggressive tendencies than fraternal twins.
   b. Children tend to behave aggressively after they have watched aggressive models.
   c. Some cultures are more aggressive than others.
   d. Milgram's study showed that people might harm others without provocation.
   Ans.: a   LG: 4   Page: 676   QT: C

108. What research evidence suggests that brain functioning plays an important role in aggression?
    a. Rape and domestic violence have increased dramatically in the United States.
    b. Higher than normal testosterone levels in young males are associated with aggression.
    c. Stimulation of the limbic system tends to produce aggressive behavior in humans.
    d. Victims of violent crimes often know their attacker.
    Ans.: c   LG: 4   Page: 677   QT: C

109. Whether or not aversive circumstances cause someone to behave aggressively depends *mostly* on the individual's
    a. internalized morals.
    b. cognitive interpretation of the situation.
    c. fear of retribution.
    d. prior experience with similar situations.
    Ans.: b   LG: 4   Page: 678   QT: C

110. Many experts agree that children may develop aggressive behavior due to observational learning. Which of the following would *not* be a source of such learning?
    a. aggressive television programs
    b. aggressive behavior of older siblings
    c. being in timeout at nursery school
    d. physical violence between parents
    Ans.: c   LG: 4   Page: 678   QT: C

111. Which of the following *best* summarizes the experts' consensus on television's impact on children's aggression?
    a. Parents, not television programs, are responsible for children's aggression.
    b. Television violence can induce aggressive behavior in children.
    c. The effect of television on children's aggression is unclear.
    d. Television violence has been identified as the *only* cause for aggression in children.
    Ans.: b   LG: 4   Page: 680   QT: C

112. The view that aggression can be learned by watching others behave aggressively represents
    a. social learning theory.
    b. psychodynamic theory.
    c. humanistic theory.
    d. Gestalt theory.
    Ans.: a   LG: 4   Page: 681   QT: F

113. Which of the following statements about Maccoby and Jacklin's research on gender differences in aggression is *not* correct?
    a. Males are more aggressive than females in all cultures.
    b. More aggression by males than females is found in animals as well as humans.
    c. Males are found to be more aggressive than females as early as two years of age.
    d. In verbal aggression, no differences are found between adult males and females.
    Ans.: d   LG: 4   Page: 680   QT: F

114. How is catharsis related to reducing aggression?
    a. Ethological theorists propose that catharsis reduces aggression.
    b. Social cognitive theorists believe that catharsis increases aggression through social learning.
    c. Psychodynamic theorists believe that catharsis increases aggression.
    d. Both a and b are correct.
    Ans.: d   LG: 4   Page: 682   QT: C

115. What does research say about reducing aggression?
    a. Rewards for aggressive behavior should be reduced.
    b. People should observe fewer incidences of aggression.
    c. Conflict management skills should be taught in schools.
    d. All of the above are true.
    Ans.: d   LG: 4   Page: 682   QT: C

116. Which of the following would be the *best* synonym for altruism?
    a. antisocial behavior
    b. pro-social behavior
    c. self-regulation
    d. extrinsic
    Ans.: b   LG: 4   Page: 682   QT: C

117. Allison collects aluminum cans on her college campus. She sells them to a recycling center and gives the proceeds to the Salvation Army. Allison is displaying
    a. reciprocity.
    b. socialism.
    c. altruism.
    d. exchange.
    Ans.: c   LG: 4   Page: 682   QT: C

118. The evolutionary explanation of altruism would argue that
    a. people are more likely to act altruistically toward a family member than a stranger.
    b. people never do anything for someone else without expecting something in return.
    c. altruism cannot be distinguished from egoism.
    d. true altruism is almost nonexistent in industrialized nations.
    Ans.: a   LG: 4   Page: 684   QT: C

119. The idea of "do onto others as you would have them do onto you" *best* describes
    a. attribution.
    b. reciprocity.
    c. ethnocentrism.
    d. conformity.
    Ans.: b   LG: 4   Page: 682   QT: C

120. Altruism is to _____ as egoism is to _____.
    a. pro-social, reciprocity
    b. reciprocity, antisocial
    c. pro-social, antisocial
    d. antisocial, reciprocity
    Ans.: a   LG: 4   Page: 683   QT: C

121. Caroline has volunteered to work with underprivileged children as a part of her professor's pet literacy project. She is hoping that the professor will take this into consideration when calculating her grade. Caroline is demonstrating
    a. altruism.
    b. egoism.
    c. ethnocentrism.
    d. compassion.
    Ans.: b   LG: 4   Page: 683   QT: A

122. Which of the following *best* describes the bystander effect?
    a. When someone is witnessing an emergency, they are more likely to assist the victim if there are others present.
    b. When someone is witnessing an emergency, they are less likely to assist the victim if there are others present.
    c. The larger the number of bystanders, the more likely someone will provide assistance in an emergency.
    d. In a study of memory, it was discovered that bystanders did not remember as much about an emergency as the individual who was the victim.
    Ans.: b   LG: 4   Page: 684   QT: C

123. Which of the following is true regarding characteristics of those who will help in spite of the bystander effect?
    a. They feel that intervention may lead to personal injury.
    b. They feel that helping may require a great deal of time.
    c. They are not clear as to what is taking place in the situation.
    d. They have been victims themselves at one time.
    Ans.: d   LG: 4   Page: 684   QT: C

124. William was injured in a fall on a busy sidewalk. As he struggled, unable to pick himself up, he noticed that a crowd had gathered around him, but no one was helping. William was witnessing
    a. groupthink.
    b. discrimination.
    c. social facilitation.
    d. the bystander effect.
    Ans.: d   LG: 4   Page: 684   QT: A

Learning Goal 5: Understand the nature of relationships.

125. Your friend Andrew is an athletic extrovert, but he has no girlfriend at the moment. You think Andrew needs someone special in his life, and you are planning to arrange a blind date. Which type of a person would you choose for Andrew's blind date?
    a. a person who chooses her friends very carefully
    b. a person who likes to read a lot
    c. a person who doesn't have a boyfriend at this time
    d. a person who has similar characteristics and attitudes
    Ans.: d   LG: 5   Page: 686   QT: A

126. Individuals tend to seek friendships and relationships with people who are similar to them for all of the following reasons *except*
    a. mutual interests.
    b. consensual validation.
    c. cognitive dissonance.
    d. shared attitudes.
    Ans.: c   LG: 5   Page: 686   QT: F

127. If you had to write a research paper on attraction, which of the following would be the *best* title for your paper?
    a. When you see aspects of yourself in your partner, watch out!
    b. Opposites attract.
    c. Differences in attitudes and behavior can expand your horizon.
    d. Like attracts like.
    Ans.: d   LG: 5   Page: 686   QT: A

128. The matching hypothesis of attraction states that
    a. individuals prefer a person more attractive than themselves.
    b. individuals are uncomfortable around attractive people.
    c. individuals choose someone close to their level of attractiveness.
    d. in enduring relationships, physical attractiveness becomes more important.
    Ans.: c   LG: 5   Page: 687   QT: F

129. Which of the following statements is consistent with the concept of consensual validation?
    a. Opposites attract.
    b. People tend to shy away from the unknown.
    c. Birds of a feather flock together.
    d. All of the above are correct.
    Ans.: c   LG: 5   Page: 686   QT: C

130. Dwayne has always perceived himself as average in attractiveness, probably a 7 out of 10 if rated. He is at a club, and he sees four women sitting alone. According to the matching hypothesis, which of them is he *most* likely to begin a conversation with?
    a. Broomhilda, who appears to be a 2 out of 10
    b. Gwendola, who is a stunningly beautiful 10 out of 10
    c. Tonya, who appears to be a 10 and intelligent
    d. Diane, who looks like an 8 out of 10
    Ans.: d   LG: 5   Page: 686   QT: A

131. Jennifer is trying to choose which of her many boyfriends to marry. According to research findings, which of the following is *least* likely to be her choice?
    a. Dwayne, whose best attribute is his good looks
    b. Bruce, whose best quality is that he is considerate
    c. Willie, who is honest
    d. Jamel, who is kind
    Ans.: a   LG: 5   Page: 687   QT: A

132. When choosing an intimate partner,
    a. men place more importance on physical attractiveness than women.
    b. men and women place equal importance on physical attractiveness.
    c. women place more importance on physical attractiveness than men.
    d. neither men nor women place any importance on physical attractiveness.
    Ans.: a   LG: 5   Page: 687   QT: F

133. When Sternberg explained the psychology of love, his theory included all of the following but
    a. passion.
    b. sex.
    c. commitment.
    d. intimacy.
    Ans.: b   LG: 5   Page: 688   QT: F

134. What is the main difference between romantic love and affectionate love?
    a. Romantic love characterizes the initial stage of a love relationship.
    b. Romantic love includes sexual attraction, whereas affectionate love does not.
    c. Romantic love includes deep caring, whereas affectionate love does not.
    d. Romantic love is characterized by commitment, passion, and intimacy.
    Ans.: d   LG: 5   Page: 688   QT: C

135. A friend of yours wonders if she is truly "in love" with her boyfriend. To help her answer her
    question, you have her write down all of the feelings she has when thinking about her boyfriend.
    The absence of which of the following might lead you to doubt whether or not she is romantically
    in love?
    a. empathy
    b. affection
    c. sexual desire
    d. understanding
    Ans.: c   LG: 5   Page: 688   QT: A

136. In the early stages of a loving relationship, sexuality and infatuation are common. These tendencies
    are strongest in
    a. romantic love.
    b. triangular love.
    c. consensual love.
    d. affectionate love.
    Ans.: a   LG: 5   Page: 688   QT: C

137. Research indicates that people get married primarily because they feel
    a. affectionate love.
    b. pragmatic love.
    c. companionate love.
    d. romantic love.
    Ans.: d   LG: 5   Page: 688   QT: F

138. Which of the following *best* explains Carol Gilligan's perspective on relationships?
    a. Females value social relationships more than males.
    b. Males are more individualistic and self-oriented.
    c. There are no longer gender differences in approaches to relationships.
    d. Both a and b are correct.
    Ans.: d   LG: 5   Page: 689   QT: C

139. Research reports gender differences in the approach to relationships. Females are found to be caring, empathetic, and supportive, whereas males are found to be independent, self-reliant, and unexpressive. When interpreting these findings, it is important to keep in mind which of the following cautions?
    a. These results have been shown to be inaccurate.
    b. These results report between-group differences.
    c. These results are based on biased samples.
    d. These results are too old to be considered valid.
    Ans.: b   LG: 5   Page: 689   QT: C

140. When it comes to relationships, women tend to emphasize
    a. independence.
    b. autonomy.
    c. connectedness.
    d. focus on self.
    Ans.: c   LG: 5   Page: 689   QT: F

141. Two individuals are having a private conversation about family, emotions, friends, experiences they have shared in the past, and other topics that are of personal significance to them.   They talk like this for two hours. According to the research on gender differences in communication, these two individuals are *most* likely
    a. two men.
    b. a man and a woman.
    c. a husband and a wife.
    d. two women.
    Ans.: d   LG: 5   Page: 690   QT: C

142. Men generally prefer
    a. report talk.
    b. socialized talk.
    c. rapport talk.
    d. small talk.
    Ans.: a   LG: 5   Page: 691   QT: F

143. Tannen argues that communication differences between males and females are due primarily to
    a. innate predispositions.
    b. differences in language development.
    c. biological factors.
    d. differential socialization.
    Ans.: d   LG: 5   Page: 691   QT: C

144. Which of the following individuals is *least* likely to report loneliness?
    — a. a divorced person
    b. a college freshman
    c. a married person
    d. a widowed person
    Ans.: c   LG: 5   Page: 691   QT: C

145. Men are more likely than women to attribute their loneliness to
    a. external factors.
    b. other people's lack of initiative.
    c. the way they were socialized.
    d. internal factors.
    Ans.: d   LG: 5   Page: 691   QT: F

146. A friend of yours is lonely at her new college where she knows almost no one. In order to help her overcome her loneliness, you would advise her to do all of the following *except*
    a. join a student club that is involved in an activity that she enjoys
    b. find a study buddy
    c. attend some social functions on campus
    d. concentrate on her studies and don't worry about her social life
    Ans.: d   LG: 5   Page: 692   QT: A

147. Which of the following is an early warning sign of loneliness?
    a. alienation
    b. compulsions
    c. involvement
    d. active interests
    Ans.: a   LG: 5   Page: 692   QT: F

148. George, a college freshman, has been feeling overwhelmingly lonely for some time. He has attempted to get to know some other students, but nothing he tries to do seems to be working—he continues to feel desperately lonely. What advice would you give George?
    a. Get out and meet new people.
    b. Make an appointment with a counselor.
    c. Attend some sporting events.
    d. Call your parents at least once a week.
    Ans.: b   LG: 5   Page: 693   QT: A

149. Which of the following is true regarding chronic loneliness?
    a. Chronic loneliness is linked with impaired physical health.
    b. Chronic loneliness is linked with impaired mental health.
    c. Chronic loneliness has been associated with early death.
    d. All of the above are true.
    Ans.: d   LG: 5   Page: 691   QT: F

150. Which of the following is *not* true of loneliness?
    a. Optimistic people are less susceptible to loneliness.
    b. Loneliness is fairly common among college students.
    c. Loneliness is a minor problem; people just need to get over it.
    d. People with good social support systems tend to be less lonely.
    Ans.: c   LG: 5   Page: 692   QT: F

True/False Items

___ 151. Attributions are the behaviors that people manifest in social settings.
___ 152. When someone does not consider situational factors in developing an opinion of another person, they are demonstrating the fundamental attribution error.
___ 153. The phrase, "What have you done for me lately?" would describe the primacy effect.
___ 154. Social comparison is an important aspect of identity formation.
___ 155. We simplify our process of forming impressions of others by using categories.
___ 156. General attitudes tend to be excellent predictors of behavior.
___ 157. When we conform in order to be liked and accepted by others, our behavior reflects informational social influences.
___ 158. Groupthink tends to lead to better decisions because of pooled resources and more information.
___ 159. Prejudice is used by some to raise their own level of self-esteem.
___ 160. Discrimination is an unjustified negative action toward another person just because he or she is a member of a group.
___ 161. Evolutionary psychologists propose that both aggression and altruism increase the prospects of survival and reproduction.
___ 162. The bystander effect is the inability of witnesses to recall the circumstances of an accident or crime.
___ 163. When choosing an intimate partner, men place less influence on physical attractiveness than women do.
___ 164. Researchers relate the gender differences found in communication patterns to socialization.
___ 165. Researchers have found a connection between a person's levels of physical well-being and loneliness.

Answer Key for True/False Items

151.	Ans.: F	LG: 1	Page: 647	159.	Ans.: T	LG: 3	Page: 671
152.	Ans.: T	LG: 1	Page: 648	160.	Ans.: T	LG: 3	Page: 672
153.	Ans.: F	LG: 1	Page: 649	161.	Ans.: T	LG: 4	Page: 683
154.	Ans.: T	LG: 1	Page: 650	162.	Ans.: F	LG: 4	Page: 684
155.	Ans.: T	LG: 1	Page: 651	163.	Ans.: F	LG: 5	Page: 687
156.	Ans.: F	LG: 1	Page: 653	164.	Ans.: T	LG: 5	Page: 691
157.	Ans.: F	LG: 2	Page: 659	165.	Ans.: T	LG: 5	Page: 691
158.	Ans.: F	LG: 2	Page: 665				

Fill-in-the-Blank Items

166. When a person attributes a failure to bad luck, he/she is making an _____ attribution.
167. According to the _____ bias, we tend to attribute our successes to internal factors and our failures to external factors.
168. Lawyers and actors tend to be very aware of the impression they are making on others; they are good at _____.
169. When you behave contrary to your attitudes, you are likely to experience discomfort, or _____.
170. Asch found that if the group has _____ social status, subjects are more likely to conform.
171. Milgram found that people were less likely to _____ when the authority figure was not perceived to be legitimate and was not close by.
172. _____ occurs when membership in a group results in the loss of personal identity.
173. _____ refers to the tendency for a group decision to be riskier than the average decision made by individual group members.
174. _____ takes place when members of a group are more concerned with getting along than critical thinking.
175. When you hold an unjustified negative attitude toward an individual based merely on that individual's membership in a group, you are holding a _____.
176. Whether or not a person will respond _____ in a particular situation depends on expectations, equity, intentions, and responsibility.
177. People's tendency to choose intimate partners who are close to their own level of attractiveness is known as the _____ hypothesis.
178. When choosing an intimate partner, _____ focus more on honesty and kindness than on physical attractiveness.
179. Sternberg's triarchic theory of love included combinations of passion, intimacy, and _____.
180. Life transitions, such as moving away to college, getting a divorce, or the death of a spouse increase the risk that an individual might begin to suffer from _____.

Answer Key for Fill-in-the-Blank Items

166.	Ans.: external	LG: 1	Page: 648
167.	Ans.: self-serving	LG: 1	Page: 649
168.	Ans.: self-monitoring	LG: 1	Page: 652
169.	Ans.: dissonance	LG: 1	Page: 653
170.	Ans.: high	LG: 2	Page: 659
171.	Ans.: obey	LG: 2	Page: 661
172.	Ans.: Deindividuation	LG: 2	Page: 664
173.	Ans.: Risky shift	LG: 2	Page: 664
174.	Ans.: Groupthink	LG: 2	Page: 665
175.	Ans.: prejudice	LG: 3	Page: 670
176.	Ans.: aggressively	LG: 4	Page: 678
177.	Ans.: matching	LG: 5	Page: 687
178.	Ans.: women	LG: 5	Page: 687
179.	Ans.: commitment	LG: 5	Page: 689
180.	Ans.: loneliness	LG: 5	Page: 691

Matching Items

181. attribution theory	A.	meeting group standard
182. attitudes	B.	favoring one's own group
183. cognitive dissonance	C.	beliefs or opinions
184. conformity	D.	unselfish interest
185. social loafing	E.	companionate
186. ethnocentrism	F.	passionate
187. discrimination	G.	causes of behavior
188. altruism	H.	reducing discomfort of inconsistent thoughts
189. romantic love	I.	less effort
190. affectionate love	J.	negative action

Answer Key for Matching Items

181.	Ans.: G	LG: 1	Page: 647	186.	Ans.: B	LG: 3	Page: 669
182.	Ans.: C	LG: 1	Page: 653	187.	Ans.: J	LG: 3	Page: 672
183.	Ans.: H	LG: 1	Page: 653	188.	Ans.: D	LG: 4	Page: 682
184.	Ans.: A	LG: 2	Page: 658	189.	Ans.: F	LG: 5	Page: 688
185.	Ans.: I	LG: 2	Page: 663	190.	Ans.: E	LG: 5	Page: 688

Essay Questions

191. Attribution theory and the fundamental attribution error are basic ideas to social psychology. Briefly describe a situation you have been in where the fundamental attribution error has occurred. What did this mean for you? What did this mean for others? (LG: 1)

Answer Guidelines: Possible options include mentioning that the fundamental attribution error means that people overestimate the importance of traits and underestimate the importance of situations when they explain the behavior of others.

192. Define and give an example of Festinger's cognitive dissonance. What can be done to resolve the state of dissonance? (LG: 1)

Answer Guidelines: Possible options include mentioning that cognitive dissonance occurs when there is an inconsistency between one's attitudes and behavior. In order to resolve the dissonance, the inconsistency has to be resolved. This can be done by changing either one's attitudes or behavior.

193. What is conformity? Describe the Asch study on conformity, and list four factors that would contribute to conformity. (LG: 2)

Answer Guidelines: Conformity involves a change in a person's behavior to coincide more with a group standard. Asch's study involved a subject agreeing with confederates regarding the length of lines, even though he knew that they were incorrect. Some factors that influence conformity are unanimity of the group, prior commitment, personal characteristics, group members' characteristics, and cultural values.

194. Describe Stanley Milgram's famous study on obedience. Generally, what were the results and how did they compare to the predictions made prior to the study? Could this study be performed today? (LG: 2)

Answer Guidelines: Possible options include mentioning that Milgram found two-thirds of the experiment participants would "shock" another person at a dangerous level of 450 volts, simply because an experimenter (a perceived authority figure) asked them to do so. These results were very different from the predictions made prior to the study. Due to stricter ethical guidelines for psychological research, this study could probably not be conducted today.

195. Certain behavior patterns are unique to group behavior. Describe some specific examples of social loafing, risky shift, and groupthink that have occurred in groups with which you were involved. (LG: 2)

Answer Guidelines: Possible options include mentioning that social loafing occurs when people in a group work less hard than they would individually; risky shift involves group decisions being riskier than individual decisions; groupthink occurs when group members, or a group leader, emphasize unanimity and harmony over critical thinking.

196. Prejudice, stereotype, and ethnocentrism all are words that have negative connotations. Explain each of these terms, and provide an example for each. (LG: 3)

Answer Guidelines: Possible options include mentioning that all three of these terms have a negative connotation because they refer to negative judgments made about others. Prejudice refers to negative attitudes about others based on group membership; stereotype involves generalizing about all members of a particular group (most often negative generalizations); and ethnocentrism refers to the tendency to favor one's own group over other groups.

197. Discuss the strategies that have been used successfully to improve interethnic relations. (LG: 3)

Answer Guidelines: Possible options include mentioning that task-oriented cooperation goals and intimate contact are strategies that have been shown to improve interethnic relations. Task-oriented cooperation requires the cooperation of groups with divergent areas of interest and varying backgrounds—all must work together to succeed. In schools, this can be done with the jigsaw classroom. Intimate contact allows people to get to know individuals from other backgrounds by sharing personal information, often resulting in the realization that we have more in common than we thought.

198. Discuss how social learning theorists explain the development of aggression. (LG: 4)

Answer Guidelines: Possible options include mentioning that social learning theorists believe that aggression is learned through reinforcement and observation. Reinforcement occurs when aggression results in attention or status. Observing aggressive behavior in models, such as in favorite television characters, can also induce aggressive behavior in children because children tend to imitate the behavior displayed by the models. Other aggressive models—such as parents, siblings, or peers—can have the same negative effect on children's behavior.

199. Describe the differences in how men and women approach and communicate in relationships. How can these differences be explained? (LG: 5)

Answer Guidelines: Possible options include mentioning that women tend to be more relationship oriented whereas men tend to be more individualistic and self-oriented. Thus, females tend to be more sensitive to relationship issues. Closely related to the different approach to relationships is the different communication patterns of males and females. Females prefer rapport talk, a conversation pattern that focuses on making connections through sharing personal thoughts and feelings. Men prefer report talk, a communication pattern that focuses on providing information. Social psychologists often explain these differences in terms of the differential socialization of males and females.

200. Describe Sternberg's triarchic theory of love. Include definitions and examples of each of his three components. (LG: 5)

Answer Guidelines: Sternberg proposed a model of love that included passion, intimacy, and commitment. Different types of love were dependent on either the presence or lack of combinations of the three. Consummate love involved the presence of all three.